CAREER STRATEGIES FOR WOMEN IN ACADEME

ARMING ATHENA

To the many incarnations of Athena
—ancient and modern

CAREER STRATEGIES FOR WOMEN IN ACADEME

ARMING ATHENA

Lynn H. Collins
Joan C. Chrisler
Kathryn Quina
Editors

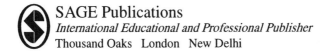

SAGE Publications
International Educational and Professional Publisher
Thousand Oaks   London   New Delhi

For information:

SAGE Publications, Inc.
2455 Teller Road
Thousand Oaks, California 91320
E-mail: order@sagepub.com

SAGE Publications Ltd.
6 Bonhill Street
London EC2A 4PU
United Kingdom

SAGE Publications India Pvt. Ltd.
M-32 Market
Greater Kailash I
New Delhi 110 048 India

Printed in the United States of America

Library of Congress Cataloging-in-Publication Data

Main entry under title:

Career strategies for women in academe: Arming Athena / edited by Lynn H. Collins, Joan C. Chrisler, Kathryn Quina.
    p. cm.
    Includes bibliographical references and index
    ISBN 0-7619-0989-3 (cloth: acid-free paper)
    ISBN 0-7619-0990-7 (pbk.: acid-free paper)
    1. Women college teachers. 2. College teaching—Vocational guidance. 3. Feminism and education. I. Collins, Lynn H. II. Chrisler, Joan C. III. Quina, Kathryn
    LB2332.3 .C38   1998
    378.1'2'082—ddc21   98-19761

This book is printed on acid-free paper.

98 99 00 01 02 03 10 9 8 7 6 5 4 3 2 1

Acquiring Editor:	Peter Labella
Production Editor:	Wendy Westgate
Editorial Assistant:	Nevair Kabakian/Karen Wiley
Designer/Typesetter:	Janelle LeMaster
Cover Designer:	Candice Harman

Contents

Foreword

A Feminist Classicist
Reflects on Athena

Who is Athena that she has been chosen as patron and paradigm of women academics in the title of this book? I'd like to begin with a review of Athena's roles and activities for those readers whose memory of Greek mythology is dim.

Athena is as respected, appealing, versatile, balanced, and fully realized a figure as any found in ancient myth. As the Greek goddess of wisdom, warfare, and handicrafts, she is the favorite daughter of the chief god Zeus, born from his head as the reified representation of his wise counsel. Associated with the owl and the olive tree, she is frequently described by the epithet "grey-eyed" (glaucopis), which many believe refers not so much to her eye color as the bright-eyed mental alertness that is her very essence. As the Roman goddess Minerva, she shared a place of distinction with Jupiter and Juno, king of the gods and his consort, and the three were revered throughout the Roman world as the Capitoline Triad.

Armed from birth with helmet, spear, and shield, she is associated with the Aegis, a distinctive armor variously thought of as either a breastplate or a fringed cape. It displayed the severed snaky head of the monstrous Gorgon, Medusa, and in common parlance has become synonymous with the notion of protection. As favored daughter of Zeus, Athena has access to his thunderbolts as well. Born shouting her war cry, she takes an active part in battle, as suggested by her epithet Promachos (fighter in the front lines), yet she is not hated for mindless blood lust, as is her half-brother Ares. Rather, she is champion of defensive war and savior of cities (Athena Polias at Athens; her icon, the Palladium, guarantees the continued existence of Troy).

A remarkably autonomous figure for patriarchal Greece, Athena is one of only three goddesses (the others are Artemis and Hestia) without consort and allowed to retain her status as virgin (Athena Parthenos) in perpetuity.

Known for her active and creative engagement with kings and later the city-state (polis), she is associated with success (either as Athena Nike or accompanied by Nike, the goddess of victory). She is consistently successful, whether in her pro-Greek partisanship during the Trojan War, or in her victory over her uncle, Poseidon, for the position of eponymous patron of the city of Athens, the city that defines Greece culturally, which was called by its leader Pericles the very "education" (paedeia) of Greece.

In fact, Athena herself is preeminently a teacher who makes the name Mentor (one of her disguises) a byword for wise nurturance. She is a force for civilization who associates herself with those movements (e.g., the defeat of the Giants) that established the younger, more enlightened Olympian gods in power. She is associated with various skills and artifacts, both those traditionally feminine and masculine: patron of textile arts, she is the teacher of these skills to female figures from Pandora to Arachne, and couturier to the gods as well. She is inventor of the war chariot, of pottery, of the flute, and of carpentry: She taught the renowned Cretan inventor Daedalus carpentry, helped build the ship Argo, and devised the Trojan horse.

Although herself a virgin by choice, she promotes fertility in the lands she favors, as evidenced by her gift of the olive tree to Athens in her contest with Poseidon. Unlike the aloof Artemis, or the often angry and vengeful Hera, Athena is a good figure to have on one's side. In fact, she is the patron of many a major hero, from Jason (leader of the Argonauts, who searched for the Golden Fleece) to the Athenian king Erichthonius, to whom she served as foster mother. Athena provides Heracles with the tools and strategems he needs to perform his labors and rid the world of monsters, as she does Perseus in his victory over Medusa. It is her idea for that hero to use his shield as a mirror, thus avoiding gazing directly at the Gorgon, who had turned other heroes to stone for doing precisely that. In the Trojan War, Athena champions the Greek hero Achilles, restraining him from making the rash mistake of slaying his commander-in-chief, Agamemnon, in the course of a quarrel, and delivering to him Hector, the Trojan champion whom she had beguiled into battle by impersonating his brother,

Deiphobos, and then deserting him. Most especially, Athena is linked with Odysseus, whose cunning matches her own, and in whom she delights for his reflection of her mental agility, power tempered by calculation, and patience in waiting for the opportune moment to act. He knows more than any other hero when to suffer abuse in silence and when to assert himself, when to assume a false identity and when to reveal himself. She is the one who helps him succeed in his contest with Ajax over the armor of the dead Achilles, and she is never far from exerting a wise and supportive influence over Odysseus, his wife Penelope, and his son Telemachus. She takes the initiative in stirring the gods to action when her favorite is held captive by the nymph Calypso, prompts Telemachus to embark on a search for his father, plants in Penelope's mind the device of challenging her unwelcome suitors to a contest for her hand in marriage, and in the guise of the family tutor, Mentor, counsels Odysseus before his battle with the suitors, and later in dealing with the slain suitors' aggrieved families.

Finally, she acts as mediator between conflicting claims; she prefers respect, reconciliation, and persuasion to brute force. Perhaps the chief expression of this aspect of Athena is in the *Oresteia* of Aeschylus, the dramatic trilogy that recounts Clytemnestra's murder of her husband Agamemnon on his return from Troy and their son Orestes's retaliatory matricide. Although he acted on Apollo's instruction, he is pursued by the matriarchal snake-haired Furies, goddesses of blood-guilt and vendetta. When the distraught youth takes refuge at Athens, a city associated—by the Athenians—with the forces of enlightenment, Athena saves him by establishing the Areopagus, a homicide court to try capital murder cases, and casts the tie-breaking vote to acquit. When the enraged Furies threaten Athens with blight, she manages to win them over and install them as Eumenides (Kindly Ones) who promote fertility and prosperity; their menacing torches are transformed into those of Athenian citizens in procession, celebrating the Panathenaia festival and bringing their gift of a new peplos (robe) to their benefactress, Athena, patron of Athens and the political process.

Wise, inventive, versatile, powerfully armed yet a skilled diplomat, autonomous yet an active collaborator in the civilizing process, a teacher, mentor, and friend, brave and successful, Athena would appear to be the perfect patron for women professors. Yet there are some aspects of the goddess that I find disturbing and problematical.

Apart from her association with textiles, Athena's experience is unlike that of actual ancient Greek women, whose place was within the confines of domesticity, and to whom the arenas of glory, war, governance, public speaking, and education were closed. In spite of the tremendous advances made in broadening the horizons of accomplishment for women since ancient times, I think we still face the danger presented by the "exceptional female": the too-easy assumption that the highly visible success of a few can be generalized to the whole sex, and the concomitant attitude that those who do not achieve similar prominence have only themselves to blame. After all, we should beware of the assumption that a society that worships and reveres a goddess (or the Virgin Mary, for that matter) is a female-dominated, or even a female-friendly, society, any more than having a queen rather than a king on the throne entails an elevation in the status of women. And as women professors, we must be all too aware of the "Queen Bee" syndrome: the phenomenon of the sole, high-powered woman in the department who "has it made," but has no desire to help other women to share her high status.

Then too, Athena was celibate and childless. Like the "school marms" of an earlier era, who were wedded to their calling and expected to devote their lives to nurturing other people's children, Athena, at least in the Greek understanding, could achieve autonomy only at the expense of her biological generativity and her sexuality. Women today, in academia as elsewhere, have and want to have choices about how and whether to express their physical and emotional as well as their mental capacities without forfeiting credibility as "professionals." Issues arise from How do we dress? to What are our institutions' policies on maternity leave and child care? How do we balance our time and energy in our attempt to live varied, satisfying lives? How do we judge ourselves—and how do others judge us—for our decisions? Athena offers us no help here. The very catalog of Athena's positive and nurturant relationships with heroes is a reflection of her asexual nature. She poses no threats, makes no demands. She is a female without specific femaleness, and only as such could the Greeks conceive of a female as being beneficent, or even self-controlled.

Furthermore, Athena as daughter can be accepted and even indulged because, unlike a son, she poses no real threat of rivalry with her father, Zeus, who had overthrown his own father, Cronos. Is it only by assuming the role of the cherished, nonthreatening daughter that female junior faculty can win the support and protection of senior male faculty?

Clearly of note is Athena's consistent pattern of identifying with males and maleness. Despite her many associations with snakes (as with water), an emblem of the Great Goddess, the tradition has her display on her (or is it her father's?!) Aegis the severed head of the Gorgon Medusa, the very representation of the male's fear of female power. The rationale that Athena offers in the *Oresteia* for siding with Apollo to acquit Orestes of his mother's murder is her own birth without a mother's agency.

Athena had likewise chosen as the site for her new homicide court the Hill of Ares, where the invading Amazons had unsuccessfully attacked the hero Theseus and the city he founded, Athens. She allies herself with the patriarchal point of view that equates civilization and progress with male usurpation and domination of female power and prerogatives.

Finally, in a later Roman myth, found in Ovid's *Metamorphoses*, explaining why spiders weave webs, Athena engages in a weaving contest with the low-born Lydian girl, Arachne. The story is ostensibly about the punishment of human hybris: Arachne's arrogant boast that she excels an immortal in the very skill the goddess had imparted to mortals, and her willful refusal to let herself be persuaded to defer to Athena's superior position (if not ability). However, one cannot dismiss as coincidental the elaborate description of the subject matter of Arachne's web: She boldly and defiantly depicts the illicit and sometimes violent amorous adventures of the powerful male Olympians Zeus, Poseidon, and Apollo. Athena can find no fault with the artistry, but she is deeply affronted by the theme of the girl's handiwork; she thinks of herself as divinity, not as female capable of understanding or identifying with female experience. Instead of fostering, she punishes the female voice speaking its own truth, its own story. She beats Arachne with her shuttle, and when the poor girl hangs herself, turns her into a spider, destined to weave its web forever. And this is not the only instance of Athena's association with the destruction of another female. She also, in one version of the story, killed her childhood friend Pallas, either by accident or in a fit of temper, and in remorse assumed her name. Likewise, the daughters of Cecrops leapt to their deaths in fear when, succumbing to "female" curiosity, they disobeyed Athena's instructions not to look in the casket that contained the man-snake Erichthonius, her fosterling.

So is Athena, in her dealings with other females, only a male Olympian in drag, indifferent at best and lethal at worst? Does she demonstrate that a woman can achieve power and success only by being accepted as an honorary male? "Gee, you don't look like a chemist!" "Wow, you think like a man!" And are we still tempted to take these remarks as compliments?

Granted, Athena is a paradigm of much that we as women can celebrate and emulate: her wisdom, craft, versatility, strength, diplomacy, initiative, and capacity for mentoring. At the same time, she is a product of patriarchal thinking, male-created (literally and figuratively) and male-identified, exceptional, removed from and even hostile to the consciousness of anything approaching sisterhood.

My long years of dealing with classical antiquity have convinced me that the Greeks acknowledged, feared, and tried desperately to tame and domesticate female power (be it sexuality, fertility, valor, or intelligence) in order to serve patriarchal purposes. Our challenge as women—and as well-educated, privileged, professional women—is to recognize and tap into that power. How do we understand and negotiate "the system" while maintaining our clearsighted ability to critique and transform it? How do we define success and achieve it without sacrificing important aspects of our humanity? How do we learn to take ourselves seriously, how do we get others to take us seriously, without turning into something we—rightly or wrongly—find distasteful? How do we keep ourselves from being co-opted to serve agendas not our own? Finally, how do we learn to acknowledge and honor our Mothers and mentor our Daughters? To negotiate these challenges requires all the wisdom, timing, diplomacy, and cunning of the armed Athena of tradition—and, as I hope I've suggested, new armor besides, our own armor, armor of which the Athena of myth could never have conceived. That is what this book is about.

—Joann Claire Silverberg

Introduction

Career Strategies for Women in Academe: Arming Athena is the book we wish we had read as graduate students. If we had known then what we know now, we would still have made the decision to pursue academic careers, but we would have been more savvy about what to expect and would have felt less alone during stressful times. We hope that the facts and the experiences described in this volume will provide information about institutional problems in academe, advice on how to handle difficult situations, and encouragement to persist and achieve one's career goals.

Athena, we knew, was the Greek Goddess of Wisdom, whose emblem, the owl, is a contemporary symbol of education. She is usually portrayed with a shield and sword, and we wondered whether those weapons would be sufficient these days to protect her against the hostilities experienced by women faculty. Perhaps, we thought, a tank or a nuclear arsenal would be necessary for a woman as strong and independent as Athena to become a tenured full professor!

In conversations with the feminist classicist Joann Silverberg, we learned that Athena's weapons were not her own. She borrowed them from her father. The design on Athena's shield is the severed head of the Gorgon Medusa, another woman. We realized that Athena needs arming in more ways than one. She needs to develop her own weapons in her fight for tenure. Perhaps the ways of men do not work for women faculty. Certainly, we hope it will not be necessary to slay other women or ruin their careers in order to achieve our own. The modern Athena must learn to work in coalition with other women in order to achieve success.

In Part I, we provide information about the current status of women in academe. Lynn Collins examines the data on the number of women who have received doctorates over the past 20 years and the number of women in the various faculty ranks. Her research shows that despite the increasing number of women who have earned advanced degrees, women faculty remain clustered in the lower ranks—the three A's: adjunct instructors, assistant professors, and associate professors. Women are also more likely to be found in lower-status institutions with teaching missions than in high-status institutions with prominent research missions. She describes the resistance to affirmative action and considers how intergroup dynamics create adverse conditions for women that may lead to their voluntary or involuntary exit through the revolving door of academe. Despite years of affirmative action and rumors of discrimination against White males, men still dominate college and university faculties and retain most of the most prestigious appointments for themselves.

Many Americans believe that sex discrimination has seriously declined and is rarely to be found these days among the educated elite. Sociologist Nijole Benokraitis demonstrates that sex discrimination is not gone; it has merely become more subtle. She describes the many levels of sexist behavior from societal to institutional to individual, and she shows us how to recognize it when it is happening to us. Unless we realize when sexism is occurring, we cannot effectively combat it.

Pay equity is another issue that is as important in academe as anywhere. Ellin Scholnick has examined a number of equity studies at various institutions, and she shows us that women faculty still earn less than their male colleagues, especially at the higher ranks. In her chapter, Scholnick shows us how we can do pay equity studies on our own campuses and how we can use social science methodologies to understand and explain salary studies. Administrations will have to make adjustments when the injustice is unavoidably clear.

In Part II, on women's roles and career decisions, Joan Chrisler discusses how the roles of teacher and researcher can conflict. The role of teacher is more compatible with women's gender role training, and it can be tempting to focus on that aspect of professional work to the neglect of research and writing. However, it is scholarly productivity that is usually more important for tenure and promotion. In her chapter, Chrisler helps us to see whether this conflict is happening to us and provides ways to bring our roles into better balance.

Susan Basow reviews the research on gender and teaching evaluations. Although it is far too simple to say that students give male professors higher ratings than female professors, Basow shows us a myriad of ways that gender of teacher, gender of student, and the qualities rated can interact.

She indicates in which situations this is most likely to produce problems for women and suggests ways to minimize the damage. This chapter is a must read for all department chairs and faculty on tenure and promotion committees.

One reason that pay inequities are worse at higher ranks is that faculty do not enter the system with the same base. Thus, even if men and women receive the same percentage increase year after year, inequality persists. Suzanna Rose and Mona Danner tell us how to find out what the range of starting salaries is, help us figure out what we most need in order to do our work effectively, and describe successful negotiating strategies to help us get what we deserve. Everyone who is searching for an academic position should read this chapter right away.

In Part III, on assuming leadership in higher education, Joan Chrisler, Linda Herr, and Nelly Murstein explain why it is so important that women faculty involve themselves in the governance system on their campuses. They show us how to recognize leadership ability in ourselves, how to encourage it in others, and how to band together with other women to increase the number of women in leadership positions. After all, if we want to change things, we must be willing to place ourselves in situations where we can become change agents.

Women who try to move up in academe, as elsewhere, frequently bump their heads on the glass ceiling. Kathryn Quina, Maureen Cotter, and Kim Romenesko review the literature on this phenomenon. They tell us how to recognize the glass ceiling and why our male colleagues don't seem to notice that it's there. Better yet, they present strategies for empowering ourselves and others and suggest ways to break through the ceiling to success.

In Part IV, on taking charge and taking care, we present group and individual ways to take care of ourselves and protect ourselves and each other from toxic environments. Bernice Lott and Lisa Rocchio discuss the problem of sexual harassment on campus and present strategies for exposing and reducing it. They believe that this cannot effectively be done by individuals, and they promote group action by sharing with us a strategy that worked on their campus as women faculty and graduate students banded together.

Linda Carli acknowledges how stressful academic life can be, especially when things are not going well. She encourages us to engage in active coping strategies, such as seeking social support, managing time efficiently, and reducing role ambiguity, in order to take control of our professional lives and move our careers ahead. This chapter is full of helpful suggestions that can be done by individuals and/or groups of women faculty.

Throughout this book, you will find short essays in boxes. We call these "success stories and cautionary tales," and we commissioned them to illustrate the points made by the chapter authors. Each describes some difficulty encountered by the author and tells what happened next. Each has at least one important lesson—what went right or what went wrong. We found reading some of these essays heartrending, but all of them, we believe, are well worth reading. We can recognize ourselves in some of them, and we're sure that you will, too. The authors of these essays can serve as your role models; if they could survive or correct the situations in which they found themselves, so can you.

We would like to thank our role models who have toiled long and hard in the vineyards of academe to open doors for other women, especially Mary Gray, Barbara Bergmann, Paula Caplan, Emily Toth (a.k.a. Ms. Mentor), Harriet Aronson (a.k.a. Aunt Academe), Mary Roth Walsh, Florence Denmark, Rhoda Unger, and Bernice Lott. This book would not exist without the authors of our chapters and essays, who shared their expertise and bared their souls in the service of this project. Some of our authors are longtime and dear friends of ours; others we have met only recently but have come to know intimately and appreciate greatly as we worked together. In addition, we offer our gratitude to those who offered us support and encouragement in the production of this book: Nancy MacLeod, Jack Powell, Carl Stenber, our editor Peter Labella and the production staff at Sage, and our colleagues at Connecticut College and the University of Rhode Island.

We enjoyed working on this project together, and we're very pleased with the results. We hope that you learn as much from reading this book as we did from writing and editing it, and that you will feel as wise as, but better armed than, Athena as you reenter the fray. Always remember how important women faculty are to women students. If you do not achieve tenure, who will look out for the welfare of your students? Who will encourage them to achieve? Who will their role models be?

Part I
The Current Status
of Women in Academe

1

Working in the Ivory Basement
Subtle Sex Discrimination in Higher Education

Nijole V. Benokraitis

Recently, our daughter handed me the 1996 Ikea catalog and said, with a grin, "Look at pages 79-81." Because Ikea, a Swedish company, launched a commercial in 1994 showing a gay couple shopping for a dining room table (which drew both protests and praise from the general public), I assumed there was another controversial advertisement. Wrong. The ad promotes "smart affordable furniture that looks good, wears well and has features that make everything easier for kids—from homework to housekeeping." The boy's bedroom is described as a "computer work station"; the girl's bedroom is crowded with such furniture as a table mirror, a wardrobe, and a huge chest. The boy is seated at his work station as he peruses computer magazines. He is surrounded by books, computer equipment, car posters, car models, and a football. The girl is lounging on her frilly bed reading a magazine. Although there's a laptop in the background, the girl is surrounded with stuffed animals, plants, knickknacks, and other decorative items.

AUTHOR'S NOTE: I am grateful to Patricia L. Camp, Sandra Donaldson, Lauraine Leblanc, Susan B. Marine, and other colleagues for providing examples of subtle sex discrimination practices.

Subtle sexism strikes again, I thought. Both of the models in the ad are White, obviously affluent, and portray sex-stereotypical images of boys and girls. The boy is interested in cars, sports, and the burgeoning computer technology. The girl's room is a cascade of ruffles and frills; she has twin beds to accommodate (presumably) all those sleepovers where girls talk about boyfriends, play with Barbie dolls, and do makeovers.

At many points in their lives, almost all women will be treated stereotypically (in Ikea ads and elsewhere) simply because they are women and regardless of other characteristics (such as intelligence and talent). Much of this sex stereotyping is subtle rather than blatant. This chapter shows how subtle sex discrimination intersects with race/ethnicity, age, and social class in higher education at the individual, organizational, institutional, and cultural levels, and suggests some remedies for challenging and diminishing this form of inequality. Consider, first, some of the ways that sex discrimination operates in our everyday lives.

SEX DISCRIMINATION: DEFINITIONS AND TYPES

In 1963, Congress passed the Equal Pay Act that prohibited sex discrimination in employment by mandating equal pay for equal work on jobs requiring equal skill, effort, and responsibility, performed under similar working conditions. Title VII of the Civil Rights Act of 1964 declared it unlawful to discriminate in hiring, firing, compensation, promotion, and other conditions of employment on the basis of race, sex, color, religion, or national origin, or to limit employees in any way that might deprive them of employment opportunities or otherwise adversely affect their status. In 1972, Title IX of the Education Amendments prohibited sex discrimination in institutions receiving federal grants, loans, or contracts. These and other laws recognized the existence of unequal employment and educational contexts for women and men but left specific definitions and interpretations of discrimination up to courts.

Sex discrimination refers here to the unequal and harmful treatment of people because of their sex (i.e., biological differences between males and females, which include hormones, chromosomes, and anatomical characteristics). That is, people may be treated differently and unequally depending on whether they have a clitoris or a penis. There are several types of sex discrimination that lie on a continuum where blatant discrimination (such as some forms of sexual harassment) is very visible, subtle discrimination (emphasized in this chapter) is less apparent, and covert discrimination (such as sabotaging someone's work or using "date-rape drugs") is clandestine and difficult to prove (for a detailed discussion of this typology, see Benokraitis, 1997; Benokraitis & Feagin, 1995).

Subtle sex discrimination refers to the unequal and harmful treatment of women that is typically less visible and less obvious than blatant sex discrimination is. It is often not noticed because most people have internalized subtle sexist behavior as normal, natural, or acceptable. It can be innocent or manipulative, intentional or unintentional, well meaning or malicious. Subtle sex discrimination is often more complex than it appears: What is discrimination to many women may not seem discriminatory to many men (or even other women). Thus, when women notice or comment about subtle sexist behavior, they may be chided for being "too sensitive" or "petty":

> I am a 28-year-old . . . female graduate student. . . . My partner, a rather large male, age 36, and I often go out to dinner. When I pay with my credit card, I have noticed that the waiter will almost inevitably return the bill and the credit card to my partner! This occurs even when I hand the credit card to the waiter myself, or when I insert the credit card into the bill folder and place it on the table near me. I find this completely infuriating. My partner, who in other ways is usually quite good about things, fails to understand why this makes me so angry. My experience with my partner's lack of understanding leads me to believe that this is so subtle a form of discrimination that most people would find it completely petty and not take it seriously. (E-mail correspondence, 1996)

This woman's and her partner's strikingly different responses to the same situation are not surprising. Gratch (1997) observed that people who are most aware of sexual harassment are usually those with firsthand, negative encounters. The same is true of subtle sexist experiences. Men—especially men of color, gay men, disabled men, and those from lower socioeconomic classes—may be victims of subtle sex discrimination as well. When, for example, Tess Pierce (1996) published an editorial in Colorado State University's student newspaper that documented sexism on the campus, one of the male students pointed out that feminists don't complain about the bookstore's selling such sexist posters as "Why chocolate is better than men." Because women are more likely than men to encounter discrimination on a daily basis, this chapter focuses on women.

5

TABLE 1.1   A Typology of Subtle Sex Discrimination Levels

	Characteristics		
Levels of Discrimination	Awareness of Subtle Sexist Acts and Practices	Visibility of Subtle Sexist Acts and Practices	Sources for Remedies
Individual	High to low	Usually low	You Family members Friends Colleagues and coworkers Lawsuits
Organizational	Low	Very low	Advocates Mentors Collective action Lawsuits
Institutional	Very low	Practically invisible	Grievance procedures Revised institutional policies Redistribution of resources Unionization Lawsuits
Cultural	Negligible	Practically invisible and blamed on the victim	Government programs and incentives Business and industry innovations Legislative action Higher education governing boards Media initiatives Lawsuits

↑   ↑   ↑   ↑

Race, ethnicity, social class, sexual orientation, age, marital status, religion, disability

LEVELS OF SUBTLE SEX DISCRIMINATION

Subtle sex discrimination operates at four levels—individual, organizational, institutional, and cultural. As Table 1.1 shows, the awareness and visibility of subtle sexist behaviors and practices decrease as the level of analysis becomes more complex and abstract. The sources of remedies, similarly, become more diffuse and bureaucratic.

Although we often hear references to *subtle sexism* or *subtle sex discrimination*, there has been little scientific analysis of these concepts. One exception is the research by Janet Swim and her colleagues. In several studies (Swim, Aikin, Hall, & Hunter, 1995; Swim & Cohen, 1997), the researchers have shown that traditional attitudinal scales are very limited. Traditional measures (such as the Attitudes Toward Women Scale) measure overt and blatant sexism rather than the more subtle varieties that have been replacing "old-fashioned" gender prejudice and discrimination. Measuring slippery concepts like subtle sexism is not an easy task. Such research is critical, however, in documenting and eliminating these "modern" forms of inequality.

Subtle sex discrimination overlaps individual, organizational, institutional, and cultural levels. Note, also, that a number of characteristics—such as race, ethnicity, sexual orientation, age, social class, marital status, religion, and disability (see Table 1.1)—increase the likelihood that many women will encounter several tiers of inequality besides "just" sex discrimination. Consider, for example, an observation by a young, Black, female attorney:

> When I go with someone to a private club, the only other Black people or women I see are the service staff—waiters, maids, gardeners, etc. There are no members who look like me. When I go to a restaurant with White women, the servers almost always look to the White woman first. I'm a lawyer, and there are times when you can work against White lawyers on the case, but when you see them outside of the courtroom, they can't remember your name or face. Yet they remember the White men they oppose in court. And, for that matter, the White women, too. When I come into one of the courts I regularly practice in, I find that I have to reintroduce myself regularly because I am mistaken for one of the few other Black women practicing here (and none of us look the least bit alike). . . . I get tired of fighting the battles sometimes. *I wish I could work in a way that people couldn't see me, like by computer, so they would have to judge me by my work and not my appearance.* (E-mail correspondence, 1996, emphasis added).

As this young woman indicates, she feels excluded at several levels— as an individual, in such organizations as private clubs, within the legal institution, and as a member of U.S. society ("I wish I could work in a way that people couldn't see me . . . ").

SUBTLE SEX DISCRIMINATION
IN HIGHER EDUCATION

According to one observer, the utopian vision of academe as a community of the wise and the soon-to-be-wise is "both medieval and unfortunate": "Elitist or not, campuses are divided by each of the diversities—race, ethnicity, gender, class, age, sexual orientation, or handicap—insidiously or overtly replicating the social [world] and its hierarchies" (Fay, 1993, p. 280). Space limitations prevent a discussion of how each of these variables divides and subdivides campuses into ivory towers and ivory basements. Some examples of subtle sex discrimination at the individual, organizational, institutional, and cultural levels in higher education should be instructive, however.

Subtle Individual Sex Discrimination

Subtle individual sex discrimination refers to the unequal behavior that occurs on a one-to-one basis and is usually targeted at specific people. Two examples of subtle sex discrimination at the individual level include professional diminution and intellectual intimidation.

Professional Diminution

Many women often experience "microinequities" or small, minor ways in which people are treated differently and thus disadvantaged (Haslett & Lipman, 1997; Rowe, 1990). One of the most common microinequities in higher education is questioning a female faculty member's professional authority:

> I teach Bibliography and Methods of Research, a required course for all new graduate students in English. Most recently, for example, one of the [graduate] students asked me if I came here with a master's degree. I was stunned and wondered what he could *possibly* be thinking—that I don't have a Ph.D. but call myself "Doctor" anyway? (E-mail correspondence, 1996).

Similarly, using different titles for male and female faculty connotes less respect:

8

What I frequently encounter as a faculty member is that my students address me as "Miss" or "Mrs." while the institutional norm at my small school—and the title they use for male professors—is "Dr." My [female] colleagues and I view this as a way students show us that we're not equal in status and expertise to our equally-educated male colleagues. (E-mail correspondence cited in Benokraitis, 1997, p. 2)

Even in engineering departments, where female faculty are rare and relationships between students and faculty are often formal and distant, Frehill (1997) found that students more often addressed women faculty by their first names, "Miss," "Ms.," or "Mrs." rather than "Professor" or "Dr."

Women faculty also report more comments about personal appearance on student course evaluations:

I get comments on evaluations such as "She ought to comb her hair differently" or "She ought to dress differently." Their comments about hair and dress suggest that they're not thinking of me first as a teacher. They look first at whether I fit the female stereotype. Teaching seems second to that. (Blakemore, Switzer, DiIorio, & Fairchild, 1997, p. 59)

Or, women may wonder how seriously they're taken because they have less access to institutional resources. A female faculty member in a political science department said, for example, "I waited for two years before I had a working computer on my desk. Two men hired after me had new working computers within three months" (Wilson, 1996b, p. A11). New faculty women in engineering have reported that they may be given the smallest labs with the oldest equipment and assigned evening courses more often than their male peers. Being given the least desirable facilities and teaching schedules at the start of a tenure-track career "can seem like one is being 'set up' to do poorly" (Frehill, 1997, p. 129).

Such "microinequities" may accumulate especially rapidly for women of color. Latina faculty, for example, may be perceived as lazy even though their professional behavior is exactly the same as that of White males:

I was in this high-powered meeting, with other people in positions of leadership in the various campuses of my university. When it was time to put our calendars together to schedule our next meeting, several White males volunteered the information that they wouldn't be able to meet on certain dates. Everybody took their statements at face value, no questions asked. When, however, I told them the dates when I couldn't meet, one turned to me and said in a very sarcastic tone: "What is this? A vacation?" (Bento, 1997, p. 102)

9

Similarly, the cultural values of minority women faculty may be misinterpreted by their colleagues. In the case of Latinas, for example, "The cultural tradition of *respeto* fosters a reluctance to openly question authority or to disagree. Showing respect for authority may be mistranslated as a lack of assertiveness, low self-confidence, or an avoidance of leadership" (Bento, 1997, p. 107).

Another professional slight is being ignored at work-related functions. In their discussion of subtle gendered racism, St. Jean and Feagin (1997) noted that Black women faculty may feel especially invisible at university social events when White male faculty "don't bother" introducing female professors to their wives or family members.

Each microinequity may seem so isolated and insignificant that one is tempted to ignore each instance of professional diminution. As these "slights" snowball, however, they undermine one's self-confidence and self-respect. Thus, an *accumulation* of microaggressions can lower many faculty women's morale, feelings of self-worth, productivity, and intellectual contributions.

Intellectual Intimidation

More than 600 higher education institutions have established women's studies programs since the late 1960s. Women's studies and feminist epistemologies have had an important impact on the intellectual development of the humanities and the social sciences (see Jacobs, 1996). Feminist scholarship is often accused of producing propaganda, however, because it challenges traditional masculine perspectives and interests (Martin & Jurik, 1996). Senior male faculty, especially, might devalue research and publications on women-related topics:

> Having served on several search committees, I'm aware of how often feminist (or even woman-topic) dissertations are dismissed as "jargony," "trendy," etc. . . . I'm not really sure if feminism is still seen as a "fly-by-night" sort of discipline, but the . . . people who make [such statements] will assure you until they're blue in the face (or you are) that they would love to hire a woman, are not opposed to feminism, etc. It's only "this" dissertation, you see, they are opposed to. . . . I think there's an awful lot of that "I'm-sure-glad-you're-not-one-of-those-(bra-burners/Marxists/marching-in-the-streeters/take your pick)" rhetoric floating around on the part of senior faculty members who have a lot of power over promotion and tenure decisions. This is a signal [to] tone down one's own voice or risk punishment. Women's publications in women's studies or feminist

journals are often dismissed as "minor pub" while men who publish in small presses/journals are heralded as having made it to a "small-but-elite/prestigious" one. (Benokraitis, 1997, pp. 15-16)

Kolodny (1996) characterized such reactions as "antifeminist intellectual harassment" because they create an environment "in which research, scholarship, and teaching pertaining to women, gender, or gender inequities are devalued, discouraged, or altogether thwarted" (p. 9). Gaard (1996) has argued that lesbian students and faculty may be especially vulnerable to intellectual harassment because lesbian topics may be deemed as lacking "academic merit," or lesbian authors may be penalized for devoting their energies to topics that are of "marginal interest" and "outside the mainstream." The combination of sexism and age discrimination, which Carpenter (1996) called "sexagism," can easily derail many academic women's careers: Even women in their 40s are likely to be perceived as "aging" or "menopausal" (with all the implications of physical and intellectual decline), whereas their male counterparts are seen as "in their prime."

Some Remedies

At the individual level, the most important source for changing subtle sexist practices is you. Becoming conscious of the ways that "professional diminution" demoralizes and alienates women students and faculty from the institution and from each other can alleviate self-doubts about one's abilities and skills. Although insecurity plagues many (if not most) academic men and women, the latter are often more susceptible to microinequities. Discussing disturbing experiences with like-minded or sympathetic peers and colleagues can allay concerns that discriminatory acts are "in my head." Although first-generation college students and faculty often feel estranged from their families because their attitudes and values may change (see Sowinska, 1993), parental encouragement and support can play a critical role in counteracting negative campus experiences (Nora & Cabrera, 1996). In addition, women faculty, especially those from working-class backgrounds (which characterizes most of us), "often feel tainted by the constant need to market myself and promote my work" (Tokarczyk, 1993, p. 320). But if we don't publicize our accomplishments, who will?

Remedies for *intellectual intimidation* are more difficult to implement because exclusion of faculty who are women, minority, older, lesbian, or

11

from working-class backgrounds is deeply entrenched in our organizational practices and institutional policies (as I will discuss shortly). Solutions are possible, however. Kolodny (1996) has suggested initiating ongoing, campus-wide dialogues on antifeminist intellectual harassment through such informal internal networks as bag lunches and e-mail and revamping promotion and tenure guidelines to include feminist scholarship. Arguing that "Being nice isn't going to get you anywhere," Gaard (1996, p. 137) has encouraged gay and lesbian faculty to organize strategies to fight homophobia, to set up hotlines to document gay-bashing, and to come out in the classroom so that straight students and faculty have an opportunity to become educated on issues of sexuality.

Forming alliances with sympathetic graduate students, faculty, staff, and administrators is an especially effective method for countering intellectual intimidation (Garner, 1996). Such alliances reduce feelings of estrangement and increase the likelihood of forging work relationships with interesting and productive colleagues.

Subtle Organizational Sex Discrimination

Subtle organizational sex discrimination persists because the practices, rules, and policies at many community colleges, colleges, and universities are often different for women and men. Most of us are less likely to be aware of subtle organizational than individual sex discrimination because day-to-day exclusionary practices are embedded in the organization's functions. Consider gatekeeping and mentoring.

Gatekeeping

Gatekeepers in college admissions may act independently (such as a college president or dean) or within a larger group (such as a search committee). Two of the recent and most highly publicized examples of gatekeeping in college admissions include the exclusion or harassment of female students by such tax-supported public colleges as the Citadel (in South Carolina) and the Virginia Military Institute (VMI).

Rather than lose its state funding, the Citadel accepted four women for the 1996-1997 academic year. Despite drastic efforts to "fit in," the female cadets were not accepted by the men. Two of the female cadets were doused with a flammable liquid and their clothing was set afire in a hazing incident.

Two female cadets also reported such physical abuse as being struck on the head with a rifle butt by a male cadet (Strosnider, 1997). Such alleged physical abuse is blatant.

Most of the sexist gatekeeping in nonmilitary higher education institutions is more subtle. During 1997, for example, some of the private liberal arts colleges were concerned that the entering class of women students has outnumbered its male counterparts in larger proportions than the national average: "[Some] administrators are concerned about the trend for a number of reasons, not least that some first-year women might have a tough time finding a date" (Gose, 1997, p. A35). Some of the private colleges wooed male students (such as sending them—but not women—a second mailing describing the college) because "alumni are more likely than alumnae to give money," because the colleges may be unable to provide "equitable athletics opportunities" for the large number of women students, and because academic programs that are less popular with women than men (such as engineering and science) might be eliminated (Gose, 1997, p. A35).

Similar gatekeeping is also common in recruiting and hiring faculty. According to Chan and Wang (1991), for example, the Asian American faculty who are most likely to be hired are those who won't "rock the boat" but, after being hired, "have never found their way into the inner circles that govern the university" (p. 59). Thus, hiring Asian American faculty is safe because it increases the visibility of affirmative action gestures without giving Asian American faculty decision-making power.

Another effective gatekeeping technique is to argue that "qualified" women and minorities are not available for hiring. According to Mickelson and Oliver (1991), such assertions are unfounded. Although Ivy League graduates are usually snapped up quickly, there are numerous Black and Latino/a candidates (including women of color) who have graduated from non-Ivy League universities but who experience difficulties in getting job offers from "second-tier" institutions.

Even when women and minorities are hired, informal gatekeeping practices may prohibit their upward mobility. One practice is the unwritten "one-minority-per-pot" rule:

A Chicano department chair [had] applied for an associate deanship at this institution. In spite of his qualifications for the position, however, he was forewarned by the academic vice president, who was Anglo, that his candidacy would not likely receive serious consideration "because there were already three

13

other Chicano administrators at the college." . . . It is important to note that when a non-Chicano applied for the same position, no one counted the number of Anglos already on the faculty or in administrative positions. (Reyes & Halcn, 1991, p. 175)

Such "one-minority-per-pot" strategies are doubly detrimental to minority women because their upward mobility is handicapped by both sex and race/ethnicity.

At some of the most privileged institutions, female academics (and faculty of color) may not be tenured despite backing from their departments. According to Wilson (1997), for example, deans and other administrators have "shot down" departmental votes granting tenure to a number of women faculty because the women's scholarship was "controversial" (i.e., feminist) or the women hadn't been "productive enough" even though they had national or international reputations as scholars.

Gatekeeping can also protect faculty who should be ousted from higher education (see Lott and Rocchio, this volume, for a discussion of sexual harassment). Suffice it to say here that even when the harasser (typically a male professor) has been found guilty of harassment, subtle administrative reactions often protect the offender. In the practice of "passing the harasser," for example, college officials negotiate with the harasser to resign quietly. In return, the university agrees never to mention the incident(s), especially if another institution calls to check his references (Leatherman, 1996). Thus, the harasser is passed on to another college and continues his preying.

Mentoring

Mentoring can incorporate a wide spectrum of activities. In higher education, mentoring can range from advising first-year students about course selections to grooming faculty as candidates for college/university president positions. One of the striking features of education in the United States is the prominence of women college students compared to the small numbers of women faculty who serve as role models or mentors. By 1993, almost 55% of bachelor's degree recipients were women. Women earned 59% of associate's degrees, 52% of master's and professional degrees, and 38% of PhD degrees. In contrast, the number of women faculty declines with rank. In the same year, women represented 48% of lecturers and instructors, 40% of assistant professors, and only 17% of professors (National Center for Education Statistics, 1995). (See Collins, this volume, for a discussion of this gender imbalance.) Thus, the pool of women faculty at senior ranks who can mentor graduate students or junior faculty is modest at best.

When gender intersects with such variables as social class, mentoring barriers increase. Women faculty from working-class backgrounds may worry that they are "impostors" who don't "belong" and are not smart enough to compete with their middle-class colleagues (see Gardner, 1993). Even middle-class students can seem intimidating:

> Like many other college teachers from working-class homes, I am amazed when I look around and see myself teaching. Sometimes . . . I feel a fraud, fearful that someone will discover I don't belong in front of the classroom. . . . I know there is something about my talk, walk, and body language that distinguishes me from my "colleagues." Since most of my teaching has been in elite institutions, these characteristics also often distinguish me from my students. Several times I have had students in my seminar declare, "Of course all of us come from middle-class families," or "I guess everyone's father here is a doctor or lawyer or something like that." (Miner, 1993, p. 81)

According to a rural Southern female faculty member, beliefs that one is different from one's colleagues may be reinforced by predominantly White, middle-class, male colleagues who pigeonhole Southerners:

> When I began to teach in the Northeast, I discovered to my surprise that many people—even some enlightened academics who would staunchly fight the stereotyping of other minorities or "fringe" cultures in American society—pretty much accepted the stereotype of the southern redneck as racist, sexist, alcoholic, ignorant, and lazy. Some of them even told me southern jokes (redneck jokes may be the last acceptable ethnic slurs in "polite" society). (Roskelly, 1993, p. 293)

Obstacles increase when race or ethnicity are stirred into the mentoring pot. Stanfield (1995) noted that "to the extent to which African American students are well mentored by Whites, the students tend to be men more so than women" because "men are much more prone to be given access to old-boy networks" (p. 328). According to Stanfield, many male faculty may avoid mentoring Black female students because the faculty fear accusations of sexual intimacy: Much of "the work of elite intellectual development is mostly informal, over cocktails and in the den at home" and "many Afro-American women get the wrong idea" (p. 328). Such claims, though unsubstantiated, justify sexist behavior and preserve the status quo.

If faculty act professionally, whether at the office or the den at home, it is highly unlikely that women students will confuse mentoring with sexual advances. Moreover, misunderstandings about sexual harassment do not explain why Black female faculty are often excluded from mentoring. For example, in a study of 14 senior-level faculty who had been awarded the New England Distinguished Black Scholars Award, Harris (1995) found that the female professors reported isolating work conditions more often than their male counterparts. One explanation for the isolation, according to Harris, was that the male professors had more active mentor relationships than did the female professors.

Some Remedies

In terms of "gatekeeping," the most obvious solution is to fling the gates open. There is no question that current gatekeepers, primarily majority faculty and administrators, have the power to increase the membership of underrepresented groups at faculty, administrative, and policy-making levels. Although she is describing gender and sexual harassment, Lorber's (1994) suggestion that senior women should use whatever power they have to implement social change is especially appropriate for challenging restrictive gatekeeping practices.

If there are few senior women in faculty ranks, a college can set up a "board of advocates" from neighboring institutions comprised of women (and men) who can investigate and address local concerns or complaints. Many colleges and universities set aside large sums of money to bring in "superstar" speakers. Although such guests may stimulate the institution's intellectual atmosphere, at least one of those speakers can be someone who addresses subtle sexist and racist organizational practices and policies. As one e-mail colleague recently wrote me:

> My experience with women scientists here is that they very much get sucked up into being one of the boys. We had a mathematician who had an epiphany about four years ago after Sheila Tobias spoke where she suddenly realized that math teaching might be structured in sexist ways. (E-mail correspondence, 1996)

16

This comment was from a woman who has long-advocated addressing sexism at her institution. It took an outsider, however, to help even some of the female faculty "see the light."

There are numerous strategies for improving mentoring practices and relationships. Noting that the scarcity of women mentors increases the higher a woman goes on the academic ladder—especially for feminist and minority students in male-dominated disciplines—Caplan (1993) has provided tips on choosing a mentor, approaching a potential mentor, connecting with nonacademic staff and administrators, and using electronic mail to contact people at other institutions. Although all of Caplan's suggestions are valuable, I would also emphasize the importance of using e-mail for networking and mentoring.[1] Electronic subscriptions are excellent avenues for responding to calls for papers at professional conferences, getting advice or information about academic issues, and networking with senior-level female (and male) faculty and administrators.

Some colleges have implemented "buddy systems" where incoming students are paired with student mentors who are already enrolled at the college. These student volunteers have been helpful in acquainting minority students with the institution's resources and student services (see Armstrong, James, & Stallings, 1995). The buddy system can be especially beneficial in steering new students to effective faculty mentors. Unless colleges recruit female and minority faculty and reward mentoring, however, buddy systems are little more than cosmetic, fraudulent gestures.

Subtle Institutional Sex Discrimination

Institutions "control human conduct by setting up predetermined patterns of conduct" (Berger & Luckmann, 1966, p. 55). Subtle institutional sex discrimination in higher education is often reinforced by subtle sex discrimination in other institutions (such as the family, economy, and political systems). Because institutions are more impersonal than organizations, discriminatory policies and ideologies are more difficult to recognize. Institutional regulations, policies, and practices were established in the United States when open sex discrimination was acceptable. Many of the policies in higher education still incorporate discriminatory mechanisms against the people they are supposed to serve and despite individual efforts to change institutional procedures. Consider, for example, gendered curricula and pedagogy and gendered campuses.

17

Gendered Curricula and Pedagogy

We often hear that academic courses are gender-neutral. There is considerable evidence, however, that our educational systems are highly gendered. Mendelsohn, Nieman, Isaacs, Lee, and Levison (1994) analyzed more than 4,000 illustrations in 12 anatomy and physical diagnosis textbooks used in medical schools. The anatomy textbooks used illustrations of male bodies more than twice as often as female bodies. In the texts on physical diagnosis, the illustrations of women were largely confined to chapters on reproduction, which falsely implied that female and male physiology differ only in respect to reproductive organs. The researchers concluded that "women are dramatically underrepresented in illustrations of normal, nonreproductive anatomy" and that "males continue to be depicted as the norm or the standard. As a result, students may develop an incomplete knowledge of normal female anatomy" (p. 1269).

Women's invisibility is reinforced by other medical institutions. Despite the fact that taxes paid by women support half of all U.S. medical research, the National Institutes of Health (NIH), a major source of funding for health care research, devotes less than 10% of its research funds to women's health problems. When the NIH recently issued guidelines that require scientists to include women and people of color as research subjects in clinical trials, a number of prestigious (White male) scientists attacked such guidelines as "ridiculous" because, biologically, women and people of color are "fundamentally" the same as White males (Burd, 1994). If this is true, why have women and people of color typically been excluded as research subjects? In fact, recent research that has included women has found that women and men may respond quite differently to such drugs as painkillers, for example (Jaroff, 1996).

Law education and legal institutions also interlock to produce and reinforce masculinist perspectives. Frug (1992) identified several ways in which apparently gender-neutral law courses and casebooks on contract law are gendered. First, the parties in cases are predominantly men: "Indeed, men not only monopolize the majority of the cases in which women do not appear but they also appear in most of the cases involving women" (p. 61). Second, men represent many different occupations and roles; the few women in illustrative cases are found in stereotypical women's occupations and domestic roles:

By confining issues that particularly concern women to domestic relations or sex discrimination courses, casebooks combine with standard law school curriculums to perpetuate the idea that women's interests are personal, concerning only themselves or their families. Men, in contrast, are concerned with the rest of life. (p. 71)

Language in both text and cases often uses "he" to refer to people of both sexes. Frug (1992) notes that historical custom might explain the exclusive use of masculine pronouns in the older decisions, but that "the casebook editors never take corrective measures through their editing prerogatives to assure readers that the particularity of women is recognized" (p. 73). In addition, because casebooks rely almost exclusively on the work of male judges and male legal commentators, the absence of women is extended to the broader legal culture.

Myths of neutrality and universality—that the perspectives of privileged White males are *the* embodiment of science, medicine, law, or literature— are rarely challenged. In describing the content and structure of her working-class courses, for example, Annas (1993) commented that "one of the continual and irritating problems in teaching working-class literature is the way much of the literature has been kept out of print or keeps going out of print" (p. 173). Because the scope and content of "academic knowledge" are still defined by majority men, new approaches are rarely embraced by majority publishers (see Maher & Tetreault, 1994). Even when materials are available, women, minorities, and other groups are often marginalized. Annas pointed out, for instance, that "teaching-a-unit-on" approach—a unit on women writers, on African American writers, on working-class writers—ghettoizes such writers into a week or two of the course:

The message [the teaching-a-unit-on] format gives to the students is that working-class literature or gay and lesbian literature, for example, do exist, but that they live in a separate room, which we can leave and shut the door, going about our business in the real world. (Annas, 1993, p. 174)

Gendered Campuses

At most colleges and universities, glass walls separate male and female students and faculty. Sometimes, the male and female campuses are almost visible, however:

19

> When we visited the school of education at one university, we entered a building and turned right. If we had turned left, we would have arrived at the physics department and met a faculty that was 100% male. As we observed students entering the building, it was like watching gender-segregated lines in elementary school: Those who turned left for physics were male, those who turned right for the school of education were female. (Sadker & Sadker, 1995, p. 167)

Such parallel campuses reflect the cumulative effects, both direct and indirect, of women's and men's gender-related experiences before they arrive on campus. Using longitudinal data in a study of why talented young women do not pursue science education and occupations, Hanson (1996) found that schools and families reinforced gender stratification throughout the elementary and high school years regardless of individual talent. For example, young men are given more resources in the home (i.e., they are more likely than young women to have a pocket calculator, to have a father who keeps track of their progress in school, and to have parents who attend PTA meetings and parent-teacher conferences). In terms of school-related variables, the young women who stay in the "science achievement pipeline" are more likely to be in academic rather than technical programs; to rate their schools high on teacher interest in students; and to have friends who are more likely to get good grades, attend classes regularly, and plan to go to college. Key family and school resources may be channeled unequally due to cultural beliefs that define science as a male realm. Thus, "young women . . . come to agree with these beliefs and develop individual and personality characteristics that conform to them" (Hanson, 1996, p. 21).

Large numbers of students who plan to major in mathematics and engineering switch to other fields. Seymour and Hewitt (1997) interviewed 460 students at 13 universities to find out why so many students were leaving engineering, mathematics, and science majors. Some of the reasons included dissatisfaction with the way introductory courses were taught in those disciplines and not achieving the high grades they had received in science and math in high school. A common problem the students raised, moreover, was that most of their professors were terrible teachers who were preoccupied with their research and were typically not available for individual questions or explanations. Such aloof and forbidding demeanors of many of the faculty had a disproportionately negative effect on female and minority students, who are more successful in the context of a teacher/learner relationship (Seymour & Hewitt, 1997). Thus, even when women and minority students stay in the science pipeline throughout high school (and overcome the institutional-level obstacles that Hanson has documented), the distancing (and masculinist) teaching techniques that most colleges and universities reward may discourage even the most capable students.

Although many students sit in the same classrooms, read the same texts, take the same exams, and are taught by the same professors, they often receive substantially different educations, which can lead to substantially unequal futures. One might expect that female and minority students who feel ignored, vulnerable, or powerless could turn to faculty—especially sympathetic, senior women faculty—to change the status quo. Unfortunately, however, most women faculty and women administrators (see Masden, this volume) themselves reside in the ivory basement of the divided campus. Consider job access, incentives to accept employment, and salaries.

In terms of job access, we often hear both from gatekeepers and well-intentioned colleagues and administrators that many women applicants are disqualified from job consideration because they don't meet "gender-neutral criteria." This is a myth. In reality, gender-relevant criteria across most institutions establish formidable obstacles for many prospective women faculty. Although the following quotation is somewhat lengthy, I include it because it provides a graphic example of how the intersection of family roles, child care policies, and religious affiliation disqualify many women from job consideration despite the application of "gender-neutral" rules:

> In a search for an administrator, a Midwest liberal arts college used guidelines that had been developed historically to find the best qualified candidate. Those rules included the standard categories of holding an earned doctorate, experience as a teacher, experience in higher education administration and active membership in the church with which the institution was affiliated. . . . I contended that women were unequally eliminated by the rigid application of these presumed neutral criteria. I tried to start a conversation on the way institutions of higher education—by first decreasing the likelihood that women would have Ph.D.s, *then* would have appropriate academic experience including sufficient publications, *then* by not promoting as many women to administration—limited the pool of candidates in the first place. *Then* by applying the religious standard inflexibly, the college further limited the pool *and* by not providing for spouses (an issue of increasing importance to both male and female faculty but given our current gender system clearly a woman has to think longer and harder about asking her husband to give up a position of status for her career) or for child care we complete the process of eliminating women without ever

having acted "discriminatorily." When I tried to point out that having any women in the pool at all was a miracle given the way they used the so-called neutral criteria, my argument was roundly dismissed as politically motivated hogwash. After all, these were neutral, standard criteria. The only thing we were to worry about was not being discriminatory against specific women. No one wished to discuss how we used standards that eliminated whole classes of people. (E-mail correspondence, 1996)

Even when women and minorities are deemed "acceptable," there may be few incentives for accepting the job offer. In a study of 840 faculty at a large southeastern university, for example, Thomas and Asunka (1995) found that the most common disincentives for African, Hispanic, and Native American faculty and women faculty were the sociocultural environment and the lack of diversity in the town and community in which the university was located. According to the Association of American Medical Colleges, minority enrollments in medical schools declined 5% from 1995 to 1996. The trend was particularly striking in California, which experienced a 19% drop. The president of the association attributed much of the drop to the recent bans on affirmative action policies in California and Texas. Although such bans have not been enforced yet because of various court challenges, some university officials believe that the mounting attacks on affirmative action are making most minority students feel unwelcome on many campuses (Mangan, 1997). Thus, legislative and judicial actions have an impact on the sociocultural environment of a university. The lack of diversity, moreover, can trigger a lack of interest in prospective women and minority faculty who are looking for positive work environments.

One of the assumptions has always been that once women had access to education, salary disparities would decrease. In fact, racial and gender inequalities become greater as one goes up the educational hierarchy (see, for example, Thomas, Herring & Horton, 1995). In most cases, as experience and seniority increase, salary gaps between men and women widen. Male faculty fare better than female faculty at *all* ranks, and the salary gap *increases* as the rank increases (see Scholnick, this volume, for a discussion of pay equity issues).

Although salary data are blatant examples of sex inequality, many of the accepted explanations for the differences in earnings are more subtle. According to many economists, for example, wages are determined by the market's supply and demand: Because employers compete with each other, they must pay the highest wages to get employees who are the most in demand. When, for example, 80% of the female professors at Illinois State

University recently joined a class action sex discrimination lawsuit, some women faculty who decided not to be part of the lawsuit blamed the salary differences on reasons other than sex discrimination. A female professor of recreation and parks management said that women simply haven't done as good a job. A female business professor wrote in a long letter to the federal court clerk that she wasn't part of the suit because "the salary differential is based solely upon principles of economics—supply and demand," that professors in fields that command high salaries outside academe tend to earn the highest salaries at the university, and that such trends were not unique to Illinois State (Wilson, 1996b).

There are several problems with the presumably gender-neutral "supply and demand" picture. First, if the labor market embodies discrimination, female jobs are devalued, and this devaluation will affect the market wages of women workers (Aman & England, 1997). At colleges and other institutions, secretaries are paid considerably less than janitors, for example, not because janitors possess more skills or are in short supply but because female-dominated clerical jobs are devalued. Second, as Hanson (1996) and others have shown, schools and families often channel resources toward boys rather than girls in preparing them for job markets. Finally, the market often responds differently to shortages depending on which sex dominates occupations:

> When there is a shortage of employees in a male occupation, the wage is often raised. But when it is a female occupation, often greater effort is expended to find a new source of cheap labor rather than raising pay. For example, U.S. hospitals have complained of a shortage of nurses for over two decades but have often imported foreign nurses instead of raising pay. (Aman & England, 1997, p. 311)

Some Remedies

Many faculty and administrators are already implementing remedies for subtle sexist institutional practices. In terms of *gendered curricula and pedagogy,* for example, colleges and universities now offer more than 20,000 women's studies courses (Guy-Sheftall & Heath, 1995). Some innovative programs include gender, race, social class, and sexual orientation issues in courses outside women's studies programs (see Fiol-Matta & Chamberlain, 1994). In lieu of the traditional term paper, many (women) faculty have their students write journals throughout the semester to integrate the students' experiences into reading (both traditional and

23

nontraditional sources), analytical thinking, and writing (see, for example, Zimbardo, 1993). Others involve students actively in the classroom to "transform the landscape of the traditional classroom, making it a space where all of us can begin the process of exposing the subtle sexisms of our everyday lives" (Gilbert, 1997, p. 246). This transformation includes role-playing, sharing the responsibility of learning (instead of relying exclusively on the instructor as the authority), and encouraging students to work together in "coming to grips" with such issues as subtle sexism.

Using a unique approach, McCaughey and King (1995) constructed a "Mean Women" video for their students to challenge popular conceptions of femininity and masculinity that support rape, rape fantasies, and men's sexual assaults. McCaughey and King strung together scenes from contemporary movies (such as *Aliens, Batman Returns, Blue Steel, Buffy the Vampire Slayer, Double Impact, Lethal Weapon 3, Terminator 2: Judgment Day*, and *Thelma and Louise*) that portrayed women in powerful roles. These faculty members emphasize that their video does not suggest that women's aggression is the only solution to rape. They are experimenting, however, with new images of women and their capabilities and men's perceptions of their own social power and physical vulnerability: "Men may assault women because they *believe* they will get away with it or because they *believe* women really want it; men may respect women because they *believe* that they won't get away with it or that women would actually become very angry" (p. 386).

In terms of *gendered campuses,* schools and families can plug the leaky pipelines that discourage girls' pursuing careers in engineering, mathematics, and science. Parents can be involved in their daughters' school and schoolwork, encourage friendships with school peer groups that value education, support progressive ideas about women's roles outside of the home, and discourage early marriage and family formation. Schools can require more math and science courses for graduation; have active, involved teachers; and have academic programs and environments that encourage interest in science (Hanson, 1996).

Higher education institutions can reward teaching techniques that include the voices of women, lesbians, older students, students from working-class families, and minorities. Women faculty should be vocal in pointing out institutional inequities and should pursue legal remedies whenever necessary. Individual lawsuits are effective, but the women may be blackballed or their professional reputations damaged even if a university settles out of court (see Saltzman, 1996). Substantiating a charge of sex or race discrimination against a university in hiring, promotion, or tenure decisions is often difficult because "unfair" decisions are not always illegal or discriminatory (see Leap, 1995).

Class action suits—such as those at Virginia Commonwealth University, the University of California at Davis, and Northern Arizona University— both protect individual plaintiffs and are more likely to be taken seriously by administrators because they attract greater media attention. In fact, academic women should follow the example of many women in blue-collar and white-collar jobs who have persisted in class action suits despite criticism, ostracism, virulent backlash, and even physical assaults by neighbors, friends, and coworkers (see Grimsley, 1996).

Some countries are much less tolerant than the United States of women's exclusion from higher education. In Sweden, for example, a 1990 law encouraged all state agencies, including universities, to use "positive discrimination" to give qualified female candidates preference in hiring. When the law was rarely used in higher education, the Minister of Education and Science proposed legislation, which was subsequently passed by the Parliament, to establish 100 new academic positions at the six universities, including 30 full professorships, that are reserved for candidates (women, in most cases) "whose gender is underrepresented" in specific disciplines. Women account for 65% of university graduates in Sweden, yet only 7% of full professors are female. The 30 professorships will have only a "tiny impact" on the overall gender imbalance because they represent only 1.4% of the 2,200 professors employed at Sweden's state universities (Bollag, 1996). Nonetheless, the Minister's and Parliament's actions are important symbolically. Can you imagine the U.S. Secretary of Education making a similar gesture?

You will recall that some private, liberal arts college administrators in the United States are considering abolishing traditionally male-dominated programs in science and engineering because male enrollments have fallen off. In contrast, several Nordic nations (such as Sweden, Finland, and Norway) have increased their efforts to attract female students to programs in mathematics, science, and technology. Some of the Swedish universities, for example, have implemented single-sex technology programs in high schools to counteract the effects of boys who "tend to take over completely in everything having to do with computers" (Bollag, 1997, p. A41). Some Norwegian universities have designed courses that offer female computer students tutorial help, the opportunity to be taught in small groups, and female computer engineers as guest lecturers. Although some students and faculty have complained that such programs are unfair because they give special help to women, the Nordic universities have justified these nontraditional efforts to overcome a chronic shortage of skilled professionals in technical fields (Bollag, 1997).

Subtle Cultural Sex Discrimination

Subtle cultural sex discrimination is very difficult to "see" because sexist (as well as racist, ageist, classist, and heterosexist) practices and values are built into our literature, art, music, language, symbols, morals, customs, beliefs, artifacts, ideology, and popular culture. Subtle cultural sex discrimination does exist, however, and is often reinforced by higher education systems. Consider, for example, what I call "the Oprah effect," the multicultural myth, and athletic programs.

The Oprah Effect

Many of us suffer from the "Oprah effect," a generalized belief that women (and especially minority women) who "don't make it" are simply not trying hard enough. After all, look at Oprah Winfrey's success, fame, and fortune. Besides being one of the wealthiest people in America, Oprah "has all the answers to such problems as domestic violence, marital strife, mental illness and other forms of social 'immorality' and disorder" (Wallace, 1993, p. 123). Her meteoric industry success gives the impression that our society welcomes and rewards hardworking and talented minority women and that other women of color fail to attain the same heights simply because they're not motivated. By focusing briefly on a few "exceptional" examples, according to Higginbotham (1995), we romanticize highly visible women (such as Oprah Winfrey) or Black historical figures (such as Sojourner Truth and Harriet Tubman) and ignore "the larger system in which the struggles of women of color, whether successful or not, take place" (p. 483).

The Multicultural Myth

The United States is the most culturally pluralistic nation in the world. This diversity rarely characterizes the typical college campus, however. Many minority students drop out of traditionally White universities because they experience social isolation, exclusion, and prejudice (Aubert, 1997). To counteract such disenfranchisement, some colleges and universities have established what Johnson (1997) calls "cultural centers," which refers to "organizations, theme houses, and residence halls or any other recognized, voluntary groupings of students on a racial or cultural basis" (p. 155). Cultural centers have enhanced multicultural experiences by bringing speakers to campus; sponsoring music, dance, and art programs; and making literature and media available for all students. In the case of Native Americans, since 1969, 30 (primarily 2-year) tribal colleges have been established to serve as bridges between reservation life and students' entry into large and predominantly White universities (Liska, 1996).

Such bridges and cultural centers have required substantial sacrifices on the part of many faculty of color, especially women faculty. For example, in a national survey of 33,986 college and university faculty, the Higher Education Research Institute (HERI) at the University of California, Los Angeles found that White and minority female faculty were more likely than their male counterparts to pursue an academic career because of the opportunity to influence social change, provide services to the community, prepare students for responsible citizenship, and develop the moral character of undergraduates. The researchers also found that African American, Native American, Asian American, Latino/a, and White female faculty were more likely than their male counterparts to report that frequent sources of stress included time pressures, a lack of personal time, seeing students, high teaching loads, and caring for elderly parents (Astin, Antonio, Cress, & Astin, 1997). Although the researchers did not imply a causal relationship between these sets of variables, it is interesting to note that the faculty (i.e., women) who appear the most interested in promoting social change in higher education are also the most likely to experience personal and professional constraints that impede realizing change-oriented interests.

These constraints will probably increase as campuses become less multicultural in the future. According to a recent report in the *Chronicle of Higher Education,* there is a widening gap between low-income (and many middle-income) students and students from high-income families because of economic and policy changes. For example, tuition has been rising steadily, whereas many family incomes have stagnated. Federal grant programs have failed to keep pace with college costs. Many institutional scholarships that were once reserved for awards based on financial need are now based on academic achievement (Burd, Healy, Lively, & Shea,

1996). In addition, as noted earlier, the recent restrictions on affirmative action programs are expected to lead to significant decreases in Black and Latino/a enrollments at many colleges and professional schools.

Between 1987 and 1994, universities and colleges increased the amount of money they spent on research and development in the sciences and engineering by about 74%, whereas support for humanities and social science programs plummeted. At some institutions, ethnic studies and women's studies budgets have been cut drastically, and the elimination of these programs may be imminent (Cordes & Walker, 1996). In addition, the proportion of people who are teaching full-time but who are not on tenure tracks or teaching part-time has increased precipitously. In the latter case, for example, the National Center for Education Statistics estimates that 43% of faculty members worked part-time in academic 1992-1993, up from 38% in 1987-1988 and 22% in 1970 (Wilson, 1996a). All of these curricular and personnel changes will invariably undermine even the modest progress that has been made in introducing multiculturalism on many campuses.

Athletic Programs

In an analysis of sports and sexism, Cahn (1994) showed how our gendered structure of athletics is the result of historical and current assumptions "that some sports are inherently and incontrovertibly masculine or feminine" (p. 217). Women have made some progress on the international athletic stage. Compared to 1896, when women were barred from the first modern games in Athens, nearly 3,700 women (about 36% of all athletes) competed in the Olympic Games in Atlanta, Georgia, in 1996. However, according to Donna Lopiano (1996), who heads the Women's Sports Foundation, there is still considerable bias in women's sports. For example, the Amateur Sports Act of 1978 mandated putting the same amount of money into women's sports as men's sports, based on the proportion of athletes in each. This has not happened, according to Lopiano. Moreover, the Olympics still do not have such women's sports as weightlifting and water polo, and, during the 1996 Olympics, many of the women's competitions were televised after 12:30 a.m. instead of during prime time (Markus, 1996).

Similar discriminatory practices are reflected in higher education. Title IX of the Education Amendments of 1972 prohibits discrimination on the basis of sex at institutions that receive federal funds. According to Lopiano, college sports are "not just fun and games." At the college level, athletic scholarships and admissions preferences for athletes translate into access to education that many young women and men would otherwise not have (Lopiano, 1996). Yet on every campus, one or two men's sports—usually football and basketball—traditionally have received a disproportionate share of the athletics budget. In 1992, nine women sued Brown University, 1 year after Brown cut off financial support for its women's gymnastics and volleyball teams. In 1996, the U.S. Court of Appeals for the First Circuit upheld a lower-court ruling that Brown had violated Title IX when, in 1991, it cut financial support for two women's sports teams. Although many women applauded the decision, some of the female athletes at Brown were reportedly "ambivalent about the decision: Many of them fear that the ruling may cause men's teams to be cut, which is not their aim" (Guernsey, 1996, p. A58).

The latter reactions by women are dismaying for two reasons. First, Lopiano (1996) noted that instead of opening up athletics opportunities for women, many college presidents (and high school principals) "take the easy way out by cutting men's 'minor' sports and blaming it on the women" (p. B7). Apparently, such subtle "blaming the victim" ploys are effective: Women "feel sorry" for reducing men's high standard of living in athletics (and elsewhere) instead of pushing for more changes.

Some Remedies

According to Garner (1996), "transforming antifeminist culture within the academy means, ultimately, transforming antifeminist culture outside the academy" (p. 201). Although this is a viable strategy for reducing blatant sexism, how do we transform subtle sex discrimination practices on the societal level?

The subtle discriminatory practices that reflect built-in patterns of gender inequality can be dismantled in several ways. The federal government can reward the recruitment and retention of women and women of color as students and faculty and can enforce penalties when institutions refuse to implement equal opportunity practices or have a history of sex discrimination. In the private sector, business and industry can target contributions (such as home computers) to the most disadvantaged groups. Instead of shoring up affirmative action programs, legislative action should earmark more funds for scholarships and living expenses. Higher education governing boards (now comprised largely of successful White businessmen) should be reconstituted to include women who are familiar with gender inequality problems in higher education.

The mainstream media are often guilty of trivializing sexism in educational systems. When the 6- and 7-year-old boys in North Carolina and New York were suspended for kissing their classmates, the media's reactions varied considerably. *Newsweek* presented the "outraged" reactions of the boys' parents. The magazine also noted that scholarly research conducted by such organizations as the American Association of University Women (AAUW) showed that sexual harassment should be taken seriously at any age because one third of those harassed said the problem began in the sixth grade or earlier (see Leland, 1996). Similarly, a *Washington Post* writer cited the AAUW study; included such educators as the National Association of Elementary School Principals, which expressed concern about sexual harassment in elementary schools; and framed the article within the larger context of the prevalence of sexual harassment as witnessed by the Navy's Tailhook scandal and the lawsuit against Mitsubishi Motors (see Sanchez, 1996).

Time, on the other hand, mocked the harassment incidents as "political correctness gone haywire." The only "experts" the *Time* journalist cited were Rush Limbaugh and Kathie Lee Gifford (that's right, the one whose line of clothes relied on child labor in developing countries), who announced that "We've gone too far with this now when we can't let a child be a child," and Camille Paglia, who described the incident as an example of "archfeminist ideology gone amuck" (Zoglin, 1996, p. 64). Clearly, sensationalism sells newspapers and magazines.

Note, also, how often the media publicize the exception in women's progress but ignore the rule. Arguing that women's basketball has come a long way, for example, *U.S. News & World Report* journalist Warren Cohen (1995) pointed out that "perhaps the best indicator of female hoops' new prominence can be found at Rutgers University, where women's basketball coach C. Vivian Stringer now earns a base salary of $150,000 a year, more than her male counterpart" (p. 81). It would have been instructive if Cohen had also compared the male and female coaches' salaries of the other five or six universities he cited in the article. According to a recent survey of the nation's largest college athletics programs (those in the National Collegiate Athletic Association's Division 1), for example, in 1996-1997, the median salary for male head basketball coaches was $290,000 compared to $98,400 for females (Naughton, 1997).

Some of this tabloid coverage could be countered by intelligent op-ed articles. How many women (and men) faculty, however, have ever submitted editorials that discuss gender inequality issues? Wood (1994) noted that "the news is not neutral, in either its representation or its effects. It shapes our understanding of the world around us in subtle and not so subtle ways, and we act on those understandings" (p. 117). Because the news is not neutral, students and faculty can (and should) challenge news media coverage that perpetuates misogynistic myths and sex stereotypes.

CONCLUSION

It is easy to feel overwhelmed when looking for solutions for sex discrimination, especially subtle sex discrimination. The status quo can be changed, nevertheless. At all levels, lawsuits, and especially class-action suits, are an effective way of showing gatekeepers and others that many of us are serious about removing discriminatory barriers. As students, faculty, administrators, and alumni, we can speak up individually about "just below the surface" discriminatory behavior that many women (and some men) experience on a daily basis. On the organizational level, senior faculty, mentors, and administrators, particularly those at decision-making levels, could alter current exclusionary policies. At the institutional level, there could be a massive infusion of women who have a greater tolerance for diverse ideas, perspectives, and practices that many in the powerful male (and some female) groups and networks do not now accept. Culture changes, albeit slowly, through both top-down and bottom-up pressures. Pressure for change will not come from those who are profiting—socially, economically, and politically—from the status quo. The action of women themselves is critical for major reforms at individual, organizational, institutional, and cultural levels.

NOTE

1. Although there are a number of informative gender-related e-mail subscriptions, one of the most comprehensive is Joan Korenman's WMST-L (Women's Studies List), which provides websites on women and gender, numerous subscription lists, and film reviews. To subscribe to WMST-L, send a "subscribe WMST-L" message in the body of the text to listserv@umdd.umd.edu. On the World Wide Web, the URL is http://www.umbc.edu/wmst/

links.html. Other informative gender-related websites include http://www.library.wisc.edu/libraries/WomensStudies/fcmain.htm and http://www.library.wisc.edu/libraries/Women's Studies.

REFERENCES

Aman, C. J., & England, P. (1997). Comparable worth: When do two jobs deserve the same pay? In N. Benokraitis (Ed.), *Subtle sexism: Current practices and prospects for change* (pp. 297-314). Thousand Oaks, CA: Sage.

Annas, P. (1993). Pass the cake: The politics of gender, class, and text in the academic workplace. In M. M. Tokarczyk & E. A. Fay (Eds.), *Working-class women in the academy: Laborers in the knowledge factory* (pp. 165-178). Amherst: University of Massachusetts Press.

Armstrong, D. G., James, F. G., & Stallings, J. A. (1995). Decentralizing the minority recruitment and retention function: A report on one college of education's experience. In G. E. Thomas (Ed.), *Race and ethnicity in America: Meeting the challenge in the 21st century* (pp. 79-89). Washington, DC: Taylor & Francis.

Astin, H. S., Antonio, A. L., Cress, C. M., & Astin, A. W. (1997). *Race and ethnicity in the American professoriate, 1995-96.* Los Angeles: UCLA Higher Education Research Institute.

Aubert, S. D. (1997). Black students on White campuses: Overcoming the isolation. In K. Lomotey (Ed.), *Sailing against the wind: African Americans and women in U.S. education* (pp. 141-146). Albany: State University of New York Press.

Benokraitis, N. (1997). Sex discrimination in the 21st century. In N. Benokraitis (Ed.), *Subtle sexism: Current practices and prospects for change* (pp. 5-33). Thousand Oaks, CA: Sage.

Benokraitis, N., & Feagin, J. (1995). *Modern sexism: Blatant, subtle and covert discrimination* (2nd ed.). Englewood Cliffs, NJ: Prentice Hall.

Bento, R. F. (1997). When good intentions are not enough: Unintentional subtle discrimination against Latinas in the workplace. In N. Benokraitis (Ed.), *Subtle sexism: Current practices and prospects for change* (pp. 95-116). Thousand Oaks, CA: Sage.

Berger, P. L., & Luckmann, T. (1966). *The social construction of reality: A treatise in the sociology of knowledge.* New York: Doubleday.

Blakemore, J. E. O., Switzer, J. Y., DiIorio, J. A., & Fairchild, D. L. (1997). Exploring the campus climate for women faculty. In N. Benokraitis (Ed.), *Subtle sexism: Current practices and prospects for change* (pp. 54-71). Thousand Oaks, CA: Sage.

Bollag, B. (1996, December 13). Sweden orders universities to develop plans to recruit female professors. *Chronicle of Higher Education*, p. A44.

Bollag, B. (1997, April 25). Universities in Nordic nations seek to attract women to scientific fields. *Chronicle of Higher Education*, pp. A43, A45.

Burd, S. (1994, April 6). NIH issues rules requiring women and minorities in clinical trials. *Chronicle of Higher Education*, p. 50A.

Burd, S., Healy, P., Lively, K., & Shea, C. (1996, June 14). Low-income students say college options are limited by the actions of lawmakers and campus officials. *Chronicle of Higher Education*, pp. A10-A12.

Cahn, S. K. (1994). *Coming on strong: Gender and sexuality in twentieth-century women's sports.* New York: Free Press.

Caplan, P. J. (1993). *Lifting a ton of feathers: A woman's guide for surviving in the academic world.* Toronto: University of Toronto Press.

Carpenter, M. W. (1996). Female grotesques in academia: Ageism, antifeminism, and feminists on the faculty. In V. Clark, S. N. Garner, M. Higonnet, & K. H. Katrak (Eds.), *Antifeminism in the academy* (pp. 141-165). New York: Routledge.

Chan, S., & Wang, L. (1991). Racism and the model minority: Asian-Americans in higher education. In P. G. Altbach & K. Lomotey (Eds.), *The racial crisis in American higher education* (pp. 43-67). Albany: State University of New York Press.

Cohen, W. (1995, December 11). Courting big-time commercial success. *U.S. News & World Report*, pp. 81-82.

Cordes, C., & Walker, P. V. (1996, June 14). Ability to win grants increasingly dictates clout of departments within universities. *Chronicle of Higher Education*, pp. A14-A15.

Fay, E. A. (1993). Dissent in the field; Or, a new type of intellectual? In M. M. Tokarczyk & E. A. Fay (Eds.), *Working-class women in the academy: Laborers in the knowledge factory* (pp. 276-291). Amherst, MA: University of Massachusetts Press.

Fiol-Matta, L., & Chamberlain, M. K. (Eds.). (1994). *Women of color and the multicultural curriculum: Transforming the college classroom*. New York: Feminist Press.

Frehill, L. M. (1997). Subtle sexism in engineering. In N. Benokraitis (Ed.), *Subtle sexism: Current practices and prospects for change* (pp. 117-135). Thousand Oaks, CA: Sage.

Frug, M. J. (1992). *Postmodern legal feminism*. New York: Routledge.

Gaard, G. (1996). Anti-lesbian intellectual harassment in the academy. In V. Clark, S. N. Garner, M. Higonnet, & K. H. Katrak (Eds.), *Antifeminism in the academy* (pp. 115-140). New York: Routledge.

Gardner, S. (1993). "What's a nice working-class girl like you doing in a place like this?" In M. M. Tokarczyk & E. A. Fay (Eds.), *Working-class women in the academy: Laborers in the knowledge factory* (pp. 49-59). Amherst: University of Massachusetts Press.

Garner, S. N. (1996). Transforming antifeminist culture in the academy. In V. Clark, S. N. Garner, M. Higonnet, & K. H. Katrak (Eds.), *Antifeminism in the academy* (pp. 201-217). New York: Routledge.

Gilbert, M. (1997). Transforming the classroom: Teaching subtle sexism through experiential role-playing. In N. Benokraitis (Ed.), *Subtle sexism: Current practices and prospects for change* (pp. 245-263). Thousand Oaks, CA: Sage.

Gose, B. (1997, June 6). Liberal-arts colleges ask: Where have the men gone? *Chronicle of Higher Education*, pp. A35-A36.

Gratch, L. V. (1997). Recognizing sexual harassment. In B. R. Sandler & R. J. Shoop (Eds.), *Sexual harassment on campus: A guide for administrators, faculty, and students* (pp. 278-292). Boston: Allyn & Bacon.

Grimsley, K. D. (1996, October 28). In court, women miners felt harassed again. *Washington Post*, pp. A1, A12.

Guernsey, L. (1996, December 6). Many female athletes at Brown are ambivalent about the appeals-court ruling. *Chronicle of Higher Education*, pp. A58-A60.

Guy-Sheftall, B., & Heath, S. (1995). *Women's studies: A retrospective*. New York: Ford Foundation.

Hanson, S. L. (1996). *Lost talent: Women in the sciences*. Philadelphia: Temple University Press.

Harris, S. A. (1995). Internal attributes of successful African Americans employed in predominantly White American schools in New England. In G. E. Thomas (Ed.), *Race and ethnicity in America: Meeting the challenge in the 21st century* (pp. 309-323). Washington, DC: Taylor & Francis.

Haslett, B. B., & Lipman, S. (1997). Micro inequities: Up close and personal. In N. Benokraitis (Ed.), *Subtle sexism: Current practices and prospects for change* (pp. 34-53). Thousand Oaks, CA: Sage.

Higginbotham, E. (1995). Designing an inclusive curriculum: Bringing all women into the core. In B. Guy-Sheftall (Ed.), *Words of fire: An anthology of African-American feminist thought* (pp. 474-486). New York: The New Press.

Jacobs, J. A. (1996). Gender inequality and higher education. *Annual Review of Sociology, 22,* 153-185.

Jaroff, L. (1996, November 11). Killing the pain. *Time,* p. 75.

Johnson, S. (1997). Ethnic/cultural centers on predominantly White campuses: Are they necessary? In K. Lomotey (Ed.), *Sailing against the wind: African Americans and women in U.S. education* (pp. 155-162). Albany: State University of New York Press.

Kolodny, A. (1996). Paying the price of antifeminist intellectual harassment. In V. Clark, S. N. Garner, M. Higonnet, & K. H. Katrak (Eds.), *Antifeminism in the academy* (pp. 3-33). New York: Routledge.

Leap, T. L. (1995, Spring). Tenure, discrimination, and African-American faculty. *Journal of Blacks in Higher Education, 7,* 103-105.

Leatherman, C. (1996, December 6). To get rid of a difficult employee, a college may hush up problems in a professor's past. *Chronicle of Higher Education,* pp. A14-A16.

Leland, J. (1996, October 21). A kiss isn't just a kiss. *Newsweek,* pp. 71-72.

Liska, A. (1996). Native Americans in higher education. In J. Tang & E. Smith (Eds.), *Women and minorities in American professions* (pp. 157-167). Albany: State University of New York Press.

Lopiano, D. (1996, December 6). Title IX: It's time to live up to the letter of the law. *Chronicle of Higher Education,* p. B7.

Lorber, J. (1994). *Paradoxes of gender.* New Haven, CT: Yale University Press.

Maher, F. A., & Tetreault, M. K. T. (1994). *The feminist classroom.* New York: Basic Books.

Mangan, K. S. (1997, January 10). Minority enrollments drop at medical schools. *Chronicle of Higher Education,* pp. A49-A50.

Markus, D. (1996, July 17). Women strive for equal play. *Baltimore Sun,* pp. 1D, 7D.

Martin, S. E., & Jurik, N. C. (1996). *Doing justice, doing gender.* Thousand Oaks, CA: Sage.

McCaughey, M., & King, N. (1995). Rape education videos: Presenting mean women instead of dangerous men. *Teaching Sociology, 23,* 374-388.

Mendelsohn, K. D., Nieman, L. Z., Isaacs, K., Lee, S., & Levison, S. P. (1994). Sex and gender bias in anatomy and physical diagnosis text illustrations. *Journal of the American Medical Association, 272,* 1267-1270.

Mickelson, R. A., & Oliver, M. L. (1991). Making the short list: Black candidates and the faculty recruitment process. In P. G. Altbach & K. Lomotey (Eds.), *The racial crisis in American higher education* (pp. 149-166). Albany: State University of New York Press.

Miner, V. (1993). Writing and teaching with class. In M. M. Tokarczyk & E. A. Fay (Eds.), *Working-class women in the academy: Laborers in the knowledge factory* (pp. 73-86). Amherst: University of Massachusetts Press.

National Center for Education Statistics. (1995). *Digest of education statistics.* Washington, DC: U.S. Government Printing Office.

Naughton, J. (1997, March 28). A confidential report details salaries of athletics officials. *Chronicle of Higher Education,* pp. A49-A50.

Nora, A., & Cabrera, A. F. (1996). The role of perceptions of prejudice and discrimination on the adjustment of minority students to college. *Journal of Higher Education, 67,* 119-148.

Pierce, T. (1996, November 5). Stop sexism by exposing it. *Rocky Mountain Collegian,* p. 4.

Reyes, M., & Halcn, J. J. (1991). Practices of the academy: Barriers to access for Chicano academics. In P. G. Altbach & K. Lomotey (Eds.), *The racial crisis in American higher education* (pp. 167-186). Albany: State University of New York Press.

Roskelly, H. (1993). Telling tales in school: A redneck daughter in the academy. In M. M. Tokarczyk & E. A. Fay (Eds.), *Working-class women in the academy: Laborers in the knowledge factory* (pp. 292-307). Amherst: University of Massachusetts Press.

Rowe, M. (1990). Barriers to equality: The power of subtle discrimination to maintain unequal opportunity. *Employee Responsibilities and Rights Journal, 3*, 153-163.

Sadker, M., & Sadker, D. (1995). *Failing at fairness: How our schools cheat girls*. New York: Touchstone.

St. Jean, Y., & Feagin, J. R. (1997). Racial masques: Black women and subtle gendered racism. In N. Benokraitis (Ed.), *Subtle sexism: Current practices and prospects for change* (pp. 179-200). Thousand Oaks, CA: Sage.

Saltzman, A. (1996, August 19). Life after the lawsuit. *U.S. News & World Report*, pp. 57-61.

Sanchez, R. (1996, October 4). In school, early lessons on sexual harassment. *Washington Post*, pp. A1, A4.

Seymour, E., & Hewitt, N. M. (1997). *Talking about leaving: Why undergraduates leave the sciences*. Boulder, CO: Westview Press.

Sowinska, S. (1993). Yer own motha wouldna reckanized ya: Surviving an apprenticeship in the "knowledge factory." In M. M. Tokarczyk & E. A. Fay (Eds.), *Working-class women in the academy: Laborers in the knowledge factory* (pp. 148-164). Amherst: University of Massachusetts Press.

Stanfield, II, J. H. (1995). Gazing through the kitchen window: Race and elite academic employment in post-1970s America. In G. E. Thomas (Ed.), *Race and ethnicity in America: Meeting the challenge in the 21st century* (pp. 325-334). Washington, DC: Taylor & Francis.

Strosnider, K. (1997, January 10). FBI investigates charges that female cadets at the Citadel were hazed. *Chronicle of Higher Education*, p. A51.

Swim, J. K., Aikin, K. J., Hall, W. S., & Hunter, B. A. (1995). Sexism and racism: Old-fashioned and modern prejudices. *Journal of Personality and Social Psychology, 68*, 199-214.

Swim, J. K., & Cohen, L. L. (1997). Overt, covert, and subtle sexism: A comparison between the Attitudes Toward Women and Modern Sexism scales. *Psychology of Women Quarterly, 21*, 103-118.

Thomas, G. E., & Asunka, K. (1995). Employment and quality of life of minority and women faculty in a predominantly White institution. In G. E. Thomas (Ed.), *Race and ethnicity in America: Meeting the challenge in the 21st century* (pp. 295-308). Washington, DC: Taylor & Francis.

Thomas, M. E., Herring, C., & Horton, H. D. (1995). Racial and gender differences in returns from education. In G. E. Thomas (Ed.), *Race and ethnicity in America: Meeting the challenge in the 21st century* (pp. 239-253). Washington, DC: Taylor & Francis.

Tokarczyk, M. M. (1993). By the rivers of Babylon. In M. M. Tokarczyk & E. A. Fay (Eds.), *Working-class women in the academy: Laborers in the knowledge factory* (pp. 311-321). Amherst: University of Massachusetts Press.

Wallace, M. (1993). Negative images: Towards a Black feminist cultural criticism. In S. During (Ed.), *The cultural studies reader* (pp. 118-131). New York: Routledge.

Wilson, R. (1996a, June 14). Scholars off the tenure track wonder if they'll ever get on. *Chronicle of Higher Education*, pp. A12-A13.

Wilson, R. (1996b, November 8). 350 female faculty members join a pay-equity dispute at Illinois State U. *Chronicle of Higher Education*, pp. A10-A11.

Wilson, R. (1997, June 6). At Harvard, Yale, and Stanford, women lost tenure bids despite backing from departments. *Chronicle of Higher Education*, pp. A10-A11.

Wood, J. T. (1994). *Who cares? Women, care, and culture.* Carbondale: Southern Illinois University Press.

Zimbardo, R. (1993). Teaching the working woman. In M. M. Tokarczyk & E. A. Fay (Eds.), *Working-class women in the academy: Laborers in the knowledge factory* (pp. 208-215). Amherst: University of Massachusetts Press.

Zoglin, R. (1996, October 7). A kiss isn't just a kiss. *Time*, p. 64.

Searching for Congruity:
Reflections of an Untenured Woman of Color

Alberta M. Gloria

As the only woman of color in an all-White department, I believe that I have a unique perspective regarding the intricacies and implicit assumptions of the academic system. In particular, I have learned the importance of personal power, survival skills, and personal and professional congruity. Perhaps it was out of my naivete as a new faculty member, or my need to believe that faculty members and administrators in higher education would respond and behave in ways that demonstrated a value for diversity, that I found myself serving as the multicultural advocate, researcher, representative, and resource to the point that I felt like the proverbial thorn in the department's side. This narrative describes a series of interrelated events that demonstrate how my cultural values and "essence" as a woman of color have been incongruent with the male-dominated Eurocentric values of the academic institution. Although there are many interpretations of the following experiences, this narrative describes *my* realities as I lived and felt them.

When first hired, I felt confident that I was selected because of my qualifications (e.g., previous teaching, research, and service) and my experience and knowledge of diversity issues. This confidence steadily deteriorated, however, as a result of several experiences and general attitudes that I faced on a daily basis. I sensed that others questioned my hire long before a colleague intimated to me that I was simply fulfilling a university racial/ethnic minority quota. Although I was never directly told that I needed to work harder than my peers, I nevertheless found myself working harder in an effort to be treated and acknowledged as an equal. The additional work required me to be more organized and to devote large amounts of energy to attend to my additional responsibilities.

Adding to my perception of having to work "double duty," there was an implicit assumption that I would work with, advise, and mentor each of the racial/ethnic minority students in the department. I was a consistent advocate for admitting qualified racial/ethnic students to the department, but I also feared that I was creating more work for myself. Students of color not only gravitated to but were directed to my office; they came not only from my department but from different colleges within the university, and eventually from local community colleges. I remember explicitly my conversation with two colleagues who advised me to better manage my time by saying no to students and community presentations. How could I say no to my community, to those who helped me get to this position in higher education, and to those who were seeking guidance and answers about academia? I was the only woman faculty of color; who else would say yes? From a personal level, how could I distance and disconnect myself from those persons who reflected my realities as a person of color in a predominantly male *and* White academic institution? White women faculty members told me that they had heavy loads of women advisees and mentees. What I was unable to communicate to them (and what I believed they were not hearing) was that there were additional roles and responsibilities for women faculty who represent a racial/ethnic minority groups (e.g., asked to participate in the racial/ethnic minority *and* women's communities). I was not trying to win some competition for who had the most work or who worked the hardest, but I did want to convey the realities of my struggles. Meeting with students on weekends became necessary for me in order to fulfill my roles and responsibilities. At the same time, I was told that the reason that I was more demanding of racial/ethnic minority students and myself was because "I had something to prove" as a woman of color. I felt stuck, alone, and greatly misunderstood. I was an untenured, unmentored, novice faculty person who was trying my best, while at every turn feeling scrutinized. I was caught in an all-too-familiar situation experienced by many faculty of color: I was torn between serving the needs of my cultural community (students included) and trying to fulfill my departmental, faculty, and tenure responsibilities. I was trying to manage the department's implicit assumptions and expectations that I work with both the racial/ethnic minority students and the community.

I recall many conversations with my racial/ethnic minority students, who were questioning their own admission into graduate school. They wondered whether they were admitted into the program for reasons other than their academic skills and abilities (i.e., racial/ethnic quota). Several of these students were told by their peers that they were admitted because of their racial/ethnic background. These students were confused, hurt, and angry; several were seriously considering dropping out of the program. Although I knew that they had a right to higher education, I struggled to assure them that their degree was worth what they had to experience and endure within academia, that someday they would help to infuse a multicultural perspective into academia. It was difficult for me to reassure them that they could find cultural congruity between their personal and academic values when I was experiencing the pain of my own doubts and struggling to find answers to these questions for myself.

When I did find time to do research, which involved collaborating with racial/ethnic minority students within the department, I was reminded of the implicit assumptions regarding publishing for a faculty person of color. To my dismay, I was told by several different students that my faculty colleagues had expressed concern and even anger about one of my recently published articles on multicultural issues in academia. Further, I was told that there had been faculty discussions and plans for continued discussion about the article (to which I had not been invited). Unfortunately, many discussions occurred in my absence, and I was unable to explain or defend my research agenda. One faculty colleague, who approached me directly, questioned my reasons for writing the article. I began to wonder if I had misunderstood the publish-or-perish concept. Was not one of my objectives as an untenured assistant professor to establish a programmatic line of research and publish the results of my queries? I was confused and disturbed by the fact that other faculty could develop a research agenda that examined the experiences of their own racial/ethnic group (i.e., White people), but when I did the same, my research agenda was discounted as a personal political agenda. I was left wondering how I could continue and survive academically with a programmatic research agenda that incited such negative emotion and energy. After all, these were the same faculty who would soon evaluate my work for tenure and promotion. I learned that the publish-or-perish rule often has an implicit caveat that research must be of a certain content (i.e., devoid of cultural realities other than those espoused by the academic establishment) in order to be considered "real" research. I found myself questioning whether I needed to formulate a new research agenda that would be more acceptable or "mainstream."

This narrative provides cautionary information for other women faculty and women faculty of color, yet I also believe it marks a history from which *all* faculty and administrators can learn. Further, I believe that this is a story of my own empowerment and efficacy and the discovery of my personal and professional congruity. Although painful, I truly value these growth opportunities and those faculty colleagues from whom I have learned valuable professional and personal lessons. My greatest lesson learned has been the importance of maintaining a sense of a cultural self in my professional life. There must be congruence between who I am personally (i.e., culturally) and professionally, and my skills, abilities, values, and beliefs. I have learned that I must always filter the male-dominated Eurocentric values of academia that have threatened and continue to threaten my "balance." In regaining my congruence, I chose to enter the "revolving door" of academia. I sought a place where I am not the only faculty of color and where all aspects of my racial/ethnic research are valued: a place where each faculty member is expected to be and is a resource for multicultural and diversity issues. Although I continue to struggle with feelings of incongruity with certain aspects of academia (e.g., the individualistic and competitive nature of tenure) and question whether I can achieve congruity between my personal and professional selves in academia, I continue my journey as a more powerful, efficacious, and better informed individual. As other faculty women of color find validation in their own experiences, it is my belief that we can reinstate and strengthen our cultural selves and senses of congruency within the academic institution. To this end, I believe that academia would greatly benefit by supporting the cultural congruity of all of its members.

On Overcoming Bureaucracy:
A Tale of a Grievance

Kathryn Quina

The year before I arrived at the University of Rhode Island, several faculty women had filed a class action lawsuit against the university for sex discrimination in promotion and salary. Although the suit dragged on for 10 years, the effect on my promotion/tenure process was unquestionable. By the time

I came up for my tenure decision, the university had realized that they were likely to lose some or all of their case, and they didn't want any more media heat. Women were talking to each other about effective strategies. The attorney for the women plaintiffs met with me beforehand, and I had an opportunity to select a comparator and make a side-by-side comparison of my strengths. Not the least important was the support from women and men who clearly believed in me (see Quina, 1986).

I owe a lot to my pioneering colleagues, who ultimately won a significant victory for most of us. Like Athena, they were brave, steady, and strong. They refused to fold under pressure. Little did I know it would fall on me someday to continue in their path.

I thrived in the URI environment of support and generosity. I worked hard to do what I needed to do to move forward. Six years after tenure, I approached my promotion to Full Professor with a sound record, great confidence, and solid support from my department. To my dismay, the relatively new dean chose to block my promotion, along with all seven other women who had been supported by their home departments. (About half of the men made it through his gauntlet.) To make matters worse, on appeal, the president promoted even more of the men, a few of the women, but not me, although every logical comparison placed me at the level of or above all of the men and equal to or above the women.

I knew I had to fight, and I knew I had to fight for the principle as well as for myself. I decided from the outset to try to make this something that set precedent, so I refused to settle out of court. This was easy for me to do—I had tenure, my case was strong, and I had the support and encouragement of almost the whole university. What could I lose, other than a year of promotion income (which was not insubstantial)?

I filed all the proper grievances, followed all the right steps, talked to the right people—I thought. We did the internal grievance based on "arbitrary and capricious" promotion, and it ended in a politically motivated denial of responsibility. (That was an interesting experience because my office was down the hall from one of the men who was handling the other side, so we had frequent interactions, which I chose to keep pleasant. Privately, he expressed support for me; publicly, he turned me down.) My union filed for arbitration, a process that takes months.

I also filed a sex discrimination complaint with the Equal Employment Opportunity Commission (EEOC), along with several other women. The

Commission found the university guilty. The press snatched up the finding and made my case (complete with a happy-faced photo) front page news. It looked to the world as if I had won a very reasonable case (the quotes of the president left no doubt that the university was guilty).

So what did I win, and what did I learn?

First, I discovered that a finding from the EEOC is only a recommendation that carries no enforcement weight. If the university doesn't comply, the Department of Justice has to decide whether to sue (through Clarence Thomas's old unit)—highly unlikely in an individual case, where the amount of money involved would be less than attorneys' fees. I had to continue in the arbitration, which dragged on and on, while the university sat on my case.

Second, I had trusted my case to my union and their attorney. It turned out that behind my back, they offered the university a settlement I had earlier explicitly deemed unacceptable, and then told me the university had insisted and I had no choice (or they would not help me further). Given the low likelihood of a Department of Justice suit, and my need to spend more time with my child, I gave in.

This was particularly galling because I had turned down a very good settlement offer earlier in the process because I wanted the decision to set a precedent. Instead I got a gag order, no precedent, and very little of the money they owed me.

Third, I learned how long even an "easy" case takes. I was not pregnant when I started the case (and wasn't for several more months); my daughter was nearly a year old when we ended the madness. I was "lucky"; some cases have taken more than a decade.

Fourth, I had an opportunity to see what being under even an obviously irrational attack can do to one's state of mind. Although virtually the whole campus, including some wonderful administrators, supported me, although the objective data were clear, sometimes I doubted myself—the old tapes of Imposter, Inferior, and Insane to Think I Was Good Enough took daily runs through my head. A dear, trusted, older feminist unplugged them, though, with a simple phone call. Out of the blue, she called one day to ask how I was feeling. Out poured my tape index. She said "I was afraid of that, we all do that. Well, just think. You managed to fool all of your colleagues who thought you were good enough, all those experts in the field who wrote letters of support, and all of us outside who believe in you. I guess it took one smart dean and one very smart president to find you out." The absurdity was immediately obvious even to self-deprecating me, and I laughed continuously for 2 days (much in relief, I'm sure!).

Finally, and most seriously, I learned how low institutional representatives will stoop when they are in a legal "battle." The same man who had earlier that year, in a legal case, praised my high moral stature (in that case, I was on the university's side) actually accused me of having problems getting along with others and falsifying an item on my vita. (This latter occurred in an arbitration meeting, and, in spite of the "rules," I lunged across the table at him, screaming in rage. They assumed it was my shortly postnatal hormones, but it was pure fury at an evil act. Even today, I can muster up the same rage at such a vile personal attack, especially because he knew it wasn't true.)

The university created thick dossiers from my two comparators by asking for information well past the deadline (they kindly documented the postdeadline requests for my use). My dossier was skinny (it helped that they left out my two books); important aspects such as my teaching evaluations were copied so poorly they were almost unreadable. Luckily, the EEOC investigator was savvy (and probably used to such tactics), and she requested materials directly from me. Such shenanigans did not help the university's defense.

But the effect on me was devastating. I had loved my university, and she trusted these people to be as honest and open as I have always been. I could accept and forgive an irrational decision; I could neither tolerate nor forgive such shameful, intentionally bad behavior. I couldn't believe my own union had sold me out. I hadn't gained anything for other women; I'd only passed by a good deal for a lousy one. I withdrew from every institutional and union committee or role, and devoted my extra time (which was limited with an infant!) to another college whose dean had supported me and to my professional associations. Whenever anyone asked me to do a task, I'd decline and let them know why.

Ultimately, justice triumphed. Two years later, not one of the handful of people on the other side was still in a position of power. The president's contract was not renewed, and a news report suggested it was because of his problems handling sex discrimination cases. A woman who had quietly supported me was promoted to provost and another to vice president by the new administration. The dean was no longer a dean (although last year, he claimed in a local magazine that he left because the university forced him to promote unqualified women and minorities, which suggests he has a slow learning curve). Before long, I was again able to walk around campus without worrying that I would run into someone I disliked. But I will never again be so naive.

What would I do differently if this happened again?
1. Get my own lawyer from the beginning; command my case more.
2. Learn the implications of every act, every word. Early on, a well-meaning supporter mentioned my gender in a university hearing, and from then on I could not pursue a personal lawsuit on sex discrimination because it was part of the binding arbitration (which otherwise was heard on the "arbitrary and capricious" grounds, which were sufficient).
3. Believe in myself more and in others less.
4. Take the best offer, and go for the principle in other ways.

What would I do the same?
1. Value my friends and colleagues who supported me so well and so long.
2. Be honest and sincere and pleasant (unless called a liar).
3. Stick with the fight as long as it was smart to do so.
4. Cherish my beautiful child more than the outcome of a grievance.

REFERENCE

Quina, K. (1986). Lessons from my first job. In S. Rose (Ed.), *Career guide for women scholars* (pp. 36-45). New York: Springer.

Competition and Contact
The Dynamics Behind
Resistance to Affirmative
Action in Academe

Lynn H. Collins

You may have heard the claims that affirmative action is causing widespread "reverse discrimination" and otherwise unfair treatment of men. For instance, I overheard one academic complain that due to affirmative action, women were stealing jobs away from far more qualified men. At the time, he was a visiting assistant professor who had applied for one of the two tenure track positions in his department. He was the men's choice for the position even before the search began. They had already invested research money in him, given him a reduced teaching load, and appointed him to one of the prestigious university committees. Only 31 other applicants materialized for his position's search at a time when such a search typically draws 100 to 200 applicants. The other search drew more than 125 applicants. He was hired.

A tenure track faculty member raised similar allegations of the unfairness of the system for White men. Shortly thereafter, his university laid off a large number of tenure track and visiting faculty, including him, but most of the faculty laid off were women. His university later rehired him, without a full search, for a position outside of his area of expertise within

AUTHOR'S NOTE: I would like to thank Lisa Basley, Shari Garsman, Reisha Kreischer, Suzanne Schroeder, and Leanne Schuh, who assisted with the data analysis and other tasks associated with the comparisons regarding women in academe.

another division. They did not find a way to rehire the women. By the time he came up for tenure, his name was on a few manuscripts, but he was not first author on either of them. He rarely presented at conferences and was not professionally active. He received tenure and was promoted. A woman in the same area who had done a great deal of service, was professionally active, and had published several chapters was denied tenure.

These two examples illustrate the widespread belief that affirmative action is threatening the ranks of potential and current male faculty in academe, as well as how inaccurate that belief is. The U.S. laws that forbid discrimination are Title IX of the educational amendments, Title VII of the 1964 Civil Rights Acts, the Equal Pay Act, and executive order 11246. The first of these was passed in 1972. In response to these initiatives, affirmative action was launched in order to open up doors previously closed to women and members of ethnic minority groups. Bergmann (1996) defined affirmative action as "planning and acting to end the absence of certain kinds of people—those who belong to groups that have been subordinated or left out—from certain schools and jobs" (p. 7).

Johnetta Cole, former president of Spellman College, believes that there is a negative attitude toward affirmative action programs and a myth that affirmative action programs lower standards (Wilson, 1993). Affirmative action may put women in a double bind because those who are hired and achieve tenure are dismissed as having made it only because of affirmative action (Rausch, Ortiz, Douthitt, & Reed, 1989) regardless of the strength of their credentials. In reality, those involved in the selection process probably would not have hired even the most talented woman if not for affirmative action, and may still not be hiring her even with it (Bergmann, 1996; Wilson, 1993).

In the recent past, one commonly given reason for the absence of successful female applicants was that there were not enough women in the pool. Few people currently use this excuse, except in the case of ethnic minority applicants and in fields such as engineering, where women are still relatively rare. The number of women earning doctorates is rising for all fields (Ries & Thurgood, 1993). As of 1994, women earned 39% of doctoral degrees conferred (National Center for Education Statistics [NCES], 1996a). Forty-seven percent of American citizens receiving doctorates are women (NCES, 1996a). Bellas (1994) claimed that the proportion of women in faculty positions has steadily increased over the past 40 years. The data tell a different story.

Despite the antidiscrimination laws, the forces that keep women from achieving success in academe are thriving; women are losing rather than gaining ground. When my students and I examined data from American Association of University Professors (AAUP) surveys, it was apparent that the rate of initial hires relative to their numbers has not changed, and women's relative representation in academe is dropping in relation to their increasing availability (AAUP, 1975, 1985, 1995, 1996; Ries & Thurgood, 1993). When one compares the number of women with doctorates to the number employed by institutions over the past 20 years, the gap is actually growing larger for women. The gap between the number of women who are qualified for faculty positions and those who hold them has almost doubled over the past 10 years, from an 8% discrepancy to a 16% discrepancy (West, 1995). Although 26% of full-time faculty in 1920 were women, this number had increased to only 31% by 1995, despite the increase in doctoral degrees conferred upon women (West, 1995). In 1981-1982, 35% of PhDs were women, but only 27% of faculty were. By 1993-1994, 39% of PhDs were women, but only 31% of faculty were (West, 1995). As of 1996, only 33% of faculty in Category I, IIA, and IIB institutions were women (AAUP, 1996; NCES, 1996b). This number is consistent with doctoral graduation rates from the early 1980s.

There are also widespread rumors that large numbers of women and minorities are being given special consideration in promotion because of affirmative action. The data tell a different story in this area as well. Women and ethnic minority faculty are promoted and tenured more slowly and less often than White men (Finklestein, 1984; Menges & Exum, 1983; NCES, 1996b; Rausch et al., 1989). Although efforts were allegedly being made to hire more women, the efforts are not reflected in women's representation in the upper faculty ranks (Rausch et al., 1989). Bentley and Blackburn (1992) noted that women's absence in the tenured ranks is due to their relatively recent entry into the workforce. However, women's entry into academic workplaces has not been that recent. If one looks at the rate at which women received doctorates 15 years ago (31.5%), one can see that there is a clear discrepancy between their availability and their representation in the senior ranks (20.6%). The availability of women with doctorates who are interested in academe is not commensurate with the current prevalence rates for women full professors, even when a time delay is added to allow for promotion. In addition, women with doctorates found less full-time employment and were more likely to be unemployed or employed part-time or outside of their field (Ahern & Scott, 1981; Billard, 1994).

Olsen and Maple (1993) stated that

> programs and policies designed to advance women in higher education must be based on accurate information about the obstacles they face and the satisfactions that sustain their development. Inaccurate assumptions about women in higher education may be as damaging to them as discrimination and insensitivity. (p. 35)

This chapter will provide a theoretical framework for understanding the resistance to affirmative action and the dynamics of backlash against women in academe. It will describe the obstacles women face in academe and offer suggestions for institutional change in the interest of warming the chilly climate of academe for women.

Two theories have been presented by Tolbert, Simons, Andrews, and Rhee (1995) to explain the dynamics within contemporary academic institutions that prevent women from flourishing. These two theories are Competition Theory and Contact Theory. Competition Theory helps to explain the current escalation of resistance to affirmative action. Contact Theory explains some of the phenomena that make academic life different for women, but also presents points of intervention.

COMPETITION THEORY

According to Competition Theory, when a minority group is relatively small within an organization, it is not likely to be seen as a threat to the majority's control of resources. This was very much the case during the first decade after affirmative action plans went into effect. In fact, when we analyzed the data from the 1975 and 1985 AAUP employment surveys, the percentage of women faculty went from 22.5% in 1975 to 26.2% in 1985, less than a four percentage-point change. The change in the percentage of women full professors between 1975 and 1985 did not reach significance ($p = .18$) despite the huge number of institutions in the survey. During that time, a larger number of both women and men were hired in order to accommodate the baby boomers who were entering colleges and universities, but the relative proportions of male and female faculty remained about the same.

As a minority group grows, however, it comes to be seen as a threat, and intergroup hostility increases. Perhaps as the real change begins to occur, the perceived threat creates resistance to entry and participation by members of the minority group. Although women are not a minority within the population, they are certainly a minority within academe. As the number of women in a department increases, intergroup relations may deteriorate (Blalock, 1967; Tolbert et al., 1995; Toren & Kraus, 1987). We examined the 1985 and 1996 AAUP employment surveys and found that the percentage of women professors went from 26.2% in 1985 to 32.8% in 1996, a 6.6 percentage-point change. The change from 1985 to 1995 in the percentage of women full professors between 1985 and 1996 finally reached significance ($p < .001$), but women were still underrepresented on faculties relative to men. This may have been enough change, however, to make women appear to be a more threatening force. Women are still underrepresented on faculties, however, especially in the higher ranks.

Similarly, outside of academe, South, Markham, Bonjean, and Corder (1987) found that as the number of female employees increased, the supportiveness of male employees toward female employees decreased. Others have found that men's satisfaction with the working environment decreases as the number of women in it increases (Tsui, Egan, & O'Reilly, 1992; Wharton & Baron, 1987). Toren and Kraus (1987) studied Israeli universities and found a significant relationship between the proportion of women in academic departments and the disparity in rank held by men and women. Women's rank distribution was more similar to men's when they constituted a smaller proportion of the faculty. The percentage of women they found in the university divisions they studied ranged from 6.5% to 20.6%. Consistent with competition theory, increases in the total number of women hired for tenure track positions at some institutions have been followed by declines (Blackburn & Wylie, 1985).

Pressures on Minorities in Organizations

Kanter's (1977) ethnographic analyses of work groups in a large corporation revealed that when minorities constitute less than 15% of the total population, there is intense scrutiny and awareness of individual minority group members by the majority, increased performance pressure among minorities, greater solidarity among majority members who feel more similar by contrast, increased social isolation of minority group members, interactions tainted by stereotypes, or rebellion as coping behavior. Kanter

49

would say that when women first start to enter a male-dominated environment, group relations decline, and the work environment for women will be unfavorable. Another way to look at this is that the dominant group resists infiltration by the minority group. Women's experiences in academe are different from men's in ways that parallel those mentioned above (Aisenberg & Harrington, 1988).

Increased Scrutiny in Academe

Women faculty are still a minority in academe. When members of a group stand out or are more salient because of one or more characteristics (such as sex or race), they will attract more attention, and attributions about them will be exaggerated (Crocker & McGraw, 1984; Taylor & Fiske, 1978). Attributions may contribute to stereotypes when not discounted and when we know little about a group's behavior (Quattrone & Jones, 1980). Many of the authors in this book describe the increased scrutiny that women faculty members experience in both personal and professional areas of their lives. Some women have reported leaving jobs due to this lack of privacy and inadequate separation of campus from community life (Rausch et al., 1989). According to the literature, scrutiny will be reduced when the number of women and their status increases.

Performance Pressure

Women and members of ethnic minority groups are held to a higher standard than are men, and that leads to increased performance pressure. More women (25%) than men (5%) believe that women have to outperform men for the same reward (Olsen & Maple, 1993). Research shows that unless it is clear from application materials that a woman is unequivocally high in ability, women's competence and career potential are devalued relative to men's (Heilman, Martell, & Simon, 1988). If such information is provided, women may be similarly or more valued. Unfortunately, in most cases for men and women, credentials are not unequivocal. In another setting, sex bias affected assessment of managerial potential. Shore (1992) found that despite superior scores on performance dimensions of an assessment for managerial potential, women did not receive superior ratings on overall managerial potential nor advance through the ranks at a superior rate. There was a tendency to diminish women's achievement when judging their potential for management roles.

It appears that women have to perform better than men to be perceived as equal to men. This bias adds to the performance pressure already felt by both women and men in academe. Notably, one of the strongest predictors of staying at an institution is perception of time pressure related to performance; the greater the pressure, the more likely people were to leave by choice (Johnsrud & Des Jarlais, 1994). Ethnic minority faculty members also experience more tenure pressure than White members of the faculty (Johnsrud & Des Jarlais, 1994).

It is difficult to partial discrimination out of evaluations of such things as scholarship and teaching, but some have started to operationalize the phenomenon by using statistical regression (see Scholnick, this volume), and others are experimenting with outside gender-blind review of credentials. If these approaches are successful, the pressure felt by women may only be as great as that felt by men.

Social Isolation

Social isolation also plays a role in academe, and it takes its toll on women. Women law students in a school with low numbers of women reported higher performance pressure and more social isolation than did women in a school with a more balanced sex ratio (Spangler, Gordon, & Pipkin, 1978). The sample for this study consisted of only two law schools, however. Other researchers have also demonstrated the existence of these dynamics in the workplace. Segal (1962) and Wolman and Frank (1975) found a negative correlation between the relative size of the minority group and the level of isolation experienced by nurses and other professionals, respectively. Finally, Rausch et al. (1989) found that women's most common complaints about the academic lifestyle concerned its limited social opportunities and limited time for family. They also found that women left universities for personal reasons such as dislike of the community or geographic location.

Interactions and Evaluations Tainted by Stereotypes

Evaluations and interactions in academe are often tainted by racial and gender stereotypes. Johnetta Cole has said that part of the problem in academe is likely to be lingering stereotypes of African American women and men as incompetent and lazy and negative images of women in general (Wilson, 1993). Benokraitis (this volume) illustrates and discusses how more subtle forms of sexism influence the experiences of academic women. Such stereotypes influence the perception of women faculty's performance.

Conditions that draw attention to traditional stereotypic conceptions of women lead to devaluation of women's achievement (Heilman et al., 1988). Gender biases in the assessment of competence are influenced by the gender association of the field and the characteristics of individuals rated (Etaugh, Houtler, & Ptasnik, 1988). Sex stereotypes play a mediating role in evaluations of competence, including the evaluation of publications. Although some have found that women perform better academically than men at all levels (Hornig, 1987), women's written work has been perceived to be of lower quality (Cole, 1979; Davis & Astin, 1978; Goldberg, 1968; Paludi & Bauer, 1983). When the number of publications and citations, and the rated quality of the research were taken into consideration, Persell (1983) found that performance criteria still affected women negatively. Even women whose work was rated "above average" were treated poorly (Persell, 1983). Recent studies show less bias in the evaluation of articles. For instance, Pirri, Eaton, and Durkin (1995) found no bias in Australian nurses against articles supposedly written by women. Swim, Borgida, Maruyama, and Myers (1989) found that the average difference between ratings of work done by men and women was small.

It may be that the demographic characteristics rather than the attitudes of the research participants have changed. The gender of the raters influences ratings of women's competence; the greater the female representation among raters, the more favorable the ratings (Haemmerlie & Montgomery, 1991; Shomer & Centers, 1970; Toder, 1980). Women also have more positive attitudes toward women (Haemmerlie & Montgomery, 1991). Studies in this area tend to be conducted on psychology majors, and psychology majors are increasingly female. Swim et al. (1989) also found that the greatest differences emerged when the quality was ambiguous, the content masculine or neutral, and ratings were done by males. Although psychology subject pools are largely female, the workplace is not. Recent studies in this area using psychology subject pools may be more profeminist and less representative of male-dominated workplace settings and the population at large. Some studies conducted in the workplace have even found that the higher the objective evaluation of her work, the less likely the woman was to be rewarded (Billard, 1994; Chamberlain, 1988; Cole & Zuckerman, 1984; Mickelson, 1989). Men devalue women more than women do, and men are still the majority in the tenured ranks, on tenure committees, and in administrations. Because those evaluating women's work are typically male, women faculty's publications may still be discounted based on stereotyping and devaluing of their work.

Gender role stereotypes play a mediating role in evaluations of competence. Women's credentials are devalued by men when the group has a male leader or authority figure (Etaugh et al., 1988). Heilman et al. (1988) found that females were generally judged less favorably than males and concluded that gender role stereotypes are to blame for sex bias in evaluations.

One of the traditional arguments against affirmative action in universities is that universities should always strive for excellence (the underlying assumption, of course, is that women and ethnic minority candidates are rarely excellent) and that candidates should be chosen by their credentials alone. However, universities seem to have difficulty operationalizing what constitutes excellence, let alone solid and acceptable work, when it comes to tenure and promotion. They claim that "they know it when they see it." The process for achieving tenure is notoriously vague and arbitrary. Most faculty receive no written guidelines for achieving tenure (Rausch et al., 1989). Tenure decisions are largely subjective. The lack of clear, consistent performance criteria allows opportunities for discrimination (Exum, Menges, Watkins, & Berglund, 1984). If criteria are vague, then they can be manipulated in the interest of personal preferences and politics. Were such standards to be specified, universities would be held responsible for sticking to them, and some "undesirables" (defined by personality, sex, race, or other factors) might have to be tenured or promoted (Hutcheson, 1996).

At this time, tenure is a highly arbitrary, subjective, political process. Johnsrud and Des Jarlais (1994) called for systematic evaluation of the concerns of junior faculty, especially women and minorities. Clearly operationalized standards and procedures would help reduce the stereotyping and bias that is inevitable in a competitive situation.

The 40% Solution

Tolbert et al. (1995) examined data from a random sample of 50 sociology departments listed in the 1977–1988 guides to graduate departments. Variables included the number of faculty of each sex at each rank who stayed or who left the department. Because tenure usually correlates with rank when an institution has a tenure system, the number of associate and full professors were combined as a measure of the number of tenured faculty. Some of the control variables included the total number of male and female faculty at a given rank, the institution's prestige, institutional control (public or private), proportion of doctorates awarded to women and men, and a correction for sample selection bias.

Tolbert et al. found that as the proportion of women in a department increases, so does the likelihood of turnover, until the number of women reaches a certain proportion of the total number of faculty members in the department. This critical percentage appears to be about 35% to 40%, which is what the overall percentage of faculty women would be now if it reflected the number of women granted doctorates in the past two decades. As the percentage of women in the environment exceeded 40%, however, Tolbert et al. found that the negative social dynamics were reduced and the turnover rate decreased. It is interesting that when the percentage of women reaches 40%, the turnover rate among men is also lower. This suggests that increasing numbers of women in departments improves the climate for men as well as women. Unfortunately, universities have been more willing to educate women than to put them on the payroll.

AAUP Survey Data

My students and I examined the results of the 1975, 1985, and 1996 AAUP surveys (AAUP, 1975, 1985, 1996) in light of Tolbert et al.'s findings. According to the 1996 AAUP survey data, only about 3% of category I institutions, 16% of category IIA institutions, and 30% of category IIB institutions have reached the 40% mark (AAUP, 1996). Average percentages of women in these three categories of institutions are 25.5%, 32.2%, and 35.4%, respectively. The percentages of women full professors are 13.3%, 19.4%, and 22.3%, respectively. Within these groups, women tend to be overrepresented at the poorest paying institutions.

The employment numbers of institutions that report in the annual AAUP survey revealed some interesting patterns. During the time period covered by Tolbert et al.'s (1995) study, the discrepancy between the percentage of women on a university's faculty and the percentage of full professors who were women gradually increased up to the point at which 40% of the faculty were women. When more than 40% of the faculty were women, the discrepancy decreased. This suggests that institutional resistance to the promotion of women may decrease once women's numbers within a university reach 40%. There also appears to be a broader phenomenon. Across all category I, IIA, and IIB institutions, the percentage of women

54

faculty is currently about 33%. In 1975, when the percentage of women faculty hovered around 22%, there was less resistance. The average maximum discrepancy between the percentage of full professors and total faculty who were women was only about 11 points. This magnitude of discrepancy was reached when women composed about 30% of the faculty, after which it dropped off. Women constituted about 26% of all faculty in 1985; the maximum discrepancy was 14.1 points and the turning point was around 40%. By 1996, however, about 33% of faculty were women. The discrepancy rose to 15.5 points and did not fall off until after the 50% mark. Although these patterns are correlational in nature, they suggest that, consistent with Competition Theory, there may be increased resistance to the promotion of women until their average representation reaches or exceeds the 40% mark across universities, at which point women cease to be a minority of the faculty. This pattern could also be due to a greater influx of new faculty into the lower ranks without similar progress in movement into upper ranks, which may have caused the maximum discrepancy to increase rather than decrease across the three decades. Unfortunately, larger numbers in the lower ranks do not result in similarity in status, a condition required for good intergroup relations.

These patterns are consistent with those found in other studies. Although there has been some disagreement in the social psychological literature about what constitutes a small versus a large minority, research shows that as the proportion of women in a workgroup rises, there is increasing resistance to their promotion and retention, perhaps up to the point at which they cease to be a minority (Blalock, 1967; Cole, 1979; Coser, 1981; Kanter, 1977; Semyonov, 1980; Toren & Kraus, 1987). This increasing resistance is reflected in current calls to end affirmation action programs.

CONTACT THEORY

Contact Theory (Allport, 1954) predicts that social prejudice is most likely to develop when cross-group interactions are low. The more frequently the group members interact, the more likely they are to be presented with evidence that disconfirms stereotypes. Disconfirming evidence serves to undermine stereotypes. Tolbert et al. (1995) discussed early conceptualizations of the contact hypothesis, in which people thought that mere contact would reduce prejudice and discrimination. Increased intergroup contact may, however, have a negative impact (Tolbert et al., 1995). Apparently, certain conditions must exist for contact to be effective in improving intergroup relations (Clore et al., 1978; Cook, 1984; Pettigrew, 1986; Stephan, 1987). These conditions include similarity in status and power (Clore, Bray, Itkin, & Murphy, 1978), sustained close contact (Weber & Crocker, 1983), a superordinate or common goal or cooperative interdependence (Blake & Mouton, 1979; Sherif, Harvey, White, Hood, & Sherif, 1961), success at achieving the common goal (Worchel, Andreoli, & Folger, 1977), a common group enemy (Dion, 1979), dissimilarity to stereotypes, and similarity in background (to reduce stereotyping and highlight similarity). Chances for success are also increased by support from authorities (Pettigrew, 1986; Stephan, 1987), including prescriptions for civility. In many academic institutions, there are a number of factors that reduce the likelihood that mere contact will improve relations. As a result, resistance to affirmative action programs continues, women continue to be seen and treated as the outgroup, and they are unlikely to be treated as equals.

Similarity in Status and Power

Bentley and Blackburn (1992) defined success for women in academe as representation in equal numbers with both equal power and equal salaries. Women need to have power in order to create new rules, alter rules, and have these rule changes accepted by others as legitimate (Bentley & Blackburn, 1992). This will not happen until women are better represented in the upper faculty ranks.

Numbers, Rank, and Status

Women, by virtue of their low numbers both overall and in tenured positions (West, 1995), are not similar to men in terms of status and power. We know from the work of Fiske (1993) that attention follows power; the dominant group may not attend to interactions with subordinates even if such interactions are numerous. If the dominant group is not paying attention, stereotype-discrepant behavior will not be noticed. According to Fiske, women will remain stereotyped and continue to be treated as subordinates unless the increased minority group size is also connected with greater power over dominants' outcomes (e.g., rewards, punishment). Others' perceptions of women become more individuated only when women gain more power (Fiske, 1993). When women and men in academe

56

become equal in status, there is a greater likelihood that contact will improve intergroup relations. Consistent with Fiske's results, Tolbert et al. (1995) found that the relationship between the number of faculty women and turnover rates among women assistant professors was weaker than that between the number of women faculty and turnover among all women. The percentage required was 45% instead of 35% to 40%. The larger percentage is required for change, because the power of assistant professors is limited, and in order for them to have an impact, their numbers need to be larger. Likewise, Tolbert et al. found that departments with few tenured women are likely to have high turnover. This is consistent with Contact Theory, which holds that intergroup interactions in which members of one group have lower status are unlikely to improve intergroup relations.

In a democratic setting, opportunities for group interaction become more frequent as sizes of groups become similar. When that happens, their voting power also becomes similar, which gives them more power. Although the number of women in a department increases the likelihood that women will have more power, it does not guarantee it. For instance, if the committee members, chair, or dean, who have decision-making power over research support, salaries, raises, assistantships, and so on, are sexist or undemocratic, the climate for women in the department can be inequitable even if their numbers are large.

These data suggest that members of ethnic minority groups will have a rough road in academe for a long time to come. Although affirmative action may eventually permit women to enter academe in numbers great enough for the resistance to them to decrease, there will continue to be resistance to entry by ethnic minority group members whose population base rate is below 40%. According to the 40% solution theory, if the percentage of any group in the workforce pool is less than 40%, it is unlikely that 40% or more of the faculty will be from that group. According to the data, if any group's representation among faculty is less than 40%, it will be difficult for them to obtain desirable positions, such as associate and full professorships. The best chances for advancement for Black academicians may be at Black universities, which is, in fact, where about half of Black professors are employed (Wilson, 1993). The situation may also be improved if there are members of one's group in positions of power, even if their numbers are low. Still, this does not bode well for African Americans, Latinos/as, and other groups that make up less than 40% of the population. It is unlikely that they will reach the critical mass required for a more satisfactory environment.

West (1995) suggested that one way to increase the ranks of women within universities is to hire new faculty at the assistant professor rather than associate professor level. Her rationale is that the pool of women is larger at this level and that, all things being equal, odds are therefore better that a woman would be chosen. Many institutions are replacing retiring males' lines with assistant professor positions, but these lines go nowhere. Colleges and universities are eliminating promotional paths as men vacate them (Cadet, 1989) by granting tenure to a lower percentage of candidates and creating more contractual (nontenure-track) positions. This limits the advancement of both new and mid-level academic women. In addition, increasing the number of women in powerless positions does little to alter the dynamics of the situation, because one of the conditions for good intergroup relations is equal status. The current trends protect men's positions in the higher education hierarchy by preventing women in the system from holding positions of power. To this end, we should be hiring women into the upper ranks in order to reduce the status differential and improve the retention of other women (Rausch et al., 1989; Tolbert et al., 1995). There are plenty of potential women candidates at the assistant professor level from whom to choose. The presence of women in authority positions has been shown to enhance profeminist attitudes (Shomer & Centers, 1970) and results in higher ratings of other women's competence (Etaugh et al., 1988). Greater exposure to women's scholarship improves female and male students' attitudes toward women (Haemmerlie & Montgomery, 1991). Women in authority positions may elicit more positive evaluations by both men and women.

Salary and Status

People are valued in relation to their paycheck. Sir Frances Galton believed that if one is paid well for something, then one must be good at it, and he used this supposition to support the idea that men are more able than women (Hothersall, 1984). This belief persists and has a deleterious impact on perceptions of the value of women's contributions to society. There has been no improvement in the discrepancy between men's and women's salaries between 1982, when academic women earned 89% of men's salaries and 1995, when they earned 88.5% (Billard, 1994). This differential is not consistently related to performance, credentials, or years in the field (Bellas, 1994; Mickelson, 1989), nor is it related to the reputation of the department or involvement in administration, research, or years at the institution for women (Billard, 1994; Mickelson, 1989). Bentley and Blackburn (1992) found that women received lower salaries within and across ranks. For a full discussion of equity issues, see Scholnick (this volume).

West (1995) suggested that institutions shouldn't match outside offers, but at some universities, competing offers and moving into administration are the only paths to career advancement (Olsen & Maple, 1993, p. 37). Better pay is the second most common reason women give for leaving their positions; one of the main ways women increase their salaries is to change jobs. Toth (1997) writes that one of her fantasies is to create "Noble University." This university would exist solely to make competing offers to women in academe, to aid them in their quest for equity. Rose and Danner (this volume) discuss the use of outside offers in salary negotiation. Women are also leaving for better opportunities for career advancement. Women are typically paid less than men and have more reason to seek better paying positions. If universities want to attract and retain women, then one step they can take is to pay them equitably and give them opportunities for advancement, growth, and development.

Sustained Close Contact

A number of authors have expressed concern about women's lack of access to important professional networks (Konrad, 1991; Simeone, 1987). At many universities, women and men are clustered within relatively gender role-consistent departments, such as women in nursing or men in engineering. This reduces the likelihood that the necessary contact will occur. Furthermore, university-wide committees are often unbalanced (see Chrisler, Herr, & Murstein, this volume), and these conditions perpetuate stereotyping and power imbalances. Furthermore, the competitive academic game is often played like a team sport, with networks making up the teams, and women are often at a disadvantage. These factors are reflected in women's greater dissatisfaction with their relationships with their department chairs and support of their colleagues (Rausch et al., 1989).

Women and ethnic minority faculty are also less likely to have had a mentor (Clark & Corcoran, 1986; Justus, Freitag, & Parker, 1987; Moore, 1982) to help them make important connections. As a result, ethnic minority and women faculty often lack information about the tenure and promotion process (Johnsrud & Des Jarlais, 1994). Mentors help faculty become part of larger networks. Not only does this increase contact, but it helps them become oriented to the priorities and practices of the academic workplace: the rules of the game. Most women (63%) and men (71%) who made it into the ranks of a highly select research institution reported having had a mentor. This mentor was usually their dissertation advisor (Olsen & Maple, 1993). Ethnic minority faculty also identify more with students (subordinates) than with faculty, which does not lead to effective networking for the faculty member. There are so few ethnic minority faculty members included in any one study, however, that it is difficult to be very confident in drawing any conclusions concerning them (Johnsrud & Des Jarlais, 1994).

If resistance to affirmative action is to be reduced, the situation will have to change structurally in order to ensure closer regular contact between men and women in academe. Change needs to begin with the alteration of "pipeline forces" (Wilson, 1993). At one New England doctoral program, the department chair urged the director of admissions to dig deeper into the male portion of the applicant pool because he believed "women are ruining the profession." When the admissions chair and committee resisted, he unilaterally admitted less qualified male applicants from the pool. Institutions or universities need to make an effort to recognize and select strong female applicants and to ensure that they are mentored as well as the male graduate students are. Bair and Boor (1988) found that top universities frequently hire their own or hire from other top 10 graduate programs. Women may lose out if there is discrimination during graduate admissions and because male faculty are more inclined to work with male students. All should establish an early connection with the academic network, beginning at the undergraduate level. At Connecticut College, women and men undergraduate and graduate psychology students work together in research groups and present their work at conferences. Their active colloquium series brings well-known psychologists to campus and helps students develop an early connection to academic networks. Duke University has started a program to prepare ethnic minority students for academic careers. College students from the historically Black colleges come to Duke to be mentored on a one-to-one basis (Wilson, 1993), with their expenses fully or partially paid.

Goals and Competition in Academe

Academe is not a mastery game; faculty members are compared with their peers and evaluated on that basis. It is an individual or at best

60

competitive team sport, played by networks of colleagues. The main goal of most academics' careers is to achieve tenure and promotion. This goal is not superordinate but individual. Preliminary goals are resource acquisition and publication; both of these goals are primarily individual and entail competition. Competition increases hostility, stereotyping, and other kinds of undesirable behavior between groups (Sheriff & Sheriff, 1969), including discrimination. Hiring, promotion, and resource allocation are all influenced by the same ingroup/outgroup phenomenon that is characteristic of all competing groups.

Competition for Resources

Scarcity of resources is another condition that cannot help but cause hostility between groups. Funding sources have been reduced in recent years; the more scarce the resources, the more fiercely the battle is fought. Faculty members compete for resources individually or in networked groups. Resource allocation can be inequitable and can have an effect on potential productivity. Resources include such things as student assistantship hours, better computer equipment, funding opportunities, summer support, software, and equipment. Because the amount of resources allocated to minority groups is less than that to majority groups, there is increased friction from within the group as well as from without. Access to grant money is becoming more equitable, but at the same time, it is becoming more competitive.

Women often report that their share of grants, research support, and committee responsibilities is inequitable (Russell, 1991). Research results confirm that women receive a smaller proportion of the resources. Although women constitute 9.6% of the workforce, they receive only 7.5% of small grants, 6.0% of federal (largest) grants, 2.5% of industrial grants, and 5.7% of other grants (Bentley & Blackburn, 1992). Bentley and Blackburn (1992) concluded that there was no longer a significant difference in the number of federal grants given to women after women's proportion of the grant awards rose from 62% of men's in 1969 to 89% of men's in 1988. However, this gap is still large, and the dollar amounts of women's grants are significantly smaller than men's.

Publications determine reputations, grant allocation, promotions, and salaries (Bentley & Blackburn, 1992). It could also be argued, however, that reputations, grant allocation, promotions, and salaries determine publication rates. Inequities in this area contribute to the pressures that push women out of academe. Men have more access to publication networks, funding networks, and grants, and they are less likely to have to resort to summer teaching and course overloads to earn a decent salary. Resources translate into an increased publication rate, and a higher publication rate translates into a greater likelihood of receiving tenure. Blackburn, Blymer, and Hall (1978) reported no significant differences in publication rate once factors such as institutional affiliation, preference for research, rank, grant support, and age were controlled, but all of these factors are impacted by discrimination. Women are in a one-down position because they are not members of the dominant group. For a further discussion of this issue, see Chrisler (this volume).

Resource allocation is another area in which better operationalization of requirements and credentials for receiving grants and an evaluation of possible bias could help reduce discrimination. Women perform less well and often choose to leave when they are not supported by their departments and universities. Administrators should examine the allocation of resources and make them as fair and as consistent as possible. Short of this, university women's committees could examine not only salary equity (see Scholnick, this volume) but resource allocation as well. Equal allocation of resources will help level the field.

Competition for Tenure

Tenure has become increasingly competitive for both women and men. The percentage of applicants denied tenure has risen from 8.7% in 1971 to 21% in 1987 (Hutcheson, 1996). Women are more likely than men to leave academe because of a negative tenure decision (Rausch et al., 1989). Although more institutions have tenure systems now than before, at least twice as many now put a cap on the number of tenure slots available (Hutcheson, 1996). Because this change is occurring simultaneously with the influx of women and ethnic minorities into the faculty ranks, some have wondered whether it is part of the resistance to affirmative action. Competition theory may explain tenure patterns over the past 20 years. In 1975, 46% of women in full-time positions had tenure. In 1992, this number was the same. In 1975, 64% of men had tenure and their number rose to 72% in 1994 (West, 1995). There appears to be resistance to granting tenure and promotion to women.

Tenure and promotion procedures and criteria are notoriously subjective and should be updated and operationalized. Women tend to do better in fields where accomplishments can be objectively evaluated. Timely, thorough, and constructive performance reviews should be given and concrete recommendations made in order to bring candidates' productivity into line with tenure requirements. Qualified faculty should be encouraged to go up for tenure as early as possible because tenured faculty are less likely to leave their institution (Rausch et al., 1989).

Acquiring tenure does not have to be a process in which faculty members compete with each other, although institutions' current fiscal policies are increasing the likelihood that it is. If tenure and promotion are awarded to those who demonstrate excellence in teaching and scholarship and dedication to the university community without regard to whoever else is up for promotion that year, then the negative dynamics encouraged by competition may be reduced. Again, clearly operationalizing excellence will help reduce bias. In turning tenure into a competition, universities run the risk of discouraging constructive collaboration on research and grants.

Dissimilarity and Similarity

Stereotypes will be perpetuated when individuals' behaviors confirm stereotypes and can be reduced when behavior runs counter to them. Changing stereotypes is not an easy process. Women who conform to the traditional gender role may be less threatening to men and experience less resistance from them. For instance, marriage and motherhood may have certain advantages. Rausch et al. (1989) and Simeone (1987) believe that married women may seem less threatening in collegial interactions because marriage accords women a protected status (Rausch et al., 1989), and they found that married women were more likely to stay at the university. They did not investigate the relationship between marital status and exit, nor did they determine whether faculty stayed because of a spouse's job; however, changing jobs because of the spouse's job was not one of the top reasons for leaving academe in that study. In following some of the traditional gender role prescriptions for behavior, however, women may reduce their effectiveness and productivity in academe.

Women who do not conform to stereotypes are given a harder time, especially by conservative male students and faculty. Students' evaluations of teaching are biased by gender of the professor, especially when the ratings are done by male students (Simeone, 1987). Basow (this volume) found that male students rate women professors most harshly when they are teaching in nontraditional fields and when they do not conform to traditional gender role stereotypes. Conservative males rated women more harshly than did any other group.

The good news and bad news is that many academic women are similar in socioeconomic background to academic men (Persell, 1983); it is easier and more socially understood for White, middle- and upper-middle-class men and women to get an education and to seek an academic career. Women from ethnic minority or lower-class backgrounds will be at an additional disadvantage in academe. Although class similarity may improve relations between the groups, when differences are present they add to the already problematic dynamic for the individuals.

Authorities and Prescriptions for Civility

Many believe that in academe, change may have to come from the top down. Bergmann (1996) pointed out the necessity of circumventing the efforts of those who employ discriminatory selection tactics to block affirmative action efforts. Those in positions of power have others' attention because they control others' outcomes (Fiske, 1993), such as funding and resources. They often have the respect of those who work for them. Their recommendations are more likely to be effective because they will at least be heard. Prescriptions for civility and respect may be communicated through antisexism and antiracism workshops as well as the enforcement of rules regarding harassment and discrimination. They can also be communicated through the existence and support of groups like WASH (see Lott & Rocchio, this volume). Under the direction of a woman president, one community college has instituted mandatory reporting of sexual harassment. This is a double-edged sword (because the individual does not have the right to decline investigation), but the rationale is that the sooner the authorities know about a problem, the faster they can act, and the stronger the message they can send that this is not acceptable. As behaviorists know, punishment is most effective when administered immediately after the offense. The college developed this approach both to protect the students and to prevent suits arising from problems too long ignored.

Institutions should develop and reinforce norms for civility. All faculty could benefit from a less hostile, more egalitarian atmosphere and more opportunities along the way to an academic career (Wilson, 1993). Johnsrud and Des Jarlais (1994) suggested that areas that need attention include relations between chairs and faculty members (e.g., career support, civil behavior, and support and development of newly recruited faculty). They say that department chairs should be selected carefully and rewarded for appropriate mentoring of faculty. Chairs should receive training in maintaining a professional work climate, staff training and development, formative evaluations, sexual harassment, and affirmative action. Efforts should also be made to reduce faculty's anxiety by identifying and eliminating structural discrimination, personal discrimination, and inappropriate faculty behavior at the department level.

BELEAGUERMENT: THE TRIALS AND TRIBULATIONS OF SUBORDINATE STATUS IN ACADEME

Not only are women competing, but they are competing as a group characterized by lower social power. Some of the other barriers to women in academe are those women face due to their subordinate position relative to men and the discrimination associated with this status. A participant in Olsen and Maples' (1993) study commented that some of the obstacles to women's progress in academe may be related to discrimination but might also be described as "beleaguerment" (p. 38). Ethnic minority and other subordinate groups are typically given the less-valued and less-desirable tasks and assignments as well as a smaller share of the available resources. Beleaguerment refers to the additional demands on women in academe, such as time devoted to teaching, advising, representing women on various committees, and duties related to home management and their role as mother.

Committee Work

Some have reported that women decrease their chances for tenure by doing too much service (Konrad, 1991). An optimist would say that women are simply in greater demand because well-meaning institutions wish to have balanced committees. Others believe that it is desirable to be on only a select group of committees; the rest are seen as undesirable. Men's mentors and chairs may help them avoid the latter. Women do seem to value campus service more than do men (Aisenberg & Harrington, 1988). Konrad (1991) found more women than men served on university committees (58% compared to 37%), and most reported that their participation was required because of their gender (70%). White women spend more hours in administrative service, more in faculty senate meetings, and more in administrative meetings than do White men. Rausch et al. (1989) found that this was not by choice, and they suggested that it may be another deterrent to productivity and therefore to promotion and tenure. Boice (1991) suggested that at the individual level, women should set limits, that is, decrease service and involvement in anything not specifically valued by the institution and rewarded with tenure and promotion. At the institutional level, administrators and faculty leaders should work to ensure equal university service workloads. Institutions should operationalize the assignment of responsibilities. For example, the University of Maryland system does annual surveys and collects data on course loads, committee work, advising, grant awards, and scholarly productivity. These are useful sources of information for determining equity in these areas. These data may be available to faculty at public institutions.

Teaching and Advising

A number of researchers (Johnsrud & Des Jarlais, 1994; Russell, 1991) have found that women have a higher teaching and advising load and spend more time on teaching activities. Rausch et al. (1989) found that only 66% of women thought that the amount of teaching responsibility given to them was equitable, whereas 81% of men thought teaching assignments were fair. Almost twice as many women (15.1%) as men (8.8%) thought that teaching loads were never or almost never equitable. Many women would prefer a lighter teaching load (Rausch et al., 1989). Women are more likely to be hired by teaching institutions and may devote more time to teaching as a result (Konrad, 1991). Women who change jobs are more likely to go to teaching universities or private industry; more men go to research institutions (Rausch et al., 1989).

On the other hand, Olsen and Maple (1993) found no significant difference in course load or number of courses taught, but that women taught more undergraduate classes and fewer graduate classes. Courses at the graduate level and advanced undergraduate classes may be designed to deal specifically with a faculty member's research interests, thus reducing the demands for course preparation time that is part of the "teaching load." Special seminars or sections of practica, field studies, or independent studies may be used to calculate course load equivalencies, but may not actually constitute work beyond one's research or an actual course. Hence, differences in teaching load may be disguised. Future studies should examine the nature of the courses taught, the number of new preparations required, and the total number of different courses taught at different points in time.

Again, it would help level the field if institutions or academic organizations could work to ensure equal teaching and advising workloads by conducting annual surveys and using the data to increase equity in workload.

Home Management

When different publication rates are found, they are likely to be due to situational, not dispositional, factors (Blackburn et al., 1978; Konrad, 1991). The rates may be a function of the large proportion of household duties carried, as was true in a study of managers (Konrad, 1991). The results of studies of the relationship between the number of children and publication rates for women and men have been mixed (Astin, 1984; Bentley & Blackburn, 1992; Cole & Zuckerman, 1987; Finkle, Olswang, & She, 1994; Hamovitch & Morgenstein, 1977; Hargins, McCann, & Reskin, 1978; Hensel, 1990). See Chrisler, this volume, for a discussion of role conflicts. It is interesting that participants in Rausch et al.'s (1989) study did not report motherhood as a reason for leaving their jobs; Finkle and Olswang (1996) found that 99% of women faculty who planned to have children did not plan to leave academe. However, women may drop out of the academic pipeline prior to taking their first job due to role conflict and time limitations. Researchers need to follow individuals from college graduation through full promotion. Although women continue to shoulder most of the responsibility for home maintenance and child care (Gmelch, Willse, & Lourich, 1986), when institution type, resources, and other factors are controlled, even some early studies found that women are as productive as men (Blackburn et al., 1978). Considering their situation as described in this chapter, it is surprising that women can come close to men's publication rate.

In 1974, the AAUP first recommended leaves of absence for childbearing, child-rearing, and family emergencies (Committee W, 1990, p. 179). AAUP noted that "career patterns of academic women vary," so "an institution's policies on faculty appointments should be sufficiently flexible to permit faculty members to combine family and career responsibilities in the manner best suited to them as professionals and parents"

(Committee W, 1990, p. 179). The issue of changing the length of the probationary period was not broached, however, Finkle et al. (1994) found support among faculty for the following changes:

1. paid leave ranging from a few weeks to several months for tenure deterrents (such as childbirth recovery and newborn care);
2. unpaid or paid leave for adoptive parents, continuing infant care, child, and dependent care;
3. a change in the institution's culture such that faculty would not be concerned that taking a leave of absence would damage their career;
4. extensions of the tenure clock; and
5. flexible work options regarding full-time or part-time schedules.

The first two suggestions entail a longer probationary period for women. The last two suggestions, however, might result in perpetual part-time, untenured status for women.

THE COST TO STUDENTS

Women faculty members are not the only ones who suffer from the effects of discrimination against them. Rothstein (1995) examined the impact of women faculty on women students' career aspirations. It is commonly believed that women faculty are important to female students because they serve as role models and mentors. Rothstein analyzed the data from a national longitudinal study of the high school class of 1972 to look at the predictors of educational outcomes. She found that a 10% difference in the number of women on the faculty accounted for a 4% greater chance of advanced degree attainment, after family income, parental degrees, SAT score, high school rank, race, religion, major field, and undergraduate institution characteristics were controlled. A chilly climate for female faculty may make it more difficult for female students to achieve their potential. Rothstein noted that a third factor, general campus attitude, could be affecting female faculty and students simultaneously.

One of the costs of turnover for all students is that they may not be able to contact former professors for recommendations if their professors have left the university. This may reduce students' chances of admission to graduate schools. Their potential accomplishments may thus be lost. They are less likely, then, to make a name for themselves that would honor their alma maters. When the number of men and women on the faculty is similar, turnover is lower for both. Furthermore, women faculty increase women students' educational attainment by serving as role models and mentors.

CONCLUSION

Although there is a widespread belief that affirmative action is threatening the ranks of male faculty in academe, this belief is clearly inaccurate. Women may be given special consideration in promotion, but the result is not in the rumored direction of favoritism. Contrary to the belief that affirmative action programs lower standards, the literature suggests that standards are actually higher for women. Women are actually promoted and tenured more slowly and less often than men and have to perform better to be seen as equally talented. Despite the antidiscrimination laws, the forces that keep women from achieving success in academe are escalating; women are losing rather than gaining ground.

Many of those involved in the hiring and promotion processes do not appear to be hiring and promoting talented women despite affirmative action plans. According to the National Center for Education Statistics, women make up slightly more than 50% of high school graduates, 54% of college graduates, and 47% of all American citizens earning doctorates (NCES, 1996a). As of 1994, women represented 39% of all doctoral recipients in the United States (NCES, 1996a). Follett, Ward, and Welch (1993) noted that standard practice in the enforcement of antidiscrimination legislation involves comparing the demographics of an institution's hiring with those of the available workforce. In cases of failure to promote, Follett et al. (1993) wrote that the benchmark would be the promotion or termination rates of other employees who have not charged the institution with discrimination. Likewise, differential pay rates and allocation of resources and responsibilities are a sign of discrimination. Based on these definitions, large numbers of institutions are currently engaging in discriminatory practices and could be deemed guilty.

Legal remedies are an option, but the long-term goal is to create a warmer climate for women in academe (Sandler, 1991). As Olsen and Maple (1993) reminded us, programs and policies designed to advance women in higher education must be based on accurate information about the obstacles women face and the satisfactions that promote their career development. Inaccurate assumptions about women in higher education may be as damaging to them as discrimination and insensitivity are. Competition theory helps to explain the current escalation of resistance to affirmative action programs. If affirmative action is to be effective in opening doors previously closed to women and members of ethnic minority groups, the challenges posed by typical intergroup dynamics will have to be surmounted. Contact theory helps to explain why affirmative action efforts have not been effective and suggests some possible points of intervention. According to contact theory, the increased intergroup contact that results from affirmative action will improve relations between the groups under certain conditions. If the climate for women in academe is to change, those conditions will have to be met. Many of these issues, as well as their solutions, are addressed in greater depth in other chapters in this book. Women must be allowed to attain equality in status and power (including an equitable distribution of desirable and undesirable duties), to work in an environment where men and women have sustained close contact, and to develop and work toward superordinate or common goals with their colleagues. Women vary in their similarity to stereotypes; both ends of the continuum have their drawbacks. Hiring a diverse selection of women will help debunk stereotypes if the rest of the conditions are met. These efforts need to be supported by the administration and by faculty leaders if they are to have the best chance at success. If these conditions required for constructive intergroup interaction and equity in duties and resources are not approximated, however, affirmative action will not succeed. Women will continue to be seen and treated as the outgroup rather than as equals and will continue to be handicapped by current inequities.

REFERENCES

AAUP. (1975, June). The annual report on the economic status of the profession. *Academe*, *61*(3), 172-183.

AAUP. (1985, March-April). The annual report on the economic status of the profession. *Academe, 71*(2), 2-74.

AAUP. (1995, March-April). The annual report on the economic status of the profession. *Academe, 81*(2), 23-78.

AAUP. (1996, March-April). The annual report on the economic status of the profession. *Academe, 82*(2), 41-96.

Ahern, N. F., & Scott, E. L. (1981). *Career outcomes in a matched sample of men and women Ph.D.s: An analytical report.* Washington, DC: National Academy Press.

Aisenberg, N., & Harrington, M. (1988). *Women of academe: Outsiders in the sacred grove.* Amherst: University of Massachusetts Press.

Allport, G. (1954). *The nature of prejudice.* Cambridge, MA: Addison Wesley.

Astin, H. S. (1984). Academic scholarship and its rewards. In M. W. Steinkamp & P. Maehr (Eds.), *Advances in motivation and achievement* (pp. 259-280). Greenwich, CT: JAI Press.

Bair, J. H., & Boor, M. (1988). Psychology of the scientist LIX: The academic elite in psychology: Linkages among top-ranked graduate programs. *Psychological Reports, 63,* 539-542.

Bellas, M. L. (1994). Comparable worth in academia: The effects on faculty salaries of the sex composition and labor-market conditions of academic disciplines. *American Sociological Review, 59,* 807-821.

Bentley, R. J., & Blackburn, R. T. (1992). Two decades of gains for female faculty? *Teachers College Record, 93,* 697-709.

Bergmann, B. R. (1996). *In defense of affirmative action.* New York: Basic Books.

Billard, L. (1994). Twenty years later: Is there pay equity for academic women? *Thought & Action, 10,* 115-144.

Blackburn, R. T., Blymer, C. E., & Hall, D. E. (1978). Correlates of faculty publications. *Sociology of Education, 52,* 132-141.

Blackburn, R. T., & Wylie, N. (1985). Current appointment and tenure practices: Their impact on new faculty careers. *College and University Personnel Association Journal, 41,* 9-15, 18-20.

Blake, R. R., & Mouton, J. S. (1979). Intergroup problem solving in organizations: From theory to practice. In W. G. Austin & S. Worchel (Eds.), *The social psychology of intergroup relations* (pp. 19-32). Monterey, CA: Brooks/Cole.

Blalock, H. (1967). Percent non-White and discrimination in the south. *American Sociological Review, 22,* 677-682.

Boice, R. (1991). New faculty as teachers. *Journal of Higher Education, 62,* 150-173.

Cadet, N. (1989). Marginalia: Women in the academic workforce. *Feminist Teacher, 4,* 16-17.

Chamberlain, M. K. (Ed.). (1988). *Women in academe: Progress and prospects.* New York: Russell Sage Foundation.

Clark, S., & Corcoran, M. (1986). Faculty development perspectives on the professional socialization of women faculty: A case of cumulative disadvantage. *Journal of Higher Education, 57,* 20-43.

Clore, G. L., Bray, R. M., Itkin, S. M., & Murphy, P. (1978). Interracial attitudes and behavior at a summer camp. *Journal of Personality and Social Psychology, 36,* 107-116.

Cole, J. R. (1979). *Fair science: Women in the scientific community.* New York: Free Press.

Cole, J., & Zuckerman, H. (1987). Marriage, motherhood, and research performance in science. *Scientific American, 256,* 119-125.

Committee W. (1990). Leaves of absence for child-bearing, child-rearing, and family emergencies. In AAUP (Ed.), *Policy documents & reports* (pp. 179-180). Washington, DC: AAUP.

Cook, S. W. (1984). Cooperative interaction in multi-ethnic contexts. In N. Miller & M. Brewer (Eds.), *Groups in contact: The psychology of desegregation* (pp. 156-186). New York: Academic Press.

Coser, R. L. (1981). Where have all the women gone? In C. F. Epstein & R. L. Coser (Eds.), *Access to power: Cross-national studies of women and elites* (pp. 16-33). New York: Allen & Unwin.

Crocker, J., & McGraw, K. M. (1984). What's good for the goose is not good for the gander: Solo status as an obstacle to occupational achievement for males and females. *American Behavioral Scientist, 27,* 357-370.

Davis, D., & Astin, H. S. (1978). Reputational standing in academe. *Journal of Higher Education, 58*, 261-275.

Dion, K. L. (1979). Intergroup conflict and intragroup cohesiveness. In W. G. Austin & S. Worchel (Eds.), *The social psychology of intergroup relations* (pp. 211-224). Monterey, CA: Brooks/Cole.

Etaugh, C., Houtler, B. D., & Ptasnik, P. (1988). Evaluating competence of women and men. *Psychology of Women Quarterly, 12*, 191-200.

Exum, W. H., Menges, R. J., Watkins, B., & Berglund, P. (1984). Making it at the top: Women and ethnic minority faculty in the academic labor market. *American Behavioral Scientist, 27*, 301-324.

Finkle, S. K., & Olswang, S. G. (1996). Childrearing as a career impediment to women assistant professors. *Review of Higher Education, 19*, 123-139.

Finkle, S. K., Olswang, S., & She, N. (1994). Childbirth, tenure, and promotion for women faculty. *Review of Higher Education, 17*, 259-270.

Finklestein, M. J. (1984). *The American academic profession: A synthesis of social inquiry since World War II.* Columbus: Ohio State University Press.

Fiske, S. T. (1993). Controlling other people: The impact of power on stereotyping. *American Psychologist, 48*, 621-628.

Follett, R., Ward, M. P., & Welch, F. (1993). Problems in assessing employment discrimination. *Economic Review, 83*, 73-78.

Gmelch, W. H., Willse, P. K., & Lourich, N. P. (1986). Dimensions of stress among university faculty: Factor analytic results from a national study. *Research in Higher Education, 24*, 266-285.

Goldberg, P. A. (1968). Are women prejudiced against women? *Transaction, 5*, 28-30.

Haemmerlie, F. M., & Montgomery, R. L. (1991). Goldberg revisited: Pro-female evaluation bias and changed attitudes toward women by engineering students. *Journal of Social Behavior and Personality, 6*, 179-194.

Hamovitch, W., & Morgenstein, R. D. (1977). Children and the productivity of academic women. *Journal of Higher Education, 48*, 633-645.

Hargins, L. L., McCann, J. C., & Reskin, B. (1978). Productivity and reproductivity: Fertility and professional achievement among research scientists. *Social Forces, 57*, 154-163.

Heilman, M. E., Martell, R. F., & Simon, M. C. (1988). The vagaries of sex bias: Conditions regulating the undervaluation, equivaluation, and overvaluation of female job applicants. *Organizational Behavior and Human Decision Processes, 41*, 98-110.

Hensel, N. (1990). Maternity, promotion, and tenure: Are they compatible? In L. B. Welch (Ed.), *Women in higher education: Changes and challenges* (pp. 3-11). New York: Praeger.

Hornig, L. S. (1980). Untenured and tenuous: The status of women faculty. *Annals of the American Academy of Political and Social Science, 448*, 115-125.

Hornig, L. S. (1987). Women graduate students: A literature review and synthesis. In L. S. Dix (Ed.), *Women: Their underrepresentation and career differentials in science and engineering* (pp. 103-122). Washington, DC: National Academy Press.

Hothersall, D. H. (1984). *History of psychology.* Philadelphia: Temple University Press.

Hutcheson, P. A. (1996). Faculty tenure: Myth and reality 1974 to 1992. *Thought & Action, 12*, 7-22.

Johnsrud, L. K., & Des Jarlais, C. D. (1994). Barriers to tenure for women and minorities. *Review of Higher Education, 17*, 335-353.

Justus, J. B., Freitag, S. B., & Parker, L. L. (1987). *The University of Georgia in the 21st century: Successful approaches to faculty diversity.* Berkeley: University of California Press.

Kanter, R. M. (1977). *Men and women of the corporation*. New York: Basic Books.

Konrad, A. M. (1991). Faculty productivity and demographics. *Thought & Action, 7*, 19-54.

Menges, R. J., & Exum, W. H. (1983). Barriers to the progress of women and minority faculty. *Journal of Higher Education, 54*, 123-143.

Mickelson, R. A. (1989). Why does Jane read and write so well? The anomaly of women's achievement. *Sociology of Education, 62*, 47-63.

Moore, K. M. (1982). The role of mentors in developing leaders for academe. *Educational Record, 63*, 22-28.

National Center for Education Statistics [NCES]. (1996b). *Statistical analysis report* [On-line]. Available: X-URL:gopher://gopher.ed.gov:10000/00/publications/postsec/ipeds/fallstaff/fstaff93.

National Center for Education Statistics [NCES] (1996a). *Degrees and other awards conferred by institutions of higher education: 1993-94* [On-line]. Available: X-URL: gopher://gopher.ed.gov:10000/00/ publications/postsec/ipeds/completions/94edtabc.

Olsen, D., & Maple, S. A. (1993). Gender differences among faculty at a research university: Myths and realities. *Initiatives, 55*(4), 33-42.

Paludi, M. A., & Bauer, W. D. (1983). Goldberg revisited: What's in an author's name? *Sex Roles, 9*, 387-390.

Persell, C. H. (1983). Gender, rewards, and research in education. *Psychology of Women Quarterly, 8*, 33-47.

Pettigrew, T. F. (1986). The intergroup contact hypothesis reconsidered. In M. Hewstone & R. Brown (Eds.), *Contact and conflict in intergroup encounters* (pp. 169-195). Oxford, UK: Basil Blackwell.

Pirri, C., Eaton, E., & Durkin, K. (1995). Australian professional women's evaluations of male and female written products. *Sex Roles, 32*, 691-697.

Quattrone, G. A., & Jones, E. E. (1980). The perception of variability within ingroups and outgroups: Implications for the law of small numbers. *Journal of Personality and Social Psychology, 38*, 141-152.

Rausch, D. K., Ortiz, B. P., Douthitt, R. A., & Reed, L. L. (1989). The academic revolving door: Why do women get caught? *Journal of the College and University Personnel Association, 40*, 1-16.

Ries, P., & Thurgood, D. H. (1993). *Summary report 1991: Doctorate recipients from United States universities*. Washington, DC: National Academy Press.

Rothstein, D. S. (1995). Do female faculty influence female students' educational and labor market attainments? *Industrial and Labor Relations Review, 48*, 515-530.

Russell, S. H. (1991). The status of women and minorities in higher education. Findings from the 1988 National Survey of Postsecondary Findings. *College and University Personnel Association Journal, 42*, 1-11.

Sandler, B. R. (1991). Women faculty at work in the classroom, or, why it still hurts to be a woman in labor. *Communication Education, 40*, 6-15.

Segal, B. (1962). Male nurses: A case study in status contradiction and prestige loss. *Social Forces, 41*, 31-38.

Semyonov, M. (1980). The social context of women's workforce participation: A comparative analysis. *American Journal of Sociology, 65*, 1090-1100.

Sherif, M., Harvey, O. J., White, B. J., Hood, W. R., & Sherif, C. W. (1961). *Intergroup conflict and cooperation: The robber's cave experiment*. Norman: University of Oklahoma Press.

Sheriff, M., & Sheriff, C. W. (1969). *Social psychology*. New York: Harper & Row.

Shomer, R. W., & Centers, R. (1970). Differences in attitudinal responses under conditions of implicitly manipulated group salience. *Journal of Personality and Social Psychology, 15*, 125-132.

Shore, T. H. (1992). Subtle gender bias in the assessment of managerial potential. *Sex Roles, 27*, 499-515.

Simeone, A. (1987). *Academic women: Working towards equity.* South Hadley, MA: Bergin and Garvey.

South, S. J., Markham, W. T., Bonjean, C. M., & Corder, J. (1987). Sex differences in support for organizational advancement. *Work & Occupations, 14*, 261-285.

Spangler, E., Gordon, M., & Pipkin, R. (1978). Token women: An empirical test of Kanter's hypothesis. *American Journal of Sociology, 84*, 160-170.

Stephan, W. G. (1987). The contact hypothesis in intergroup relations. In C. Hendrick (Ed.), *Group processes and intergroup relations* (pp. 13-40). Newbury Park, CA: Sage.

Swim, J., Borgida, E., Maruyama, G., & Myers, D. G. (1989). Joan McKay versus John McKay: Do gender stereotypes bias evaluations? *Psychological Bulletin, 105*, 409-429.

Taylor, S. E., & Fiske, S. T. (1978). Salience, attention and attribution: Top of the head phenomena. In L. Berkowitz (Ed.), *Advances in experimental social psychology* (pp. 249-288). New York: Academic Press.

Toder, N. L. (1980). The effect of the sexual composition of group on discrimination against women and sex role attitudes. *Psychology of Women Quarterly, 5*, 292-310.

Tolbert, P. S., Simons, T., Andrews, A., & Rhee, J. (1995). The effects of gender composition in academic departments on faculty takeover. *Industrial and Labor Relations Review, 48*, 562-579.

Toren, N., & Kraus, V. (1987). The effects of minority size on women's position in academia. *Social Forces, 65*, 1090-1100.

Toth, E. (1997). *Ms. Mentor's impeccable advice for women in academia.* Baltimore, MD: University of Pennsylvania Press.

Tsui, A., Egan, T., & O'Reilly, C. (1992). Being different: Relational demography and organizational attachment. *Administrative Science Quarterly, 37*, 554-579.

Weber, R., & Crocker, J. (1983). Cognitive processes in the revision of stereotypic beliefs. *Journal of Personality and Social Psychology, 45*, 961-977.

West, M. S. (1995, July/August). Women faculty: Frozen in time. *Academe, 81*(4), 26-29.

Wharton, A., & Baron, J. (1987). So happy together? The impact of gender segregation on men at work. *American Sociological Review, 52*, 574-587.

Wilson, R. (1993). Why the shortage of Black forces? *Journal of Blacks in Higher Education, 1*, 25-34.

Wolman, C., & Frank, H. (1975). The solo woman in a professional peer group. *American Journal of Orthopsychiatry, 45*, 164-171.

Worchel, S., Andreoli, V. A., & Folger, R. (1977). Intergroup cooperation and intergroup attraction: The effect of previous interaction and outcome of combined effort. *Journal of Experimental Social Psychology, 13*, 131-140.

A Woman's Search for Belonging in Academia

Chris D. Erickson

As a junior female faculty member, I wage a constant battle with academia to fit in and an even fiercer battle within myself to feel like I belong. Some days I win, but more often, my days end with a lot of doubts and insecurities about my place in the academic system. What follows are some reflections on my experiences thus far and an account of the obstacles I have faced in my attempts to enter and belong in the professoriate.

My struggle to feel like I belong in academia began in graduate school, where my advisor treated me more paternally than he did male students, as if I needed more or gentler hand holding. He clearly conveyed to me the message that I would be nothing without him, that he had made me what I was, and referred to other eminent scholars (also women) that he had "made." He introduced me to others in the field as "his" protégée, so that my professional identity became completely associated with his. He suggested that if I stuck with him, I would go on to great things, but he never commented on the good things I was doing or was capable of doing as an individual. Eventually, I changed advisors, but at great personal and professional expense in terms of his retaliatory behaviors.

As a new faculty member in an almost all-male department, I immediately found myself very unwelcome, beginning with the orientation dinner when the university president assumed that my husband was the new faculty member. Then came the invitations to social functions that were arranged by the "Faculty Wives Club." At one point, a senior faculty member laughed as he described to me how university administration had told the all-male department for years that eventually they would have to hire a woman, but that they had refused to do so. He described with pride how the faculty had found creative ways to avoid hiring women, but that, alas, eventually they had been forced to hire two. His point in telling me this had been to inform me about how lucky I was to have been selected for my position, and he implied that I should really appreciate what I had been given (which was, apparently, the privilege of working among them). All of the faculty acted as if I was lucky to be there because I could not possibly have earned my position by way of my abilities. They assumed that I was not, nor could I ever hope to be, as talented as they were. Needless to say, this was a very lonely introduction to academic life.

Eventually, another new woman faculty was hired, and she was treated the same way. I was not surprised when she left after 1 year, and when she had gone, the male faculty openly bashed her. "I knew from the start she was never cut out for academia," they would say, even though they had selected her from a national search. As a group, they concluded that her professional career would never amount to anything. The recurrent theme of their discussions, and the message I received, was that I was beneath them in status and ability by means of my gender.

My colleagues consistently made light of the work that I was doing, as if it were a hobby or insignificant. They were not interested in my professional activities, and, in fact, they assumed I was doing nothing. When they would learn about my professional activities via a travel request, for example, they were genuinely surprised but completely uninterested in the merits of the work I was doing, as if my efforts were not worth their attention.

As I became even more productive, they found ways to imply that my work was of such poor quality as to be worse than if I were not doing anything at all. For example, at one point, the department chair called on the faculty to submit grant proposals to increase the department's financial resources. I was the only one who wrote a proposal, and when the department chair brought it before the faculty for their approval, they concluded that it would "not hurt the department," so I was therefore allowed to submit it to the funding agency. If a male faculty member had submitted the only grant proposal, it would have been heralded as a masterpiece.

One of the facts of academic life that I have found most troubling is universities' recent efforts to raise the requirements for faculty tenure and promotion. The effect of this change has been that senior faculty, mostly White men, have had to publish only a few articles and perform some amount of service to achieve tenure and promotion, whereas the recent influx of women and racial/ethnic faculty are faced with much more rigorous standards and increasingly enormous demands on their time and energy merely to survive in academia. Now that women and racial/ethnic faculty have begun to join the academic ranks, junior faculty have to have several publications a year, excellent teaching evaluations, and perform considerable amounts of service to earn tenure.

I have no doubt that this raising of "standards" is the direct result of the increase (in some cases, unwanted) in hiring of diverse faculty members. It is as if the system were saying that it has to raise its standards now that the "riffraff" have arrived. A more malicious interpretation is that the system would like to wash out those who are not members of the "old boys' network."

These kinds of messages have taken a large toll on my self-confidence and caused me to get off to a slow start in publishing my research. After all, it was apparently not interesting and was obviously of substandard quality, so what was the point? Another effect has been my hesitance to assert myself or my ideas, because they were frequently not taken seriously, or to discuss my accomplishments, because no one seemed interested in them.

When I first began preparing for a career in academia, I naively thought that I would be welcomed with open arms for the new or different perspectives I had to offer. Eventually, I developed an expectation of rejection. For several years, I just assumed that I would not do well; after all, I was trained to believe that I was not able to think for myself and that I needed someone to assist me in my work. As a result, I limped along professionally, trying to avoid humiliation rather than working to share my ideas and opinions.

Sadly, it has taken some time for me to realize that not only am I not bad at this job, but I am actually very talented and capable in my work, and may even have a lot to offer my profession. Although it is unfortunate that all of those messages detracted from my energies to do my job, and that it has taken me several years to realize my worth as an academician, somehow I managed to persist and have come to realize that I do have a reason for being here. Eventually, I may even feel like I belong.

It seems to me that part of the problem is that change is threatening, and that including new faculty who are different can be confusing or troubling for some senior faculty. As with everything, however, change is going to come no matter what. Unfortunately, I have borne the brunt of the system's attempts to remain the same, and it has taken a lot of the fun out of the dreams I had for my career. I have become disillusioned and now have to take pride in mere survival, rather than in the work that I had planned to do.

Some days, I still wonder whether I will ever feel like I belong in academia, or whether it will manage to drain me of my essence before I reach that point. Until then, I must be satisfied that I have done my best to make my mark, to have at least scratched on the walls of academe: "Chris was here."

Come and Be Black for Me

Ethel Morgan Smith

I am glad February is almost over. It's during this month that everyone is looking for me—or rather, anyone who can come and be Black for them.

I'm the only African American professor in my university department of 50 faculty members. I reside in a world that is predominantly White and male: a land-grant state university with about 20,000 students, 5% of whom are African American.

During February, my mailbox is overflowing. Most of the mail wants me to represent "my people" for some worthwhile organization during the month of February and February only. Sometimes the tone is pleasant. I generally accept those. Most often the tone is not pleasant. I group the mail into categories of "accept for sure," "decline for sure," "maybe," and "I'll get back to you."

I've had letters that point out (if not in so many words) that their tax dollars pay my salary and they rightfully deserve a piece of me. The least I can do, these letters imply, is come and be Black for them. I dump those requests in my recycling bin. I also get numerous calls. A pleasant woman from the arts council needed someone to attend her luncheon book-club meeting at her house. One of my colleagues, whom I haven't even met, gave her my telephone number. Her group is thinking of including a Black writer on its reading list next year. I accept her pleasant invitation. It doesn't conflict with my calendar. I can be Black that Wednesday.

Someone knocks on my door. A graduate student, White male, wants me to be a member of his thesis committee. A portion of his writing will be on the impact of contemporary African American women authors on American literature. He's a good student. I accept and thank him for thinking of me. I want to know when I can expect some of his work.

Another student drops by. She is African American and can't decide if she's angry with me or not. Last semester I thought she was being self-

This piece was published in the Pittsburgh Post-Gazette on February 24th, 1997. A different version was published in an anthology called *Honey Hush! African-American Women's Humor*, edited by Daryl Dance. Used with permission of the author.

righteous (as I think many students are) when she screamed at me in class for selecting a novel whose protagonist, a Black man, was married to a White woman. The student said that the protagonist wasn't really Black because he was married to a White woman. I blew up at her in class and asked her who made her God of Blackness? I don't think I apologized to her. She wants to talk about what to do with the rest of her life. I suggest improving her grades. She leaves before I can thank her for coming. I get back to sorting the mail. Five more organizations have submitted requests for me to come and be Black.

Another knock on my door. It's two White students, male and female, from last semester's African American literature class. They (well, he, since the male speaks for the female) liked my class and learned a lot, but thought they would offer me some advice. He tells me that the Black kids, all four of them, wanted to speak too much in class when I asked for comments or specific questions about the text. I remind them that everyone was given ample opportunity to speak. The student tells me that it was also annoying that "they" always sat together. I point out that all of the White students sat together as well. My two visitors leave.

Someone else knocks on my door. It's my colleague whose office is down the hall. He calls himself a folklorist. He, too, wants me to come and be Black for his group. Another colleague drops by. A White male who's fascinated by Africa wants me to know that if I have any interest in going to see my homeland, he is the man to help me get there. I tell him that Alabama is my homeland. My boss comes by next. He wants me to be a part of a new task force on diversity. I accept and thank him for thinking of me.

I have to get home. It's nearing the end of "come-and-be-Black-for-me" month and I need my rest.

Paying Athena
Statistics, Statutes, and Strategies

3

Ellin Kofsky Scholnick

The absence of equal pay for equal work haunts women in every occupational setting. Although the problem is widespread, each context offers particular challenges and possible means of redressing inequities. Institutions of higher education are designed specifically to generate and disseminate knowledge. The very expertise required to enter and survive in academe can also be used by women to gain information about institutional and personal inequities. In a research culture, personal command of the scholarship on salaries also provides the ammunition for combating inequities because it is difficult for scholarly institutions to ignore scholarship on their own practices. If structures and rules have not been designed to create salary equity, many institutions of higher education have a tradition of faculty governance that serves as a critical counterweight to administrative processes. The same formal and informal committees that debate the nature of the curriculum, student admission standards, and parking fees can be used to recruit allies in the fight for pay equity. The government also

AUTHOR'S NOTE: I wish to thank Erica Fener for her help in gathering the statistical data presented in this chapter and Barbara Bergmann, who fed me lunch and many insights into the analysis of faculty salary.

provides the same weapon to faculty that it provides for the entire labor market: legislation and judicial rulings on gender discrimination. None of these resources guarantees equity; using each may involve costs and risks; but command and enrichment of these resources are vital to the ultimate achievement of equal compensation for women.

This chapter discusses these weapons and strategies. It begins with demographic information about faculty and the relation between women's position in the academic labor market and salary equity. A second section discusses the implications of these data for career choices and salary negotiations. The third section describes the laws designed to bar salary discrimination, and the chapter ends with suggestions for actions designed to prevent and redress problems.

ARE WOMEN UNDERPAID?

I used to think that understanding salary issues was easy. You had merely to peruse the statistics published yearly by the American Association of University Professors (AAUP) in *Academe* or by the U.S. Department of Education in *The Digest of Education Statistics*. For example, in the 1994-1995 academic year, the mean wages of male full-time instructional faculty on 9-month contracts was $51,228, whereas women's wages averaged $41,369 (U.S. Department of Education, 1996). Women faculty were earning 80 cents of the males' salary dollar. But the figures are uninterpretable and misleading. What causes the disparity? Are the differences equally prevalent across the spectrum of women faculty in diverse departments, ranks, and institutions?

Determinants of Salary

Two classes of determinants, human capital and institutional structure, have been used to explain wage differences (Bellas, 1993; Nettles & Perna, 1995; Youn, 1988). Human capital refers to the qualities the individual brings to the workplace. These characteristics, which are acquired by individuals in order to make themselves valuable commodities, include education, years of experience, scholarly attainment, and area of expertise. In a perfect world, salary is determined by merit, which in turn is defined by these variables. Theoretically, individuals determine their own human capital. Even though faculty in various fields, such as business or the humanities, may be paid different salaries due to differing market values, individuals can freely choose their academic specialization based on their interests and assessments of relative supply and demand.

Sociologists emphasize a second set of determinants of salary: structural factors. Institutions differ in the amount and source of their budgets, their prestige, their student population, and their missions. These characteristics are associated with variations in activities rewarded and salary levels. In addition to the structure of the internal (institutional) labor markets, external structural factors, such as the political and economic climate, influence the budget and reward structure in higher education (Szafran, 1984).

This neat categorization is deceptive because it presumes that the structural and the personal are independent of one another. The very human capital that the educational system rewards (e.g., education, scholarly attainment, and scholarly productivity) is garnered in the educational system. Arguably, the Ivy League undergraduate is already on a fast track to gaining the credentials that will promote later success, including entry into the most prestigious and highest paying academic positions. So, if the system is biased in its dispensation of capital by failing to admit certain people or failing to encourage them to move into higher-paying fields or the most prestigious institutions, then the attainment and reward of human capital cannot be understood without reference to structural analyses.

This interdependence is particularly clear when a third set of salary determinants, demographic variables, such as race and gender, is introduced. It would be unnecessary to find special ways to arm Athena if the attainment of academic credentials were equally easy for males and females (Astin, 1969; Caplan, 1993). Although this chapter focuses on women, the pattern of underrepresentation and salary inequities is also pronounced for African American, Hispanic, Asian American, and Native American male academics, and there is double discrimination for women of color. Determination of the extent and causes of salary differences is complicated by the inextricable, reciprocal interaction of the acquisition of human capital; the structure of the institutions that govern the acquisition and reward system; and implicit, historical biases.

Analyses of salary equity hinge on the employment of statistical techniques to divide the gap between male and female salaries into portions that are due to the human capital (merit) that each person possesses, the institutional structure, and bias that occurs when people in the same institution with the same human capital are paid inequitably. This statistical methodology is part of the armamentarium women need to detect, prevent, and combat salary abuses. But these neat intellectual and quantitative partitions are addressed to one issue. Do women who are in the same situational location and with the same human capital as men receive the same salary as men do? There is a second issue inextricably intertwined with the first. Do women have the same access as men to those locations and human capital? The economist Barbara Bergmann (1986, 1996) has studied the impact of implicit segregation on salary structures. It is well known that there is a glass ceiling that impedes the progress of women in corporations and limits their earning power. Bergmann drew attention to the pervasiveness of segregation in other sectors of the workplace. For example, most people who sell appliances, cars, and insurance are male. Men outnumber women in supervisory positions. White females and African Americans are relegated to less prestigious positions that are associated with lower salaries. In addition, because the range of positions for which women and minorities can compete is narrowed, there is more competition for these positions, which further contributes to lower salaries.

Where the Women Are

Bergmann's analysis will be the basis for my discussion of faculty salaries. A crucial component in understanding gender differences in salary is access to higher-paying positions. Just as in the general labor market, there is an occupational hierarchy in higher education determined by the prestige, location, and mission of the educational institution, and the rank and discipline of faculty. Position in the hierarchy is a critical determinant of faculty salaries (Bell, 1997), and women are least likely to be found in the positions that are the most prestigious and the most highly paid.

In support of this claim, I will use data from the 1992-1993 academic year to illustrate the pattern of positions and salaries of women faculty. A cautionary note is in order. Getting precise data is complicated by the existence of different databases, which were collected at different times with different samples and category systems. Where possible, I have used recently published data from this one time period and one database to make comparisons, but there are inconsistencies within this system and constant updates of the analysis of 1993 faculty surveys. Thus, the statistics are only approximate descriptions.

In 1992, women accounted for 36.6% of the professoriate (U.S. Department of Education, 1995, Table 223). But they were more likely to be found

84

TABLE 3.1   Comparison of Percentage of Female Faculty and Faculty Salaries in Various Types of Institutions (1992-1993)

Type of Institution	Full-Time Faculty: Percent Female	Part-Time Faculty: Percent Female	Average Salary: Female & Male Full-Time Faculty
Public Research	23.4	43.1	$56,443
Private Research	30.9	41.3	$63,967
Public Doctoral	30.2	44.6	$51,497
Private Doctoral	23.7	36.7	$56,011
Public Comprehensive	33.9	51.1	$43,487
Private Comprehensive	35.1	43.5	$43,255
Private Liberal Arts	38.9	53.5	$37,623
Public Two-Year	45.3	43.2	$39,351

SOURCE: U.S. Department of Education. National Center for Education Statistics, National Study of Postsecondary Faculty, 1993, *The Digest of Education Statistics*, 1996, Table 225.

in part-time positions that usually do not afford job security, participation in departmental governance, or research careers. Women accounted for 44.6% of the part-time positions, but only 33.2% of the full-time faculty positions (U.S. Department of Education, 1996, Table 226).

Educational institutions are often ranked with institutions that grant doctorates at the top. Table 3.1 presents data on the representation of women in the full-time and part-time faculty of diverse institutions in 1992-1993 (U.S. Department of Education, 1996, Table 225). Among full-time instructional faculty, women held a smaller percentage of appointments in public research institutions and private doctoral institutions (23%) than in public 2-year colleges (45%). The contrast between the representation of women in full- and part-time posts is striking. Within the context of elite institutions, full-time women faculty are in short supply, yet they constitute the majority of part-time faculty in private liberal arts colleges and public comprehensive universities.

The type of institution and type of position (full- vs. part-time) might be considered structural variables. Field of specialization and rank are constituents of human capital. Table 3.2 presents the percentage of women faculty in different disciplines in 1992 (U.S. Department of Education, 1996, Table 226). At that time, women comprised the smallest proportion of faculty in fields that are held in high esteem by institutions because of the contracts and grants faculty obtain. Among full-time faculty, just 6% of

TABLE 3.2   Salaries and Percentages of Female Faculty in Various Disciplines (1992-1993)

Discipline	Full-Time Faculty: Percent Female	Part-Time Faculty: Percent Female	Average Salary: Female & Male Full-Time Faculty
Engineering	6.1	8.0	$55,569
Natural Sciences	20.1	32.2	$48,192
Agric.-Home Economics	24.7	52.0	$47,809
Social Sciences	27.5	43.2	$45,960
Business	31.2	30.0	$49,223
Fine Arts	33.0	48.3	$40,574
Humanities	41.4	59.0	$40,972
Health	50.1[a]	56.5	$55,624
Education	51.1	67.3	$42,046

SOURCE: U.S. Department of Education. National Center for Education Statistics, National Study of Postsecondary Faculty, 1993, The Digest of Education Statistics, 1996, Table 226.

a. This includes Nursing, where more than 95% of full-time and part-time faculty are female, and Medicine, where less than 30% of full-time and part-time faculty are female.

engineers and 20% of natural scientists were women. Yet more than 50% of the faculty in allied health fields and in education and 41% of the humanities faculty were female. It could be argued that the scarcity of women reflects their unavailability in the labor pool. Yet in almost every discipline, the representation of women in part-time positions exceeded their representation in full-time positions.[1]

The most dramatic gender differences occur in the ranks faculty hold (U.S. Department of Education, 1996, Table 226). In 1992, among full-time instructional faculty, women constituted 16.7% of the full professors and 29.4% of the associate professors. About 42.5% of the assistant professors and 46.7% of the instructors were women. Another way of examining these data is to compute the percentage *within* each gender who are full professors. In the 1992-1993 academic year, approximately 44% of the men who were employed as full-time faculty held the rank of full professor, but only 17% of women faculty had been promoted to this rank (Hamermesh, 1993, Table 16). A greater percentage of men (71%) than women (60%) in full-time tenure-track positions had earned tenure. Only 56% of women of color had earned tenure (American Council of Education Fifteenth Annual Status Report on Minorities in Higher Education).

Who Is Paid the Most?

There are financial consequences associated with one's specific faculty position. Discussion here will be confined to full-time instructional faculty because the diversity of part-time arrangements precludes comparisons within and among institutions. But it should be noted that this diversity of arrangements and the lack of job security create a situation where inequity can flourish and remain undetected (Caplan, 1993). As institutions begin to rely more heavily on part-time contractual faculty, women are placed at risk.

Bell (1997) noted that faculty who are in highly rated institutions and prestigious disciplines earn more than their counterparts in other institutions and disciplines. Women are scarce where the rewards are greatest (see Table 3.1; U.S. Department of Education, 1996, Table 228). Women are least likely to be found in public research institutions and private doctoral institutions. In 1992, the average salary in these universities was in excess of $56,000, but in the community colleges and private liberal arts schools, which tend to have the highest proportion of women faculty, the average salary was below $40,000. Table 3.2 indicates that the highest salaries are earned in disciplines with the fewest women.

There are very few women full professors, but women are highly represented in nontenured and nontenurable positions. In 1992-1993, the average salary for full professors was $58,788; associate professors earned, on average, $43,945; assistant professor salaries averaged $36,625; and instructors earned $28,499 (U.S. Department of Education, 1996, Table 229). The average full professor at a public university earned $63,452. A full-time instructor in a public 2-year college received half that much ($31,039; U.S. Department of Education, 1995, Table 227).

Where are the women? They are more likely to be junior faculty in 2-year colleges and in nontechnical fields. Therefore, one problem in evaluating salary inequities is the underrepresentation of women in highly paid positions. The academic fields that women have entered are often ones that either historically have been less well remunerated or have become less financially rewarding as women enter them (Cantor et al., 1995). In academic life, not all fields are considered equal, not all institutions pay equally, and higher academic rank is associated with higher salary. The same problems women face in the general labor market beset women in academia. Women will need to break occupational and institutional barriers if they are to earn higher salaries. There are several hurdles to overcome. The

87

first is access. But even if institutions recruit women, are there salary inequities?

Gender Equity

Men and women faculty often have the same job title in the same department of the same university. Do they earn the same salaries? Why not simply look up the data for female and male assistant professors in English who teach full-time at a comprehensive university and compare them? A measure of salary equity would be the percentage of the average man's salary that the average woman makes. This approach is problematic. The data are local. They indicate what happens in a particular situation, not what happens across the board.

Moreover, determination of salaries is based on several factors that constitute the structural and human capital variables we have already discussed. Salary differences may also reflect the differential weighing of criteria for males and females. A salary committee may weight research productivity more for one gender than the other or may use the same criteria but set a higher standard for raises for one group than another. So how much of the difference in pay is due to bias and how much to gender differences in human capital and job placement?

The One-Equation Approach

To answer these questions, some variant of multiple regression analysis is the method of choice. Salaries vary, and regression analyses are used in an attempt to find factors that explain the variability. If all professors earned $50,000, all associate professors earned $40,000, and all assistant professors earned $20,000, then rank alone determines differences among individuals. Because there is uniformity in pay within a rank, rank predicts 100% of the variation among salaries.

We already know that there are multiple factors that are associated with salary variations. One way to determine salary equity is to include all of them within a single regression equation in order to determine how much singly and in combination they account for variations in salary (Moore, 1993; Toutkoushian, 1994). Gender and ethnicity are also included. These analyses indicate how much of the variation in salaries is due to gender when all the other predictor variables, such as rank or discipline, are held constant. Consequently, the analyses can estimate the gender bias in salary allocation.

The value of any regression analysis is dependent on the power of the variables that are included. If the analysis accounts for only 30% of salary variation, then it is hard to evaluate the impact of gender because so much variation is unexplained, and the addition of other variables might alter what is known about the impact of gender biases.

A regression analysis is only as good as the variables it includes. What counts as worthy behavior is often gendered. For example, teaching and advising effectiveness and institutional service are rarely found in regression equations. Some variables usually entered into regression equations may be biased. Rank is a major determinant of salaries. When different standards are used to determine promotion for women and men, then the impact of gender is apparent not only in the weight assigned to gender in a regression equation but in the weight assigned to rank (Smart, 1991; Snyder, Hyer, & McLaughlin, 1994; Weiler, 1990). Sometimes, crucial determinants of salary, such as research productivity, are omitted, and the usefulness of the regression analysis is thereby diminished. The following discussion of salary studies highlights analyses of national databases that include measures of research productivity because of its central role in salary and promotion (Fairweather, 1993).

An example is a set of regression analyses computed by Nettles and Perna (1995), who used data from a 1992-1993 survey conducted by the National Study of Post-Secondary Faculty. The sample consisted of full-time tenured or tenure-track instructional faculty in the full spectrum of accredited institutions from 2-year colleges to research universities. Their initial analysis included the three types of variables thought to affect faculty salary: human capital variables (e.g., rank, field, highest degree, and productivity), structural variables (e.g., category of institution, geographic location), and demographic variables (e.g., gender and ethnicity).

The analysis explained 42% of the variance in salaries. Among the variables that had a strong impact on salary were holding the rank of associate or full professor, working at a research or doctoral university, and career scholarly productivity. Productivity was defined by a standardized and composite measure. Certain measures of productivity tend to cluster together, such as refereed articles, chapters, and books. For each type of activity, such as articles in refereed journals, the output in the category was compared to the mean output of scholars in the discipline, and then the different standardized productivity measures were combined. But even when rank, productivity, field, and category of institution were controlled, women received 11% less pay than men.

The results of this regression analysis confirm other studies of national databases collected in the past. When Fairweather (1993) analyzed data within four different categories of institution ranging from liberal arts colleges to research universities, he uniformly found that gender was a significant predictor of salaries. In five of nine disciplinary groupings, being a female was also associated with lower salary.

The preceding analyses focused on the factors that predicted salary. But each of the predictors is also affected by structural and demographic factors. Investigators have sought to determine the "causal chain." Langton and Pfeffer (1994) evaluated the factors that contribute to the impact of academic discipline on salary. Their data support Bergmann's (1996) claim that fields such as the humanities—with low mobility, an oversupply of faculty, and an oversupply of women, in particular—tend to pay less. These fields often have wide variations in salaries and show the greatest male-female wage differential.

Nettles and Perna (1995) used the same tactic with their data. If rank and productivity are predictors of salary, what predicts them? The women appeared to be 21% less productive than male faculty. But productivity is related to length of career and serving on thesis and dissertation committees, as well as being at a research or doctoral institution. Women are disadvantaged on each of these indices. When these attributes are statistically controlled, Nettles and Perna found that women actually exceeded men in scholarship. Hence, when both pertinent structural and human capital variables were held constant, women were paid less and the very variables used to predict salary—rank and productivity—were themselves contaminated because women did not have equivalent access to the conditions that fostered career advancement.

The Decomposition or Multiple Equation Approach

Users of the single equation model assume that men and women are rewarded in the same way and that women may fare badly because they lack certain attributes. Were those attributes equated, women would not fall behind. But Nettles and Perna (1995), as well as other researchers (Bellas, 1993; Langton & Pfeffer, 1994), also discovered instances where possession of the same attribute had a different impact on females than on males.

Consequently, a different approach to salary analysis has been employed (Oaxaca, 1973; Szafran, 1984; Weiler, 1990). Regression equations are computed separately for each gender in order to compare whether the variables are weighted the same for each gender. The regression equation that accounts for the salaries of one gender can then be used to predict what people of the other gender would earn if the person's salary were governed by the same criteria. For example, what would a woman be paid if her accomplishments were evaluated by the criteria that govern men's wages? The resultant salary would be women's "fair" wage given whatever human capital characteristics they possess. The actual salary differential is the sum of two components, "explained" differences in human capital as estimated by using the males' equation to compute females' earnings, and "unexplained" differences that may reflect discriminatory practices. Note, however, that the distinction between discriminatory and nondiscrimina-tory sources of variation is simplistic because some of the explained difference in human capital may still be the result of discriminatory practices. The unexplained differences include both the effects of discrimi-nation that lead to underpayment and other factors not included in the regression analysis.

Let's take a hypothetical example (see Barbezat, 1988, for more detail). Suppose the average salary of men is $50,000 and the average salary of women is $40,000. This illustrates the current wage gap where women earn 80% of what men do. What accounts for the 20% gap? Data on women's status on predictor variables are plugged into the males' equation, and by those calculations, women should earn $48,000. The gap between $50,000 and $48,000 reflects the human capital differences between the sexes. We have accounted for $2,000 of the $10,000 disparity. The rest may reflect gender discrimination. The 20% gap is comprised of 4% ($2,000/$50,000) due to gender differences in credentials and 16% due to discrimination. In this hypothetical example, 80% of the gap is accounted for by discriminatory wage practices.

The partition can be calculated for all variables simultaneously or for each separate variable. There are also alternative ways to compute the extent of inequity. Some researchers base their estimates on additional equations in which women's salaries are used as the standard for men, and others use a single equation to estimate the alleged overcompensation of men and undercompensation for women (Becker & Toutkoushian, 1995;

Cotton, 1988; Moore, 1993; Toutkoushian, 1994). Both the amount attributed to discrimination and the cost of redressing the disparities "depends greatly on the combinations of models, methods, and estimators" (Becker & Toutkoushian, 1995, p. 209).

Ashraf's (1996) analysis presents an elegant example of the decomposition approach. Ashraf used five national surveys from which he selected data on full-time tenure-track faculty in American 4-year colleges and universities. Although the information is dated because the surveys were conducted in 1969, 1972, 1977, 1984, and 1989, the data span 20 years and include more than 50,000 participants, with the largest samples in the 1969 and 1972 cohorts. The data are also of interest because the earliest samples predate legislation on gender discrimination in salaries.

The same predictors of salary were used for each data set. Among the structural variables were teaching load and type of institution. The regression equations also included human capital variables, such as age, rank, experience, and publication record. For each field and each type of institution, Ashraf ascertained the number of publications faculty produced and then assigned faculty a score based on how far above or below the mean their publication records fell. In three of the surveys, all of these measures predicted 60% to 67% of the variation in faculty salaries.

The first four surveys showed an encouraging wage trend. The gap in earnings declined from 28.11% in 1969 to 17.75% in 1984, but the greatest disparity in wages appeared in 1989. Women earned 31.61% less than men. The gap was widest where the fewest women were found, at the full professor level and at research and doctoral institutions.

How much of the wage gap was due to discrimination?[2] (See Table 3.3.) Part of the gap is explained by gender differences in rank, seniority, and productivity. In each survey, about a third of the wage gap reflected these differences. The remainder reflected gender bias. This was divided into two sources, the extent of female undercompensation as judged by plugging their data into the regression equation used to predict males' salaries, and the extent of male overcompensation as judged by what they would have been paid if the prediction of females' salaries had been applied to men. Each source accounted for approximately a third of the wage gap.

Just as the single regression models have inspired causal models that examine the factors that influence the predictors and the degree to which these factors may reflect biases, researchers who used decomposition models have incorporated more specific analyses to pinpoint the source of salary discrimination. For example, we know that women earn less than

TABLE 3.3   Earnings Gap Between Male and Female Faculty

Year	Total Gap	Explained by Predictors	Overpayment to Males	Underpayment to Females
1969	28.11%	9.64%	8.78%	9.69%
1972	20.28%	7.07%	6.47%	6.74%
1977	21.52%	7.67%	6.75%	7.10%
1984	17.75%	6.54%	5.61%	5.60%
1989	31.61%	11.81%	9.74%	10.04%

SOURCE: Ashraf (1996).

men earn, and that part of the disparity is due to the relative absence of women full professors. Is the problem due to the paucity of women with seniority and sufficient accomplishments or to bias in promotions?

Weiler (1990) used data from a portion of the 1969 sample to determine the variables that predicted rank and salary for each gender. When he applied the same set of weighted predictors of rank to females that had been applied to males, there were fewer female full and associate professors than would be expected given women's careers. He then partitioned the differences in pay into three components, the human capital components such as publication record that are often used as promotion criteria, discrimination in awarding rank, and gender bias. Like Ashraf (1996), he found that approximately one third of the wage difference between females' and males' salaries was explained by gender differences in accomplishments. An additional half of the gap was attributable to promotion discrimination, and the remainder reflected salary discrimination. Szafran (1984) and Barbezat (1988), who used part of the same data set, have also found discrimination in the awarding of promotions.

Weiler's data are from 1969. Johnson and Kovacevich (1997) recently examined patterns of promotion at Kent State University. They examined the career patterns of all faculty hired as assistant professors, and so their sample included both relatively recent hires as well as those hired more than a decade ago. In their sample, women took longer to be promoted and were less likely to be promoted than men; this promotion discrimination accounted for a substantial portion of salary differences. There are some preliminary local indicators of change. Both the Oregon State System and my own institution, the University of Maryland, College Park, have tracked recently entering cohorts of faculty through the promotion process and have found that males and females hired at the same time are promoted at about the same rates to both associate and full professor (Oregon State System of Higher Education, 1996; Struna, Berlin, & Scholnick, 1997).[3]

FROM KNOWLEDGE TO ACTION

Why is it important to understand the salary structure of colleges and universities? Salary is not just another indicator of career advancement; it dictates one's lifestyle. It is one of the factors to consider in making career decisions at various junctures. The economic picture of academic life may influence choices of discipline. If one were contemplating enrolling in a technical school that offered courses in mechanics, automobile repair, or computer programming, it would be wise to inquire about job prospects and pay scales upon graduation. Then why not ask the same questions before embarking on graduate study?

Understanding of the salary picture ought to influence when and where one applies for faculty positions. Mobility is often restricted once a particular entry point is chosen. It is hard to move from part-time positions to full-time posts and from 2-year colleges to institutions granting doctorates. These considerations might influence whether one tries to push forward to complete a doctorate or takes a part-time position.

One crucial determinant of wages is starting salary. It is hard to recover from initial inequities because subsequent merit increments and cost-of-living increments are usually awarded as percentages of salary. Therefore, people receive different raises if their base pay differs, and the gap between the highest- and lowest-paid faculty will widen. Department chairs or deans often have considerable flexibility in setting an initial salary because they want to recruit the most talented applicants. Perhaps women come into the bargaining process with lower expectations of salary, or the dynamics of bargaining for salaries disadvantages women in the same way that bargaining for car prices does (Ayres, 1991).

One aid in the bargaining process is information about current pay levels. Annual reports of salaries at specific institutions for the current academic year are published by the American Association of University Professors (the March/April issue of *Academe*) and in the *Digest of Educational Statistics*. The Integrated Postsecondary Education Data System website lists salaries by gender and rank for every institution. The reference list at the conclusion of this chapter lists its website and other sites where data can be found. In some states, the budget lines for salaries at state institutions of higher education are a matter of public record and are available at public and college libraries. The data are useful in gauging appropriate starting salaries and in evaluating fairness in treatment at any point in one's career.

Caplan (1993) noted that faculty life is governed by a set of invisible rules that new entrants to the faculty culture need to understand in order to adapt and succeed. Often, this information is provided informally by mentors, but women have few mentors (Bergmann, 1986). The scarcity of senior women in some fields means that new women faculty often lack the information they need about career expectations, the reward system, and ways to handle the demands of the faculty role. They also lack the advocates on committees that make crucial decisions about salary and promotions, as well as the colleagues who will tell them how to handle grievances and who will provide political support. Whereas male faculty are easily adopted into a mentoring relationship, women may need to actively seek mentors in their own and other departments. There are other sources of information that women can use to discern the nature of an institutional culture. Often, secretarial and administrative staff can provide useful insights. Colleagues in one's cohort who are going through the same process may provide information and support.

Another source of information is the research on faculty salaries that makes the reward system explicit. Despite all the rhetoric about institutions with different missions, research productivity is generally given a high priority (Fairweather, 1993). Caplan (1993) advises faculty to include in their negotiations written agreements about the expectations of faculty for teaching, research, advising, and institutional or professional service, and the implications of these activities for both promotion and pay. It is reasonable to ask for additional compensation when these assignments exceed the norms for a department. When service, advising, or course overloads are not remunerated and do not enhance credentials for promotion, it pays to be judicious in involvement.

Women need not work in isolation. Even before selecting a position or before encountering salary discrimination, look for and support organizations and structures that may help prevent and deal with pay discrimination. (See Friedman, Rimsky, & Johnson, 1996, for a guide.) These organizations help create a female-friendly environment. In their absence, women need to create these activities and organizations. Many campuses have strong Women's Commissions or Caucuses or academic officers whose responsibilities include advocacy for women. When these groups are effective, they monitor and report the status of women students, staff, and faculty, and work for change. They also advocate for the working conditions that foster productivity and satisfaction, such as on-site day-care centers.

Inequity can flourish when there is an unwritten tradition. Fair and explicit policies may dampen discrimination. More than 25 years ago, the faculty in my department developed a written handbook to describe the procedures and standards by which faculty are evaluated for promotion and tenure. An elected faculty committee advises the chairperson on salaries, and it is mandatory that people at each rank be represented on the committee. My university has moved toward similar specification of the procedural guidelines, including formal appeals processes for promotion and tenure. A faculty ombudsperson is empowered to negotiate disputes, including salary complaints. I think that this has led to the current situation, in which the data suggest equity in promotion and salary. It is important for women to push for overt and equitable guidelines and standards and for formal and responsive procedures for handling disputes. Because women are not alone in distrusting the unwritten rules and hidden power structure within institutions, they have allies across the faculty. These procedures do not guarantee fairness, because the effectiveness always depends upon the attitudes of the people who carry out the procedures, but they are necessary first steps.

Creating explicit rules is not enough. Just as institutions review departments for their effectiveness, they need to have procedures to monitor and report on the effectiveness of recruitment, retention, promotion, and rewards for faculty. Salary studies are part of the monitoring process. Because faculties are decentralized, it is difficult to keep track of all the cases where people are cognizant of their own undercompensation, much less the instances where faculty members are unaware of the problem. Usually, problems appear to be so diverse that it might be hard to discern a pattern. A well-designed salary study of the entire faculty makes explicit the variables the institution uses in its reward structure and may reveal a discriminatory pattern. Committee W of the American Association of University Professors can provide guidance in conducting salary surveys on campuses. Salary studies provide the kinds of evidence that administrators are likely to find more persuasive than specific anecdotes. Ideally, an institution that knows itself can initiate institutional changes and plan its future better.

Regression analyses can be used to pinpoint individuals who seem grossly undercompensated. The analyses are also useful for designing strategies for remediation. Administrators can use the analyses to estimate the costs of across-the-board raises or raises that reflect the degree to which the individual deviates from expected salaries (Becker & Toutkoushian, 1995; Snyder et al., 1994; Toutkoushian, 1994). Thus, there is a direct link between the regression model and the implementation of an action plan.

Salary analyses also can become institutionalized and so provide a means of monitoring. After applying a monetary remedy, subsequent analyses can reveal the effectiveness of attempts to achieve wage parity. Even carefully established pay equity plans can be vitiated by faculty attempts to garner retention bonuses or continuing biases in setting starting salaries.

Systematic salary monitoring sends a message to administrators who set salaries that there is institutional oversight and institutional concern for race and gender inequities. When salary studies work well to reduce or eradicate inequities, it enhances the institution's reputation. The outcome may lead to easier recruitment of women and ethnic minorities in areas where they were underrepresented.

Salary studies are also a weapon in the affirmative action debate that threatens the status of women faculty. A persuasive argument in the debate is the proportion of the wage gap that reflects differences in accomplishments as opposed to discrimination. As the partitioning produces a greater proportion due to discrimination and a smaller proportion due to differences in achievements, then affirmative action is supported. Women perform as well as men, but institutional barriers have been erected against their just compensation.

WOMEN AND THE LEGAL SYSTEM

Salary studies are time consuming and expensive. They may be pushed by women in power, women legislators, or women appointees to boards overseeing higher education (e.g., Maryland Higher Education Commission, 1996). Some salary studies are an attempt to ward off lawsuits or are in response to lawsuits. The Equal Pay Act of 1963 and Title VII of the Civil Rights Act of 1964 are applicable to faculty salaries and set the grounds for defining discrimination as well as the scope of affirmative action (see Berry, 1994, and Moore, 1993, for concise, readable explanations).

The Equal Pay Act

The Equal Pay Act of 1964 bars employers from sex discrimination in salaries when the employees perform jobs that require "equal skill, effort, and responsibility and which are performed under similar working conditions." Four exceptions are permitted: merit, seniority, quantity and quality of production, and differentials based on any criterion other than sex. The plaintiff must supply evidence that the positions where there are salary differentials are indeed equal, whereas defendants usually try to prove that the jobs are unequal or that the permissible exceptions are applicable to the case (Berry, 1994). The human capital variables included in regression equations are consistent with the language of the law. Equal skill might be interpreted as educational attainment, and effort might refer to full- or part-time status. Seniority refers to years of experience or rank. Quantity and quality of production can be translated into publications, teaching ratings, and so on.

Definitions of merit are open to debate. What constitutes a gender-neutral merit system? When the basis of merit judgments is not public, or the system is not employed systematically or evenhandedly, there are grounds for complaint that the system may be biased. Each of these grounds is hard to define, and their impact is hard to prove. When pay corrections are made to compensate underpaid women, the law can be used by men whose salaries are also similarly below expectations (Moore, 1993).

The inclusion of other presumably gender-neutral factors in salaries has been particularly controversial (Fiss, 1992). For example, the comparative market value of different fields has been used as a defense of salary differences, even though women's entry into some high-paying fields has been slow and difficult. Often holding prestigious posts, such as journal editor, or officer or fellow of professional organizations, is included in merit judgments, but if these honors are not accorded to women very frequently, would such qualifications be considered gender neutral, and would they be considered criteria that are relevant to or necessary for faculty performance?

Title VII

These issues have become even murkier under Title VII, which does not require that the salary dispute refer to jobs that require exactly equal work. This law prohibits discrimination in all terms and conditions of employment, not just salary (Berry, 1994). Title VII bars employers from asking questions during hiring that are irrelevant to job qualifications, such as marital status or child-bearing plans.

One ground for litigation is wage discrimination based on *disparate treatment*. The use of practices that overtly discriminate against certain people of a given gender or race violates Title VII. If most of the women who were hired as assistant professors right after completing their doctorates were paid less than newly hired male assistant professors, the salary procedure would be suspicious unless the institution could justify its actions by citing merit, seniority, productivity, business necessity, or some other qualifications (Moore, 1993). What constitutes a justifiable exception is open to debate.

The discussion of salary studies illustrates the nature of the evidence used by plaintiffs in Title VII cases (Berry, 1994). The data have included direct comparisons of the salary disparities between females and males in comparable ranks in a given department. Regression analyses have also been used as evidence. But the most persuasive evidence appears to be anecdotal. So, when a chairperson in a department remarks that most women cannot do good research or sustain a career commitment, and these women are not promoted as quickly or as frequently and receive lower pay, the statements may be actionable.

Title VII also covers cases where employers do not intentionally discriminate but where a specific policy or practice has *disparate impact* or a disproportionate effect on a particular group. A policy may appear gender-neutral, but in reality, it narrows the applicant pool, biases the selection process, or produces salary inequities. Suppose there were an all-male salary committee in a psychology department who weighted grantsmanship as the most important factor in merit raises. Grants differ in availability across fields in psychology, and the applied fields, where grants are less available, are disproportionately female. Is this a violation of the law? It depends on whether garnering grants is relevant to the performance of one's role as a faculty member (Berry, 1994; Fiss, 1992). To the extent that the department overtly values entrepreneurial activities and grants foster higher productivity, judgments of disparate impact are hard to make.

The timing of disparate impact is even more controversial. Should the impact be measured now, or is a history of past treatment relevant? Suppose an engineering department deliberately sets out to hire women and pays larger salaries to attract them because they are a scarce commodity. The department is trying to overcome past discrimination by diversifying the applicant pool and the professoriate, but it may lead to claims of discrimination against men.

Unlike the Equal Pay Act, which enables individuals to sue, Title VII permits class action suits. In addition, the law permits more government intervention. Prior to litigation, EEOC officers will attempt conciliation. Failing this, the agency can initiate suits. The Attorney General may also initiate suits to reverse patterns of discrimination. Title VII also permits a wider range of penalties than the Equal Pay Act, including compensatory and punitive damages.

Other laws are also designed to prevent and punish salary inequities. Title IX of the Education Act of 1972 prohibits sex discrimination in institutions that receive federal funding. Many states have local laws that bar sex discrimination.

CHOOSING STRATEGIES

The very existence of these laws and the administrative apparatus for their enforcement support the quest for pay equity. There are government agencies through which complaints can be made and litigation can be initiated. Educational institutions that receive government funding are under strict guidelines for reporting and monitoring recruitment procedures. Nevertheless, equity has not been achieved. The emotional and financial cost of suits is high. The Equal Employment Opportunity Commission is understaffed. Only a small proportion of cases are tried, usually after considerable delays (Bergmann, 1996). The courts are divided in their interpretations of the laws, and there are constant attacks on affirmative action (Bergmann, 1996).

Therefore, the best strategy is prevention. The initial step is careful scrutiny of one's contract. Make sure the expectations and methods of evaluation are spelled out. Check with potential colleagues about the contents of their recruitment package and initial letter of appointment.

Building a curriculum vitae is important. Ultimately, the most powerful tactic in preventing salary inequity is a solid list of accomplishments that makes one competitive in the academic marketplace. Women often fail to document their achievements and undersell the achievements they do document. Keep careful records of the nature of accomplishments, including letters from appreciative students and even appreciative reviewers. Keep track of departmental assignments and their outcomes. Also, if necessary, keep a diary of harmful practices.

Find a comparison group that entered the department at about the same time, and monitor its progress and assignments. Look at subsequent hires to determine whether their initial salary is markedly different from yours.

Be informed. Know the institutional practices and the salary structure. Often, there is a faculty handbook to provide needed information. Know who makes the key decisions. Go beyond abstract information. If there is insider information, know the insiders, such as the Dean of your college or the Dean of the Faculty, so that you can share news of your accomplishments. Get to know the equity officer, who can provide past institutional history and tips that may prevent or ameliorate problems. Choose your service obligations to the university partly on the extent to which they expose you to decision makers or enable you to provide input to decision makers. Find senior colleagues who can provide information about the activities that are highly valued by those who set salaries and recommend promotions. These colleagues may also provide entries into the political and professional networks that foster career development.

Engage in political action. Find women in your discipline or in related disciplines who can help in acculturation to the set of invisible rules and practices that influence success in the institution. Women full professors and faculty stars may be willing to advocate for female colleagues who have experienced unfair treatment. Share information with new colleagues, and create a climate that fosters development. One example is informal lunches to welcome new faculty and establish contacts for them.

At the campus level, join and support your Women's Commission or Caucus. The members will provide a network of allies. Effective commissions are engaged in political action to create a female-friendly and female-fair environment. Women's studies programs may also provide allies. Join the campus branch of AAUP's Committee W or the American Association of University Women. When none of these organizations exists, try to create them, using already existing models on other campuses. Many national organizations, such as AAUP and the American Council on Education, professional disciplinary organizations, and e-mail networks (e.g., WMST-L) can provide models and hints for forming organizations and information on policies of interest to women. Women's groups can serve as a watchdog for the institution and an initiator of institutional change. When pay equity problems surface, the group may have the clout and resources to initiate the study.

Concern about pay equity is not confined to women faculty. It is also a concern of the support staff and of people of color. They may provide information and be allies in the push for monitoring recruitment, promotion, and salaries and for creating activities that are aimed at fostering career development.

Become a member of your campus governance structure, because it may have the power to change institutional practices, such as provisions to stop the tenure clock. Within this governance structure, women need to run for budget and salary committees to be in a position to spot injustices and recommend changes. Sometimes, an active and responsive faculty union may provide a source of support.

Anything educational institutions do to foster the career development of women and publicize their accomplishments becomes a tool in achieving salary equity. This book provides weapons for handling diverse areas of academic life, but they are drawn from the same armory. Victories on one front produce victories on other fronts.

The skirmishes are not confined to the institution. Educational institutions are responsive to outside pressures. For public institutions, liaisons with members of the women's caucus within the legislature or state women's commissions may be useful. Active women's groups within alumnae organizations may provide support for monitoring equity within the institution. And the battle over affirmative action illustrates the fundamental premise of this book. Higher education is neither a meritocracy nor an ivory tower isolated from society. Instead, colleges and universities are institutions with practices that incorporate larger cultural values. The civil rights laws were designed to combat social discrimination, and Athena's weapons must also be directed toward those sources of inequity.

NOTES

1. Women may also be in part-time positions due to family responsibilities, restrictions in mobility, or as a way station while completing more advanced degrees. Often, men teach part-time to supplement income from full-time positions.

2. Be wary of these figures because they are approximations. The magnitude of discrimination estimated depends on the precise regression equation used and the definitions of

predictor variables. However, the pattern reported in these national data sets is consistent across diverse analyses.

3. These data do not take into account those who left prior to promotion review.

REFERENCES

American Council on Education. (1997). *Fifteenth annual status report on minorities in higher education.* Washington, DC: Author.

Ashraf, J. (1996). The influence of gender on faculty salaries in the United States, 1969-1989. *Applied Economics, 28,* 857-864.

Astin, H. (1969). *The woman doctorate in America: Origins, career, and family.* New York: Russell Sage.

Ayres, I. (1991). Fair driving: Gender and race discrimination in retail car negotiations. *Harvard Law Review, 104,* 817-872.

Barbezat, D. (1988). Gender differences in the academic reward system. In D. W. Breneman & T. I. K. Youn (Eds.), *Academic labor markets and careers* (pp. 138-164). Philadelphia: Falmer.

Becker, W. E., & Toutkoushian, R. K. (1995). The measurement and cost of removing unexplained gender differences in faculty salaries. *Economics of Education Review, 14,* 209-220.

Bell, L. A. (1997). Not so good: The annual report on the academic status of the profession. *Academe, 83*(2), 12-20.

Bellas, M. L. (1993). Faculty salaries: Still a cost of being female. *Social Science Quarterly, 74,* 62-75.

Bergmann, B. R. (1986). *The economic emergence of women.* New York: Basic Books.

Bergmann, B. R. (1996). *In defense of affirmative action.* New York: Basic Books.

Berry, D. B. (1994). *Equal compensation for women: A guide to getting what you're worth in salaries, benefits and respect.* Los Angeles: Lowell House.

Cantor, D. W., Astin, H. S., Bernay, T. M., Fox, R. E., Goodheart, C. D., Hall, C. C., Kenkel, M. B., Mednick, M. T., & Pion, G. M. (1995). *Report of the task force on the changing composition of psychology.* Washington, DC: American Psychological Association.

Caplan, P. J. (1993). *Lifting a ton of feathers: A woman's guide to surviving in the academic world.* Toronto: University of Toronto Press.

Cotton, J. (1988). On the decomposition of wage differentials. *Review of Economics and Statistics, 70,* 236-243.

The Equal Pay Act of 1963 (29 U.S.C. §206(d)).

Fairweather, J. S. (1993). Faculty reward structures: Towards institutional and professional homogenization. *Research in Higher Education, 34,* 603-623.

Fiss, O. (1992). An uncertain inheritance. In H. Zuckerman, J. R. Cole, & J. T. Bruer (Eds.), *The outer circle: Women in the scientific community* (pp. 259-273). New Haven, CT: Yale University Press.

Friedman, D., Rimsky, C., & Johnson, A. A. (1996). *College and university reference guide to work-family programs.* New York: Families and Work Institute.

Hamermesh, D. S. (1996, March-April). Not so bad: Annual report on the economic status of the profession. *Academe, 82*(2), 14-22.

Integrated Postsecondary Education Data System of the National Center for Education Statistics. URL: http://www.ed.asu/aaup/ntlf2.html (faculty salaries) and http://129.219.88.111/cgi-bin/9495salsexdif.pl (sex differences)

Johnson, R. J., & Kovacevich, D. (1997). *Promotion and salary inequities between males and females at Kent State University.* Kent, OH: Kent State University.

Langton, N., & Pfeffer, J. (1994). Paying the professor: Sources of salary variation in academic labor markets. *American Sociological Review, 59,* 236-256.

Maryland Higher Education Commission. (1996). *The status of women in Maryland public higher education, 1984-1994.* Annapolis: Author.

Moore, N. (1993). Faculty salary equity issues in regression model selection. *Research in Higher Education, 34,* 107-126.

Nettles, M. T., & Perna, L. W. (1995, November). *Sex and race differences in faculty salaries, tenure, rank, and productivity: Why on average do women, African-Americans and Hispanics have lower salaries, tenure and rank?* Paper presented at the Association for the Study of Higher Education annual conference, Orlando, Florida.

Oaxaca, R. (1973). Male-female wage differentials in urban labor markets. *International Economic Review, 14,* 693-709.

Oregon State System of Higher Education. (1996). *The status of women faculty in the Oregon state system of higher education.* Office of Institutional Research, Oregon State System of Higher Education. URL: http://www.osshe.edu/irs/statwomn/index/html

Smart, J. C. (1991). Gender equity in academic rank and salary. *Review of Higher Education, 14,* 511-526.

Snyder, J. K., Hyer, P. B., & McLaughlin, G. W. (1994). Faculty salary equity: Issues and options. *Research in Higher Education, 35,* 1-19.

Struna, N. L., Berlin, A., & Scholnick, E. (1997). *The status of women faculty at the University of Maryland: Moving toward our goal.* College Park: University of Maryland President's Commission on Women's Issues.

Szafran, R. F. (1984). *Universities and women faculty: Why some organizations discriminate more than others.* New York: Praeger.

Title VII of the Civil Rights Act of 1964 (42 U.S.C. §2000e).

Toutkoushian, R. K. (1994). Issues in choosing a strategy for achieving salary equity. *Research in Higher Education, 35,* 415-428.

U.S. Department of Education, National Center for Education Statistics. (1995). *1995 Digest of Education Statistics.* Washington, DC: U.S. Department of Education.

U.S. Department of Education, National Center for Education Statistics. (1996). *The Digest of Education Statistics 1996.* Washington, DC: U.S. Department of Education. URL: http//nces01.ed.gov/NCES/pubs/d96

Weiler, W. C. (1990). Integrating rank differences into a model of male-female faculty salary discrimination. *Quarterly Review of Economics and Business, 30,* 3-15.

Youn, T. I. K. (1988). Studies of academic markets and careers: An historical review. In D. W. Breneman & T. I. K. Youn (Eds.), *Academic labor markets and careers* (pp. 8-27). Philadelphia: Falmer.

Part II

Women's Roles and

Career Decisions

Teacher Versus Scholar
Role Conflict for Women?

Joan C. Chrisler

Jessie Bernard (1964) divided faculty into two categories: Teachers and men of knowledge. Teachers, she wrote, serve as communicators of knowledge, whereas men of knowledge serve as collaborators with the original authors as well as authors themselves of the knowledge they present. Bernard chose the term "men of knowledge" advisedly; they were, she found, most likely to be men, whereas "teachers" were most likely to be women.

Teachers, wrote Bernard, typically deal with the established, elementary aspects of their disciplines. Their task is to conserve, not to innovate. Thus, teachers are most often found in the introductory or other required courses where the students' interest in the subject matter cannot be taken for granted. Teachers must, therefore, coax their students into becoming interested in the material. They focus much more than do men of knowledge on the process of teaching and the class dynamics; this leads them to define their productivity in terms of the number of students stimulated rather than the amount of scholarly work published.

Men of knowledge, on the other hand, are typically found teaching the controversial, advanced courses in their disciplines. In advanced courses, the motivation of the students may be taken for granted, leaving the

AUTHOR'S NOTE: An earlier version of this chapter was presented at the conference on Gender in Academe: The Future of Our Past, University of South Florida, Tampa, November 1989.

professor free to focus more on scholarship than on teaching. The man of knowledge systematizes research findings and puts them in perspective, takes a point of view and argues for or against the views of others, and has a clear role in the shaping of the direction of the field, either through publication or training graduate students who will later publish similar views (Bernard, 1964).

Are women still less likely to be "men of knowledge"? Do women prefer teaching to scholarly research and writing? Are the roles of teacher and scholar compatible with societal expectations for women? These are some of the questions this chapter will address.

WOMEN AS TEACHERS

A number of studies (Astin, 1973; Astin & Snyder, 1982; Centra, 1974; Theodore, 1986; Tuckman, 1979) have found that women professors are more likely than men to list teaching as their principal activity; more men than women list research as their principal activity. The division of activities varies to some extent according to discipline; women in the arts, humanities, and social sciences spend more time teaching, whereas women in the natural sciences spend more time in research activities (Astin, 1973). More women than men (39.9% vs. 22.4%) teach only undergraduates; more men than women (15.9% vs. 11%) teach only graduate students (Centra, 1974). Again, this varies somewhat by discipline. In the modern languages, men were three times as likely as women to teach only graduate students; in sociology, women were twice as likely as men to teach only undergraduates and half as likely to teach only graduate students (Morlock, 1973). More recent data indicate that men continue to be offered more opportunities than women to teach graduate-level courses (Jones, Hoenack, & Hammida, 1994). In a report on their 1989 faculty workload study, the Carnegie Foundation (1990) noted that 58% of women but only 48% of men taught only undergraduates; a HERI faculty survey (Astin, Korn, & Lewis, 1991) conducted the same year found that 20% of women but only 13% of men taught a remedial course.

In the late 1970s, surveys of faculty at 4-year institutions indicated that women spent more hours in the classroom than did their male colleagues. Fifty-three percent of male faculty and 35% of female faculty taught 8 or fewer hours per week; 28% of female faculty and 15% of male faculty taught 13 or more hours per week (Hornig, 1980). In the late 1980s, teaching loads became more equitable, but the gap had not closed. Forty-three percent of male faculty and 36% of female faculty taught 8 or fewer hours per week; 27% of female faculty and 20% of male faculty taught 13 or more hours per week (Astin et al., 1991). Furthermore, women faculty report spending more time than do their male colleagues preparing for classes and advising students (Astin et al., 1991).

These data clearly support Bernard's (1964) contention that women are more likely to be teachers and men more likely to be scholars (men of knowledge), both in terms of the differential amounts of time spent on teaching versus research and in the fact that men are more likely to spend significant amounts of time teaching specialized, upper-level or graduate courses. One might argue that the fact that women are more likely to be employed at community colleges and liberal arts colleges, whereas men make up the majority of the university faculty accounts for most of these findings. In other words, women may spend more time teaching because their employers require that they do so, rather than because they choose to do so. There has been a debate in the literature over whether women choose the lower-paying, lower-status positions at 2- and 4-year colleges because they prefer to spend more time teaching (Brown, 1967) or whether they would prefer, were employment discrimination not prevalent, to work at higher-paying, higher-status research universities where scholarly activities are encouraged and supported (Simeone, 1987).

Regardless of the extent of their scholarly interests, it seems that women professors generally spend more time with the students than do men (Park, 1996). This is true not only of classroom contact hours, but also of time spent in academic and club advising, socializing, and personal counseling. Many women academics have spoken eloquently about their concern for their students. Florence Denmark (1988) wrote,

> I think I'm different from my male colleagues. I tend to give more time to my students. However, I think this is generally more true of women than men. We're more willing to nurture. Whether we're socialized to do so is irrelevant . . . some men . . . don't have much time for students. . . . I think it is important for students to feel someone cares and is concerned so that they will believe they can achieve and be successful. (pp. 290-291)

A minority woman professor told an interviewer (Thomas, Spencer, & Sako, 1983),

Students come to my office for advising. Male professors do not care in many instances to listen and to give solutions to problems that are very real to students. My reputation as an advisor is such that I get students from all programs. I care for students but while I spend 45 minutes with each one of them, my male colleagues write books, reviews, publish, and get promoted. Then I go home and I have to cook and be a mother.

In a 1973 survey of faculty conducted by the American Council on Education, 20% more women than men endorsed the importance of student emotional development and helping students achieve deeper levels of self-understanding as goals of college teaching; 10% more women than men endorsed the relevance to the undergraduate curriculum of the development of moral character, the development of responsible citizens, and providing the local community with skilled resources. These gender differences persisted across institutional type (Finklestein, 1984).

Commenting on her study of women scientists, Bernard (1983) wrote that

> self-actualization for them in academia lies in the less well-rewarded areas of teaching, counseling, or administration. They really do care about students as people rather than as potential disciples. They really do see teaching as an important contribution in training future scientists, and they really do feel good when they can help students master difficult skills. They really do feel satisfied when they salvage a student whose family problems are interfering with his or her academic or scientific achievements. (p. 76)

Brushing aside any suggestion that women's emotional involvement in teaching and counseling is the result of innate nurturing ability, Aisenberg and Harrington (1988) suggested that women see learning as a tool for personal empowerment. A common theme in their interviews with academic women was a transformational experience: a change from a passive to an active persona, a movement toward autonomy and independence, a new worldview—all of which resulted from their passionate involvement in the study of their discipline. The attraction to teaching and otherwise working with students may be the desire to provoke this same transformational experience in others. Rather than simply transferring their mothering abilities from the home to the professional scene, academic women may be bent on the radical purpose of invoking change and empowerment in others. Oddly, despite women's apparently greater involvement with students, they are not generally perceived by students as being better teachers than their male colleagues (Fandt & Stevens, 1991; Finklestein, 1984; Kaschak, 1978; Loeb & Ferber, 1973). (See Basow, this volume, for a discussion of student evaluations of teaching.)

Many women are surprised to learn that the activities they find so challenging and rewarding are considered by tenure and promotion committees to be less valuable than research and publication. This lower value is also reflected in graduate programs, which emphasize research skills and provide little or no pedagogical training (Bess, 1990). Shelley Park (1996) believes that the gender imbalance in professors' task preferences influences as well as is influenced by what universities and colleges value. The lack of graduate training in pedagogy suggests that teaching is something that anyone can do, that it is instinctual or natural (like parenting), and that working with students is "uncreative, unchallenging, and unskilled" (Park, 1996, p. 52) as compared to research and writing, which require skills and rigorous standards that must be learned. As long as teaching, academic advising, and other student-related service activities are seen as women's work, male professors will be less likely to choose these roles for themselves (Park, 1996), and women will continue to be encouraged to see these tasks as comfortable and compatible with the feminine gender role.

WOMEN AS SCHOLARS

In the report on their 1958 study of the American higher education system, Caplow and McGee wrote,

> Women scholars are not taken seriously and cannot look forward to a normal professional career. . . . Women tend to be discriminated against in the academic profession, not because they have low prestige but because they are outside the prestige system entirely and for this reason are of no use to a department in future recruitment. (Lewis, 1975, pp. 123-124)

Although women have made significant strides since the 1950s, their credibility as scholars may still be in question.

Advice to beginning academics often contains references to the fact that women and minority men are not considered credible scholars and must therefore focus on their research and writing in order not to feed the stereotype (Caplan, 1993; Gibbons, 1986; Taylor & Martin, 1987;

Thomas et al., 1983). The lack of credibility is a larger problem when the scholar's work focuses on issues of concern to women (Gibbons, 1986; Simeone, 1987) or minorities (Gregory, 1995; Thomas et al., 1983)—issues on the periphery of traditional disciplinary concerns. It is difficult to get such research past the gatekeepers and into the mainstream disciplinary journals (Burgess, 1997). Most gatekeepers (e.g., editors, reviewers, advisors) are White men who may not see the importance of such work and whose judgments set the parameters of discussion and debate in their fields (Spender, 1981). As a result, women publish more frequently than do men in interdisciplinary and women's studies journals, which are not given much weight in tenure and promotion reviews, where the quality of the article is often defined by the name recognition of the journal in which it appears (Abramson, 1975; Kawawe, 1997). Regardless of where women's articles are published, their male colleagues are less likely to cite them than they are to cite articles written by other men (Ferber, 1986, 1988).

In her 1986 study of 470 women who filed sex discrimination complaints against higher-education institutions, Theodore (1986) found that the women complained bitterly of not being taken seriously as scholars. Both innuendoes and open criticism were reported to occur routinely.

> The women lacked proper focus; they were not analytical; they deliberately avoided quantitative approaches when these were necessary; their skills were limited because of their feminine nature. . . . Women are not theoretical, they cannot conceptualize, they think irrationally, they do not know how to reason, they are too emotional to do creative work, and they do not have the stuff to be good researchers. Women simply are not serious scholars. . . . Despite the evidence women produce of their [scholarly] productivity, some men openly indicate resentment of the ideas and scholarship of their women colleagues. . . . Such negative attitudes discourage women from doing scholarly work. (pp. 7-19)

Many studies have attempted to compare the scholarly productivity of men and women. These studies are confounded in a variety of ways. First, the typical measure of productivity is simply to count published items—a measure of quantity, not quality. Item counting typically gives equal weight to books, reviews, and articles. An edited book is not differentiated from an original monograph, nor is a long article from a short one, nor a multi-authored article from a single-authored one (Finklestein, 1984). Second, publication rates vary by discipline (Astin, 1978). The highest publication rates are found in the natural sciences, where a high priority is placed on research and where, in addition to articles and books, one publishes notes, abstracts, laboratory reports, and technical bulletins. Publication rates are lowest in the arts and humanities, where most women scholars are working; the social sciences fall in between. Third, publication rates tend to increase with rank (Astin, 1978). Full professors publish more than associate professors, who publish more than assistant professors. One's research and writing abilities, one's ability to "target" journals, one's reputation, one's professional contacts, and one's invitations to contribute articles and chapters all increase with experience and rank. Men have been promoted much more quickly than women, and many more men than women have reached the rank of full professor (Bentley & Blackburn, 1992; Billard, 1994). Fourth, publication rates vary with institutional setting (Astin, 1978). Universities and research institutes have the highest publication rates. Research and writing are priorities there and have considerable institutional support. Publishing does not have the same high priority at liberal arts colleges and is not expected of faculty at community colleges. Thus, one can see the inequity of comparing the publication rate of a female associate professor of English who is teaching six introductory courses on a 5-day teaching schedule at a community college with that of a male professor of chemistry who is teaching two advanced courses on a 2-day teaching schedule at a university where he has the help of graduate teaching and research assistants. As Hornig (1979) has commented about the typical academic woman, "We need only remind ourselves that with the facilities and the students of the institutions in which she is commonly employed, the truly remarkable fact is that she is publishing at all" (p. 130).

As a result of the problems described above, the studies on publication rates are inconclusive. Some researchers (e.g., Astin, 1973; Helmreich, Spence, Beane, Lucker, & Matthews, 1980; Jones et al., 1994; Long, 1992) have found that women published significantly less often than men, whereas others (e.g., Boice, Shaughnessy, & Pecker, 1985; Davis & Astin, 1987; Simon, Clark, & Galway, 1975) have found no significant difference in publication rate. Loeb and Ferber (1973) studied the scholarly productivity of the faculty at the University of Illinois. They found that men published slightly more books and articles than women, whereas women published slightly more bulletins, technical reports, reviews, and edited books than men. In general, men who obtained their doctorates prior to 1964 had published more than women with the same degree dates and years of experience; however, among those with more recent degrees, women tended to have published more than men. This latter finding is of considerable interest because 15% of the women faculty were part-time versus only 1% of the men. More recently, Boyer (1990) reported that the 1989 Carnegie Foundation Survey found that 35% of men and 13% of women had published 11 or more articles during their careers; 49% of men and 36% of women had ever written or edited a book.

In her study of the scholarly activity of zoologists, Bernard (1964) found no differences between women and men in the numbers of books, articles, notes, or abstracts published. Men, however, had published significantly more laboratory reports, technical bulletins, reports to "special publics" (e.g., wildlife commissions, legislators), and more teaching aides (e.g., lab manuals, charts, demonstration materials, bibliographies). This may be due to the men having more contacts (the "old boys" network) that led to invitations to do this type of work, as well as more access to grants and other forms of recognition that can be influenced by sex discrimination. More recently, Bernard (1983) noted that "when questions of interest to women began to be raised and publication outlets to be available . . . there was a veritable explosion of productivity among women" (p. 76).

Several studies have examined what resources are necessary for scholarly productivity. Astin and Davis (1985) asked professors what they thought was most important in facilitating their work. Women most often answered that they needed motivation and support from their spouses and/or families; men most often answered that they needed research assistants. When asked to what they attributed their research productivity, women referred to personal variables such as hard work, motivation, interest in the topic, and having the necessary skills. Men attributed their productivity to institutional resources such as release time, grant funds, student assistants, and secretarial help. Astin and Davis (1985) wondered whether women may be underutilizing institutional resources and, thus, lowering both their productivity and visibility. Perhaps the women didn't even know what resources were available to them.

In her study of scientists Bernard (1964) found that the most productive researchers were those

in the most favored positions to know what was going on in their fields, in closest contact with the people and laboratories doing the most important work, in the closest and most frequent contact with the leaders in their fields, and most likely,

114

therefore, to get the unexpected, unanticipated, even accidental information which . . . is so important in this day and age. (p. 158)

She also found that women scientists were less likely than men to edit journals, belong to professional societies, attend conferences, or visit other labs. The women were also less likely to maintain regular mailing lists for their reprints, to be on the reprint lists of others, or to engage in regular correspondence or telephone conversations with other researchers in their fields. It is no surprise that men have an easier time joining a mostly male network or that women with young children and/or low-paying jobs are less able to travel to professional meetings. However, some of the differences Bernard found are undoubtedly traceable to poor mentoring, a topic I shall address later. Some women simply may not know how to place themselves in positions where they will hear the latest information.

High producers also seem to organize their lives around their research and writing; they make productivity a way of life (Bernard, 1964). This may be a particular difficulty for women academics given the number of other demands that are placed on them. In examining her own work habits, Valian (1985) discovered that she did not feel entitled to put her scholarly work first and to schedule uninterruptible time for it. When asked when she could attend a meeting or see a student privately, she did not exclude her writing time. The desire to appear unselfish, to give others whatever they seem to need, and to fit one's own work into the leftover spaces may be typical of women and a result of gender role socialization. Simeone (1987) also noted that this willingness to be accessible to others may be counterproductive to scholarly development. One of the women academics she interviewed said of students,

I have always known that they don't respect my time as much as they respect that of men in the department who are much less busy than I am. . . . There is a feeling on the part of many of our students that men's time is sacrosanct and women's time is theirs. (p. 59)

Women who put their own work before the needs of others are perceived as "tough, cold, heartless, or pushy" (Simeone, 1987, p. 79), an image that most women will seek to avoid, and particularly those women who are untenured faculty.

Preparing grant applications and sending one's work out to journals involves a willingness to take risks. One needs self-confidence and the ability to withstand rejection in order to be a productive scholar. In light of the harsh criticisms that have been leveled against women scholars, it would not be surprising to learn that their confidence in their scholarly abilities was shaken. If so, their lack of confidence may move them away from scholarship and toward teaching and student-centered activities, in which they do not have to prove their abilities continually. Furthermore, the long delays and the uncertainty of rewards associated with research and writing pale beside the relatively immediate satisfactions of good teaching; the negative consequences of teaching poorly will be encountered daily, whereas the negative consequences of failing to publish may be in the distant future (Stevens, 1978).

Social psychologists who have studied patterns of attribution about success and failure (see Frieze, 1978, for a review) have found that the successes of women are often attributed to unstable factors such as luck or hard work, whereas the successes of men are generally attributed to stable factors such as ability. This cognitive pattern is probably most likely to be found when the activity at which the people are successful is one that is considered stereotypically masculine (e.g., scholarship). Thus, when women are successful at obtaining a grant or publishing an article, because their success is attributed to unstable factors, they will not expect continued success in the future. When women fail, however, their failures are likely to be attributed to stable factors, such as lack of ability, whereas men's failures are generally attributed to unstable factors, such as lack of effort. In other words, when her article is accepted for publication, a woman (and her colleagues) may think, "That was lucky!" When her article is rejected, she (and others) may doubt her scholarly abilities. Obviously, these scenarios do nothing to enhance women's self-confidence. These differential attributions have been part of women's lives since childhood, and they can have serious consequences.

Studies (see Frieze, 1978) have found that women and girls do not expect to do as well as men and boys expect to do on novel tasks, athletic tasks, and academic tasks. Women typically underestimate their future performance, and men typically overestimate theirs. For example, Feldman (1974) found that women graduate students in five scientific disciplines were less likely than their male peers to agree with the statement, "I hope to make significant contributions to knowledge in my field." These women were also less confident in their ability to do original work. Expectations can have powerful effects on performance. Frieze (1978) found that research participants who were randomly given high expectations for their performance actually performed significantly better on a task than did participants who were randomly given low expectations.

I have heard many anecdotes about the extreme reaction to editorial criticism experienced by some women, particularly new authors. These women have filed manuscripts away after having received rejection notices, with the expectation that some day they would revise and resubmit them. Time passed, and the papers remained unpublished. As the level of scholarly activity is reduced, the amount of scholarly success cannot rise, nor can the scholar's confidence (Stake, 1986). Aisenberg and Harrington (1988) believe that women may have more extreme reactions to editorial criticism because they see their written work not merely as products but as extensions of the self, that is, the chosen or transformed self. Thus, rejection strikes at the core of the woman's most valued identity. Aisenberg and Harrington (1988) found in their interviews that many women are not satisfied with competence as a criterion for publication. They were holding out for important work that they thought would make a significant contribution to their disciplines. Such significant work takes much longer to produce than the merely competent work that makes up most of our literature. Thus, these scholars produced fewer articles and fewer addresses at meetings, engaged in longer term research, and wrote more complicated books. Rejection of such work would presumably be more painful. Even if the work is accepted and valued, its success may not come in time to impress tenure and promotion committees.

WOMEN'S PROFESSIONAL SOCIALIZATION

A number of authors (Aisenberg & Harrington, 1988; Chrisler, 1995; Clark & Corcoran, 1986; Denmark, 1988; Payton, 1988; Schoenfeld & Magnan, 1992; Toth, 1997; Yoder, 1986) have commented on the importance of mentors to professional socialization (i.e., learning the rules of the game). "The game includes publishing, networking, and public speaking" (Yoder, 1986, p. 83), each of which has its own set of rules to which young professionals are best introduced by mentors. Because of their tendency to view women students as dilettantes who are unlikely to make serious scholarly contributions, male professors have tended to focus their attention on and direct their advice to male students. The relative lack of female mentors has no doubt affected women's career development.

117

The men in Adler's (1976) study of graduate students reported talking more frequently with faculty about both academic and nonacademic matters than did the women students. Furthermore, those students who have close relationships with their professors are more likely to publish while in graduate school (Feldman, 1974), thus getting a head start in the job market. Women are less likely than men to have had such close relationships with faculty (Aisenberg & Harrington, 1988; Feldman, 1974) and, thus, are viewed as less promising scholars by potential employers.

Dale Spender (1981) has written about the frequent "assumption that with publication comes legitimization and that personal opinions, interpretations, and conclusions move closer to 'truth' and credibility when they are contained between the covers of a respectable academic journal or book" (p. 188). It is essential that this assumption be communicated early and often to aspiring scholars so that they enter the profession expecting to publish and understanding that it is necessary for their career advancement. Spender (1981) described a colleague who insisted that his graduate students

> undertake an analysis of relevant journals to determine what topics were favored and from what perspective, what length and language was preferred, and so on. . . . [This man] was considered to be an excellent advisor by his students who claimed he had helped them "crack the code" of publishing. (p. 190)

Some may view this exercise cynically and express concerns that his students will produce research projects that are "tailor-made" for acceptance by particular journals with a view only to career advancement, yet there is no doubt that this type of exercise is an important contribution to the mentoring process. His students are learning a valuable lesson about how to target journals that many women academics have had to learn on their own through years of trial and error.

Professional socialization takes place not only in the classroom and in one-to-one advising sessions, but in a myriad of less formal situations. Theodore's (1986) interviewees complained of not being invited to closed seminars or "social gatherings where a great deal of discussion related to . . . studies and job prospects took place" (p. 6). Lillian Troll (1988) discovered when she joined all-male lunch groups from time to time that they talked about grantsmanship, gossip, academic policy, and money. Her women friends talked mostly about personal matters, especially home life and family pressures. They were not invited or expected to hear the news or other information that would help them to find or keep jobs. The isolation of women students can be so severe that when they graduate, they're unsure of what to do next. When Carolyn Payton (1988) described her attempt to find her first academic position, she wrote, "I knew nothing of submitting resumes and cover letters to potential job sites. I had no idea as to what would be an appropriate salary; I had no dollar value to attach to my degree" (p. 233).

Aisenberg and Harrington (1988) found that the women in their study had suffered so from the lack of mentoring that they had little knowledge of how to plan a professional life. Some entered graduate school with no plans other than to continue studying the subject matter in which they were immersed, others "with only a vague, long-distance vision of scholarship and teaching in mind" (p. 45). Without clear goals or professional advice, "women tend not to plan intermediate five- and ten-year strategies. Rather they take smaller steps, almost literally feeling their way along. . . . Lacking instruction in general career strategy, women frequently remain unaware of specific steps important to their advancement" (p. 45).

"Naive" and "innocent" were the adjectives most frequently used by the women in Aisenberg and Harrington's (1988) study to describe themselves in the early years of their careers. A composer working on her degree told the interviewers that she is not sure how to go about getting her work performed and doesn't know why she doesn't know this information. Other interviewees said the following: "I have never had the feeling that anybody carefully read my thesis and evaluated it and argued with me and so on" (p. 161). "I see people sort of hanging at their professors' doors with weekly appointments; I certainly never had anything like that" (p. 160). "No one encouraged me to be scholarly. No one even taught me about footnotes" (p. 167). "You see, I wrote the wrong thesis. . . . It was not only interdisciplinary, on literature and myth, but out of the main-stream . . . but I loved it. . . . It didn't become clear to me for a long, long time that my advisor should never have let me write that thesis in terms of having something to turn into a book . . . If he had been looking after my professional interests, which he wasn't" (p. 184).

Denmark (1988) has suggested that beginning professionals need both a supportive mentor to encourage their career development and a political mentor to teach them how to build their reputations and toot their own horns. The political mentor, she believes, is most important "because, unless you know those ropes, it sometimes doesn't matter how good you are—no one notices" (p. 290). Many women have learned this the hard way. In an essay in which she described the isolation she felt in the early years of her career, Judith Stiehm (1985) wrote, "When my first book was finished it went quietly onto library shelves. Almost no one knew it was being written; no audience expected it; it went largely unread" (p. 379).

Peer relationships are as important to professional socialization (Chrisler, 1995; Clark & Corcoran, 1986) as the standard senior/junior mentoring relationships. As Troll (1988) noted, much information and professional advice is imparted in the everyday, informal discussions among peers. In graduate school, peers facilitate learning, exchange practical assistance, supply emotional support, and practice engaging in the type of collegial interactions they will experience later as faculty (Clark & Corocoran, 1986). Older women faculty and women in male-dominated fields, of course, had peer groups composed almost entirely of men. Many of these women have reported (Aisenberg & Harrington, 1988; Clark & Corcoran, 1986; Rose, 1985, 1986) that they have had difficulty becoming included in their peer networks, either because the men deliberately excluded them or because they felt awkward or unwelcome when it became clear to them that the men did not know how to relate to them as colleagues. Exclusion from professional networks can have a lasting effect on women's careers and contribute to an accumulative disadvantage as well as to a perception of female faculty as outsiders or marginal professionals (Aisenberg & Harrington, 1988; Clark & Corcoran, 1986; Gallant & Cross, 1993; Rose, 1986; Tierney & Bensimon, 1996).

WOMEN'S GENDER ROLE SOCIALIZATION

Even as women move into new roles in society, they are influenced by the old ones they seek to escape. Women must, therefore, fight against traditions they have absorbed into their own psyches as well as fight discrimination in the outside world. Traditionally, "women's identity was located in the body and emotions, men's in the mind. Women . . . provided sympathy, enchantment, inspiration. Men learned, calculated, . . . wrote, . . . philosophized" (Aisenberg & Harrington, 1988, p. 4).

Thinking itself is seen by some as an aggressive trait (Theodore, 1986) that is located firmly in the province of men. Many women have been warned from childhood not to speak up or to question, challenge, or criticize others (Aisenberg & Harrington, 1988). Social sanctions still exist for women who violate gender role expectations. Those who raise their voices in intellectual argument may find themselves "stigmatized . . . as shrewish, shrill, whining, or complaining" (Aisenberg & Harrington, 1988, p. 71).

Women who fit the traditional gender role display a number of characteristics that are likely to work against those needed to succeed as a scholar. Femininity has been equated with low assertiveness (Russell, 1979; Schwartz & Lever, 1973), low competitiveness, dependency (Schwartz & Lever, 1973), patience, receptivity, modesty, unselfishness, and nonaggressiveness (Aisenberg & Harrington, 1988). In addition, women are expected to avoid taking risks (Schwartz & Lever, 1973) and to be accommodating and peace-keeping (Aisenberg & Harrington, 1988). These characteristics are well suited to maintaining social activities. They are maladaptive, however, to building and maintaining a reputation as a scholar.

The "feminine modesty effect" (Berg, Stephan, & Dodson, 1981; Gould & Slone, 1982) in causal attribution, which I described earlier, can interfere with women's ability to draw attention to their work and take credit for their successes. Denmark (1988) believes that it is difficult for women to learn to "toot their own horns" because they have been taught not to boast about themselves. However, if women don't do this, their work will be overlooked. Crittenden and Wiley (1980, 1985; Wiley & Crittenden, 1992) have conducted several studies of faculty attribution patterns and colleagues' reactions to them. Their results clearly indicate that modest accounts of publication success (e.g., "I was lucky that my manuscript was sent to helpful reviewers") enhanced femininity but decreased professionalism in the eyes of colleagues. Similarly, self-serving accounts of publication failures (e.g., "My manuscript was sent to incompetent reviewers") decreased femininity but increased professionalism in the eyes of colleagues. Therefore, women, but not men, must choose between their professional and their gender roles (Wiley & Crittenden, 1992); whichever choice they make, they risk rejection by those who will evaluate them for tenure and promotion. Furthermore, those women who showed the modesty effect in describing their failures (i.e., blamed themselves rather than the reviewers or editors) were less likely to make attempts to publish their articles elsewhere (Crittenden & Wiley, 1980).

A study (Roe, 1953) of the personalities of productive research scientists found that they shared four main characteristics. The scientists displayed high intelligence, persistence in their work (from which they derived their primary satisfaction), extreme independence, and low interest in social activities. All four characteristics were evident in childhood. This contrasts with the observation that girls are unwilling to display high intelligence and unlikely to develop the other three characteristics, which run contrary to the traditional feminine gender role (Rossi, 1965). In this same vein, according to Hornig (1979), the typical male scientist is able to ignore the stereotype that he is cold, unconcerned about others, and completely absorbed in his work. "If he pays attention to this critique at all, it does not seem to bother him much, since he believes it to be clearly unrelated to his chief mission in life, the pursuit of objective truth" (Hornig, 1979, p. 128). Such a critique would bother most women because it is incompatible with women's traditional social and nurturing responsibilities. Whether or not sociability and nurturing are important to one's self-concept, women who are seen by others as cold or insensitive are socially ostracized. This realization may lead women to prefer the role of the science teacher to that of the research scientist.

CONCLUSION

The answer posed in the title of this chapter—is being both teacher and scholar a role conflict for women—is "yes." This is not because women cannot or do not perform both roles. Rather, it reflects the fact that women's scholarly impulses have been restricted and negated for millennia. Women's long history of intellectual discouragement (Lerner, 1993) has affected the way we see ourselves and the way others, including our colleagues and students, see us. At the same time, our nurturing abilities have been practiced and praised throughout our lives; this experience makes teaching a particularly rewarding activity.

Most of us became professors because we wanted to be both teachers and scholars. We need to find ways to encourage and support each other to fulfill both roles. This should start with frank discussions among ourselves about the ways in which we have experienced and dealt with our own role conflicts. Some may want to organize writing support groups with women colleagues (Hood, 1985). Other women can provide not only emotional support but editing and other practical help. More experienced authors can mentor beginners.

It is also essential to set up a schedule in which priority time is allocated for scholarly activities (Valian, 1985) and to stick to it. I find it much easier to write at home on nonteaching days than to ignore knocks on the door and a ringing telephone at the office; this plan also allows me to make myself very available to students when I am on campus, without compromising my own needs too much. Taylor and Martin (1987) have suggested that a minimum of 10 hours per week must be devoted to scholarly work if one intends to be productive, and I have also found this to be true.

Be creative in scheduling writing time. Several women I know trained themselves to become early birds. They were at their desks by 5 a.m. in order to work for two or three hours before their children woke up. Don't wait for long blocks of free time that may never materialize (Gallos, 1996); short blocks will help keep you going. In less than an hour, one can organize materials, check references, draft an outline, write a few paragraphs, edit last week's work, and so on. If you're having trouble scheduling time for writing, start by making a list of all the times you can't write, then block out some of what's left for your scholarly projects.

Difficulty in writing is sometimes a sign of lack of enthusiasm for the topic. Although it may not be practical to abandon a project on which one has made considerable progress, it is always possible to find new areas for future work. Some authors (Gallos, 1996; King, 1996) have noted that their productivity soared when they could be passionate about their topics and use methodologies they found congenial. I have several areas of expertise, and I keep my enthusiasm high by moving back and forth among them. I also like to vary the kinds of things I write (e.g., research reports, book reviews, literature reviews, public policy pieces, teaching tips) in order to keep from being bored.

If you're not sure how much you have to write or what types of scholarship are valued for tenure and/or promotion, ask your department chair, dean, and colleagues who have served on the tenure and promotion committee. The more people you ask, the better you'll be able to figure out what the rules are. Ask people who have recently been tenured or promoted if you can look at their files. Study a few. See what the successful ones contain and how they are organized. Share what you learn with other women in your situation.

Finally, women must make better use of institutional resources (Astin & Davis, 1985) in order to become productive scholars. Find out what resources are available, and ask for your fair share. If your department chair responds vaguely when you ask questions, ask someone else. The office of the Dean of the Faculty is a good resource, as are senior women faculty in your own or other departments. Over the years, I have discovered most of what I needed to know by asking questions at meetings of the faculty who teach women's studies.

Include time spent tracking down and applying for research funding in your scheduled writing time. If your institution does not provide research or teaching assistants, solicit volunteers. Upper-level undergraduates who are interested in attending graduate school are eager for such opportunities, and they may be eligible for work-study funds. With careful training and supervision, they make competent (and sometimes excellent) assistants. Thus, in addition to advancing your own career, you can serve as a mentor to young women by introducing them to the life of the mind.

REFERENCES

Abramson, J. (1975). *The invisible woman*. San Francisco: Jossey-Bass.

Adler, N. E. (1976). Women students. In J. Katz & R. T. Hartnett (Eds.), *Scholars in the making: The development of graduate and professional students* (pp. 197-255). Cambridge, MA: Ballinger.

Aisenberg, N., & Harrington, M. (1988). *Women of academe: Outsiders in the sacred grove.* Amherst: University of Massachusetts Press.

Astin, A. W., Korn, W. S., & Lewis, L. S. (1991). *The American college teacher: National norms for the 1989-90 HERI faculty survey*. Los Angeles: Higher Education Research Institute, UCLA.

Astin, H. S. (1973). Career profiles of women doctorates. In A. Rossi & A. Calderwood (Eds.), *Academic women on the move* (pp. 139-161). New York: Russell Sage.

Astin, H. S. (1978). Factors affecting women's scholarly productivity. In H. S. Astin & W. Z. Hirsch (Eds.), *The higher education of women: Essays in honor of Rosemary Park* (pp. 133-157). New York: Praeger.

Astin, H. S., & Davis, D. E. (1985). Research productivity across the life and career cycles: Facilitators and barriers for women. In M. F. Fox (Ed.), *Scholarly writing and publishing: Issues, problems, and solutions* (pp. 147-160). Boulder, CO: Westview.

Astin, H. S., & Snyder, M. B. (1982). A decade of response. *Change, 14*, 26-31, 59.

Bentley, R. J., & Blackburn, R. T. (1992). Two decades of gains for female faculty? *Teachers College Record, 93*, 697-709.

Berg, J. H., Stephan, W. G., & Dodson, M. (1981). Attributional modesty in women. *Psychology of Women Quarterly, 5*, 711-727.

Bernard, J. (1964). *Academic women*. New York: Meridian.

Bernard, J. (1983). Benchmark for the 1980s. In M. L. Spencer, M. Kehoe, & K. Speece (Eds.), *Handbook for women scholars: Strategies for success* (pp. 69-79). San Francisco: Americas Behavioral Research Corp.

Bess, J. L. (1990, May/June). College teachers: Miscast professionals. *Change, 22,* 19-22.

Billard, L. (1994). Twenty years later: Is there parity for academic women? *Thought & Action, 10,* 115-144.

Boice, R., Shaughnessy, P., & Pecker, G. (1985). Women and publishing in psychology. *American Psychologist, 40,* 577-578.

Boyer, E. L. (1990). *Scholarship re-considered: Priorities of the professoriate.* Princeton, NJ: Carnegie Foundation for the Advancement of Teaching.

Brown, D. (1967). *The mobile professors.* Washington, DC: American Council on Education.

Burgess, N. J. (1997). Tenure and promotion among African American women in the academy: Issues and strategies. In L. Benjamin (Ed.), *Black women in the academy: Promises and perils* (pp. 227-234). Gainesville: University of Florida Press.

Caplan, P. J. (1993). *Lifting a ton of feathers: A woman's guide to surviving in the academic world.* Toronto: University of Toronto Press.

Carnegie Foundation. (1990, Sept/Oct). Women faculty excel as campus citizens. *Change, 22,* 39-43.

Centra, J. A. (1974). *Women, men, and the doctorate.* Princeton, NJ: Educational Testing Service.

Chrisler, J. C. (1995). *Desperately seeking succor: How to manage if you haven't got a mentor.* Unpublished manuscript.

Clark, S. M., & Corcoran, M. (1986). Perspectives on the professional socialization of women: A case of accumulative disadvantage? *Journal of Higher Education, 57,* 20-43.

Crittenden, K. S., & Wiley, M. G. (1980). Causal attribution and behavioral response to failure. *Social Psychology Quarterly, 43,* 353-358.

Crittenden, K. S., & Wiley, M. G. (1985). When egotism is normative: Self-presentational norms guiding attributions. *Social Psychology Quarterly, 48,* 360-365.

Davis, D. E., & Astin, H. S. (1987). Reputational standing in academe. *Journal of Higher Education, 58,* 261-275.

Denmark, F. L. (1988). Florence L. Denmark. In A. N. O'Connell & N. F. Russo (Eds.), *Models of achievement: Reflections of eminent women in psychology* (pp. 281-193). Hillsdale, NJ: Lawrence Erlbaum.

Fandt, P. M., & Stevens, G. E. (1991). Evaluation bias in the business classroom: Evidence relating to the effects of prior experience. *Journal of Psychology,* 469-477.

Feldman, S. D. (1974). *Escape from the doll's house: Women in graduate and professional school education.* New York: McGraw-Hill.

Ferber, M. A. (1986). Citations: Are they an objective measure of scholarly merit? *Signs, 11,* 381-389.

Ferber, M. A. (1988). Citations and networking. *Gender & Society, 2,* 82-89.

Finklestein, M. J. (1984). *The American academic profession: Synthesis of social scientific inquiry since World War II.* Columbus: Ohio State University Press.

Frieze, I. H. (1978). Psychological barriers for women in science: Internal and external. In J. A. Ramaley (Ed.), *Covert discrimination and women in the sciences* (pp. 65-95). Boulder, CO: Westview.

Gallant, M. J., & Cross, J. E. (1993). Wayward puritans in the ivory tower: Collective aspects of gender discrimination in academia. *Sociological Quarterly, 34,* 237-256.

Gallos, J. V. (1996). On becoming a scholar: One woman's journey. In P. J. Frost & M. S. Taylor (Eds.), *Rhythms of academic life: Personal accounts of careers in academia* (pp. 11-18). Thousand Oaks, CA: Sage.

Gibbons, J. (1986). Pitfalls on the way to tenure. In S. Rose (Ed.), *Career guide for women scholars* (pp. 27-35). New York: Springer.

Gould, R. J., & Slone, C. G. (1982). The "feminine modesty" effect: A self-presentational interpretation of sex differences in causal attribution. *Personality and Social Psychology Bulletin, 8*, 477-485.

Gregory, S. T. (1995). *Black women in the academy: The secrets to success and achievement.* Lanham, NY: University Press of America.

Helmreich, R. L., Spence, J. T., Beane, W. E., Lucker, G. W., & Matthews, K. A. (1980). Making it in academic psychology: Demographic and personality correlates of attainment. *Journal of Personality and Social Psychology, 39*, 896-908.

Hood, J. C. (1985). The lone scholar myth. In M. F. Fox (Ed.), *Scholarly writing and publishing: Issues, problems, and solutions* (pp. 111-125). Boulder, CO: Westview.

Hornig, L. S. (1979). Scientific sexism. In A. M. Briscoe & S. M. Pfafflin (Eds.), *Expanding the role of women in the sciences* (pp. 125-133). New York: New York Academy of Sciences.

Hornig, L. S. (1980). Untenured and tenuous: The status of women faculty. *Annals of the American Academy of Political and Social Science, 448*, 115-125.

Jones, L. K., Hoenack, S. A., & Hammida, M. (1994). Career development of tenure track assistant professors. *Thought & Action, 9*, 147-172.

Kaschak, E. (1978). Sex bias in student evaluations of college professors. *Psychology of Women Quarterly, 2*, 235-243.

Kawawe, S. M. (1997). Black women in diverse academic settings: Gender and racial crimes of commission and omission in academia. In L. Benjamin (Ed.), *Black women in the academy: Promises and perils* (pp. 263-269). Gainesville: University of Florida Press.

King, T. C. (1996). Rounding corners: An African American female scholar's pretenure experiences. In P. J. Frost & M. S. Taylor (Eds.), *Rhythms of academic life: Personal accounts of careers in academia* (pp. 193-199). Thousand Oaks, CA: Sage.

Lerner, G. (1993). *The creation of feminist consciousness: From the middle ages to 1870.* New York: Oxford University Press.

Lewis, L. S. (1975). *Scaling the ivory tower: Merit and its limits in academic careers.* Baltimore: Johns Hopkins University Press.

Loeb, J. W., & Ferber, M. A. (1973). Representation, performance, and status of women on the faculty at the Urbana-Champaign campus of the University of Illinois. In A. S. Rossi & A. Calderwood (Eds.), *Academic women on the move* (pp. 239-254). New York: Russell Sage.

Long, J. S. (1992). Measures of sex differences in scientific productivity. *Social Forces, 71*, 159-178.

Morlock, L. (1973). Discipline variation in the status of academic women. In A. S. Rossi & A. Calderwood (Eds.), *Academic women on the move* (pp. 255-312). New York: Russell Sage.

Park, S. M. (1996). Research, teaching, and service: Why shouldn't women's work count? *Journal of Higher Education, 67*, 46-84.

Payton, C. R. (1988). Carolyn Roberston Payton. In A. N. O'Connell & N. F. Russo (Eds.), *Models of achievement: Reflections of eminent women in psychology* (pp. 229-242). Hillsdale, NJ: Lawrence Erlbaum.

Roe, A. (1953). Psychological study of research scientists. *Psychological Monographs, 67.*

Rose, S. M. (1985). Professional networks of junior faculty in psychology. *Psychology of Women Quarterly, 9*, 533-547.

Rose, S. (1986). Building a professional network. In S. Rose (Ed.), *Career guide for women scholars* (pp. 46-56). New York: Springer.

Rossi, A. S. (1965). Women in science: Why so few? *Science, 148*, 1196-1202.

Russell, D. H. (1979). How a scientist who happens to be female can succeed in academia. In A. M. Briscoe & S. M. Pfafflin (Eds.), *Expanding the role of women in the sciences* (pp. 283-295). New York: New York Academy of Sciences.

Schoenfeld, A. C., & Magnan, R. (1992). *Mentor in a manual: Climbing the academic ladder to tenure.* Madison, WI: Magna Publications.

Schwartz, P., & Lever, J. (1973). Women in the male world of higher education. In A. S. Rossi & A. Calderwood (Eds.), *Academic women on the move* (pp. 57-77). New York: Russell Sage.

Simeone, A. (1987). *Academic women: Working toward equality.* South Hadley, MA: Bergin & Garvey.

Simon, R. J., Clark, S. M., & Galway, K. (1975). The woman Ph.D.: A recent profile. In M. T. Mednick, S. S. Tangri, & L. W. Hoffman (Eds.), *Women and achievement: Social and motivational analyses* (pp. 355-371). New York: Wiley.

Spender, D. (1981). The gatekeepers: A feminist critique of academic publishing. In H. Roberts (Ed.), *Doing feminist research* (pp. 186-202). London: Routledge & Kegan Paul.

Stake, J. E. (1986). When it's publish or perish: Tips on survival. In S. Rose (Ed.), *Career guide for women scholars* (pp. 57-65). New York: Springer.

Stevens, V. J. (1978). Increasing professional productivity while teaching full time: A case study in self-control. *Teaching of Psychology, 5,* 203-205.

Stiehm, J. H. (1985). A feminist in military academy land; or men and their institutions as curiosities. In P. A. Treichler, C. Kramarae, & B. Stafford (Eds.), *For alma mater: Theory and practice in feminist scholarship* (pp. 377-392). Chicago: University of Illinois Press.

Taylor, S. E., & Martin, J. (1987). The present-minded professor: Controlling one's career. In M. P. Zanna & J. M. Darley (Eds.), *The compleat academic: A practical guide for the beginning social scientist* (pp. 23-60). New York: Random House.

Theodore, A. (1986). *The campus troublemakers: Academic women in protest.* Houston: Cap and Gown Press.

Thomas, S., Spencer, M. L., & Sako, M. (1983). Conversations with minority women scholars. In M. L. Spencer, M. Kehoe, & K. Speece (Eds.), *Handbook for women scholars: Strategies for success* (pp. 41-59). San Francisco: Americas Behavioral Research Corp.

Tierney, W. G., & Bensimon, E. M. (1996). *Promotion and tenure: Community and socialization in academe.* Albany: State University of New York Press.

Toth, E. (1997). *Ms. Mentor's impeccable advice for women in academia.* Philadelphia: University of Pennsylvania Press.

Troll, L. E. (1988). Lillian E. Troll. In A. N. O'Connell & N. F. Russo (Eds.), *Models of achievement: Reflections of eminent women in psychology* (pp. 105-117). Hillsdale, NJ: Lawrence Erlbaum.

Tuckman, B. H. (1979). Salary differentials among university faculty and their implications for the future. In T. R. Pezzulla & B. E. Bittingham (Eds.), *Salary equity* (pp. 19-38). Lexington, MA: D. C. Heath.

Valian, V. (1985). Solving a work problem. In M. F. Fox (Ed.), *Scholarly writing and publishing: Issues, problems, and solutions* (pp. 99-110). Boulder, CO: Westview.

Wiley, M. G., & Crittenden, K. S. (1992). By your attributions shall you be known: Consequences of attributional accounts for professional and gender identities. *Sex Roles, 27,* 259-276.

Yoder, J. D. (1986). Challenges during the transition from graduate student to assistant professor. In S. Rose (Ed.), *Career guide for women scholars* (pp. 81-88). New York: Springer.

The ABD Faculty Blues:
Getting Organized for the Dissertation and Beyond

Michelle R. Dunlap

Proposing a dissertation idea, conducting the research, and writing the dissertation are all part of an extremely complex, overwhelming, and time-consuming process. The challenges of the process can be exacerbated by personal responsibilities. When I completed my doctoral qualifying exams to reach the all-but-dissertation (ABD) status, I was working two part-time jobs and later a full-time one. I was also raising a young child by myself. It seemed that starting my dissertation work and finishing my PhD were light years away from the realities I was facing on a daily basis. It was very difficult to find and manage the time I needed to move from ABD to PhD.

In addition to these challenges, I was dealing with the reality that it had been nearly 10 years since the last African American or the last woman had graduated from my program. That fact is an indicator of the kind of exclusionary and poor retention practices that exist in academia and other social institutions. There was a part of me that feared that I might suffer from such exclusion as an African American woman no matter how hard I might work and how much I might excel in my studies. In spite of my fears, I grew more determined to persevere, and I tried to develop strategies for successfully completing my degree.

I started my efforts by consulting with a colleague, who loaned me a book titled *How to Complete and Survive a Doctoral Dissertation* (Sternberg, 1981) and recommended that I first read the chapter about the emotions involved in writing a dissertation. Over the course of the next week (between work, parenting, and a zillion other responsibilities), I read the entire book. I did begin with Chapter 7, which is titled "Down in the Dumps: How to Get Out." The author described the self-doubts, anxieties, fears, depression, procrastination, alienation, emotional extremes, and other negative thoughts, emotions, and behaviors that can be associated with the dissertation process. Then he offered self-help techniques and suggestions for finding support. I found this chapter very useful because it helped me to realize that many of the negative feelings that I was experiencing at the time were a normal part of the dissertation process.

A task such as writing a dissertation can be so overwhelming that one may not really know how to get started. Using ideas from the other chapters in Sternberg's book, I first spent some time reassessing my priorities and decided that I needed to devise some strategies for getting more time out of what was very little time availability. I also made assessments regarding my physical space needs. One of my first steps was the creation of a corner of space that would have the basic items that I would need for writing. These items included, for example, my faithful old word processor and printer, my books, a thesaurus and other reference materials, and a tape player (for inspirational music, which is very important to me). I bought a portable box file, file folders, index cards, an index box file, and other supplies that were recommended in Sternberg's book. These supplies cost about $20 altogether. I organized the portable file by dissertation section from "introduction" to "references." I organized the index card file box by literature review themes, with lots of blank cards so that themes and resource summaries could be added as I searched the literature on my topic at various libraries. From that point on, all materials, resources, and ideas related to any aspect of my dissertation were filed appropriately. This was very helpful when I actually began composing the dissertation proposal because I could go through my files section by section, using my notes and resources as organizational tools. Also, I could research and brainstorm for any part of the dissertation and then place the notes into the appropriate file for later composition on the computer.

The greatest challenge to staying on target was the lack of large blocks of time for writing, analyzing data, and so on. When I started, I was working two part-time jobs as an adjunct instructor at two colleges, and later, I was working a rigorous 40-hour per week job as a family counselor. In an effort to create large blocks of time to devote to my dissertation work, I renegotiated with my supervisor for a schedule that would allow me to work four 10-hour rather than five 8-hour days per week. I was thus able to devote the entire Wednesday of each week to my dissertation work. In addition, I made every effort to arrange my clients' counseling hours during the day and did my chart noting and paperwork hours at home during the evening. Therefore, only a couple of nights per week required baby-sitting arrangements. I also spent 2 to 4 hours each night at the computer at home after I put my child to sleep.

Getting organized and strategically creating these blocks of time were crucial for making progress and completing my graduate work. I am now a junior faculty member, and I often feel the strain that comes with trying to balance teaching, student advising, research, community service, and parenting. I find myself returning to, adapting, and testing the kinds of strategies described above as I continue to work to develop longer and more productive blocks of time for my research, publishing, and grant-writing activities. By applying and modifying some of these same strategies, my scholarly output has improved significantly in the past year. In addition to making time whenever and wherever possible for scholarship, I have managed to keep my entire Thursdays during the academic year and most of my summers for my writing.

Investing in a laptop computer also helped me to increase my flexibility and ability to find blocks of time for working. In my opinion, however, nothing takes the place of a pencil and a legal pad when one has a hectic schedule. For example, in the midst of a busy teaching semester, while waiting for my child during his karate class, I wrote a very rough outline of a book proposal. I found these notes to be extremely valuable 3 months later when I wrote the formal proposal during the summer. I also make an annual "productivity schedule" that consists of target deadline dates for rough drafts, final drafts, and soliciting comments from colleagues prior to the journal submission.

Most crucial, however, to my current productivity has been the adoption of three mentors whom I consider to be role models for academic and personal success. They have each committed to reading my manuscript drafts and commenting frankly on them, and they have done so for the past year. All three of my mentors have been available for collegial discussion and advising on a range of professional goal setting and decisions. Other colleagues have also agreed to make themselves available for critiquing my work whenever I need to rely upon them. In gratitude for their generosity, I promised myself that I will serve as a mentor and role model for others as I continue to become better grounded as a scholar.

It is my hope that *Career Strategies for Women in Academe: Arming Athena* will do for women faculty what Sternberg's book has done for graduate students who were battling the ABD blues. I know that being a graduate student and being a junior faculty member can feel overwhelming at times. First, we have to understand how these experiences affect us emotionally. Then, we have to organize strategically and formulate plans to get the social support and resources necessary for our personal and professional success. Creating and implementing such plans can move us beyond the ABD or junior faculty blues and on toward meeting our professional goals.

REFERENCES

Sternberg, D. (1981). *How to complete and survive a doctoral dissertation*. New York: St. Martin's.

Career Strategies I Stumbled Upon

Loraine K. Obler

For a long time, I've appreciated how important working for 9 years in a research institution postdoctorally was for me professionally. Until I wrote this essay, however, I hadn't realized the importance that feeling—and being—connected has had for me professionally. A number of the strategies I've found for getting along in academe are related to being connected.

GETTING SUPPORT OUTSIDE OF THE OBVIOUS PLACES

I never felt comfortable in my doctoral program. The faculty were unavailable or dismissive when I attempted to speak with them, and I was not comfortable with any of the students; I simply didn't connect to them. I was fortunate, however, to fall in with a group of friends in my secondary field of interest. We still, 20 years later, get together whenever we can. Only one of them became an academic because the "market" changed so dramatically in the mid-1970s, but I was also lucky to make a couple of friends from other disciplines who moved to my university town. Having academics to consult about how to deal with colleagues, students, administration, negotiating a new job, planning a sabbatical, and so on, has been very important to me all along. For example, I was finding writing my first short article terribly difficult to do, so I pulled together a group of women graduate students and one friendly faculty person to find out how other people get writing done.

When looking for a place to connect to other academic feminists and lesbians, as I was wanting to identify myself publicly, again my field of origin was quite inhospitable. So I turned to a related one and happened upon the Association for Women in Psychology (AWP). Working with a Boston-based group to put together the national conference around 1980 was a revelation: how differently meetings could be run from "the usual"; how people could work together and resolve, or at least get through, severe tension. For many years to come, AWP remained an important source of support and catalyst for growth for me.

Several years later, I helped initiate a Feminist Research Methodology Group that met for nearly a dozen years. Here I was able to talk about topics that interested me but that none of my colleagues would have wanted to or could have discussed intelligently. Although the focus of this group was on the work we were doing, we also used this group to talk about career issues, as we were virtually all in the first decade of our academic careers.

GETTING WELL-MENTORED

Being mentored has been important to me in a number of ways. In graduate school, I was in a field—linguistics—where one wrote relatively independent dissertations. Rather than choosing as my advisor one or another problematic faculty person whose areas were closest to those of my dissertation, I chose the nicest professor I'd had, from my minor area, who was always wonderfully supportive to me. I was thus able to feel very good about that relationship, as he supported me through my oral and written exams and dissertation defense.

I was extremely fortunate to find a second mentor as I moved into my new field of interest—neurolinguistics—and have continued working with him for more than two decades. Through working with him I got involved in a fast-paced post-doc research position for 9 years. Here I learned how to publish articles—that is, how to work with colleagues, how to get research done, and how to get articles written and out for review when they were as good as we could make them (not waiting until they were perfect). This experience proved invaluable in getting me my academic position when I was tired of living off soft money, as I had a substantial list of publications. I also learned to write grant proposals through this position, and, most crucially, how to get over the anger at rejections, and revise, resubmit, and write letters of appeal.

LEARNING HOW TO GET RESEARCH DONE

That research position also proved invaluable in teaching me how to involve others in research (in my current field—neurolinguistics—virtually all work is done collaboratively), so I have been able to maintain productivity in my next job—an academic one—despite my teaching commitments. I was lucky, I believe, to continue straight from undergraduate to graduate school, and then to postgraduate research as I had not acquired a desire for

132

living at a higher economic level. I feel sorry for students who take academic jobs immediately upon graduation, as the teaching is so compelling day-to-day that it is extremely hard to set up a research program.

BECOMING VISIBLE IN THE FIELD

At my "post-doc" institution generally, and by watching my mentor in particular, I learned the importance of visibility. I pushed myself to speak up, writing down the questions I would force myself to articulate so I could at least have the right words, both at our internal meetings and at national conferences. I have learned, too, the subtle art of boasting about the presentations I get invited to give and about prestigious conferences when my papers get accepted there; I have realized that, although our society prohibits undue boasting, it is necessary to remind one's colleagues that one is respected nationally or internationally. (I do this by referring to these invitations in embedded clauses, e.g., "when I was at the conference on X in Guadeloupe last week, I heard..." or "I'm afraid I won't be able to be at that meeting next week because I've been invited to speak at the XYZ meeting in London." I'm currently fighting with the realization that one cannot maintain national or international visibility these days without participating in e-mail discussions; I'm dystechnologic and am most comfortable reading others' messages without contributing my own.

GETTING CONNECTED IN ACADEME

When I took my current academic job, I found that my department, apart from my woman colleague, was not particularly welcoming. (In her I was lucky; she made a point of inviting me for a welcoming faculty dinner at a time when my partner could be in town.) To my surprise, none of my other departmental colleagues has ever asked about my partner, nor even our child, who was born while I was in this position, now 9 years ago! One strategy I took in the first year was contacting all the feminists I knew of in the school and having lunch with them to get to know them a bit and learn about the school through their eyes. I make a point, as well, of having lunch individually with most of my departmental colleagues once a year as otherwise we would never speak directly outside of faculty meetings. Naturally, these aren't the same sort of personal, getting-to-know-each-other meetings that I continue to maintain with many of the feminists (and women faculty in other departments who would not identify as feminists); I set them up around some issue I'd like to discuss—problems with doctoral students, the future of the department, and so on. But they serve my "feeling connected" needs nevertheless.

I also learned to consult the Ombuds Officer at the school when I wanted someone to discuss problems about which I thought that I could not turn to anybody in my department or any of these outside-the-department colleagues. Indeed, I have found ombudsing so helpful that I have taken on being the Ombuds Officer this year, and it has permitted me a new way to connect within the university, an expanded view of problem solving, plus a way to return to the feminist work I gave up for a period when our son was young.

BE PREPARED TO BE "JUNIOR" FOR A DECADE

I have had to make compromises at a number of points. My post-doc mentor, for example, was first author on a book that he proposed doing; I wrote 90% of it. After a couple of years, just as we were sending the book off to the publisher, I found the courage to ask him if I should be first author. He said it would be inappropriate, and the book, much cited in my small subfield, has his name first on it. He did see to it that any invitation that came to him to talk about it went to me, and I came to realize that he had just finished second-authoring a book he had written "with" a more senior colleague. Over the years, I have learned to find ways to respond to unfairnesses that a senior person proposes in ways I think are more effective, but I also believe that my preparedness to be a junior person for the first decade of my collaboration has been extremely useful to my career throughout. Had I left in anger at an earlier stage, I would have lost many of the tangible and intangible benefits that have accrued to me, for example, through being associated with my research institution and continuing to work in our extremely productive laboratory.

Student Evaluations
The Role of Gender Bias
and Teaching Styles

Susan A. Basow

Although women as a group have made significant advances into the professoriate, they remain a minority on campuses across the United States. Furthermore, women faculty are overrepresented in community colleges and in the lower, untenured ranks, where they remain for longer periods than do equally qualified men. In this chapter, I will examine the ways in which student evaluations of instructors affect women's chances of retaining a position in academia and show that women faculty frequently get evaluated differently from their male peers. Reasons for these differential evaluations to be explored include perceptual bias and differences in teaching styles. I will conclude with some strategies for dealing with these issues.

GENDER ISSUES IN STUDENT EVALUATIONS

Student evaluations are used on most college campuses as a major (sometimes the sole) way to assess college teaching (Seldin, 1993). Such evaluations may consist of open-ended questions (e.g., "What did you like/dislike about this course?") or Likert-scale-type questions (e.g., "On a scale of 1-5, how effective is this professor?"). The scale-type questions may be single items that tap different aspects of teaching (such as, "How well/timely did the professor provide feedback on assignments?"), or the questions may be clustered into a smaller number of factors (e.g., "Organization," "Clarity"). On many campuses, both open-ended and specific questions may be used to provide different types of feedback to the instructor and personnel committees. Research on student evaluations, however, has focused predominantly on questions answered on a numerical scale.

The results of most field research suggest that teacher gender is not a strong main effect (Bennett, 1982a; Cashin, 1988; Feldman, 1993; Seldin, 1993). That means that if one looks only at the average rating of all male instructors compared to all female instructors, there probably would not be many significant differences. This is a very reassuring finding; it is also deceptive. When one starts to examine some of the variables found to be important in the laboratory research on gender bias, such as gender-typed qualities and gender of rater, a more complex pattern emerges. Depending on the methodology, the gender-typing of the discipline, the gender-typed characteristics of the instructors, and the types of questions asked, female professors sometimes do receive significantly lower ratings than do male professors, especially from male students (Basow, 1995; Basow & Silberg, 1987; Bennett, 1982a; Sidanius & Crane, 1989).

Let's take a brief look at the laboratory research. A more in-depth examination of how gender variables may affect student evaluations of actual teachers in the field will follow.

LABORATORY RESEARCH

The typical research paradigm for studying gender bias in evaluations is to present evaluators with information, such as job applications, job performance descriptions, or journal articles, that is identical in all respects except for the applicant's or the author's gender. Classic results from the 1960s and 1970s are that a professional article, a job performance description, or a job application all were rated more highly when thought to belong to a man than when thought to belong to a woman (Dobbins, Cardy, & Truxillo, 1986; Fidell, 1975; Freeman, 1977; Goldberg, 1968). In the Fidell (1975) study, for example, written profiles of job candidates were submitted to psychology department chairs (all male) for assessment of suitability for a position in their department. The profiles varied only by name and pronouns. Female applicants for academic positions were less likely than identically qualified male applicants to be offered tenure-track positions, and when they were offered a position, women started at a lower rank and with lower salaries.

Recent review articles and meta-analyses of gender bias research (Eagly, Makhijani, & Klonsky, 1992; Feldman, 1992, 1993; Lott, 1985; Swim, Borgida, Maruyama, & Myers, 1989; Top, 1991) suggest that such bias is more subtle today than 30 years ago and probably is evident only under certain conditions. That is, the gender of the person being evaluated does not appear to affect ratings across all raters and all situations. Rather, the effects of gender may only appear in interaction with other variables. Important variables to examine are gender-typed characteristics of the rating context or field, the gender of the rater, the status of the person being rated, and the gender-typed characteristics of the person being rated.

Most discrimination occurs against individuals who are in contexts viewed as nontraditional for their gender (Basow, 1992; Lott, 1985). Thus, we may find more discrimination against women who teach engineering than we do against women who teach English (Hancock, Shannon, & Trentham, 1993). Men who violate gender-role norms also may be deval-ued, as are male nurses; however, this devaluation tends to occur less consistently for men than women. Furthermore, men in such situations tend to be paid more and harassed less than their female coworkers and women in jobs traditionally held by men (Etaugh & Riley, 1983; Ott, 1989).

Another important variable in evaluation research is the gender of the rater. In the past 20 years, men have shown more bias against women and against people violating gender-prescribed behaviors than have women (Basow, 1992; Kaschak, 1978). For example, Dobbins and his colleagues (1986) found that male undergraduates rated male professors, whose teaching was described using written profiles, as more effective than identically described female professors, at least when the students thought the evaluation would be used for personnel decisions (as opposed to being used for instructor feedback or for an experimental purpose). Female students showed no differential rating of male and female professors in this study. The greater gender bias shown by males probably is a product of changes in social attitudes toward women that resulted from the second wave of the women's movement. Many surveys have found more change in women's attitudes than in men's (e.g., Twenge, 1997).

A third important variable in ratings of women and men is the status of the applicant or person being rated. Most discrimination occurs against aspiring individuals or people with unproven or moderate abilities rather than against award-winning or experienced applicants. In the teaching arena, untenured women professors at the beginning of their careers might be more vulnerable to negative ratings than women professors holding endowed chairs. In circumstances where a woman is viewed as certifiably competent, such as being an award winner, she may be perceived as equivalent to her male counterpart or even as his superior (Abramson, Goldberg, Greenberg, & Abramson, 1977; Basow & Howe, 1979; Kaschak, 1981). This latter effect, when a highly qualified woman is rated more highly than an identically qualified man, has been termed by Paul Abramson and his colleagues (1977), "the talking platypus effect." As they explained: with a talking platypus, what is remarkable is not what it says but the fact that it can talk at all.

Other research suggests the importance of gender-typed attributes in student ratings. In two studies that involved written profiles of male and female teachers, which included adjectives described as stereotypically masculine or feminine, Harris (1975, 1976) found that, on all measures except warmth, both male and female students rated teachers with "masculine" teaching styles more positively than they did those with "feminine" teaching styles.

It would not be correct to assume that only masculine traits are appreciated, however. In the Harris studies, "warmth" in teachers was very positively rated, at least by female students. Other research supports the importance of teacher warmth and nurturance, especially in combination with teacher competence and dynamism. Androgynous professors, those high in both stereotypic masculine (active/instrumental) traits and stereotypic feminine (nurturant/expressive) traits, appear to be the most highly rated (Basow & Howe, 1987; Erdle, Murray, & Rushton, 1985; Freeman, 1994; Wheeless & Potorti, 1989). In fact, it may be *particularly* important for female professors to demonstrate both sets of characteristics—those traditionally viewed as feminine, such as friendliness and support, and those traditionally viewed as masculine, such as competence and confidence (Bennett, 1982b; Bernstein, Blaisdell, et al., 1995; Bray & Howard, 1980; Kierstead, D'Agostino, & Drill, 1988; Martin, 1984). Indeed, this heavier set of expectations for women professors appears to be one of the subtle ways that gender bias operates in student evaluations.

One way of understanding this double set of expectations on female faculty is to picture two circles that overlap slightly. One circle represents social expectations of a woman (warm, nurturant, domestic, low status); the other, social expectations of a professor (competent, knowledgeable, professional, high status). The area of overlap is very small. In contrast, social expectations of a man (strong, dominant, knowledgeable, high status) overlap quite a bit with social expectations of a professor. Because we like people to fit our expectations and feel quite uncomfortable when they don't, women have a more difficult time than men in being accepted as professors. Women professors may have to satisfy both sets of expectations in order to receive positive ratings, whereas their male counterparts may have to live up to only one set of expectations. Thus, women faculty must squeeze themselves into that narrow area of overlap between the two circles of expectations, whereas men faculty have a wider range of behavioral possibilities. I believe it is precisely those female professors whose behavior doesn't fit into the narrow boundary allotted them for whom gender variables in evaluation are most important.

FIELD RESEARCH

Most of the research reported above is somewhat artificial; it occurred in controlled settings and was based on written descriptions or videotapes of professors. Let's now consider research that has been carried out in actual classrooms with real-life professors. In the natural environment, it is difficult to control completely for all the variables that may affect student ratings; therefore, significant results found in such settings carry a great deal of weight.

Bennett (1982a, 1982b) investigated the effect of both gender and gender-role variables on teaching evaluations. She used student ratings of their teachers at a small, private, women's liberal arts college and at five larger universities. Bennett did not find evidence of direct gender bias in student evaluations of teachers, although female professors were perceived as having a warmer interpersonal style than male professors. Female professors also were rated as more effective and engaging than male professors, but this did not translate into better overall ratings.

These findings and others suggest that gender-role stereotypes were influencing evaluations of female professors but not those of male professors. In particular, Bennett found that greater demands for student contact and support are placed on female professors than on male professors and that students do in fact receive greater time and personal support from their female teachers. However, students are more critical of their female professors' availability than their male professors'. Bernstein, Sumner, and their colleagues (1995) reported similar results. In their study at a large state university, they found that women faculty spent the same amount of time with students as did men faculty, but the women were rated by students as less available.

Students seem to be less tolerant of their female faculty in several ways. Certain aspects of teaching style are more important to teaching performance ratings of female professors than of male professors; for example, in the Bennett (1982a, 1982b) studies, in order to get good ratings, it was more important for women than men professors to use a highly structured instructional approach and to act experienced and professional. Bernstein, Blaisdell, and their colleagues (1995) found that for women faculty to receive high evaluations, they had to demonstrate more effort (through more time spent with students and preparing for class), more teacher-student interactions in class (through class discussions and cooperative learning), as well as fewer demands (through reduced workload expectations and higher grades) than their male counterparts. Remember the point that women professors must walk a fine line to be accepted.

Bennett (1982a) concluded from the results of her first study that "in the institution studied, women invested considerably in both the formal aspects of teaching and the informal interpersonal aspects of the instructor role in order to earn parity with their male colleagues" (p. 178). The old aphorism that "Women have to be twice as good as men to get half as far" may be operating here. Certainly, the double effort required by women to obtain comparable ratings with their male peers seems to be borne out in Bennett's study.

To examine in more detail the effects of gender and gender-typing on ratings of college professors in an actual classroom setting, Nancy Silberg and I conducted a field study at a small liberal arts college that was formerly all-male (Basow & Silberg, 1987). Because a major problem in previous research was not controlling for the variables that may interact with gender, we tried to control for these variables by asking all female faculty who had been at the college at least 1 year to participate. We then matched each with a male professor in the same discipline, at the same rank, and with the same number of years at the college. We wound up with 16 women and 16 men, most of whom were in the social sciences; a few were in the humanities and natural sciences.

By asking all students in these 32 professors' classes to participate, we were able to survey more than half the student body (more than 1,000 students). Each student received two questionnaires during class time, midway through the semester. They rated their professor using a standard student rating form that consisted of 25 questions, which were summarized into five factor scores that tapped different aspects of teaching, plus an overall rating question. Students also used the Bem Sex Role Inventory (Bem, 1974) to rate their professors with respect to instrumental and expressive personality traits.

The results revealed a consistent pattern. Although male professors received slightly better ratings than female professors on all factors (Scholarship; Organization/Clarity; Instructor-Group Interaction; Instructor-Individual Student Interaction; Dynamism/Enthusiasm), the more important and meaningful finding was that male students rated female professors more negatively than they rated male professors on all six measures of the student rating questionnaire. Other field studies of student ratings typically neglect to ask the gender of the student rater or fail to match professors on important variables such as rank and discipline (Bennett, 1982a; Elmore & LaPointe, 1974, 1975).

The fact that college teaching is considered a male occupation may help to explain why male students rate female professors less favorably than they rate male professors. Less favorable ratings of women are most likely to occur when women are seen as not fitting gender stereotypes, in this case by participating in a gender-atypical profession (e.g., Etaugh & Riley, 1983). If male students show a greater bias than female students, it may be because males tend to be more traditional than females in terms of their attitudes toward women, and traditional attitudes toward women are associated with more gender bias (Holahan & Stephen, 1981). Student major is also relevant here—the most negative male students were Economics/Business and Engineering majors. As a follow-up to this study (Basow, 1986), students' attitudes toward women as a function of their major fields were assessed. Male students in Economics/Business and Engineering were found to be the most traditional (see also Haemmerlie, Abdul-Wakeel, & Pomeroy, 1986).

Both male and female students in the Basow and Silberg (1987) study, however, rated female professors less favorably on the factor that measured

141

Instructor-Individual Student Interaction. This factor involves questions related to a professor's availability to and contact with students. Because of gender stereotypes, female professors may be expected to be more "accessible" to students than are male professors, as Bennett (1982b) found. The poorer ratings of female professors on the factor Instructor-Individual Student Interaction may be the result of not having conformed to this expectation or of not appearing sufficiently "nurturant." This latter possibility is supported by the finding that when student-perceived gender-typed personality traits of the faculty were controlled for statistically, the lower ratings of female professors disappeared.

The relatively poorer ratings received by female professors compared to male professors by both female and male students on the Overall Teaching Ability question may be attributed to the strong correlation between the Overall Teaching Ability question and the Dynamism/Enthusiasm factor ($r = .88, p < .001$). This explanation is supported by other studies (Abrami, Leventhal, & Perry, 1982; Marsh & Ware, 1982; Murray, 1997; Williams & Ceci, 1997), whose results indicate that teacher expressiveness (i.e., the utilization of emphatic gestures, facial expressions, and vocal variations) strongly influences student ratings, sometimes even more than does lecture content.

Why do female professors receive poorer ratings on dynamism and enthusiasm than do male professors, especially from male students? Perhaps male professors are stronger in active/instrumental personality traits, a finding confirmed in our study. But when these traits were controlled for statistically, female professors were still rated less favorably than were male professors, especially by male students.

It may be that the ratings on Dynamism/Enthusiasm are not based on these personality traits but rather on either differences in gender-based expectations or differences in actual classroom behavior. Both possibilities will be examined in more detail below. For now, it should be remembered that male students rated female professors even less favorably on this variable than did female students.

More recently (Basow, 1995), I completed a study of 4 years of student evaluations at the same private liberal arts college used in the earlier (Basow & Silberg, 1987) study. Using the data from the standard student evaluation questionnaire, which consisted of 14 questions about the instructor and included an overall rating, I looked at the professor-gender-by-student-gender interactions, and also whether these patterns varied by division. The three divisions examined were humanities, social sciences, and natural sciences, although the number of females in the latter was small, and half were in the psychology department.

As previously found, there was a student-gender-by-professor-gender interaction each semester on at least some of the questions, with the most common pattern being similar ratings for male professors and differential ratings of female professors. Other field researchers also found such an interaction. The most common pattern is for students to give higher ratings to same-gender faculty members (Freeman, 1994; Hancock et al., 1993; Tatro, 1995). The highest ratings frequently are given by female students to female professors. Academic division or discipline may also be important, especially in interaction with professor gender and student gender. In my study (Basow, 1995), the strongest professor-gender-by-student-gender interactions occurred in the humanities and social sciences.

There were interesting interactions on specific questions as well, especially those related to teaching style. For example, I found that female students tended to rate their female professors particularly high on the item "speaks in an appropriate manner," whereas male students tended to rate their female professors particularly low on this item (Basow, 1995). Male students also tended to rate female professors particularly low on the items "stimulates your thinking" and "is fair and impartial."

Female faculty generally received higher ratings on interpersonal questions, especially from female students. This pattern is a frequent one, as Feldman found in his 1993 meta-analysis of field studies. Women faculty typically receive higher ratings on concern for students and other interpersonal items than do men faculty. In contrast, male faculty generally receive higher ratings on "knowledge" (Basow, 1995; Feldman, 1993). (See Chrisler, this volume, for a discussion of "men of knowledge.") Given that I did not find this latter difference accounted for by such variables as rank and number of years teaching, it is likely that these differences are due to the operation of gender stereotypes, as well as gender differences in teaching style (Basow, 1995). For example, lecturing (as opposed to class discussions) may make a professor seem knowledgeable. As we will see, men professors tend to use the lecture style more than women professors.

Overall, the picture that emerges from my studies and others is a complex one. Women tend to be rated more highly than men on interpersonal items, especially by female students. Men tend to be rated more highly than women on "knowledge" items and on dynamism and enthusiasm. Students tend to rate same-gender professors most highly overall; this is particularly true of female students. Male students may devalue women faculty, at least on certain items. Many of these patterns appear only in certain disciplines.

The complex picture that emerges from field research is further complicated by the fact that male and female professors are not similarly situated in real life. Men are overrepresented in the higher professorial ranks and in science and technical fields as compared to the humanities. Women are overpresented in introductory courses. All of these variables have an effect on student evaluations. For example, tenured professors tend to receive better ratings than untenured professors and teaching assistants; humanities courses tend to be rated higher than those in science and engineering; upper-level courses tend to be rated higher than lower-level courses (Feldman, 1983; Marsh & Dunkin, 1992). Thus, some women faculty may be at a disadvantage because of structural factors beyond their control.

Type of institution also may be important. My studies were conducted at an institution that was previously all male with a relatively homogenous and traditional student body. Results may be different at larger, more heterogeneous institutions, especially those with a long history of coeducation.

Race of instructor is also likely to be important, but with so few minority faculty in the professoriate, little research has examined this variable, especially with respect to gender issues. Bernstein, Blaisdell, and their colleagues (1995) examined race of professor in their study, but with so few ethnic minority faculty, they did not find any significant patterns. Given the hegemony of racism and of White norms for behavior, we can expect that minority women are held to an even stricter standard of behavior than are White women. The same situation exists with respect to sexual orientation of the professor; we simply do not know how such a factor affects student evaluations. There is every reason to think that lesbians and gay men might be perceived more negatively than their heterosexual counterparts given the high level of homophobia among many college students and the assumptions of gender nonconformity that are associated with homosexuality (Basow, 1992; Herek, 1994). We do know that feminist instructors tend to receive lower evaluations than other female professors (Hartung, 1990; Lewis, 1994). Clearly, this is an area where research is sorely needed.

It should be pointed out that the magnitude of the mean differences and of the effect sizes in research on gender and student evaluations is small, and they account for less than 3% of the variance in student evaluations (Basow, 1995; Basow & Silberg, 1987; Feldman, 1993). Nonetheless, for certain female professors, gender variables may play more than a negligible role. For an untenured woman faculty member in a male-dominated discipline with a no-nonsense style of teaching and a classroom of predominantly male students with traditional attitudes, gender factors may indeed affect student ratings.

GENDER BIAS OR BEHAVIORAL DIFFERENCES?

When men and women professors receive somewhat different evaluations from their students, we can conclude that (a) men are engaging in different classroom behaviors than are women, (b) the same behavior is perceived differently when it is performed by a man than by a woman, or (c) both of the above are true. The evidence suggests that the third option is most accurate.

Perceptual Biases

Many studies have documented that when men and women engage in the same behaviors, they are perceived differently. Some of this research has already been reviewed. Results with regard to written and videotaped material indicate that we evaluate behaviors in context and that gender is a salient part of any context.

For example, based on classroom observations and student ratings, Statham, Richardson, and Cook (1991) found that the more classroom time a male professor spent presenting material, the higher his likability ratings, but the reverse was true for female professors. For women, the more time spent presenting material, the lower her likability ratings. Conversely, when female professors attempt to involve students by soliciting student input, encouraging questions, or responding to questions, the lower students' ratings of her competence. These behaviors, less common in male professors' teaching style in the first place, had no effect on students' ratings of his competence.

My studies of faculty expressiveness also support the conclusion that students perceive and react to the same behavior differently when it is displayed by female and male professors (Basow, 1987; Basow & Distenfeld, 1985; see also Kierstead et al., 1988). Because expressiveness is linked to both gender-typed feminine qualities (e.g., smiling and facial move-

145

ments) and gender-typed masculine qualities (e.g., dynamism and enthusiasm), it merits closer examination.

Faculty expressiveness tends to enhance student ratings of professors in general (Abrami et al., 1982; Basow, 1987; Basow & Distenfeld, 1985; Marsh & Ware, 1982; Winocur, Schoen, & Sirowatka, 1989). In particular, expressiveness appears to enhance the ratings of scholarship and instrumental ("masculine") personality traits for a female professor, whereas it impairs those ratings for a male professor. Furthermore, in my studies (Basow, 1987; Basow & Distenfeld, 1985), students' achievement also varied depending on their own gender and the female professor's level of expressiveness. For example, when a female professor was nonexpressive, male students learned the least.

In general, it appears that students are more variable in their reactions to a female professor than to a male professor, a finding in line with other research (e.g., Basow, 1995; Basow & Silberg, 1987) and with the hypothesis that a different standard is used to judge women than is used to judge men. For example, warmth and relationships with students appear to be more important for female professors than male professors in terms of student evaluations (Cooper, Stewart, & Gudykunst, 1982; Martin, 1984; Van Giffen, 1990). These findings also relate to the idea that women professors must meet a double standard. That is, women professors must demonstrate traditionally feminine traits of warmth, friendliness, helpfulness, and interest in students, in addition to professional competency, in order to get good student ratings. These nurturant/expressive qualities are important for men professors, but not as important as they are for women. For male professors, competency ratings are much more important to student evaluations.

Expected grade may be another way students perceive faculty nurturance or warmth. Researchers have repeatedly found that expected grade correlates significantly with global student ratings of faculty (e.g., Marsh & Dunkin, 1992), but female professors may be particularly affected. If students expect to receive a low grade, they tend to evaluate their female professor lower than they would a male professor from whom they expected to receive that same grade (Bernstein, Blaisdell, et al., 1995; Langbein, 1994). A demanding female professor may violate students' gender-related expectations of female nurturance (as in the ever-forgiving mother).

In many cases, especially with respect to interpersonal interactions, female students rate female professors significantly higher than do male students. This is similar to others' findings that teacher "warmth" and teacher availability are more highly rated by female students than male students (Basow, 1995; Harris, 1975, 1976; Hearn, 1985; Winocur et al., 1989). These findings suggest that there may be a same-gender preference for gender-appropriate teaching styles (i.e., female students prefer warmth in their female professors; male students prefer displays of scholarship in their male professors), at least in humanities and social science classrooms.

This qualification by professional discipline is important, yet it is all too frequently neglected in student evaluation research. Discipline may matter either because of teaching method employed (e.g., lecture vs. discussion) or because of gender visibility. Both factors have been found to matter in student evaluation research. Where a woman professor's gender is particularly salient, whether because she's in a department with few women, or in a gender-atypical field, or is teaching a women's studies course, her teaching evaluations may be significantly affected by her student-perceived personality characteristics and by the gender of her students (Basow, 1995; Bennett, 1982b; Hartung, 1990; Sidanius & Crane, 1989; Tieman & Rankin-Ullock, 1985).

Behavioral Differences

So far, we have been examining how perceptual biases may affect student evaluations. Another important question is whether women professors behave differently in the classroom than do their male counterparts. Brophy (1985), in a review of a wide range of classroom studies from preschool through college, concluded "that male and female teachers are much more similar than different, both in their general approaches to instruction and in their interactions with male and female students" (p. 137).

However, despite no dramatic differences in behavior, Brophy did find certain consistent patterns that differentiated women and men professors. On the college level, male faculty were found to be relatively more teacher-centered and direct; female faculty were found to be relatively more student-centered, indirect, and supportive of students. Some studies (Brooks, 1982; Crawford & McLeod, 1990) have found that students participate nearly twice the amount of class time in female professors' classes as they do in male professors' classes in the same discipline.

In the study by Statham and her colleagues (1991), observations of more than 160 classes at a large state university revealed that women professors encouraged student participation significantly more than did men professors, a finding that is supported by the results of many other researchers (Bennett, 1982a; Constantinople, Cornelius, & Gray, 1988; Feldman, 1993). Women were also significantly more likely to vary their lecture styles than were men. In-depth interviews with 15 full-time women professors and 15 full-time men professors matched for rank, discipline, and gender ratio of their departments suggested that male and female professors view the classroom in different ways, at least they do when they hold the rank of assistant or associate professor.

In discussions of four common classroom management problems—students' inattentiveness, classroom disruptions, challenges to the competency of the professor, and students' nonparticipation—women assistant and associate professors were "less harsh, more accepting, more likely to interpret student challenges as an 'awakening' of interest, and more likely to engage in the give and take of free discussion than were their male counterparts" (p. 285). The women faculty demonstrated authority, but softened it at the same time.

In contrast, men at the assistant and associate professor level were found to "reprimand students publicly and harshly, directly correct students' misconceptions, 'point-prove' outside of class, and have difficulty in getting students to partake in classroom discussions" (p. 285). Male faculty used their authority to maintain classroom control, even when it had a dampening effect on students. In general, women professors "tended to focus more on the student as the locus of learning; men, on themselves" (p. 126). Student evaluations of male and female faculty, however, were equally positive, which suggests that students appreciate both styles, or, at least they appreciate gender-consistent styles.

It is interesting that Statham and her colleagues did not find any differences between how male and female full professors viewed these classroom problems. The women's views were more similar to those previously found for men. The researchers speculated that the lack of gender differences is due to the full professors having been fully accepted in their community, although it is possible that women who become full professors are selected because their style resembles men's. Or it may be that older faculty resemble each other more than younger faculty, who may have been influenced by feminist pedagogy or doubt the need to conform.

In the Statham et al. study (1991), faculty were matched for discipline and rank. Even in such a controlled situation, most female faculty (at least assistant and associate professors) appeared to be more student-centered and discussion-oriented than were the male faculty. In real life, women and men tend to be in different disciplines (e.g., women are overrepresented in English, men in engineering), which lend themselves to different teaching styles. Thus, in actual practice, gender distinctions in teaching style may be even more marked. Indeed, other researchers have found that female faculty are more likely than their male counterparts to use a variety of teaching techniques other than lecturing, such as cooperative learning, class discussions, and small group work (Astin, Korn, & Lewis, 1991; Murray, Rushton, & Paunonen, 1990).

Gender differences in student reactions to male and female professors may contribute to these different teaching patterns. Canada and Pringle (1995) observed classroom interactions during the first 5 years of co-education at a previously all-women's college. They found that gender mattered in a mixed-sex classroom in ways it did not when classes were all female. Women faculty had to adopt various strategies to deal with male students' challenges to their authority, challenges that did not occur when all the students were women. Male faculty did not seem to change their teaching behavior in the transition from single-sex to mixed-sex classes.

In sum, there is evidence both for the hypothesis that women and men may have some different classroom behaviors and for the hypothesis that even when female and male faculty demonstrate the same behavior, they may be perceived and reacted to differently. This adds to our understanding of classroom gender dynamics and of how evaluations of female and male faculty members may be influenced by gender-based norms.

SUMMARY AND SUGGESTIONS FOR COPING

The pattern that emerges is a complex one. Women faculty may get the same, lower, or higher ratings than their male counterparts depending on many different factors aside from their teaching competence. The specific questions asked of students are important. Consistent gender differences do not typically occur on an overall rating question, but women faculty tend to be rated higher on interpersonal qualities and interactions with students than do men faculty. In contrast, men faculty tend to be rated more highly than women faculty on questions relating to knowledge and dynamism/enthusiasm. These differences may relate to gender-typed personality traits or gender-related teaching styles or gender-related student expectations.

149

TABLE 5.1   Basow Checklist for Evaluation Bias Risk

_____ female professor
_____ male students
_____ traditional gender role attitudes of students
_____ stereotypic male discipline/subject area
_____ nonexpressive/non-nurturant personality traits
_____ nonexpressive/non-nurturant behaviors
_____ lecture-based teaching style
_____ untenured professor status
_____ lower-level (e.g., introductory) course
_____ "tough" grader
_____ feminist reputation
_____ additional minority cue (race, ethnicity, sexual orientation)

Student gender appears to interact with professor gender such that each sex may rate a same-sex teacher more positively, at least on some items. This seems especially to be the case with male students, who frequently rate female faculty lower than female students do. This pattern may be most pronounced with male students who have traditional attitudes toward women, especially when rating women faculty in traditionally male fields. In contrast, female students tend to rate their female professors very positively, especially on interpersonal questions.

Women faculty appear to be expected to be strong in nurturant and expressive characteristics as well as in instrumental and active traits. Although also desirable for men, these double qualities appear critical for women, especially if they are in gender-atypical fields. These results can best be understood by viewing gender as a "marked" characteristic for female professors. That is, male professors are professors; female professors are female professors. Thus, women faculty have to earn their status, whereas men faculty simply assume theirs. We need to understand the complexity of gender factors in student evaluations if we are to use them effectively.

Table 5.1 lists the risk factors for bias that women faculty might use to determine the likelihood that gender bias may be influencing their ratings. Remember that the effect of any one factor tends to be very small, but the cumulative effect of several factors may be noticeable.

Strategies

Many of the factors that contribute to negative ratings of women faculty appear to be beyond our control. Certainly, students come to college with gender-role expectations that are difficult to modify. Society as a whole needs changing. But the woman faculty member can do several things to arm herself against unfairly negative student evaluations. Some of these suggestions (especially #1 and #2 below) may not fit an individual woman's personality or ideology. Indeed, it's not fair that women professors have to be concerned about gender-stereotyped expectations. However, because those expectations do exist, it might be helpful for those who want to build an academic career to know how to try to get around them.

1. Educate others about the ways gender can affect student evaluations. If done early enough, especially with students and supervisors, such material is less likely to be seen as defensive. Many are able to learn of and overcome their own potential biases if they are made aware of them.

2. Women faculty must signal that they are competent and knowledgeable. For example, you might talk about your qualifications on the first day of class—anything associated with status, knowledge, competence, and connections.

   a. Dressing in a professional way appears more important for women faculty than for men. A woman professor who dresses informally (e.g., jeans) may seem more approachable, but she does not get high ratings for respect or knowledge (Lukavsky, Butler, & Harden, 1995).

   b. Women faculty also may gain respect by using their title (Dr. or Professor) and last names, rather than their first names. Because women frequently are thought of as belonging to the domestic sphere, using professional titles may help students break the gender-stereotype set.

3. Women faculty must appear nurturant and expressive, but not too much so. These traits must go along with competent behaviors or else the woman risks being seen as a "mother" and similarly devalued. For example, along with telling students your qualifications on the first day of class, you might also inform them of your willingness to help students and some ways in which you do so; for example, review sessions, help with papers.

   a. Smiling and eye contact appear to be particularly important for women faculty, especially with male students (Kierstead et al., 1988; Martin, 1984). These signs may make a competent woman less threatening.

   b. It is also important to be accessible to students (e.g., post and keep regular office hours). Do not, however, be endlessly available to your

151

students. You will not get any other work done, and you will not be particularly appreciated or rewarded with high evaluations (Bernstein, Sumner, et al., 1995).

4. Teach female students. Female students tend to give higher ratings than male students overall, especially to female professors.

5. Avoid too much lecturing. Women who use the lecture format are rated lower than men who do so. Encouraging active participation by students is a good predictor of student evaluations, especially for women professors (Bernstein, Blaisdell, et al., 1995).

6. Try to get your institution to adopt standardized and objective assessment instruments, especially those that tap different teaching factors. Beware of forms that emphasize only some aspects of teaching, or that ask only vague general questions.

7. If your institution doesn't have a good evaluation form, you might be able to substitute or supplement with your own. Try to get students to focus on behaviorally based questions that relate to your course objectives rather than on subjective, vague ones.

8. Before handing out evaluations, review the course objectives and ask students to consider what they've learned during the term. This may help to focus students on your effectiveness as a professor rather than on your personality.

9. Ask peers to observe your classes and evaluate your teaching using behavioral rating forms. Although peers may be as vulnerable to bias as students, they may also provide a different, more objective view.

10. Document the student learning in your classes using a portfolio approach. If you teach one section of a multisection course that has a common final exam, document how well your students did relative to those in other sections. Include your grade distributions in your personnel file because women faculty may be penalized more than male faculty for being tough graders.

11. If you think the variables discussed in this chapter have affected your student ratings, include some of the research cited here in your personnel file or tenure packet. Encourage your Chair to read some relevant literature before writing the recommendation to the tenure and promotion committee.

REFERENCES

Abrami, P. C., Leventhal, L., & Perry, R. P. (1982). Educational seduction. *Review of Educational Research, 52*, 446-464.

Abramson, P., Goldberg, P., Greenberg, J., & Abramson, L. (1977). The talking platypus phenomenon: Competency ratings as a function of sex and professional status. *Psychology of Women Quarterly, 2*, 114-124.

Astin, A. W., Korn, W. S., & Lewis, E. L. (1991). *The American college teacher: National norms for the 1989-90 HERI faculty survey*. Los Angeles: UCLA Higher Education Research Institute, Graduate School of Education.

Basow, S. A. (1986). *Attitudes toward women as a function of college major*. Unpublished manuscript, Lafayette College, Easton, PA.

Basow, S. A. (1987). Effects of teacher expressiveness: Mediated by teacher sex-typing? *Journal of Educational Psychology, 82*, 599-602.

Basow, S. A. (1992). *Gender: Stereotypes and roles* (3rd ed.). Pacific Grove, CA: Brooks/Cole.

Basow, S. A. (1995). Student evaluations of college professors: When gender matters. *Journal of Educational Psychology, 87*, 656-665.

Basow, S. A., & Distenfeld, M. S. (1985). Teacher expressiveness: More important for males than females? *Journal of Educational Psychology, 77*, 45-52.

Basow, S. A., & Howe, K. G. (1979). Evaluations of college professors: Effects of professors' sex-type and sex, and students' sex. *Psychological Reports, 60*, 671-678.

Basow, S. A., & Silberg, N. (1987). Student evaluations of college professors: Are female and male professors rated differently? *Journal of Educational Psychology, 79*, 308-314.

Bem, S. L. (1974). The measurement of psychological androgyny. *Journal of Consulting and Clinical Psychology, 42*, 155-162.

Bennett, S. K. (1982a). Student perceptions of and expectations for male and female instructors: Evidence relating to the question of gender bias in teaching evaluations. *Journal of Educational Psychology, 74*, 170-179.

Bennett, S. K. (1982b). Undergraduates and their teachers: An analysis of student evaluations of male and female instructors. In P. Perun (Ed.), *The undergraduate woman: Issues in educational equity* (pp. 251-273). Lexington, MA: Lexington Books.

Bernstein, B. L., Blaisdell, S. L., Perez, M. J., St. Peter, C. J., Sumner, A., & Burke, L. (1995, August). *Faculty gender, effort, style and rigor: Relative contributions to student evaluations*. Paper presented at the meeting of the American Psychological Association, New York.

Bernstein, B. L., Sumner, A. J., Blaisdell, S. L., Perez, M. J., St. Peter, C. J., & Burke, L. (1995, August). *Women faculty's role demands, work effort and student evaluations of instructor's concern and availability*. Paper presented at the meeting of the American Psychological Association, New York.

Bray, J., & Howard, G. (1980). Interaction of teacher and student sex and sex role orientations and student evaluations of college instruction. *Contemporary Educational Psychology, 5*, 241-248.

Brooks, V. R. (1982). Sex differences in student dominance behavior in female and male professors' classrooms. *Sex Roles, 8*, 683-690.

Brophy, J. (1985). Interactions of male and female students with male and female teachers. In L. C. Wilkinson & C. B. Marrett (Eds.), *Gender influences in classroom interaction* (pp. 115-142). Orlando, FL: Academic Press.

Canada, K., & Pringle, R. (1995). The role of gender in college classroom interactions: A social context approach. *Sociology of Education, 68*, 161-186.

Cashin, W. E. (1988, September). *Student ratings of teaching: A summary of the research*. IDEA Paper No. 20. Manhattan: Kansas State University, Center for Faculty Evaluation and Development.

Constantinople, A., Cornelius, R., & Gray, J. (1988). The chilly climate: Fact or artifact? *Journal of Higher Education, 59*, 527-550.

Cooper, P. J., Stewart, L. P., & Gudykunst, W. B. (1982). Relationship with instructor and other variables influencing student evaluations of instruction. *Communication Quarterly, 30*, 308-315.

Crawford, M., & McLeod, M. (1990). Gender in the college classroom: An assessment of the chilly climate for women. *Sex Roles, 23,* 101-122.

Dobbins, G. H., Cardy, R. L., & Truxillo, D. M. (1986). Effects of ratee sex and purpose of appraisal on the accuracy of performance evaluations. *Basic and Applied Social Psychology, 7,* 225-241.

Eagly, A. H., Makhijani, M. G., & Klonsky, B. G. (1992). Gender and the evaluation of leaders: A meta-analysis. *Psychological Bulletin, 111,* 3-22.

Elmore, P. B., & LaPointe, K. A. (1974). Effects of teacher sex and student sex on the evaluation of college instructors. *Journal of Educational Psychology, 66,* 386-389.

Elmore, P. B., & LaPointe, K. A. (1975). Effects of teacher sex, student sex, and teacher warmth on the evaluation of college instructors. *Journal of Educational Psychology, 67,* 368-374.

Erdle, S., Murray, H. G., & Rushton, J. P. (1985). Personality, classroom behavior, and student ratings of college teaching effectiveness: A path analysis. *Journal of Educational Psychology, 77,* 394-407.

Etaugh, C., & Riley, S. (1983). Evaluating competence of women and men: Effects of marital and parental status and occupational sex-typing. *Sex Roles, 9,* 943-952.

Feldman, K. A. (1983). Seniority and experience of college teachers as related to evaluations they receive from students. *Research in Higher Education, 18,* 3-124.

Feldman, K. (1992). College students' views of male and female college teachers: Part I—Evidence from the social laboratory and experiments. *Research in Higher Education, 33,* 317-375.

Feldman, K. (1993). College students' views of male and female college teachers: Part II—Evidence from students' evaluations of their classroom teachers. *Research in Higher Education, 34,* 151-211.

Fidell, L. S. (1975). Empirical verifications of sex discrimination in hiring practices in psychology. *American Psychologist, 25,* 1094-1098.

Freeman, B. C. (1977). Faculty women in the American university: Up the down staircase. In P. G. Altbach (Ed.), *Comparative perspectives on the academic profession* (pp. 166-190). New York: Praeger.

Freeman, H. R. (1994). Student evaluations of college instructors: Effects of type of course taught, instructor gender and gender role, and student gender. *Journal of Educational Psychology, 86,* 627-630.

Goldberg, P. (1968). Are women prejudiced against women? *Trans-Action, 5,* 28-30.

Haemmerlie, F. M., Abdul-Wakeel, A., & Pomeroy, M. (1986). Male sex bias against men and women in various professions. *Journal of Social Psychology, 125,* 797-798.

Hancock, G. R., Shannon, D. M., & Trentham, L. L. (1993). Student and teacher gender in ratings of university faculty: Results from five colleges of study. *Journal of Personnel Evaluation in Education, 6,* 235-248.

Harris, M. B. (1975). Sex role stereotypes and teacher evaluations. *Journal of Educational Psychology, 67,* 751-756.

Harris, M. B. (1976). The effects of sex, sex-stereotyped descriptions, and institution on evaluations of teachers. *Sex Roles, 2,* 15-21.

Hartung, B. (1990). Selective rejection: How students perceive women's studies teachers. *NWSA Journal, 2,* 254-263.

Hearn, J. C. (1985). Determinants of college students' overall evaluations of their academic programs. *Research in Higher Education, 23,* 413-437.

Herek, G. (1994). Assessing heterosexuals' attitudes toward lesbian and gay men. In B. Greene & G. Herek (Eds.), *Lesbian and gay psychology: Theory, research, and clinical applications* (pp. 206-228). Thousand Oaks, CA: Sage.

Holahan, C. K., & Stephen, C. W. (1981). When beauty isn't talent: The influence of physical attractiveness, attitudes toward women, and competence on impression formation. *Sex Roles, 7*, 867-876.

Kaschak, E. (1978). Sex bias in student evaluations of college professors. *Psychology of Women Quarterly, 3*, 235-243.

Kaschak, E. (1981). Another look at sex bias in students' evaluations of professors: Do winners get the recognition that they have been given? *Psychology of Women Quarterly, 5*, 767-772.

Kierstead, D., D'Agostino, P., & Drill, H. (1988). Sex role stereotyping of college professors: Bias in students' ratings of instructors. *Journal of Educational Psychology, 80*, 342-344.

Langbein, L. I. (1994, Sept.). The validity of student evaluations of teaching. *PS: Political Science & Politics*, pp. 545-553.

Lewis, E. M. (1994, March). *The selective rejection of feminist faculty*. Paper presented at the meeting of the Association for Women in Psychology, Oakland, CA.

Lott, B. (1985). The devaluation of women's competence. *Journal of Social Issues, 41*(4), 43-60.

Lukavsky, J., Butler, S., & Harden, A. J. (1995). Perceptions of an instructor: Dress and students' characteristics. *Perceptual and Motor Skills, 81*, 231-240.

Marsh, H. W., & Dunkin, M. J. (1992). Students' evaluations of university teaching: A multidimensional perspective. In J. C. Smart (Ed.), *Higher education: Handbook of theory and research, Vol. VIII* (pp. 143-233). New York: Agathon Press.

Marsh, H., & Ware, J. E., Jr. (1982). Effects of expressiveness, content coverage, and incentive on multidimensional student rating scales: New interpretations of the Dr. Fox effect. *Journal of Educational Psychology, 74*, 126-134.

Martin, E. (1984). Power and authority in the classroom: Sexist stereotypes in teaching evaluations. *Signs, 9*, 483-492.

Murray, B. (1997, May). How important is teaching style to students? *APA Monitor*, p. 48.

Murray, H. G., Rushton, J. P., & Paunonen, S. V. (1990). Teacher personality traits and student instructional ratings in six types of university courses. *Journal of Educational Psychology, 82*, 250-261.

Ott, E. M. (1989). Effects of the male-female ratio at work: Policewomen and male nurses. *Psychology of Women Quarterly, 13*, 41-57.

Seldin, P. (1993, July 21). The use and abuse of student ratings of professors. *Chronicle of Higher Education*, p. A40.

Sidanius, J., & Crane, M. (1989). Job evaluation and gender: The case of university faculty. *Journal of Applied Social Psychology, 19*, 174-197.

Statham, A., Richardson, L., & Cook, J. (1991). *Gender and university teaching: A negotiated difference*. Albany: State University of New York Press.

Swim, J., Borgida, E., Maruyama, G., & Myers, D. G. (1989). Joan McKay versus John McKay: Do gender stereotypes bias evaluations? *Psychological Bulletin, 105*, 409-429.

Tatro, C. N. (1995). Gender effects on student evaluations of faculty. *Journal of Research and Development in Education, 28*, 169-173.

Tieman, C. R., & Rankin-Ullock, B. (1985). Student evaluations of teachers: An examination of the effect of sex and field of study. *Teaching Sociology, 12*, 177-191.

Top, T. J. (1991). Sex bias in the evaluation of performance in the scientific, artistic, and literary professions: A review. *Sex Roles, 24*, 73-106.

Twenge, J. M. (1997). Attitudes toward women, 1970-1995. *Psychology of Women Quarterly, 21*, 35-51.

Van Giffen, K. (1990). Influence of professor gender and perceived use of humor on course evaluations. *Humor, 3*, 65-73.

Wheeless, V. E., & Potorti, P. F. (1989). Student assessment of teacher masculinity and femininity: A test of the sex role congruency hypothesis on student attitudes toward learning. *Journal of Educational Psychology, 81*, 259-262.

Williams, W. M., & Ceci, S. J. (1997, September/October). "How'm I doing?": Problems with student ratings of instructors and courses. *Change*, pp. 13-23.

Winocur, S., Schoen, L. G., & Sirowatka, A. H. (1989). Perceptions of male and female academics within a teaching context. *Research in Higher Education, 30*, 317-329.

6 Money Matters
The Art of Negotiation
for Women Faculty

Suzanna Rose
Mona J. E. Danner

If "location, location, location" is the single most important consideration in real estate, the likely parallel motto for career success in academe is "negotiate, negotiate, negotiate." Negotiation is the use of information and power to affect behavior; more specifically, it is an endeavor that focuses on gaining the favor of people from whom we want things (Cohen, 1980). For women faculty, the idea of developing their negotiation skills may run counter to a well-ingrained belief that academe is a meritocracy in which rewards presumably are given to those possessing the greatest talent. In reality, few are recognized based on their expertise alone; success usually requires both job competency and the ability to negotiate. In other words, in academe as in business, "you don't get what you deserve, you get what you negotiate" (Karrass, 1992).

Knowledge about how to negotiate has been shown to have a significant impact on one's likelihood of success. Those who know that negotiation requires tactical skill, as well as distinct types of information such as knowing deadlines and the other party's reputation, generally are more successful at bargaining than those who have little awareness of the task-specific components of negotiating (Stevens, Bavetta, & Gist, 1993; Weingart, Hyder, & Prietula, 1996). Elements of the task environment also play a role in negotiating, including the behavior of the other party, the success of attempted strategies, and the content of the task itself (Weingart et al., 1996). The other negotiator's possible gender bias has been identified as an aspect of the task environment that may significantly affect women's success as well (e.g., Gerhart & Rynes, 1991). Nevertheless, actively preparing oneself for the negotiating process may help women achieve better outcomes even when the task environment is uncontrollable or unfavorable.

One of the most crucial negotiations from the standpoint of academic careers is the salary negotiation. In general, women faculty fare less well than men in this process. Research indicates that women faculty are paid lower salaries than are men—about 20% less, on average. Translated into dollars, colleges and universities pay women nearly $10,000 a year less than men. Gender differences remain greatest at the full professor rank, where women earn 80% of men's salary, but are still present at the associate and assistant professor levels, where women earn 93% of men's earnings. The salary gap persists across academic disciplines and types of institutions (NCES, 1993, 1996; Sax, Astin, Arrendondo, & Korn, 1996).

Despite the importance of negotiating salary and other conditions of employment in academe, how to proceed is seldom discussed. For example, *Career Guide for Women Scholars* (Rose, 1986), *The Academic Job Search Handbook* (Heiberger & Vick, 1996), *Lifting a Ton of Feathers: A Woman's Guide to Surviving in the Academic World* (Caplan, 1993), *Promotion and Tenure: Community and Socialization in Academe* (Tierney & Bensimon, 1996), *Rhythms of Academic Life* (Frost & Taylor, 1996), and *Black Women in the Academy* (Benjamin, 1997) contain much information pertinent to the academic job search and how to establish and maintain a successful career, but mention little about salary or contract negotiations. The graduate school experience is similarly lacking in instruction concerning negotiation for most, although informal networks may convey relevant information from senior to junior men (e.g., Dreher & Cox, 1996). As a result, new women PhDs may enter the job market with little experience or knowledge about how to position themselves for the first job. In addition, subsequent opportunities for significant salary negotiations may be infrequent in an academic career. Thus, women could be quite senior, and the wage gap with senior men quite large, before they could benefit from trial-and-error learning.

In the present chapter, our intent is to illustrate why women faculty should acquire the art of negotiating, as well as to provide practical advice concerning how to negotiate. Although faculty jobs involve numerous types of bargaining, the primary focus will be on negotiating the academic contract, with a particular emphasis on salary negotiation.

MONEY MATTERS

Negotiation is important because money matters in academe. Your salary is a sign of your worth to the institution, as well as a source of self-esteem. Your economic security or that of your family also depends on your income. Moreover, your earning power affects not only your current living conditions, but also your retirement benefits, which generally are calculated partly as a percentage of your base salary in the years before retirement. Thus, the most important negotiation you are likely to make during the first phase of your career is the entry-level salary negotiation. Opportunities to increase your salary throughout your career are similarly crucial for you to negotiate successfully.

The long-term financial and career implications of entry-level salary may be best illustrated with an example. Suppose a woman assistant professor, Linda, is newly hired at $42,000, and earns 93% (i.e., the average wage gap) of a newly hired male assistant professor, Bob, who is hired at $45,150. Now suppose both Linda and Bob get average merit raises of 5% for the next 5 years. At this juncture, when they are likely to be undergoing tenure review, the institution will have invested $17,400 more in Bob than Linda (enough for a down payment on a house or relaxing vacations every year!). Bob also may be more enthusiastic about his job because he has been more amply rewarded and may even be seen as more valuable to the department simply because the institution has invested more in him, even though their performance has been similar. Even if the salary differential is only $1,000, the difference calculated over 40 years, given 3.5% yearly raises, is a loss to the woman of $84,550 (Haignere, 1996).

Research indicates that gender plays a role at each stage of the negotiation process that is detrimental to women. The extent and success of negotiating academic salaries depends on four steps:

1. the applicant's pay expectations,
2. the initial salary offered by the institution,

3. whether or not a counteroffer is made by the applicant, and

4. the final salary agreed upon by the applicant and the institution.

First, women tend to have lower pay expectations than do men regardless of occupational field (Jackson, Gardner, & Sullivan, 1992; Major & Konar, 1984). Lower salaries emerge as one consequence of lower salary expectations. For instance, applicants who conveyed lower pay expectations in one laboratory study were offered less pay than equally qualified applicants who had higher pay expectations (Major, Vanderslice, & McFarlin, 1984). Thus, women's lower pay expectations may partly influence the second step of the negotiation, the initial salary offer.

Second, research shows that the initial salary offer given by the institution's representative (usually a White man) has a strong impact on the final outcome of negotiation (i.e., higher initial offers are associated with higher final offers). The evidence also is clear that men (particularly White men) receive better initial offers for both commercial negotiations and salary discussions than do women. In a study of car sales, Ayers (1991) found significant differences in the initial offers made by sales associates based on the buyer's gender and race. White men received lower initial price quotes than did White women and minority women and men. Experimental simulations of various retail buyer-seller interactions confirm that men procure lower prices and higher profits than do women (Neu, Graham, & Gilly, 1988). Similarly, men obtain better initial salary offers in both laboratory and field studies. Male prospects who were hypothetical job applicants were assigned higher starting salaries by research participants than female prospects, even when they had the same qualifications and pay expectations (Major, McFarlin, & Gagnon, 1984). The finding of higher initial salary offers to men also held true in an investigation of the actual experiences of recent MBA graduates, who were surveyed about the outcomes of their wage discussions with employers (Gerhart & Rynes, 1991).

An applicant's gender also may affect whether she or he makes one or more counteroffers during the third step of a salary negotiation and what tactics are used to negotiate. Women may have less knowledge or skill at negotiation than men. In a hypothetical salary negotiation, men college students were found to use significantly more active tactics (e.g., ask for a larger salary than that offered), whereas women were significantly more indirect in their self-promotion tactics (e.g., emphasize their motivation to work hard; Kaman & Hartel, 1990). When confronted with a competitive negotiator, women MBAs in a simulated salary negotiation were less likely than men either to match this style or to use diverse negotiation tactics (Renard, 1992). In one of the few studies to examine salary negotiation directly, Gerhart and Rynes (1991) found that 56% of the MBA students who negotiated for larger salaries received increases from $1,000 to $7,000. Although men and women showed the same proclivity to initiate salary negotiations, men received $742 more, on average, for their efforts. Propensity to negotiate also depends on the attractiveness of the offer and other options available to the applicant. If women are offered less initially, the offer may be viewed as less attractive, and they may be less likely to bargain (Bacharach & Lawler, 1981; Chamberlain, 1955). In addition, applicants who have alternate job offers will have more bargaining power and will be more likely to negotiate (Mannix, Thompson, & Bazerman, 1989). Thus, a woman's skill at negotiating is not the only determinant of whether she will bargain or obtain outcomes equal to men.

The persistent wage gap between women and men in academic salaries indicates that men obtain better final salary offers at the last stage of negotiation. This difference cannot be explained solely by individual differences in ability, education, or training. Academic women's salaries lag significantly behind men's even when academic rank, type of institution, and experience are taken into account (NCES, 1993). Gender stereotyping also results in the differential valuation of women and men by male supervisors with respect to vocationally relevant characteristics (Rosen & Jerdee, 1978). Beliefs that women are willing to work for less pay or deserve less pay than men also remain common among administrators and supervisors (Rynes, Rosen, & Mahoney, 1985). Possible negotiator bias as expressed in the form of final salary offers, then, is one of the likely barriers to successful salary negotiation for women.

The first empirical study of negotiation in academe recently completed by Danner (1996) illustrates how the four steps just described operated for a national faculty sample of sociology PhDs in their first academic job. Women expected significantly lower salaries than men, initially were offered less, and were given final offers lower than those reported by men, congruent with previous research. Contrary to earlier findings, women were significantly more likely to initiate negotiations than were men. When women did not bargain, it was usually because they had been told that a higher salary simply was not possible. The major reason men did not initiate negotiations was because they were offered a salary equal to or exceeding their expectations. Despite the disparity in salary offers, it paid for both women and men to negotiate. About 92% of those who made a specific salary counteroffer won a salary higher than that offered initially.

In sum, the evidence concerning gender and salary negotiation indicates that women are underbenefitted in terms of salary in a variety of occupations, including academe. It appears that women have little control over some aspects of the salary negotiation, such as negotiator bias with regard to the initial and final salary offer, but that high pay expectations and the use of diverse negotiating tactics translate into higher salaries for women. These results suggest that even in adverse circumstances, women faculty may be able to improve salary negotiation outcomes by pursuing two goals:

1. developing high pay expectations and
2. planning a negotiation strategy.

PAY EXPECTATIONS

It is problematic enough for women faculty that administrators may give them lower initial and final salary offers than they do men, but research on gender and perceived pay entitlement indicates that women also may undervalue themselves. It has been shown that women pay themselves less than men do when asked to determine their own pay for work done in an experimental task. In one study, women and men undergraduates worked alone on a task for about an hour and were told to compensate themselves. On average, women took $2 for their work, whereas men took $3 (Major, McFarlin, & Gagnon, 1984). Even in situations where women have outperformed a coworker, they have been found to allocate less pay to themselves (e.g., Major, 1994). Research done on actual full-time workers confirms the laboratory findings, with women reporting that they deserve less pay for the jobs they held than did men (Desmarais & Curtis, 1997). In addition, women have been found to work more efficiently and longer than men when paid the same amount for performing a task. For example, when women and men undergraduates were given an equal wage and told to work as long as they wished on a routine task, women accomplished more in the same time period, made fewer errors, and worked 30% longer than men who performed the same task (Major, McFarlin, & Gagnon, 1984).

Part of the explanation for gender differences in pay expectations pertains to lack of information about or gender differences in available social comparison standards. At least three types of social comparisons may operate, including comparing one's current salary with male peers, female peers, or with one's own recent pay experience. First, research indicates that when women lack knowledge about male peers' earnings, they tend to have lower pay expectations (Bylsma & Major, 1992). Conversely, when women receive comparison information about men's earnings, they expect to be paid equally. The first author's experience as a career consultant to women faculty at several universities suggests that many women scholars are not aware of what male peers earn. Junior women faculty typically assume that their salaries are comparable to men peers and do not seek verification. Senior women faculty may not want to know peers' wages because they fear being demoralized if inequities are discovered. Not every woman knows where to look for information, either. Some are not aware that public colleges and universities make all salaries available to the public, usually through a listing obtainable at the reference desk of the campus library. Others are unfamiliar with salary scales that are regularly published by the *Chronicle of Higher Education* and the AAUP.

Comparative salary information and career support also may be lacking for women who are excluded from mentoring relationships and networks with senior men. For instance, Dreher and Cox (1996) reported that MBA graduates who had established a mentoring relationship with White men earned an average of $16,840 more than those with other mentors. However, White women and African American and Hispanic MBAs of both genders were significantly less likely than White men to form such relationships. Thus, women may not have or seek enough information concerning male peers' salaries to allow them to negotiate effectively.

Social comparisons with female peers' salaries may be another source of women's low pay expectations. Women may be more familiar with women colleagues' salaries via informal same-sex networks. If women colleagues also are underpaid, this comparison will not reveal the top of the scale for salaries at a similar rank. Furthermore, women's pay expectations have been shown in at least one study to depend upon whether a female or male comparison group was chosen. Women in high-prestige jobs were asked by Zanna, Crosby, and Lowenstein (1987) to indicate what they earned and to name what peers they used when making salary comparisons. Results indicated that women whose comparison group was predominantly men earned more than women whose comparison group was mixed-gender or predominantly women.

One's previous pay experience also has been shown to affect pay expectations. For instance, using undergraduate students, Desmarais and Curtis (1997) demonstrated that both women and men who had higher previous income levels for their most recent job paid themselves more for completing an experimental task than did others. These results suggest that the more one earns, the more one will expect to earn. Conversely, being lower on the pay scale, as is the case for most women faculty, is likely to reduce one's initial pay expectations.

How might women faculty raise their pay expectations, then, given that low salary expectations may be internalized? We propose four strategies. First, women need to seek comparative salary information quite assiduously; in other words, you need to "do your homework." Fortunately, doing research represents an important component of our training as academics. If you are a graduate student, start preparing for the job search by learning as much as you can about the salaries of faculty at your own and comparable institutions. If you are already in a faculty position at a public institution, regularly check on peers' salaries in the library. Research indicates that the wage gap between women and men faculty is largest at private, elite institutions, where it is also most difficult to obtain information about salaries (e.g., Szafran, 1984). Therefore, if you are at a private institution, you may have to rely on salary norms published annually in the *Chronicle of Higher Education* or talk about salary to peers at other universities or in similarly ranked departments at your institution. Evaluate where you stand in terms of these markers.

Second, seek multiple opinions concerning what is possible in salary negotiations as well as what is likely or usual. Do not trust any one person's opinion. The person with whom you typically negotiate (e.g., your department chair or dean) may not always be the most reliable source of information concerning what you deserve or what is possible. If he or she has offered your peers a higher entry-level salary or a larger raise, he or she may justify having given you a poor bargain by impugning your performance. Because it is widely believed that academe is a meritocracy, you also may regard a below-scale salary or raise as objectively reflecting poorer quality work on your part. Verify any information concerning your salary and performance using several independent sources. Develop a network outside of your department to corroborate opinions. Women's studies programs are often a critical source of comparative data for women faculty. It is important not to rely solely on departmental colleagues as your knowledge base because myths about what is possible sometimes get solidified within departments. For example, one of us was told by colleagues, including the department chair, that no raise was likely to accompany a promotion, but was able to obtain one when negotiating directly with the dean.

Third, develop connections that will help you raise your pay expectations and improve your negotiating skill. Seek out colleagues whom you trust who also have been effective at building their careers in ways you find commendable. A colleague who is a good strategist is one who is able to answer the question, "Under what conditions have exceptions to this rule, policy, or practice been made?" Conversely, a colleague who insists that "nothing can be done" to improve your salary or job conditions will not be that helpful to you. Select individuals who have high pay expectations for women, and be aware that even very high-achieving women sometimes underrate themselves or other women. For example, one of our colleagues, an extremely able woman negotiator who had recently achieved an objective very much desired by the university, also had received another job offer at a prestigious university. She was at a point where her current dean was going to make a counteroffer. She called a friend to discuss the salary figure that would be needed to keep her, one she perceived to be extremely high. Others had told her the amount was more than she could realistically expect to get. Her friend suggested that she raise her target by at least $5,000 based on what she knew men faculty more senior to but with less responsibility than the woman were earning, even though the figure sounded high to her, as well. The woman got the money she requested as well as many other concessions, and the university got her to stay. This example demonstrates that women faculty need to learn what is "outlandish" in terms of salary, due to internalized low pay expectations, as opposed to being truly beyond market price.

In summary, women faculty with low pay expectations may need to counteract them strongly by using several strategies to raise their aspirations. By educating yourself about faculty salaries, you will develop more confidence in what you might be able to achieve.

PLANNING A NEGOTIATION STRATEGY

Part of planning a specific negotiation strategy requires that you know your personal wants and professional needs, as well as how congruent these are with the mission of the institution you hope to join or are at already. This means that you should make an honest assessment of your skills, accomplishments, and potential. Every negotiator must be able to give something that is wanted by the other party. Faculty either must be able to do the job the institution perceives needs to be done, or must convince the other negotiator that the skills the faculty member offers are what the institution wants.

Your personal goals will help guide you in making choices about what to negotiate for and how to pursue an appropriate strategy. If you are at the job search stage, identify your personal preferences regarding the type of institution you hope to join. Teaching or research? Small or large? Geographic location? City size? Type of student body? In combination with a realistic assessment of your skills, accomplishments, and potential, the answers to these questions reveal a realistic indication of your power in negotiating during the hiring process. For example, limitations on moving due to personal or partner preference or family responsibilities will restrict one's personal job market. However, casting a narrow net and applying for positions in specific geographic regions mean that a woman will not get or be able to use another job offer to increase her bargaining power at her first-choice institution.

Assessing your situation differs to some extent for graduate students who are going on the job market versus established faculty. A tight academic job market exists in nearly every discipline. Many institutions replace retiring faculty with part-time or temporary hires, and tenure is under attack in many states. In addition to acquiring a thorough understanding of their discipline, graduate students must prepare early to position themselves as viable candidates. Job ads increasingly request some teaching experience and at least one research publication for even entry-level positions. Do your very best to get these while a student. Also make certain that you attend professional association meetings, present your research there, meet students and faculty at other institutions, investigate the employment exchange room, and volunteer to serve on a committee. Your goal in these activities is to begin to earn recognition for yourself and develop relationships that can provide valuable information and contacts. Be aware that as a woman you may need more credentials than a man to compete effectively for the same job.

Planning for tenured senior faculty also necessitates an assessment of how one's talents fit the institution's mission, how one is progressing toward promotion to full professor or toward other professional goals, and one's likely marketability. Because senior faculty cost more to hire, few jobs are advertised at the senior level, and the competition for them is quite stiff. The average tenured faculty may not have much chance of getting a job elsewhere, and this will limit her bargaining power with administrators. A woman's personal life (e.g., spouse employed, children in school) more so than a man's may be seen by administrators as reducing the likelihood that she would seriously consider leaving. Senior women who seek to negotiate a better contract at their current institution must confront the assumption that they will not really leave if their requests are not met. If you are tenured and not marketable or not planning on moving, one of the most effective ways to increase your salary is to assume administrative responsibilities (e.g., Lewis, 1975). On the other hand, if you are a highly successful scholar who wishes to promote her research career, seriously applying for jobs may help you to find a better one or to use a job offer at another institution to improve your current situation.

Knowing what to negotiate for is equally important. We emphasize base salary because salary is forever. However, there are numerous things you may need—not want, but need—to do the job the institution wants you to do. These will be discussed more fully in the next section on the negotiation process.

Thus, planning a negotiation strategy begins first with knowing what you want and need and knowing the institution with which you're dealing. Both require thoughtful consideration and extensive research before any initial offer is received or sought. Once you have identified your goals as described above, you are ready to move on to planning the actual negotiation strategy.

Planning the negotiation strategy itself requires that you carefully analyze the total situation and the goals on which you have decided in light of three tightly interrelated variables: power, information, and time (Cohen, 1980). It also is important to realize that a negotiation is a process, not a single event, that involves all three in concert.

Power

Power is defined as the capacity or ability to get things done; to influence others to think or do what you would like them to do; or to exercise control over people, events, situations, or oneself. The concept of power sometimes has a negative connotation to women, particularly the notion of having coercive power over someone. However, power also has many positive aspects that are important to keep in mind (e.g., power is required to implement one's goals and facilitate one's own and others' development). Several types of power that are relevant to negotiating will be discussed below, including self-confidence and persistence; expert power; and the power of investment, identification, and formal procedures. Self-confidence, or the perception of one's own power, will enhance your power in any negotiation. Granted, it is not easy to perceive yourself as personally powerful if you have been discriminated against, disregarded, or otherwise treated badly. The cumulative effect of a hostile environment cannot be ignored as a factor that affects the self-esteem and career confidence of women graduate students and faculty. If you feel demoralized or inadequate in your role as a professional, you may need to obtain a considerable amount of support in order to present yourself in a positive and self-confident manner. Women have reported finding this kind of support through role-playing, creative visualization, feminist support networks and professional organizations, and therapy. Presenting yourself in a positive way requires that you honestly appraise how you come across to others through a process of self-examination, seeking feedback from supportive others, and getting the help you need to build self-confidence.

A self-defeating self-presentation that has been observed among some women job candidates by one of the authors is when the candidate's first move is to enumerate her weakness for the current position. The most recent example of this strategy was used by a candidate who had numerous recent publications and a considerable amount of federal funding for her work. Early in her interview with various individual faculty, the candidate stated that she knew she hadn't published as much as she should have in the past few years. By framing her performance in a negative light, the candidate provided a "lens" for the review of her work that was to her detriment. It is a much better idea to focus on your strengths in any negotiation and leave the responsibility for finding your supposed weaknesses to the other side.

It is also wise in terms of projecting self-confidence to review your probable limitations for the position you are applying and consider ways they may be either deemphasized or turned into a source of power and strength. Do not leave it solely to your interviewers or colleagues to determine your contribution. You are a major player in influencing how your work is viewed. For instance, perhaps your publication record is not up to competitive standards in terms of quantity. It is important, then, to provide information about the high quality of your work, such as including rejection rates of journals in which you publish, the ranking of journals or presses in which your work appears, or citation counts or favorable reviews of your publications. Or perhaps you have published less because you do time-consuming field research instead of laboratory studies. You may want to point out that recent trends in your area indicate that field research is "the cutting edge." Always be prepared to educate your colleagues about your contribution. Few faculty have time to read much outside their own area, so it is important not to assume they know a lot more about what you're doing than what you tell them.

An aspect of power that is related to self-confidence is persistence. According to Cohen (1980), "Most people aren't persistent enough when negotiating" (p. 83). This may apply especially to women. For instance, some of the women faculty in Danner's (1996) research did not bargain because they were told that the offer they had been given was nonnegotiable. However, other research has shown that individuals who bargained for salary increases in response to a nonnegotiable offer generally obtained a higher final offer (Gerhart & Rynes, 1991). Persistence also refers to holding one's position over time. Be prepared to make a case on your own behalf more than once, perhaps even over a period of years. The "squeaky wheel" strategy works. Most people who may find it easy to say no once or even several times may find it difficult to do so continually and eventually may grant some concessions.

A second type of power that is highly valued in academe is expert power. Presumably, an outstanding or solid scholarly reputation will be justly rewarded by your institution. Expert power is likely to provide one of your strongest power bases; however, it does not automatically translate into better job conditions for women faculty, who often work harder and longer than men to get the salary and recognition they deserve for comparable work. For instance, Wenneras and Wold (1997) found that reviewers for postdoctoral fellowships in biomedicine in Sweden had consistently given female applicants lower scores than equally productive men. The researchers reported that, in some cases, the women applicants would have had to publish three extra papers in top-tiered journals or 20 extra papers in less prestigious journals to be ranked the same as the male applicants. Likewise, research on admissions to the National Academy of Sciences indicated that, on average, women were admitted nine years later than men, even though the research that led to their election did not appear to be done any later (Zuckerman & Cole, 1975).

With these caveats in mind, expert power as reflected by your competitive standing in the job market still provides one of the major bargaining points in an academic salary negotiation. Having other institutions interested in hiring you provides verification of your credentials. Although you are in the strongest position to negotiate when you have another job offer in hand, some faculty have used the job application process effectively to negotiate at earlier stages. For example, one woman, Jane, had received a job offer at one university and was deliberating over whether to accept it. In the meantime, she had been called for an interview by another institution. She used the second institution's interest in her to raise her counteroffer to the first school, and successfully negotiated a higher salary and better terms of employment than had been offered.

The investment that the institution and specific individuals have made in you is another source of power. In any hiring situation, the department and university will have spent a considerable amount of time and money to consider you for a position before offering you the job. After such an investment, most of the people running the job search may prefer not to start over with a new candidate and probably will try quite hard to meet reasonable requests (e.g., extend the deadline for considering the contract, provide additional resources). If you are a senior faculty member, administrators will be looking for evidence that they have gotten a good return on their investment from you before being willing to invest more. Develop ways to educate relevant administrators about what you have accomplished. For example, you might send a note to your department chair, dean, or chair of the funding committee about an article or book you wrote or got published during a leave or summer fellowship funded by your institution. Keeping a few key people informed of your successes also will make it easier to approach them later if you need allies when seeking a promotion, raise, grant, sabbatical, or whatever. The more familiar they are with your work, the more effectively they will be able to advocate for you.

Others' identification with you is yet another source of power that influences the negotiation process. This power base may be less available for women faculty to use than men with regard to superiors who also are likely to be male. Research indicates that women are often excluded from informal networks and protégée relationships in the professions (e.g., Clark

& Corcoran, 1986; Dreher & Cox, 1996; Zuckerman, Cole, & Bruer, 1991). Dreher and Cox (1996) have pointed out that individual characteristics such as race and gender are of considerable importance in understanding how existing opportunity structures work. Sexual orientation and class background might be added to this list, as well. Opportunity structures are influenced by these characteristics because influential decision makers (who are mostly White men) are more likely to form close relationships with individuals who are similar to themselves (other White men; Dreher & Cox, 1996). Thus, White men will have more access to and benefit more from relationships with powerful White men in academe than will White women, women or men of color, lesbians, women faculty from poor or working-class economic backgrounds, or someone with a combination of these identities (e.g., Gregory, 1995; Tokarczyk & Fay, 1993).

The way the power of identification with similar others may work to the detriment of women faculty may be illustrated with two actual case examples. The first case pertained to two women faculty hired by the same department in the same year, one White and one African American. The older White men in the department identified more strongly with the White woman than the African American woman, who intimidated them by her outspokenness. The White woman was labeled the "star" of the two, even though both had graduated from prestigious institutions and had similar records. The department chair gave the White woman her preferred courses to teach, which were in her research area and involved little course preparation. Against department policy, the African American woman was given an above-average course load and numerous new courses to prepare, none of which was in her research area. This problem was not corrected until higher administration became aware of it. Besides demonstrating race discrimination, this example shows that the identification of the White woman as "like us" worked in her favor, whereas the social distance between the African American woman and the White male faculty made it easier for them to disregard her concerns. In a second recent case, a department chair (a White man) went to the dean (also a White man) to advocate successfully for a higher salary for a younger White male faculty member with whom he played golf. The younger man said he needed a raise because his wife just had a baby. The department chair refused to advocate for a raise for the young man's similarly accomplished female colleague, who was the sole support of her husband and child at the time. In order to get a raise, she had to go onto the job market, obtain an invitation to interview, and bargain with the dean herself. It is reasonable to conclude that the older man's identification with the younger man's role as a provider played a part in his advocacy for the man, but was not a motivator in the woman's case.

Given that women faculty may have difficulty becoming "one of the boys," they may have to rely on power bases other than identification. Those who are ineligible for recruitment into the elite based on gender, race, sexual orientation, or class are in a position similar to that of a dissenting male scholar who has been judged not to fit in. According to Lewis (1975), such individuals will be left to make their own careers; it is only in this case that the rule of publish or perish will be operative. Otherwise, there is little evidence that one's publication record is tied to faculty rank or salaries (e.g., Doering, 1972, Lewis, 1975; Szafran, 1984). The four possible outcomes for the dissenting scholar, then, are:

> First, he [*sic*] may voluntarily leave the department. Second, if he fails to engage in any scholarly activity, he may be asked to leave, regardless of his skill in the classroom. Third, he may become an industrious scholar, put a minimum amount of effort into his teaching and other departmental responsibilities, and be harassed, or treated unfairly; eventually he may leave to maintain his self-respect. Fourth, he may become a productive scholar and a skilled teacher, and since his senior colleagues would be flagrantly violating academic norms by denying promotion or tenure, he can expect eventually to receive either or both. (p. 41)

Although it has been more than 20 years since Lewis (1975) described these outcomes, they describe the options for many women faculty today very well. They also suggest that, because they lack identification power with the gatekeepers, women would do well to enhance their expert power as much as possible to achieve the fourth outcome.

Formal procedures constitute a final power base for women that will be discussed here. At times, women faculty have been forced to use grievances and legal remedies to maintain their rights. Because of the emotional and financial cost of such actions, it is preferable to negotiate using other strategies, if possible. It also is best to forego using the threat of initiating a formal procedure when bargaining; to do so is likely to shut down the negotiation. However, to indicate that you are concerned about the "equity" or "fairness" of salary or contract decisions suggests that you see your rights as being violated and implies that you may pursue the matter further if not satisfied. Providing clear evidence of your performance in comparison with that of better paid male (or White) colleagues could demonstrate that you have a strong case for a grievance or other action.

Most savvy administrators will realize that it would be better to take care of your situation at this point, rather than later. Grievance panels in faculty-administration disputes at most universities tend toward compromise, so if you go to the effort to conduct a grievance, there is a good chance you will get something you request. Due to the high personal cost of this strategy and possible (illegal) retaliation, it is recommended only as a last resort. It also is wise, when pursuing this option, to seek legal advice.

Time

Most people tend to think of the time frame of a negotiation as that period in which the actual bargaining takes place. In fact, the negotiation often involves a much longer process. If you are looking for a job, you may already have laid a series of connections by using your network to locate openings or influence perceptions of your application. Once you are hired, you will have an ongoing relationship with many people with whom you will negotiate. This means that you and the other party may have considerable information about each other and a history with which you will have to contend. Your strategy should take this longer time line into account. You also will need to know or should learn the formal and informal deadlines for making requests, so as to time your actions appropriately. Asking for a raise after all the funds have been distributed is not likely to yield the outcome you desire and will make you appear naive. Keep in mind that you may need to develop a strategy that involves repeated contacts over several years to get your desired goals. Finally, recognize that time may require you to change your strategy, because circumstances change with time. Keep an open mind and be flexible.

Information

The information you gather before the formal negotiation itself will be crucial to the outcome you achieve. Most of the information you will need will have to be obtained by word of mouth from your network. Thus, the benefits of developing a university-wide and national network cannot be overestimated. Several types of information you will need to be a successful negotiator already have been described in the earlier discussion on pay expectations, including learning peers' salaries at your own and comparable institutions, what exceptions there have been, and under what circumstances they were granted. Two types of information that have been useful to the authors in addition to those described earlier include information about precedence and about the other party's or institution's needs. First, finding there has been a precedent for a specific action has helped a number of women known to one author to obtain maternity leaves or have the tenure clock stopped. In one instance, a woman was told by her department chair that because there was no official maternity leave policy, she would have to teach that semester. When the woman learned that someone else in another department had been granted an unofficial maternity leave by the chair, she went to the dean to negotiate a similar leave for herself. In another case, a woman who had two children in the years before the tenure decision (and no maternity leave) was given a negative tenure vote by her department. When she established that a precedent had been set for other women in some departments to stop the tenure clock during a maternity leave, she was able retroactively to receive a 2-year stop in the tenure clock. Two years later, she obtained tenure.

Second, having information about the other party's needs may be invaluable in a negotiation. For example, one woman colleague who was negotiating with a chancellor to retain funding for an endowed professorship had heard immediately prior to the meeting that the chancellor had endorsed a new research initiative for the university aimed at getting more federal funding. The woman was able to argue successfully with the chancellor to keep the endowed professorship funding at a high level based on the argument that cuts would make it difficult to attract faculty who had federal funding for the position, subsequently jeopardizing the chancellor's goals.

In summary, planning the negotiation requires that you identify your personal and professional goals and incorporate them into a strategy that uses your strongest power bases and the information you have gathered over a period of time to achieve your goals. In the next section, the tactics that can be used to implement your strategy will be explained.

THE NEGOTIATION PROCESS

The process of coming to agreement about salary and other terms of the academic contract often is correctly described as a game. Some tactics that may be used in playing the negotiating game will be described below using:

a. case studies,

b. examples of items that have been negotiated successfully by women faculty, and

c. a step-by-step description of the negotiation process.

CASE STUDIES

The two case studies that follow provide a more in-depth picture of how the actual bargaining session is conducted. The two cases chosen show how the process occurred for actual women faculty, one at the hiring stage of her career, and one negotiating for a raise at the senior level. In Case Study A, Susan was able to achieve a successful negotiation by using several strategies. First, because the offer was given late in the season, the timing of the negotiation was in her favor. Other job candidates for the position may have taken other offers, making her bargaining position more favorable. Second, the institution had already shown its willingness to make an investment in her, so it was only a small step for the dean to take to make increases in the investment in order to secure a top-ranked candidate. Third, the example illustrates that the dean was prepared to negotiate even though he described the offer as nonnegotiable. Finally, Susan's enthusiasm conveyed that she was likely to accept the position if her offer was met.

The situation for Ruth as a senior faculty in Case Study B was quite different. Ruth had a considerable amount of information about how the dean had operated in the past and what other faculty earned. She planned her raise strategy to correspond with a promotion and linked her request to a pay equity issue rather than using a strictly merit raise approach. Knowing that she had little support from the department chair, Ruth found another ally for her cause in the director of another program on campus of which she was a faculty member. Ruth also refused to let the chair's pessimism about an increase affect her target salary figure. The fact that the dean met twice with Ruth and once with both the chair and director about Ruth's salary may have worked in her favor by increasing the time investment the dean had made in her. Ruth was also able to convey the seriousness of her intent by mentioning her peer's salary grievance, thereby implying she might consider other avenues if her request was not met. However, throughout the negotiation, Ruth maintained an upbeat, professional attitude about herself and the university that seemed to be appreciated by the dean.

CASE STUDY A

Susan was offered a tenure-track assistant professor position following her interview at a nationally recognized PhD program. The dean told Susan that the $35,000 salary was at the high end of the range and that it, and the $500 moving expenses allowance, was nonnegotiable. She was given 10 days to think about it. Although she wanted the job very much and thought that the offer was a fair one, Susan's mentor encouraged her to make a counteroffer. He explained to her that it would cost her nothing, that the hiring institution had very few women faculty in the program, and that it was already mid-March. He also reminded her that she was a good candidate with some teaching and research experience. (During graduate school, Susan had worked on her mentor's grant, which had produced two minor coauthored publications, and had taught two introductory courses. Although ABD, she would finish the dissertation before starting the faculty job.)

Susan took her mentor's advice and, after 10 days, asked for a salary of $37,000 and moving expenses of $1,500. Also, for the first time, she requested specific computer hardware and software, graduate faculty status, and guaranteed summer teaching. In making the requests, Susan followed her mentor's advice and emphasized her experience, her research agenda, and her excitement at coming to the program and working with graduate students. The dean countered with a salary of $36,500 and moving expenses of $1,000, all the computer equipment requested, and graduate faculty status. He said Susan probably would be able to teach in the summer, but was unable to guarantee it. The dean was cordial throughout the negotiations and never reminded Susan that he had said earlier that his offer was not negotiable. Susan accepted the offer.

The two case studies demonstrate that each negotiation is unique and may involve quite different goals and tactics. No one formula may be applied to every negotiation.

Negotiable Items in an Academic Contract

Once you have identified your personal and professional goals, you must translate these into specific requests in the negotiation. Although base salary is the most important negotiation, there are many hidden expenses

CASE STUDY B

Ruth had been at her current institution for about 15 years and had just been promoted to full professor. As is typical in the case of many senior faculty, salary inversion had resulted in her salary being close to the level of that of many newly hired faculty. This occurs when merit raises for established faculty fail to keep pace with the salaries for new hires, which must be at market level in order to be competitive. Ruth's reputation as a feminist activist also had done little to endear her to the department chair. Thus, even though Ruth's publication record was similar to male peers, her salary had fallen well below theirs. Ruth planned to request a "salary adjustment" from the dean once she obtained final confirmation of her promotion. If she did not receive her requested increase, she planned to file a grievance.

Ruth first approached her chair with a list of faculty salaries (obtained from the library) for faculty at similar rank in the social sciences to demonstrate that a considerable increase would be required to bring her salary into line. Ruth named $58,000 as her target figure for the following year, an amount $2,000 over what her most immediate male peer would earn. The chair sent her to the dean to negotiate, but did not offer to accompany her. The dean said he would not discuss salary until the following month. Ruth made her points concerning her performance and the issue of equity anyway. She also gave the salary data to the director of another program on campus of which she was a faculty member, and asked that person to advocate for her as well. In the meantime, the chair told Ruth that she would "never get" the figure she had requested.

A month later, Ruth again met with the dean. She reviewed her performance, using her recent promotion to indicate that her work was nationally recognized. She also let the dean know that she was aware that a faculty grievance by a colleague who was less productive than herself had been settled in the colleague's favor. The dean offered to increase her salary over a 3-year period. Ruth had calculated an amount 3 years hence that would place her $2,000 ahead of her most immediate peer and named that as her target figure. Several offers and counteroffers were made, and Ruth accepted as the final offer a salary that would place her $1,000 above her target goal.

involved in living the academic life that may become part of the negotiation process. Other forms of financial compensation and personal satisfaction may come in the form of other benefits you may be able to negotiate. Ask yourself what you need from the institution in order to fulfill your professional goals, and then consider what you need to fulfill the institution's goals for you: Laboratory space? Few service requirements? Computer equipment? We have compiled a list of things below that you may be able to negotiate for in addition to base salary. The negotiation for these items should occur after you have been offered the job. Everything you request above the initial offer made to you should be justified in terms of getting the job done that the institution wants you to do. All of the items below were obtained by assistant professors in actual negotiations, though not all for the same job.

- Base salary increases (most important)
- Moving expenses
- Higher rank
- Office specifications (e.g., window, central location, size)
- Start-up money for research (e.g., cost of laboratory or equipment)
- Research space
- Graduate or undergraduate student assistants
- Summer supplements for teaching or research
- Computer equipment, including software and printer
- Conference and/or research travel expenses
- Reduced teaching load, at least during the first or second year
- Agreement to repeat courses annually to reduce number of new course preparations
- 2-day-per-week teaching schedule
- Reduced service expectations (but be cautious)
- Spousal or partner hire
- Time toward tenure reduced

If this is your first job, realistically appraise the contradictions inherent in the items above, especially those surrounding teaching and service. Although your institution may privilege solitary research, remember that first impressions matter. For example, new faculty who are frequently in the office are seen by faculty and students and able to develop relationships and reputations. Likewise, service on committees demonstrates one's competency and citizenship.

At the senior level, negotiations can be quite complex. If you are being considered for another job or have been offered another job and your current institution is eager to keep you, you may be able to bargain for a number of additional benefits that may be limited only by your creativity. Some actual benefits that have been obtained by various senior faculty in this situation are listed below:

- A considerable salary increase
- Promotion from associate to full professor
- Ample funding for start up of research program or laboratory
- Funds to build a program(s), including other faculty positions
- Postdoctoral fellow positions for research program
- Funding or fellowships for graduate students
- Funding for colloquium series
- Space for self and research staff
- Resources for journal editorship role
- New building or reconfiguration of current space
- Journal subscriptions or other library resources

Once you have decided on which possible items you might want, prioritize your list into two or three categories, including which items are essential to you, which are moderately important, and which are your "dream list." Now you are prepared to negotiate using the steps below.

Steps in the Negotiation Process

After you have done the preparation described in this chapter, you should be ready to proceed with implementing your strategy in the actual bargaining session. Below, we suggest some general rules and steps in the negotiation process, and we provide a cautionary note to accompany them. Every situation is different. You may break nearly every rule and still be very successful, although that would be the exceptional case. Perhaps the most important rules are to be reasonably flexible and most gracious. Flexibility demonstrates your interest in serving the institution as well as yourself. A professional attitude ensures that good feelings about you will persist despite the outcome. Academe is a very small community and one in which you need to maintain an excellent reputation. Unfortunately, many women (and men) encounter negotiators who are neither flexible nor gracious. In those cases, if you are in the hiring process, we suggest viewing this as an important insight into the nature of the administrator and institution and the likely conditions of work.

Set Goals

Set a high explicit goal for the negotiation based on your homework. Be sure this goal is high enough; do not underestimate yourself. The goal should be higher than the minimum you are prepared to accept.

Conduct the Negotiation in Person, if Possible

In the hiring process, telephone negotiations are common, but it is generally recommended that negotiations be conducted in person even if they involve more expense (Cohen, 1980). Face-to-face interactions are less likely to result in misunderstandings, are more informal, more collaborative, longer, and make it harder to say no. If the negotiation must take place over the telephone, you are in the best position if you plan the call carefully beforehand and are the caller, not the one called.

Let the Other Party Name the First Figure

The first dollar amount mentioned sets either the floor or the ceiling for future negotiations. In hiring situations, the institution sets a salary range for a particular position, and it behooves the candidate to find out what the range is early on. This should be done as discreetly as possible. Some shrewd negotiators may attempt to pressure the candidate to name "what it will take to get you here" during the interview process before even offering her the job, especially if they perceive the candidate to be uncomfortable with negotiating. Immediate agreement with your named salary is likely to indicate that the administrator was playing a game and has won. We have heard many stories like this. Indeed, one of the authors had this experience. She politely refused to name a figure by asking about the salary range and stated that she had not yet learned the local cost of living, tax structure, or other benefits. The administrator persisted in asking her. After four rounds of this, and clearly exasperated, he named the figure that was her actual expected salary. She feigned disappointment and stated that it was below her expectations.

Resist the pressure to name a figure first, particularly in a hiring situation where you may have little knowledge about the salary structure. Instead, wait to begin negotiations until you are offered a specific job at a stated salary. Then counter the offer with a higher one, a full justification for why you are worth the extra money, and other items you need in order to do your job. The only exception to this rule generally occurs among more senior job candidates or current faculty who know exactly what it will take to get or keep them, know that the institution has paid comparable wages to peers, can justify their worth, and are prepared to stand firm.

Remember That Almost Everything Is Negotiable

Nonnegotiable final offers, deadlines, and a host of other rules that have been legitimized by being put in writing or strongly asserted may nevertheless be negotiated under the "right" circumstances (Cohen, 1980; Nierenberg, 1981). For instance, one of the authors received a grant recently from her institution that specified in bold type that if the same proposal was funded elsewhere, the funds must be returned to the institution. When she received funding from another source, she casually mentioned to a colleague that she was going to return the first grant award. She then learned that it was possible to negotiate to keep funds from the first grant if she had a "good reason," despite the rule, and was successful in keeping part of the funding.

Be Self-Confident

Convey the message that you will not back down on your negotiation position. Be confident that you are worth what you are requesting. Flexibility should only come into play when the negotiation seems to require it in order to keep it moving. At this point, be certain that the institution offers the same degree of flexibility as it requests of you.

Use Persuasive Arguments

Use substantive arguments to persuade the other person to change her or his mind about an issue. For instance, perhaps you have not been the top-ranked faculty member in your department in terms of publications over the past few years, but you have consistently been publishing above the department mean for a number of years. You might argue that a greater-than-average raise is warranted in your case as recognition for "sustained superior contribution." Emphasize all the skills you bring to the institution.

Exchange Information

Get information about the other person's preferences on a specific issue, either by asking directly what issue is most important ("What consideration have you given to my 2 years of post-doctoral experience in your salary offer?" and "To what extent have you taken my record of federal funding into account?") or by indirectly judging the other's reactions to your offers.

Approach the Negotiation as a Win-Win Event

Assume that your gain will be beneficial to the other person, and, if possible, make this reasoning part of the negotiation process. For example, you might argue that it is advantageous for the university hiring you to pay you at the upper end of the assistant professor scale because you are already a seasoned teacher and researcher who will be able to pull her weight in the department immediately.

Trade Off Issues

Be prepared to trade off issues that are lower in value to you for issues that have higher value. For instance, it may be wise to negotiate for a reduced teaching load rather than a guaranteed summer teaching appointment to increase your income, in order to provide more time for research in your schedule. Likewise, a higher salary is preferable to a better computer when the extant one will do.

Pay Attention to Time

Two aspects of time are important. First, a new faculty's starting salary may well affect her for the rest of her career, especially once she is "tenured-in" or otherwise place-bound. Indeed, this may be the most opportune time of one's career to negotiate salary because new salaries frequently come from the university's budget line, whereas adjustments for current faculty often come from within departmental resources. In addition, the hiring institution may be willing to offer a good beginning salary in order to compete successfully with other universities. Moreover, recent graduates enter their first jobs with many positives; their graduate school success lies behind them and their potential before them. Current faculty have established and often complex reputations within their institutions and disciplines. Few people negotiate the terrain of academe, indeed of life itself, without ruffling a few feathers, including some that belong to influential administrators or scholars. Thus, current faculty may need to initiate salary negotiation in concert with some significant milestone, such as a promotion, a recent grant award or other type of scholarly recognition, and possibly even news of a salary grievance that has been settled in favor of someone in a position similar to yours.

Second, knowing the employer's timetable in a hiring situation and gracefully stretching it to its limits increases the institution's investment in a job candidate. Generally, faculty and administrators make job offers only to people they want and need, a decision they have come to following a lengthy and painstaking process that may not be completed until near the end of the academic year. Thus, ask for time to make your decisions regarding a job offer, and remember that even time can be negotiated.

In summary, successful negotiation requires that you utilize power, time, and information effectively within the context of the actual negotiating session, as described above.

CONCLUSION

It is important to realize that the effectiveness of your negotiation skill cannot be judged solely by the dollar outcome or additional benefits of the bargain you obtain. Women faculty experience serious salary inequities in academe, regardless of their performance. Research consistently indicates that discrimination is more severe at the later stages of women professors' careers than at the recruitment stage (i.e., recruitment equity is easier to obtain than rank or salary equity for women; Szafran, 1984). These findings suggest that women faculty have their best chance to achieve equity during the hiring process and should carefully plan their negotiation strategy before the job search. They also indicate that senior women will be required to do some hard negotiating at later stages of their careers if they hope to reduce the gender salary gap by a significant amount. In other words, negotiation may not necessarily result in a "win" with you earning more than others; it may just keep you from falling as far behind as you might.

The positive aspects of negotiation for women extend far beyond the actual outcome of the deal, and it is these we wish to emphasize in this chapter. By accepting responsibility for what you can do to advance yourself, you are likely to feel more self-confident and satisfied with your job, as well as obtain better outcomes for yourself. In addition, self-blame is likely to be reduced by the realization that your negotiating skill alone may not be sufficient to counteract sex discrimination. Finally, as women faculty become more aware that, as a group, they are disadvantaged in the salary process, we hope there will be a collaborative response to improve the situation for women as a whole on their campuses. One strategy is for women faculty to conduct their own faculty salary study. Lois Haignere successfully implemented such a strategy with 29 New York state universities using a procedure described in *Pay Checks: A Guide to Achieving Salary Equity in Higher Education*. The result was a $2 million settlement for women and minority faculty. Similar individual and collective efforts to challenge pay inequity eventually should strengthen women's position at the negotiating table.

REFERENCES

Ayres, I. (1991). Fair driving: Gender and race discrimination in retail car negotiations. *Harvard Law Review, 104*, 817-872.

Bacharach, S. B., & Lawler, E. J. (1981). *Bargaining*. San Francisco: Jossey-Bass.

Benjamin, L. (Ed.). (1997). *Black women in the academy: Promises and perils*. Gainesville: University of Florida Press.

Bylsma, W. H., & Major, B. (1992). Two routes to eliminating gender differences in personal entitlement. *Psychology of Women Quarterly, 16*, 193-200.

Caplan, P. (1993). *Lifting a ton of feathers: A woman's guide to surviving in the academic world*. Toronto: University of Toronto Press.

Chamberlain, N. W. (1955). *A general theory of economic progress*. New York: Harper.

Clark, S. M., & Corcoran, M. (1986). Perspectives on the professional socialization of women faculty: A case of accumulative disadvantage? *Journal of Higher Education, 57*, 20-43.

Cohen, H. (1980). *You can negotiate anything*. New York: Bantam Books.

Danner, Mona J. E. (1996). *Gender and the process of negotiating the academic contract*. Unpublished research.

Desmarais, S., & Curtis, J. (1997). Gender and perceived pay entitlement: Testing for effects of experience with income. *Journal of Personality and Social Psychology, 72*, 141-150.

Doering, R. (1972). Publish or perish: Book productivity and academic rank at twenty-six elite universities. *American Sociologist, 7*, 11-13.

Dreher, G. F., & Cox, T. H., Jr. (1996). Race, gender, and opportunity: A study of compensation attainment and the establishment of mentoring relationships. *Journal of Applied Psychology, 81*, 287-308.

Frost, P. J., & Taylor, M. S. (1996). *Rhythms of academic life*. Thousand Oaks, CA: Sage.

Gerhart, B., & Rynes, S. (1991). Determinants and consequences of salary negotiations by graduating male and female MBAs. *Journal of Applied Psychology, 76*, 256-262.

Gregory, S. T. (1995). *Black women in the academy: The secrets to success*. Lanham, MD: University Press of America.

Haignere, L. (1996). *Pay checks: A guide to achieving salary equity in higher education.* Albany, NY: United University Professions, Local 2190.

Heiberger, M., & Vick, J. M. (1996). *The academic job search handbook* (2nd ed.). Philadelphia: University of Pennsylvania Press.

Jackson, L. A., Gardner, P. D., & Sullivan, L. A. (1992). Explaining gender differences in self-pay expectations: Social comparison standards and perceptions of fair pay. *Journal of Applied Psychology, 77,* 651-663.

Kaman, B. D., & Hartel, C. E. J. (1990, August). *Anticipating pay negotiation strategies and pay outcomes during recruitment: An exploration of gender differences.* Paper presented at the annual meeting of the Academy of Management, San Francisco.

Karrass, C. L. (1992). *The negotiating game.* New York: HarperBusiness.

Lewis, L. (1975). *Scaling the ivory tower.* Baltimore: Johns Hopkins University Press.

Major, B. (1994). From disadvantage to deserving: Comparisons, justifications and the psychology of entitlement. In M. P. Zanna (Ed.), *Advances in experimental social psychology* (Vol. 26, pp. 293-355). New York: Academic Press.

Major, B., & Konar, E. (1984). An investigation of sex differences in pay expectations and their possible causes. *Academy of Management Journal, 27,* 777-792.

Major, B., McFarlin, D., & Gagnon, D. (1984). Overworked and underpaid: On the nature of gender differences in personal entitlement. *Journal of Personality and Social Psychology, 47,* 1399-1412.

Major, B., Vanderslice, B., & McFarlin, D. B. (1984). Effects of pay expected on pay received: The confirmatory nature of initial expectations. *Journal of Applied Social Psychology, 14,* 399-412.

Mannix, E. A., Thompson, L. L., & Bazerman, M. H. (1989). Negotiation in small groups. *Journal of Applied Psychology, 74,* 508-517.

NCES (National Center for Education Statistics). (1993). *Salaries of full-time instructional faculty on 9- and 10- month contracts in institutions of higher education, 1982-83 through 1992-93.* Washington, DC: U.S. Department of Education.

NCES (National Center for Education Statistics). (1996). *Salaries of full-time instructional faculty 1994-1995.* Washington, DC: U.S. Department of Education.

Neu, J., Graham, J., & Gilly, M. (1988). The influence of gender on behaviors and outcomes in a retail buyer-seller negotiation simulation. *Journal of Retailing, 64,* 427-451.

Nierenberg, G. I. (1981). *The art of negotiating.* New York: Pocket Books.

Renard, M. K. (1992). *Salary negotiations and the male-female wage gap.* Unpublished doctoral dissertation, University of Maryland.

Rose, S. (Ed.). (1986). *Career guide for women scholars.* New York: Springer.

Rosen, B., & Jerdee, T. H. (1978). Perceived sex differences in managerially relevant characteristics. *Sex Roles, 4,* 837-843.

Rynes, S. L., Rosen, B., & Mahoney, T. A. (1985). Evaluating comparable worth: Three perspectives. *Business Horizons, 28,* 82-86.

Sax, L., Astin, A. W., Arrendondo, M., & Korn, W. S. (1996). *The American college teacher: National norms for the 1995-96 HERI Faculty Survey.* Los Angeles, CA: Higher Education Research Institute.

Stevens, C. K., Bavetta, A. G., & Gist, M. E. (1993). Gender differences in the acquisition of salary negotiation skills: The role of goals, self-efficacy, and perceived control. *Journal of Applied Psychology, 78,* 723-735.

Szafran, R. F. (1984). *Universities and women faculty: Why some organizations discriminate more than others.* New York: Praeger.

Tierney, W. G., & Bensimon, E. M. (1996). *Promotion and tenure: Community and socialization in academe.* Albany: State University of New York Press.

Tokarczyk, M. M., & Fay, E. A. (Eds.). (1993). *Working class women in the academy: Laborers in the knowledge factory*. Amherst: University of Massachusetts Press.

Weingart, L., Hyder, E. B., & Prietula, M. J. (1996). Knowledge matters: The effect of tactical descriptions on negotiation behavior and outcome. *Journal of Personality and Social Psychology, 70*, 1205-1217.

Wenneras, C., & Wold, A. (1997, May 22). Nepotism and sexism in peer-review. *Nature, 387*(6631), 341-343.

Zanna, M. P., Crosby, F., & Lowenstein, G. (1987). Male reference groups and discontent among female professionals. In B. Gutek & L. Larwood (Eds.), *Women's career development* (pp. 28-41). Newbury Park, CA: Sage.

Zuckerman, H., & Cole, J. R. (1975). Women in American science. *Minerva, 13*, 82-102.

Zuckerman, H., Cole, J. R., & Bruer, J. T. (Eds.). (1991). *The outer circle: Women in the scientific community*. New York: Norton.

Part III

Assuming Leadership
in Higher Education

Women as Faculty Leaders

Joan C. Chrisler
Linda Herr
Nelly K. Murstein

Higher education has had a long-standing and rather romantic ideal of the university as a community of scholars who devise their own curriculum, set their own policies, and in all other ways govern themselves (Williams, Gore, Broches, & Lostoski, 1987). Political and socioeconomic changes, the proliferation of "professional" staff, increasingly powerful governing boards, and increasingly interested state legislatures have eroded the traditional ideal of faculty as "a community of self-governing scholars" (Williams et al., 1987, p. 630). Most institutions today hold as their ideal a model of "shared governance" that requires active participation by representative groups of faculty in committees that devise and implement educational and other institutional policies (Williams et al., 1987). The model of shared governance is described in the 1966 Statement on Government of Colleges and Universities, which was written and adopted by members of the American Association of University Professors (AAUP), the American Council on Education (ACE), and the Association of Governing Boards of Universities and Colleges (AGB). The statement delineates which areas of policy and decision making are primarily the responsibility of the faculty, the administration, and the governing board, and it urges that decisions be made in a spirit of respectful consultation of all parties concerned.

The importance of shared governance to the smooth running of our institutions of higher education suggests that it should be a major part of the socialization of new faculty. Yet handbooks for new faculty and their mentors (e.g., Boice, 1992; Schoenfeld & Magnan, 1992; Tierney & Bensimon, 1996; Zanna & Darley, 1987) have little to say about faculty governance other than to warn junior faculty not to do too much service because it interferes with scholarly productivity. "Service" is a catch-all term that is understood to mean faculty governance, involvement in the affairs of professional associations, department business, student advising, and local activities off-campus (e.g., talks to community groups); in other words, service is anything faculty do that is not teaching or research. Although most tenure and promotion committees are charged to examine the triangle of faculty activity (i.e., teaching, scholarship, and service), it is clear to almost everyone that service is the triangle's weakest leg.

If faculty lose interest in serving on campuswide committees, then the ideal of shared governance will be lost. More and more decisions will be turned over to professional staff and administrators. The faculty will lose its traditional control over the curriculum, subject matter, methods of instruction, faculty status, the requirements for and awarding of degrees, and aspects of student life that relate to the educational process (AAUP, 1995). If junior faculty wait until after they are tenured to involve themselves in faculty governance, they fail to develop the track record that earns them the opportunity to be perceived as faculty leaders. Furthermore, shared governance requires representative groups of faculty; that means not only diversity of scholarly disciplines, but diversity in age, gender, ethnicity, faculty status, and so on. Any missing segment of the whole diminishes the strength of the faculty's voice in the governance process.

WOMEN AND CAMPUS SERVICE

There is no doubt that over the years, men have wielded more power and influence in campus governance than have women (Twale & Shannon, 1996a). Early studies of faculty activity showed that although both sexes were equally interested in and willing to serve on faculty committees (Muller, 1978), male professors were actually much more involved in the governance structure than their female colleagues (Baldridge, Curtis, Ecker, & Ripley, 1978; Hollon & Gemmill, 1976; Muller, 1978). Women perceived themselves as less involved in decision making on campus (Denton & Zeytinoglu, 1993; Hollon & Gemmill, 1976), and, as a result, they were less satisfied with their current positions than were their male colleagues (Hollon & Gemmill, 1976).

More recent studies have documented an increase in the participation of women in campus service. McElrath (1992) surveyed 250 faculty in departments of criminology, criminal justice, and sociology and found no significant differences in committee membership between the sexes. In a study of faculty at Ball State University, Kite and Balogh (1997) found that women and men were perceived to be equally active in campus service. It is important to note that McElrath did not consider the nature (only the number) of committees on which her respondents participated, and the Kite and Balogh survey examined perceptions rather than reality.

Two major national surveys of faculty activities purported to show an even rosier picture. A 1988 survey by the U.S. Department of Education found that women faculty devote a larger percentage of their time to campus service than do their male colleagues. Furthermore, women were found to be more likely than men to volunteer their time for committee work and other service (U. S. Department of Education, 1991). In analyzing the results of their 1989 survey, the Carnegie Foundation for the Advancement of Teaching (Carnegie Foundation, 1990) discovered that women were more involved than men in the day-to-day governance of their campuses. Only at the full professor rank did women and men do equal amounts of committee work. In a smaller but more recent survey of arts and sciences faculty at Purdue University, Blakemore, Switzer, DiLorio, and Fairchild (1997) found that tenured women were the faculty who do the most campus service. Their respondents grumbled about men who were not doing their share; they believed that they were repeatedly elected or appointed to committees because they take committee work seriously.

Does this apparent increase in women's service activity translate into greater power and influence in university governance structures? We caution against that conclusion. First, some of the surveys asked about "service participation." As we noted earlier, service is a loosely defined term that has been applied to committee work as well as to a variety of other activities, including academic and club advising, personal counseling of students, and attendance at (or organization of) departmental social or cocurricular activities. A number of researchers have concluded that women faculty are more likely than their male colleagues to advise and otherwise interact with students outside the classroom (e.g., Astin, Korn, & Lewis, 1991; Bernard, 1983; Park, 1996; Thomas, Spencer, & Sako, 1983). These activities are valuable, but they should not be confused with involvement in the campus governance structure. Second, some of the researchers were concerned only with the number of committee assignments the respondents had. Thus, their data tell us nothing about whether the committees were departmental, divisional, collegewide, or university-wide; whether the members of the committees were elected or appointed; whether the respondents were committee members or committee chairs; whether the tasks of the committees were central to the governance structure (i.e., policy-making or implementing) or peripheral (e.g., approving student-designed majors or hearing appeals of parking violations).

Gender stereotypes can and do influence which faculty are appointed to or nominated for committees. Ernst (1982) noted a tendency for faculty from the English department (especially women) to serve on library committees, faculty from the mathematics department and business school (especially men) to serve on budget committees, and faculty from the engineering department (especially men) to serve on facilities committees. Search committees for presidents and provosts (Ernst, 1982) and faculty confronted with a nomination ballot for the budget committee often share a bias that women lack budgetary experience or interest.

Twale and Shannon (1996a) found that the women in their survey reported more committee service than the men, but they were less likely than the men to chair important committees. There was a gender difference in the types of committees to which women and men were elected or appointed with high frequency. Women were more likely to be elected to admissions, curriculum and program design, and faculty search committees. Men were more likely to be elected to grievance, promotion and tenure, advisory, strategic planning, and policy committees. Women tended to be appointed to committees on the library, graduation, traffic appeals, teaching awards, sexual harassment, and "Greek life"; men were appointed to academic honesty, grievance, educational policy, academic and admissions standards committees, and the faculty senate. Women were more likely to chair committees on sexual harassment, affirmative action, curriculum, and admissions, whereas men chaired promotion and tenure, academic standards, personnel review, and research and administrative policy committees. The authors (Twale & Shannon, 1996b) noted a similar gender difference in faculty activities in professional organizations. Women reported more service on nominating, membership, awards, and graduate student committees, whereas men reported more service on leadership, policy, and assessment committees.

We examined a list of the Spring 1997 members of the "big six" committees on our campus, all of which are elected by the faculty. Women constitute approximately 40% of our faculty, and they made up 33% of the members of the Faculty Steering and Conference Committee (FSCC)—our most important policy-making committee. Women accounted for 56% of the membership of our educational planning committee, 40% of our curriculum committee, 40% of our promotion and tenure committee, 27% of our budget committee, and 14% of our grievance committee. Only one of these committees was chaired by a woman—the promotion and tenure committee, which selects its own chair. The three committees whose chairs are elected by the faculty at large were all chaired by men. Gender balance was not much better on most of the committees whose members are appointed by the FSCC. We were surprised to discover that all faculty on the information services (technology) committee and the continuing education committee were men, whereas all faculty on the committee on academic standing were women.

Twale and Shannon (1996a) also noted that faculty status affected the type of service their respondents reported. Untenured faculty were more likely to serve on departmental and college committees. Tenured faculty were more likely to serve on university committees. This pattern is undoubtedly influenced by name recognition and length of time at the institution. The Carnegie Foundation (1990) found that, in general, faculty became increasingly active in governance processes the longer they were at the institution. However, the pattern may also be influenced by the type of work others think best suits untenured women.

Tierney and Bensimon (1996) interviewed 54 department chairs and deans and 202 assistant professors at 12 colleges and universities of various sizes and types. When they spoke to untenured women about the type of service they did, they found it to consist in large measure of what they described as "mom work," that is, nurturing and caretaking functions. The women were assigned such tasks as editing the department newsletter, serving as pre-med advisor or advisor to student clubs, and organizing student-faculty social activities. The pressure to do mom work was greatest in small private colleges where the dependence on tuition revenues leads to considerable pressure for faculty to be popular with students and their parents. The pressure to be popular may be greater for female faculty than for their male colleagues, and, of course, women who do mom work at home are thought to be well suited to doing it on campus.

Department chairs can wield considerable power and influence, especially in colleges and universities that have strong departmental cultures, but there is no evidence that the number of women department chairs is approaching parity. Handbooks for department chairs (e.g., Gmelch & Miskin, 1995; Tucker, 1993) have little to say about gender issues. Index entries about women and gender concern how to recruit and retain female faculty and how to deal with sexual harassment complaints. The authors seem to assume their readers will be men.

Turk (1981) noted that women chairs were increasing most in traditionally female disciplines and in new interdisciplinary departments and programs. We examined the Spring 1997 list of department chairs at our college and found that 41% were women. The majority of them chaired departments in the humanities and social sciences that were traditionally (or have recently become) of particular interest to women students, such as languages, art history, child development, education, dance, anthropology, sociology, and psychology. No women chaired departments in mathematics or the natural sciences; nor did any women chair departments with large numbers of male majors (e.g., government, history, economics). Four women (40%) chaired interdisciplinary programs, but three of these were also chairs of regular departments. Only one woman (17%) was serving as an academic dean or associate dean; she was the Dean of Freshmen. These results are disappointing in an institution such as ours, a former women's college with a history of strong women presidents and deans and, until a recent wave of retirements, an unusually high number of tenured women full professors.

WHAT MAKES A GOOD LEADER?

A leader is a person who can motivate a group of people to attain a common goal (Brehm & Kassin, 1996). Good leadership is based on social influence, which can be acquired through such various means as winning supporters, solving problems, building coalitions, stirring emotions, negotiating deals, mending fences, or by virtue of one's position in the organization (Brehm

& Kassin, 1996). Leadership that is based on one's position, such as department chair, is called assigned (or legitimate) leadership (Northouse, 1997). Individuals who are perceived by others as influential members of a group, regardless of their official position, are known as emergent leaders (Northouse, 1997). Emergent leaders often become assigned leaders.

Personality Characteristics

Early psychosocial research on leadership took what has become known as the trait approach. It was originally known as the "great man" theory because the researchers focused on trying to understand how the personal characteristics of individual leaders (all of whom were men, of course) contributed to their success. It was believed that leaders were born, not made; that only those "great" people who possessed these characteristics from birth would emerge as leaders (Northouse, 1997). Although most contemporary researchers believe that leadership is more situationally based and interpersonally interactive and that it can be developed, there is no doubt that personality traits are also influential.

Northouse (1997) has examined dozens of trait studies, and he concluded that five traits occur most frequently in the findings and thus seem most central to the definition of leadership ability. These traits are intelligence; self-confidence (includes self-esteem and the belief that one can make a difference); determination (includes initiative and persistence); integrity (includes responsibility, honesty, and trustworthiness); and sociability (includes friendliness, tact, and concern about others). None of these traits is the exclusive province of one sex or the other, although some have argued that women's gender-role socialization makes it more likely that women will excel at sociability. Regan and Brooks (1995) believe that women's traditional sensitivity to others and concern about others' welfare leads to the development of leadership styles based on cooperation, collaboration, and caring; they call this style "relational leadership."

When we first began work on this chapter, we sat down together to make a list of qualities that we thought were important in determining faculty leaders. All of the above traits were on our list, but we found ourselves focusing primarily on the integrity cluster. We believe that these traits are especially important to faculty who are voting for colleagues who will represent the faculty's views (e.g., faculty senate, department chairs); advise the administration on policy matters; or determine faculty status (e.g., tenure and promotion or grievance committees). Faculty are most likely to be selected by their peers for these duties if they have reputations for being candid, judicious, trustworthy, assertive, fair, loyal, principled, and willing to accept responsibility for their actions. Faculty with integrity inspire confidence in their colleagues as well as in administrators, who may not always agree with them but respect them nonetheless.

We then had an amusing and ego-enhancing conversation in which we recounted instances of having noticed these traits and behaviors in each other and other women leaders on campus. We decided that it was important to tell other women when we noticed their leadership ability (e.g., "I admire your persistence in getting that done," "Congratulations on speaking up at the faculty meeting; you made an important point"). This, we believe, will help to encourage them to display their abilities again and to begin to think of themselves as potential leaders. This type of encouragement may be especially important to young, untenured women.

Situational Behavior

Leadership, by definition, takes place in a group; therefore, the situation in which the group finds itself and the patterns of interactions among the group members affect who is perceived as an emerging leader. Groups usually gather to communicate or to accomplish a task. Both communication behaviors and task-related behaviors contribute to leadership.

Communication behaviors exhibited by emerging leaders include verbal involvement, seeking the opinions of others, suggesting ideas, being well-informed about the issues, and being firm but not rigid (Fisher, 1974). Social psychologists (e.g., Mullen, 1991) have found that people who speak most often in groups are perceived to be the groups' leaders. We cannot emphasize enough how important it is to speak up during meetings. Professors like to talk, and it can be difficult for new or junior members of a group to get a word in edgewise, but women who want to develop their leadership abilities will have to learn to interrupt or speak quickly when opportunities arise. We realize that taking our advice may mean overcoming cultural and/or gender role messages about one's place in the public sphere; speaking up may be uncomfortable, but it is necessary. Here are some strategies to try: suggest a plan or a time line, ask other quiet people what they think, summarize the discussion, comment on others' comments (e.g., "What a great idea!" or "I agree with X."). People too new in the group to feel comfortable stating their opinions can always ask questions, second motions, suggest taking a break when others look tired, or move for adjournment (Chrisler, 1995).

Fiedler (1967) noticed that there are two types of leaders: task-oriented (almost single-mindedly focused on getting the job done) and relations-oriented (concerned about good working relationships and group morale). Both types of leaders are important, and large groups may need more than one of each type. In high-stress situations such as a looming deadline, task-oriented leaders tend to be more effective, whereas in ambiguous situations or long-term assignments, relations-oriented leaders may be more successful (Brehm & Kassin, 1996). Although we believe that people have preferences for one style or the other, we do think it is possible to shift from one role to the other. A flexible leader is alert to group dynamics and can see what the group needs. If there's no clear task-oriented leader, women can assume that role by reminding the group of what remains to be done, suggesting a way to divide up the tasks, encouraging the group to set deadlines, and gently but firmly returning the group to the task at hand when they drift off on tangents. If there's no clear relations-oriented leader, women can assume that role by thanking people for their work, complimenting them on their ideas or initiative, ensuring that everyone gets a chance to speak, bringing a snack to the meeting, making a joke if things get tense, encouraging teamwork, and making sure that credit is appropriately shared when the task is done.

Other behaviors that emerging leaders display are showing up at committee meetings (keeping absences to an absolute minimum and letting the chair know the reasons), reliably and responsibly carrying out assignments, volunteering only for tasks whose deadlines they think they can meet, practicing teamwork, being tactful, accepting challenges, acting self-confident (regardless of whether they are self-confident), and generously acknowledging the work of others. Emerging leaders take the initiative to suggest new projects or procedures, but they don't try to change too many things at once. The successful completion of one assignment often leads to the invitation to take on another. Emerging leaders say yes as often as possible.

Gender Stereotypes and Leadership Perception

Lingering stereotypes that portray men as leaders and women as followers still affect women's opportunities to become faculty leaders; many people feel uneasy in the presence of women leaders, although they may not come right out and say so. In a classic study (Porter, Geis, Cooper, & Newman, 1985), participants were shown photographs of same-sex or mixed-sex groups seated around a table and asked to identify the groups' leaders. In cases of same-sex groups, the participants chose the person at the head of the table as the probable leader. In mixed-sex groups, the head-of-the-table bias occurred only when men were seated there. In another important study (Butler & Geis, 1990), the researchers observed through a one-way mirror participants in a discussion group with trained confedeartes. Male and female confederates who were assigned to play assertive roles were equally likely to be perceived by the participants as leaders. However, the researchers noted that the participants smiled and nodded more often in response to male leaders; they frowned more often when female leaders were speaking. These subtle but certain differences in approval are probably familiar to many women leaders.

Gender stereotypes of women as communal or relational and men as agentic or instrumental may affect the types of opportunities faculty are given to participate in committee work and governance activities. As we saw earlier, women are more likely to be asked to do mom work and to be elected or appointed to committees that deal with student concerns, social issues, or routine matters, whereas men are more likely to be on committees that deal with policy making or implementation, faculty status, or grievances. Furthermore, women faculty, especially untenured women and women of color, often find themselves appointed to committees for balance; that is, someone decided to add a woman, a minority, or a junior person to a search committee to make it more representative. These situations can be problems or opportunities. It is a problem in cases where there are too few of a particular type of faculty (this is often so for women of color), so the same people are tapped again and again for committees or task forces.[1] If the committees are always unimportant or the woman's status too marginalized for her to make a contribution, then these assignments are taking her away from scholarship, teaching preparation, or more important service, and she will have to find a comfortable way to refuse at least sometimes. (We believe that women leaders should watch out for these situations and try to stop the exploitation of more vulnerable women.) However, every committee—no matter how small or relatively unimportant—can be seen as an opportunity for women to gain experience, polish their leadership skills, and meet and impress people who might later vote for them for a leadership position. Potential faculty leaders, perhaps especially women, need to build a track record of quality service to the institution.

If members of a group do not expect women to exhibit leadership, they may not pay much attention to what women say. Most of the women reading this chapter have probably had the experience of making a suggestion to a group, getting no reaction, and later hearing a man make the same suggestion, which the group then discusses avidly. This is a common situation, and one that is difficult to handle. To let it go is disempowering. To say "Yes, I agree it's a good idea; that's why I suggested it 15 minutes ago" may result in being perceived as obnoxious (although Joan still recommends it!). Sometimes, a similar phenomenon occurs after a meeting or event when people do not remember who said what. Women's ideas or witticisms may be attributed to men, or quiet people's to those who were more talkative. In both cases, we believe that it is important for women to watch out for other women. A firm statement, such as "That wasn't Pete's idea; it was Pam's," can be an effective correction, and it prevents Pam from being forced to speak up for herself.

In a recent series of experiments on how stereotypes affect judgments, Biernet and Kobrynowicz (1997) found that people set lower minimum competency standards but higher ability standards for women than for men and for Blacks than for Whites. This means that it is easier for low-status than for high-status groups to meet minimum standards but harder for them to prove that their performance is based on their abilities. These results are both interesting and disturbing. They help to explain why women (especially women of color) can be seen as good enough for some kinds of tasks, yet, despite their various successes, not good enough for leadership positions.

We have seen this phenomenon in action when faculty are deciding how to mark their nomination ballots for the "big six" committees. Both women and men are quick to dismiss their women colleagues ("Oh, she won't want to do it," "She doesn't have enough experience yet," "She's difficult to work with"), whereas men who are equally difficult or inexperienced are cheerfully nominated. We have seen men nominate or vote for other men who seem to us to be clearly unsuited to the jobs because "the experience will be good for him." Never have we seen women be so easy on other women, not even those of us who want to see more women in leadership positions. Why do women judge each other more harshly than men seem to judge other men? Do we hold women to higher standards of competence? Are we quicker to criticize women because we know each other better and are more familiar with our flaws? Whatever the cause, we end up with a small group of "electable women" who get nominated again and again because they are seen as likely to win. Other women don't get the chance to try, and the electable women are overworked.

WHY SHOULD WOMEN BECOME FACULTY LEADERS?

There are many reasons why women should assume positions as faculty leaders. The reasons range from principled approaches to the common good to more individual reasons, such as career or personal development. All are important.

We began this chapter by discussing the tradition of shared governance in colleges and universities and the key role that faculty play. It worries us that younger faculty are repeatedly advised to shy away from service because the rewards are elsewhere. If everyone follows this advice, soon there will be no one willing to do the faculty's business or able to be the faculty's voice. Untenured faculty should take care not to become over-committed, but we don't think that one committee assignment (outside the department) per year is too much. After one or two peripheral committees, try to move into committees that are central to faculty governance. These are usually the elected committees, but check your faculty handbook to be sure. If it's hard to tell which committees are the important ones, ask someone who is an active faculty leader.

Remember that the Statement on Government of Colleges and Universities (AAUP, 1995) requires representative groups of faculty. If the same people are elected again and again, faculty governance is not representative. If the same type of people (e.g., men, senior faculty) dominate the committees, then the interests, needs, and opinions of the unrepresented groups (e.g., women, untenured faculty) may never be heeded or addressed. If someone tells you not to run for an important committee until after you're tenured, seek a second (and third and fourth) opinion.

The status of women students, faculty, and administrators is unlikely to change for the better if there are no women leaders on campus to push a women's agenda. It's essential, for example, for the health of the women's studies program to have women on the budget and curriculum committees.

Feminist scholars undergoing evaluation can feel more sure of a fair hearing if there are women on the tenure and promotion committee who understand the value of women's studies and appreciate new forms of scholarship. For the same reason, women are needed on committees that evaluate faculty for sabbatical requests, travel funds, merit pay, or internal grants for research or curriculum development. Women are needed on the grievance committee to hear complaints about sex discrimination or harassment and on high-level search committees to be sure that some women candidates make the short list. There are countless (and often unpredictable) opportunities for women leaders to make a contribution to women's general welfare on campus, but they have to be at the decision-making locus.

If women want to become faculty leaders, they have to remain on campus long enough to become electable, that is, they have to become tenured. Remember the three legs of the triangle? The center of the triangle is "collegiality," and the networking and reputation faculty develop through committee work help to demonstrate this important trait. It is also good to know people outside the home department, especially if things aren't going well or there's no mentor inside the department. Friends developed through committee work can provide advice, social support, and information, especially the kind one wouldn't want to ask one's department chair. Most tenure files allow candidates to include letters from on-campus colleagues not in the home department, and the faculty leaders met through committee work are exactly the type of people to approach for such letters. They can comment on the candidate's talents, abilities, and contributions to governance work, as well as suggest how valuable future contributions might be.

Women who think they might like to become administrators at some point in their careers can gain valuable experience by participating in a wide variety of campus committees. Committee activities can teach faculty how the university runs, how policies are made, how budgets are constructed, how to get things done, how to work with others effectively, how to negotiate, how to write reports, and so on. These are the skills and knowledge search committees rank high.

Finally, researchers (Carnegie Foundation, 1990; Hollon & Gemmill, 1976) have found that faculty who are more involved in campus committees are more satisfied with their jobs, are less likely to consider leaving for another position, report that they have a greater sense of community, and

201

feel more empowered. They believe that they have an opportunity to influence policy and participate in decision making—and they do!

Nelly's Story

I must begin by stating that I am a "foreigner." I came to the United States in 1949 with a French baccalaureat, which is to say that I was already formed by a different culture when I arrived in Texas to begin my studies at Rice University. I knew that I wanted to teach, but I really did not understand the American university system. I didn't even know that classes start in September, and when I arrived in October, I learned that I had to wait a year to enroll.

After receiving my PhD I attended my first professional meeting. At the MLA presidential address, I learned that professors of foreign languages and literatures did not have a strong voice in universities because they didn't understand "the system" and were not well integrated into the academic community. Right then and there, I decided that I would be different. I decided to welcome (and did) every opportunity to serve on faculty committees. In the beginning, of course, these committees were small ones and not threatening to me.

My first real challenge came when, as a young associate professor, I was asked to chair the Department of French and Italian at Connecticut College. I was terrified. I feared I could not do it, but I forced myself to accept. In my first year as Chair, I reorganized the structure of the department in order to share with my colleagues the various tasks and responsibilities, rather than doing it all myself as previous Chairs had done. I was also able to spend time rethinking the curriculum and to implement many of my ideas. It was a most rewarding experience, and since then, I have chaired the department several times.

The experience I've just described has become a pattern for me. Every time I have been elected or appointed to an important committee (e.g., Faculty Steering and Conference Committee once, tenure and promotion committee twice), fear of not understanding the system was my first reaction. Then, I think of that address at the MLA and remind myself that as an "electable woman," I owe it to myself and others to overcome my fears. Each time, I end up accepting and finding it a worthwhile experience.

Recently, I was asked to chair a faculty hearing committee on a matter that was crucial to a colleague's career. My anxiety was such that I lost five pounds in a week! All this is to say that even at age 65, more than 30 years after taking up that first challenge, I still have to fight the same battle, and always come out stronger for doing so.

I accepted my first leadership positions so that foreign language faculty would have a stronger voice in college governance. Then, having become sensitized to women's issues, I have continued to lead as a woman for other women. Working for causes has given me the strength and the support I needed to surmount my fears. Now, as I approach the end of my career, I realize that although I have always been oriented toward working for others, the greatest beneficiary has been myself.

Linda's Story

During the 21 years that I have worked at Connecticut College, I have managed to do a good deal of service. In fact, when, in preparation for this chapter, I sat down to list my committee and administrative work, I was surprised. I found I'd done a lot more than I'd realized. I have chaired the Department of Theater for 20 years: 18 as Chair and two as Cochair. I have served as Acting Director of the Gender and Women's Studies Program and Acting Chair of the Department of Dance. I have been elected twice to the Faculty Steering and Conference Committee, which I chaired for 2 years, and twice to the budget committee, which I chaired for a year. I have chaired a major administrative search committee and served on the grievance committee, a strategic planning team, and a variety of smaller committees. I have also served as director or codirector of several major arts events on campus, including a celebration of the Eugene O'Neill Centennial and a celebration of New London, Connecticut's 350th birthday.

The ethics and importance of service were very different when I first arrived at Connecticut College. Service was considered to be extremely important for tenure, and I also knew that my participation in the governance structure would help to improve the position of the Department of Theater. Therefore, I accepted every opportunity that came my way, and I learned a great deal about how the campus worked and how to get things accomplished. I am amazed, when I think back, to realize that, although I was a feminist, I was not at all aware of the importance of being a woman leader or of helping other women to achieve leadership positions. Opportunities came to me—notice that I view them as opportunities, not simply as onerous requests for service—but I did not translate these opportunities into ways of opening doors for other women to learn leadership skills. These notions came to me much later, but once the idea of using my positions to help other women achieve their leadership goals took root, I attempted to mentor and support others as much as possible.

I now believe that the women of my generation must dedicate ourselves to mentoring and talking openly about our experiences to our younger colleagues. I am proud of my participation in our women's studies telephone tree, which we are using to change the profile of women's leadership on our campus. Sticking one's neck out is risky, of course, as I have learned the hard way, but I have no regrets. There's no change without risk, so take a chance. You may be surprised at what you can accomplish.

Joan's Story

I have worked at Connecticut College for 11 years, during which time I have been elected twice to the grievance committee and twice to the Faculty Steering and Conference Committee (FSCC), which I chaired for 1 year. I have served as Chair of the Department of Psychology and as Associate Dean of the Faculty. I had several early appointed positions: as faculty teller for one year, as the untenured "token" on a strategic planning team, and as a member of the affirmative action committee (which never met!).

I believe that I was able to move from the minor committees to the major committees so quickly because I knew a lot of people on campus. I had two senior faculty friends who made it a point to introduce me to others, and I became active almost immediately with the women's studies program, where I met feminists from all over campus. Although I don't tend to talk a lot in groups, I have never been shy about expressing my opinions on the issues of the day, and I soon had a reputation for my candor.

As Associate Dean, I was the only woman on the staff of the Provost/Dean of the Faculty. At our weekly meetings, the others would look to me to deal with anything that concerned "out-groups": women's issues, multiculturalism, gay and lesbian rights, affirmative action. I was often annoyed that my presence provided an excuse for the others to avoid these matters, but I felt my responsibility keenly, and I never missed an opportunity to speak up. As a member of the FSCC, I made sure that our committee appointments were gender-balanced, supported the women's studies program, tried to prevent the disenfranchisement of underrepresented groups of faculty, and, as Chair, served as a role model for younger women faculty and students. These, I believe, have been my major contributions thus far.[2]

HOW TO BECOME A FACULTY LEADER

To increase the number of women faculty leaders, we will have to take both individual actions and group actions. First, we'll discuss individual actions that should be taken by women who want to move into leadership positions.

Networking is very important, and the larger the faculty, the more important it is. Women have to find ways to connect with colleagues across the campus. We know that this can be difficult for new faculty, especially for those in their first tenure track job, but no matter how busy they are, they must make time to get to know people. They should take a lunch break daily and go to the faculty dining room, attend social events from time to time, and volunteer for activities that give them the opportunity to meet new colleagues.

It is important to cultivate a reputation as an independent thinker who is not afraid to express opinions. This can be done in casual conversation over lunch or at meetings of committees or one's department. Faculty are always interested in intelligent, clear-thinking, assertive, honest individuals, and when they find such people, they tend to tell others about them. Potential faculty leaders should always vote their conscience, be discreet, and learn to separate the personal from the professional. Ad hominem (or feminam!) remarks are never appropriate.

Remember that one cannot make intelligent comments if one doesn't understand the issues. Women who want to become leaders should keep well informed, ask questions of others in order to get the details and the history of the situation, and only then make suggestions. Future leaders should make sure to attend as many open meetings as possible in order to hear members of the faculty senate or its committees report out on current issues and policy development.

It is not necessary to wait until one is elected to a committee to demonstrate leadership ability. Faculty who have good ideas can often implement them outside committee and departmental structures. For example, Nelly decided that the faculty in the foreign language departments ought to meet from time to time to discuss curricular issues, teaching strategies, and other common concerns. She called the first meeting, which went so well that the group decided to continue to meet. Nelly also has a long-standing interest in the fine arts. When the college canceled its summer arts festival, she called a colleague with similar interests and suggested that they get a group together to brainstorm about new arts activities that might help to replace the one that was canceled. In acting on her concerns, Nelly also showed her organizational ability, creativity, and initiative.

Leaders need to be familiar with Robert's Rules of Order. Those who are not should obtain a copy and read through it. It's very frustrating to be caught in a parliamentary maneuver one doesn't understand and be kept from making one's point. Faculty who are less familiar with Robert's Rules respect those who know the ins and outs.

Finally, women must be willing to accept appointments and/or assignments in areas in which they haven't had much experience (Ernst, 1982). It's important to do things, even if one isn't sure how. There's always someone who can explain it, so accept the challenge and learn. The more experience we get, the more opportunities we'll have.

Senior women who want to encourage more women to participate in faculty governance must be prepared to nominate other women and, when possible, appoint them to committees. We ought to reach out to new faculty and pull them into our network. We need to be alert for signs of leadership ability in our colleagues and encourage them to step forward. We have to stop being so hard on other women when we consider their qualifications. There are no perfect candidates; the important thing is to place women in situations where they can learn and develop their skills. Never let a nomination ballot drop unmarked into your wastebasket, and remember that it is okay to campaign for yourself. If you'd like to be nominated for a committee, tell people. They may be happy to hear it.

Department chairs can play an important role in educating new faculty about the campus governance structure. Explaining the importance of service, as well as what the committees do and how they interact with each other, is an important part of mentoring. Faculty colleagues who are serving on important committees could be asked to give brief reports at department meetings. This would serve to illustrate the value of participation in governance activities and to educate everyone about what is currently being discussed.

We believe that group action is necessary in order to prevent talented women from being stymied by the gender stereotypes we discussed earlier. Feminist faculty may have to organize themselves into a phone or e-mail tree in order to be effective in voting as a block. A few years ago, the women's studies faculty on our campus got disgusted with how few women were on the ballots for the "big six" committees, and we decided to take action. If one of our group decides she would like to run for a committee, she notifies the Director of Gender and Women's Studies, who puts out a voice mail message to us all. She says something like, "The nominations ballot for the budget committee is in your mail. Professor X is willing to serve. Please keep that in mind when you mark your ballots." Most people throw out their nomination ballots unmarked. If they know someone wants to run, they are usually willing to nominate her. Everyone we've done this for has made it onto the election ballot. When an election ballot arrives with women's names on it, the director sends a message like this: "The ballot for the budget committee is in your mail. I'd like to draw your attention to the fact that Professors X and Y are running." We keep the messages low key so as not to pressure anyone, but we've probably increased the number of ballots returned and we've seen how effective women can be when we vote together!

We hope you'll try some of our suggestions or find your own ways to increase the number of women faculty leaders on your campus. When women use all of their talents, everybody wins.

NOTES

1. If you find yourself too much in demand, you will have to learn when to accept and when to reject requests to serve on committees. Committees with high visibility (such as major search committees or task forces appointed by the president or provost) or committees that are central to the campus governance structure will usually be more important to accept than those that are more peripheral. It is always possible to resign from a less important committee in order to accept a more important committee or to balance a committee that meets frequently with one that meets rarely. Remember that you do not have to answer immediately when you are asked to serve or stand for nomination. Say, "May I get back to you on this? I need to think about how it fits with my other responsibilities." Then ask for advice from your department chair, mentor, or any woman campus leader. Try to avoid the mistake made by a colleague of ours who turned down a request from the President to serve on a short-term, major search committee near the end of the academic year because she was already on a minor committee whose work was winding down.

2. See Dawson (1997) and Green (1997) for career accounts and advice from successful women administrators.

REFERENCES

AAUP (American Association of University Professors). (1995). Statement on government of colleges and universities. In *Policy documents and reports* (pp. 179-185). Washington, DC: Author.

Astin, A. W., Korn, W. S., & Lewis, L. S. (1991). *The American college teacher: National norms for the 1989-90 HERI faculty survey.* Los Angeles: UCLA Higher Education Research Institute.

Baldridge, J., Curtis, D., Ecker, G., & Ripley, G. (1978). *Policy making and effective leadership.* San Francisco: Jossey-Bass.

Bernard, J. (1983). Benchmark for the 1980s. In M. L. Spencer, M. Kehoe, & K. Speece (Eds.), *Handbook for women scholars: Strategies for success* (pp. 69-79). San Francisco: Americas Behavioral Research Corp.

Biernet, M., & Kobrynowicz, D. (1997). Gender- and race-based standards of competence: Lower minimum standards but higher ability standards for devalued groups. *Journal of Personality and Social Psychology, 72,* 544-557.

Blakemore, J. E. O., Switzer, J. Y., DiLorio, J. A., & Fairchild, D. L. (1997). Exploring the campus climate for women faculty. In N. V. Benokraitis (Ed.), *Subtle sexism: Current practice and prospects for change* (pp. 54-71). Thousand Oaks, CA: Sage.

Boice, R. (1992). *The new faculty member: Supporting and fostering professional development.* San Francisco: Jossey-Bass.

Brehm, S. S., & Kassin, S. M. (1996). *Social psychology* (3rd ed.). Boston: Houghton Mifflin.

Butler, D., & Geis, F. L. (1990). Nonverbal affect responses to male and female leaders: Implications for leadership evaluations. *Journal of Personality and Social Psychology, 58,* 48-59.

Carnegie Foundation. (1990, Sept./Oct.). Women faculty excel as campus citizens. *Change,* pp. 39-43.

Chrisler, J. C. (1995). *Desperately seeking succor: How to manage if you haven't got a mentor.* Unpublished manuscript.

Dawson, M. E. (1997). Climbing the administrative ladder in the academy: An experiential case history. In L. Benjamin (Ed.), *Black women in the academy: Promises and perils* (pp. 189-200). Gainesville: University of Florida Press.

Denton, M., & Zeytinoglu, I. U. (1993). Perceived participation in decision-making in a university setting: The impact of gender. *Industrial and Labor Relations Review, 46,* 320-331.

Ernst, R. J. (1982). Women in higher education leadership positions: It doesn't happen by accident. *Journal of the College and University Personnel Association, 33*(2), 19-22.

Fiedler, F. E. (1967). *A theory of leadership effectiveness.* New York: McGraw-Hill.

Fisher, B. A. (1974). *Small group decision making: Communication and the group process.* New York: McGraw-Hill.

Gmelch, W. H., & Miskin, V. D. (1995). *Chairing an academic department.* Thousand Oaks, CA: Sage.

Green, P. S. (1997). Rites of passage and rights of way: A woman administrator's experiences. In L. Benjamin (Ed.), *Black women in the academy: Promises and perils* (pp. 147-157). Gainesville: University of Florida Press.

Hollon, C. J., & Gemmill, G. R. (1976). A comparison of female and male professors on participation in decision making, job related tension, job involvement, and job satisfaction. *Educational Administration Quarterly, 12,* 80-93.

Kite, M. E., & Balogh, D. W. (1997). Warming trends: Improving the chilly campus climate. In N. V. Benokraitis (Ed.), *Subtle sexism: Current practice and prospects for change* (pp. 264-278). Thousand Oaks, CA: Sage.

McElrath, K. (1992). Gender, career disruption, and academic rewards. *Journal of Higher Education, 63,* 269-281.

Mullen, B. (1991). Group composition, salience, and cognitive representations: The phenomenology of being in a group. *Journal of Experimental Social Psychology, 27,* 297-323.

Muller, J. K. (1978). Interest and involvement of women in university governance. *Journal of the National Association for Women Deans, Administrators, and Counselors, 42*(1), 10-15.

Northouse, P. G. (1997). *Leadership: Theory and practice*. Thousand Oaks, CA: Sage.

Park, S. M. (1996). Research, teaching, and service: Why shouldn't women's work count? *Journal of Higher Education, 67,* 46-84.

Porter, N., Geis, F. L., Cooper, E., & Newman, E. (1985). Androgyny and leadership in mixed-sex groups. *Journal of Personality and Social Psychology, 49,* 808-823.

Regan, H. B., & Brooks, G. H. (1995). *Out of women's experience: Creating relational leadership*. Thousand Oaks, CA: Corwin Press.

Schoenfeld, A. C., & Magnan, R. (1992). *Mentor in a manual: Climbing the academic ladder to tenure*. Madison, WI: Magna Publications.

Thomas, S., Spencer, M. L., & Sako, M. (1983). Conversations with minority women scholars. In M. L. Spencer, M. Kehoe, & K. Speece (Eds.), *Handbook for women scholars: Strategies for success* (pp. 41-59). San Francisco: Americas Behavioral Research Corp.

Tierney, W. G., & Bensimon, E. M. (1996). *Promotion and tenure: Community and socialization in academe*. Albany: State University of New York Press.

Tucker, A. (1993). *Chairing the academic department: Leadership among peers* (3rd ed.). Phoenix, AZ: Oryx Press.

Turk, T. G. (1981). Women faculty in higher education: Academic administration and governance in a state university system, 1966-1977. *Pacific Sociological Review, 24,* 212-236.

Twale, D. J., & Shannon, D. M. (1996a). Gender differences among faculty in campus governance: Nature of involvement, satisfaction, and power. *Initiatives, 57*(4), 11-19.

Twale, D. J., & Shannon, D. M. (1996b). Professional service involvement of leadership faculty: An assessment of gender, role, and satisfaction. *Sex Roles, 34,* 117-126.

U.S. Department of Education. (1991). *Profiles of faculty in higher education institutions, 1988*. Washington, DC: National Center for Education Statistics.

Williams, D., Gore, W., Broches, C., & Lostoski, C. (1987). One faculty's perception of its governance role. *Journal of Higher Education, 58,* 629-657.

Zanna, M. P., & Darley, J. M. (1987). *The compleat academic: A practical guide for the beginning social scientist*. New York: Random House.

Women Administrators in Higher Education

Mary K. Madsen

The number of women administrators in higher education falls far short of the proportion of women on university faculties. More women are desperately needed in the administrative ranks to ensure that the needs of women students, staff, and faculty are adequately addressed. Do you have what it takes to become a dean, vice president, provost, president, or chancellor? Here are some tips on how to prepare yourself for the challenge of administrative work.

Academic administrators must understand the missions of the institutions they serve. Because colleges and universities nurture scholarship through service, teaching, and research, women administrators must themselves be curious scholars. They must be people of vision who follow world, national, regional, state, and local trends, movements, and forces. They must be voracious readers, ponderers, examiners, screeners, and critics of vast amounts of information. Women who want to move up must exhibit a keen interest in the entire university community. They must learn as much as they can, yet avoid clogging their minds with minutiae. It is more effective and efficient to learn where to locate some types of information than to try to learn and store in one's memory ever-changing or infrequently needed details.

Membership in networks is essential. If a good woman's network does not exist on your campus, start one. If the men accept women into their networks, wise women gladly join. Networks give people access to significant information and to opportunities for career advancement. Loners rarely advance through the administrative ranks in academe.

Management and leadership are not exercises in a vacuum. Successful leaders learn who the movers and shakers are on their campuses. A college or university is an organization, and, like other types of organizations, the productivity of its employees ranges from those who excel to those who just putt along. A woman who seeks to move up must align herself with the doers, both to get things accomplished and to be identified as a doer by others inside and outside the institution.

A sense of humor is imperative for survival in a milieu as highly charged as most campuses. People who cannot relieve pressure by stepping outside a tense situation and finding some humor in it are likely to be perceived as cold and lacking vitality. Interpersonal relationships are strengthened when people who work together see the comic as well as the serious aspects of events. A sense of humor is an indication of balance in one's personality. To recognize and respond to funny situations reflects a sense of joy in one's work.

Women administrators need to develop a cooperative spirit, which will, in turn, enhance their ability to compromise when necessary. Although some people find this difficult, it is important if one wishes to be viewed as willing to listen to the ideas of others, work on teams, and accept credit for accomplishments through group membership. Women who seek to move up through the administrative ranks must respect people at every level of the university. If they turn off people at any level of the system, they can seriously jeopardize their ability to be effective. Maintenance people, deans, secretaries, faculty, vice presidents, and bus drivers are all valuable human resources who deserve respect. A woman should carefully select her battles, and always be as positive and constructive as possible. Administrators must be able to say forthrightly what they think and assertively what they want. Neither shyness nor aggression will open doors.

Women must master math skills; math anxiety is not befitting an administrator. A woman who desires an administrative post must understand budgeting—budget control, regulations, restrictions, and development. Women who do not have adequate knowledge of financial management can teach themselves, enroll in formal courses, or seek on-the-job training. Women faculty who think they might be interested in moving into administration should try to get elected to the budget committee and seek other faculty positions (e.g., department chair) that provide the opportunity to work with budgets.

Other skills needed by administrators include time management, public speaking, research, and writing. There are seminars and books on these topics easily available to help sharpen one's skills. Women who want to become administrators should seek opportunities to write and to give talks, both to practice their skills and to bring their ideas to the attention of those who might nominate them for administrative positions.

Mentors may be the single most important factor in an academic administrator's career development. Mentors can suggest strategies for career mobility, and they are often the best and toughest critics of their protégées. Mentors are people who can open doors, initiate contacts, and make recommendations for new professionals. Female mentors in academic administration are scarce and precious; you might have to look for them on campuses other than your own. They are important, however, because they can offer first-hand advice about handling the often sensitive situations unique to women. An aspiring professional should not sit and wait for a mentor to find her; she must actively seek out and cultivate appropriate mentors.

People who make strides in any career usually have high energy levels. This can be achieved by careful monitoring of one's health, proper exercise, a nutritious diet, and sufficient rest. Regular medical examinations are also important. A woman on the move in her career is also physically on the go and at risk of developing a stress-related illness known as burnout. One of the best ways to avoid this condition is to allow time for relaxation and leisure. Workaholics may pay a terrible price for eliminating leisure from their lives.

Professional women interested in both career mobility and family life will find it necessary to employ a reasonable birth control strategy. Careers and families are not mutually exclusive, but rare is the successful career woman who can also manage a large family. A cooperative spouse or partner who understands the ebbs and flows of career pressures makes the most desirable mate.

Although the 1970s and 1980s were not very encouraging times for women in higher education administration, change is firmly under way in the 1990s, and I'm eager to see what the 21st century will bring. I wonder who among my readers will be leading the way. Could it be you?

Strategy Notes for the Equity Struggle: Women Academics in a Canadian Context

Clare Porac

I have been an academic for 22 years, and currently, I am one of 23 women at the rank of professor at my university. Since 1990, I have been involved in the implementation of employment equity programs, which are the Canadian equivalents to affirmative action initiatives in universities in the United States. I have chaired the Faculty Association Status of Women Committee, served four terms on the Faculty Association Executive Committee, and served three terms on the Steering Committee of the Faculty Women's Caucus. During the 1990 to 1996 period, my university increased the percentage of tenure track women faculty from 19% to 28%. Gender parity has been achieved at the assistant professor rank (54% women faculty), but the percentages of women at the associate (28%) and professorial (9%) ranks indicate that only a few women successfully achieve Professor status.

The women mentors of newly appointed women faculty share the opinion that the current academic system can be a revolving door for women academics. During the same 1990 to 1996 period, my university experienced a highly publicized departmental incident involving male and female colleagues that resulted in two of the three women faculty in the department at the time requesting reassignment to another academic unit. Three women in the same faculty have left the university for other reasons, and two of these have abandoned academic careers.

Carolyn Heilbrun (1990), in her writings about women faculty members and universities, says,

> Having taken the young women to its institutional bosom, it wishes to confine the energies it found so attractive to the already designated duties of a girlfriend or coed, or eventually of a consort. Where the university must change is in allowing the energy of women to be exercised fully and to its own ends. (p. 263)

When mentoring newly appointed women faculty, I encourage them to maintain their exuberant intellectual energies while simultaneously acculturating them to a male-dominated institutional culture, a culture that values conformity and is resistant to new ideas. Given the paradoxical nature of this task, I am not surprised when some young women faculty give up the struggle and leave academic life or when women faculty mentors suffer burnout and retreat back to a safe life of scholarship and institutional passivity.

My cautionary advice is simple. Along with the development of effective scholarly and teaching skills, women faculty must attend to their career management. Ideally, you should start the untenured years by opening a chronological file labeled "ME." This file should contain documentation of all conversations and correspondence with department/university administrators or evaluation committee members about your career progress. Beware of the Chair (Head) who practices the "fireside chat technique," or the informal, seemingly spontaneous office drop-in to discuss your teaching performance or scholarly activities. When these situations are encountered, write a follow-up memo to confirm what was said during the visit. The memo should give a summary of the conversation and end with a statement such as, "If you disagree with the above summary, please let me know and we can meet again to discuss our differing views. Otherwise, if I do not hear from you, I will assume that you agree with the substance of these comments."

Many women faculty resist implementing such a practice; they often view it as confrontational, legalistic, and likely to provoke a negative reaction from their colleagues. Newly appointed women faculty members are still likely to have been mentored by men during their graduate training, and they assume that the congenial, often older, usually male Chair (Head) is similar to their graduate advisor. However, congeniality is not to be interpreted as professional collegiality. You have moved, as Carolyn Heilbrun contends, from coed to colleague-competitor status, and the kindly, career-established, male colleague may not be motivated by benign intent. Particular caution is warranted in departments where women faculty are a numerical minority or where male faculty members believe that the department has been "forced to hire women" and to engage in "reverse discrimination." Rapid turnover in administrative positions also makes caution necessary. Undocumented verbal agreements made with one Chair (Head) upon hiring may not be honored by a different Chair (Head) when your tenure decision is made 5 or 6 years later.

Make it clear to colleagues that you prefer a formal, documented approach to discussions of your career progress. Women faculty who have taken this advice sometimes find that colleagues act with surprise, a reaction that, in and of itself, could be a warning signal for extra vigilance. However, conscientious administrators appreciate the opportunity to provide a "paper trail" because they know that written documentation is a valuable asset in career progress matters. Careful and regular documentation of performance expectations results in unambiguous communication about evaluation criteria, and you can avoid problems that arise from conflicting interpretations of informal discussions that occurred in years past.

I advised a woman faculty member who had received notice that her promotion decision was negative. Fortunately, there were enough procedural irregularities in the decision-making process to predict a successful outcome upon appeal. My questions about a written record of past conversations with her Chair concerning her performance produced a common response, "I didn't think it was necessary at the time." After I tried to reassure her about the likelihood of a successful appeal, she said, "But why does it [promotion] have to be so hard?" I cannot answer this question; all I know is that it often is.

REFERENCE

Heilbrun, C. (1990). *Hamlet's mother and other women*. New York: Ballantine.

8 Breaking the (Plexi-)Glass Ceiling in Higher Education

Kathryn Quina
Maureen Cotter
Kim Romenesko

The term "glass ceiling" has been used to capture the almost universal experience of middle-management women in U.S. corporations and government who, after finally climbing onto the career advancement ladder, now find the executive levels closed to them. Women now comprise nearly 50% of the labor force but are clustered at the lowest levels of salary and position, with a clear male dominance in almost any hierarchy one reviews. For example, a 1991 survey by the U.S. Department of Labor (DOL) of *Fortune* 1000 corporation employees found that although women held nearly 40% of the jobs, and minority group members held 15%, only 17% and 6% of all supervisors were women or minorities, respectively; fewer than 7% and 3%, respectively, held senior executive positions. This difference cannot explained by education, length of service, or other factors (DOL, 1991).

This glass ceiling effect can be observed at every rung up the academic career ladder. Nationally, women now constitute more than 52% of all college students, but less than one third of the faculty. Only about 10% of full professorships, the highest academic rank, are held by women; among

215

these, African American women hold less than 1% (Wechsler, 1995). A large 1984 survey found that only 10% of college presidents were women; 1.3% are African American women, and percentages for other ethnic minority groups were negligible. The few women deans were clustered in nursing, education, continuing education, and home economics, and were rare in business, engineering, law, and medicine. Greater proportions of women—about one third—were found among other administrative positions, such as registrars, librarians, and student affairs personnel, but the authors also noted that these areas do not have the same upward career tracks as academic administrative posts, where women held less than 15% of the positions (Tinsley, Secor, & Kaplan, 1984).

The invisible nature of the barriers has led to the label "glass ceiling"—it is, after all, illegal to deny anyone a promotion because they have brown skin, speak with a "foreign" accent, move about in a wheelchair, or have two X chromosomes. However, other construction materials may better fit the analogy. For example, the ceiling's resistance in the face of so many competent women hammering from the underside is more like layered Plexiglas®. Past efforts to break the glass by sheer force of numbers have not been very successful. Therefore, it is time to consider other options. Plexiglas, after all, is sometimes more easily broken by bending it (a lot), sawing a window through it, or drilling it full of holes. Better yet, replacing it with a flexible screen would allow fresh air to flow throughout the system!

Furthermore, our experience has been that the barriers that have led to the glass ceiling are actually quite visible to those experiencing them, especially those who are underneath it doing the hammering. In fact, the barriers are invisible only to those who choose not to look. Thus, our Plexiglas ceiling is also opaque. In this chapter, we will argue that what is necessary for change is a more comprehensive and aggressive approach to assessment of the reasons for the ceiling, along with equally comprehensive and aggressive actions to make the ceiling visible to those who are not looking, for they have the power to remove it.

Any examination of the Plexiglas ceiling effect in academia must recognize that career paths for higher education faculty, academic staff, and administrators are different from those in business and industry. Unlike industry, public universities are large organizations whose records are open to scrutiny because of state and federal legislation and funding. Thus, they may be ideal models for testing assessment models and intervention approaches.

The Plexiglass ceiling may also be experienced differently within each major category found in a university (clerical staff, professional and academic staff, faculty, and administration). Our work revealed an array of definitions of power and career goals within and between these categories. It is important to recognize that in academia, a PhD is a prerequisite to advancement to the positions with the most power. Thus, top-level advancement is, realistically, available only through faculty lines. Although we ultimately want to dissolve the ceiling, this problem isn't only about breaking through the top. Ceilings are only a problem after one has been able to rise off the "sticky floor" (hired but unable to move further up) and break down the "glass walls" (moved up but in a limited area; Kelly, 1993).

There are highly skilled professionals in nonfaculty positions, such as academic staff, who will not advance to a faculty or top administrative position because the hierarchy doesn't include that path, but they could move from, say, an advisor to a mid-management role. We have tried to set up this discussion to appreciate and accommodate this breadth of interest while remaining focused on our ultimate goal of advancing women to positions of real power in academia.

This chapter draws from two studies conducted by the authors:

1. an extensive review of the status of girls and women as students, faculty, staff, and administrators in the Rhode Island education system, carried out for the RI Advisory Commission on Women (Quina, Cotter, & Adler, 1992); and

2. an intensive case study of a large midwestern public university, including data collected for, and gathered from, 90 participants in a working seminar titled "Breaking the Glass Ceiling in Higher Education," funded by the DOL Chicago Women's Bureau (Quina & Romenesko, 1993).

Each set of data demonstrates that 20 years after Title IX legislated sex equity in education, there are significant areas where one can safely say that little has changed. Many of the gender opportunity differences we observed have direct implications for long-term development as a top-level executive or scholar. Selected examples are presented here to underscore our conclusions about the contemporary barriers for women.

EXPLAINING THE GLASS CEILING EFFECT

There are three kinds of explanations in the literature for the glass ceiling effect: personal, situational, and societal. A person-centered explanation,

217

popular in psychology and business, focuses on characteristics of women (e.g., women do not have enough management experience, femininity is incompatible with leadership, women fear success). In fact, research data tend not to support this explanation: Women managers do as well as men on various measures (Astin & Leland, 1991). Furthermore, women have been changing and preparing themselves for decades, learning how to be assertive and dress for success, yet the ceiling remains solid.

A societal approach, in contrast, focuses on the biggest picture, often the socialization of men and women as dominant and submissive, or corporations as too masculine and women employees as too feminine (e.g., Miner & Longino, 1987). Although these roles are evident and affect the work setting enormously, to focus on societal issues sets us up for differences and defeat because they can be changed only through widespread social change, which is beyond the scope of any single person or group.

Although both of these types of explanations have some merit, the bulk of the research literature supports an institutional explanatory model, which suggests that formal and informal institutional policies and practices differentially affect women and minorities (Riger & Galligan, 1980). Focusing on institutional strategies has further merits. First, problems perceived to be "personal issues," such as family-work stress, can be solved through institutional approaches such as providing appropriate day care. Societally based attitudes may not be changed, but the problems they create can be mitigated (or their impact reduced) by enforcing behavioral changes such as curbing derogatory language or requiring more objective, open decision making.

Institutional barriers to promotion were identified by 90 university employees who attended workshops on the glass ceiling funded by the DOL (Quina & Romenesko, 1993). In those workshops, faculty, academic staff, and administrators, in separate working groups, came up with amazingly similar lists of barriers to promotion. The similarity across their lists, despite widely disparate job classifications, points to the commonalities of their experiences and the pervasiveness of an institution's problems. These barriers, plus additional issues identified by the authors from our data and from the research literature, are found in Table 8.1.

We will address four overall areas of concern that emerge from our work, and discuss strategies to address each of them.

TABLE 8.1   **Barriers to Advancement in Academia**

Power within the system
  Are women administrators clustered in traditional women's areas or human resources?
  Are women responsible for budgets, and do they have decision-making power?
  What support staff and budgets are provided for women administrators?
  What is the gender ratio in better-paid departments (business, engineering)?
  Is salary equity assessed using appropriate techniques?
  Are merit allocations fair and equitable?

Hiring practices
  How do credentials of those hired compare to those not hired?
  Does tokenism appear: one woman per unit, one woman administrator, and so on?

Promotion practices
  Who initiates promotions?
  Are promotions delayed or denied?
  How much time is spent in rank or position before promotion?
  Are career tracks for professional staff and clerical staff clearly defined?

Professional development, formal (small grants) and informal (course releases)
  Are internships publicly available and equitably awarded?
  How much, and what kind, of informal mentoring is received?
  How much, and what kind of, contact do women have with their supervisors?
  How comfortable are women about contact with supervisors/administrators?

"Tracking"
  Are women found only in stereotypical areas?
  Are women "fast-tracked" without suitable opportunities to do research?
  Are women in higher positions underemployed or underutilized?
  Are women undertitled (i.e., doing the work of a higher-level title)?
  Are service expectations and commitments greater for women?

Information availability
  Who makes decisions, and who knows how and when decisions are made?
  Are there clear job descriptions with unchanging expectations for promotion?
  Do individuals receive information about how they are meeting expectations?

Attitudes toward and stereotypes of administrators
  What are the attitudes and stereotypes of women and minority administrators?
  Are women administrators treated like tokens?
  Are women administrators allowed to "fail" without penalty?

Perceptions of peers and administrators
  Is women's competence devalued?
  Are complaints about sexism trivialized?
  Is there support for women's studies, a Women's Center, and gender scholarship?
  Are administrators held responsible for discriminatory decisions?

(continued)

TABLE 8.1   Barriers to Advancement in Academia

Family issues
    Is there a parental leave policy which takes it into account in time toward tenure?
    Are day care and sick child care available on campus?

Working environment
    Is there an "old boy network" operating at the top levels?
    Is there a chilly climate (harassment, stressors, perceived lack of support)?
    What reasons are given for leaving (comparative exit interviews)?
    What is the overall quality of life (including demoralization and fear)?

Safety issues
    Do women curtail their professional activities because of safety concerns?
    How does the administration respond to women's safety concerns?

SOURCE: Quina and Romenesko, 1993.

ASSESSMENT CONCERNS

Data are, of course, a key feature of a contemporary Athena's armament. But data are often presented as summaries across a large institution. Such aggregate data can be misleading and should be used cautiously. There are more women faculty, more women administrators, more women athletes and coaches, and more women students at colleges and universities than ever. However, if you break the data down further, by title, discipline, or responsibilities, the gender inequities remain glaring.

Quina et al. (1992) and Quina and Romenesko (1993) reviewed data from two public university campuses. These more detailed analyses revealed:

- Women faculty are clustered at the lower ranks of instructor and assistant professor, and they are more likely to be at community colleges than at research universities (consistent with national statistics presented in Lie, Malik, and Harris, 1994, and Wechsler, 1995). The increase in women administrators has come primarily in "Assistant to" or "Assistant" positions; women senior administrators rarely number more than one per campus.
- In many departments, women continued to hold fewer than 5% of the positions; we consistently counted one tenured woman per business or engineering department (out of from 23 to 52 members) on each campus. Salaries of male and female members of departments with 90% or more men

220

TABLE 8.2   Associate/Full Professors, Wisconsin–Milwaukee, 1991-1992

	Sex	
School	*Male*	*Female*
Nursing	0	33 (100%)
Allied Health	10	17 (63%)
Social Welfare	12	8 (40%)
Education	45	19 (30%)
Letters & Science	287	65 (18%)
Business Administration	21	1 (5%)
Architecture & Urban Planning	22	1 (4%)
Engineering & Applied Science	44	1 (2%)

SOURCE: Masland (1993).

were as much as $12,000 higher than salaries of faculty in more balanced or female-dominated departments (Table 8.2).

- Just as women are beginning to set foot on the stage of academic success, that stage is being pulled out from under them by assaults on tenure, downsizing, and utilization of part-time instructors on campuses across the country. This picture is not improved when we look at the regular "pipeline" of tenure-track hires. In spite of increases in the number of women receiving their PhDs in underrepresented areas, these women do not seem to be arriving in academia—in part because a smaller proportion of graduates are arriving at all. Although some areas show great promise—for example, at one of our institutions, four of six assistant professors in computer science and mathematics were women; as were two of four new hires in business (Quina & Jackson, 1996)—when the absolute number of new hires is so low, there is not a great hope for eradicating the enormous differences that exist.

- As Tinsley et al. observed in 1984, the few women who had moved into administrative positions were in traditionally "female" areas. Women deans were found in education and nursing. Women administrators were more likely to be responsible for human resources and personnel, and they rarely had decision-making or budgetary responsibilities, or career tracks that would lead to top management.

- Although Title IX has had an extraordinary impact on women students' participation in sports, it appears that their postgraduate opportunities are as limited in coaching as they are on the playing field. For example, Quina et al. (1992) found that among teams in the Rhode Island higher education system, women and men shared coaching responsibilities for women's teams, but men's teams were coached only by men (Table 8.3).

221

TABLE 8.3   Coaches of Rhode Island Intercollegiate Athletic Teams, 1990

	Teams	
Sex of Coach	Men's	Women's
Female	0%	48%
Male	100%	52%

- Even the one statistic we often point to as progress, that more women are in college than men, is misleading. Women are more likely to be attending community colleges or other public institutions, part-time, whereas men are more likely to be located in private schools, full-time (the exception among the Rhode Island data were men attending evening MBA programs part-time). Men's doctorates are far more likely to be from higher-status private institutions (Rhode Island Office of Higher Education Report No. 1/90, RI Higher Education Fall Enrollment 1989, in Quina et al., 1992).

In these analyses, as in any other review, numbers cannot tell the whole story. Qualitative data are essential. We need to understand the process behind the numbers—how this ceiling is experienced by the people above and below it, why women and minorities get stuck or walled in, and what a successful path looks like.

CAREER DEVELOPMENT CONCERNS

Recently, authors have attributed the lack of career advancement of women and minorities in academia as well as in corporations to the way in which the ladder to success is installed and maintained. Reports identify the following concerns about the promotion processes in woman- and minority-unfriendly organizations:

1. lack of organizational commitment to recruitment practices;
2. failure to share notices of advancement opportunities; and
3. failure of the institution or company to own the responsibility for equal opportunity (DOL, 1992; Kelly, 1993; "Reaching Past the Glass Ceiling," 1993).

We think of the promotion process as a reward for past performance, but it should also be recognized as an opportunity to learn new roles and

TABLE 8.4   Promotions Within RI Department of Elementary and Secondary
Education: Management and Nonclassified Employees, 1989

	Women	*Men*	*% Women*
Management-initiated	6	11	35
Employee-initiated	9	6	60
Open position	6	5	55
Total	21	22	49

skills (and hence advance even more). Cannings and Montmarquette (1991) analyzed "managerial momentum" throughout a large Canadian firm and found that several factors worked against women. First, women made formal requests for promotion more often than men, yet men achieved more promotions. Men were much more likely to perceive their superiors as encouraging them to advance, and they perceived nearly a three times greater chance of actual promotion. Men reported more access to informal networks, which no doubt boosted their momentum. Ironically, when Cannings and Montmarquette examined performance ratings, women had earned higher evaluations than did men.

This kind of ceiling may be difficult to detect in overall data, which underlines our earlier point about assessment. In one analysis within the systems we examined, it appeared that women staff had been promoted at rates equal to men, albeit for lower-level positions (Latham, 1989). On closer examination, however, the promotion process was different for women. Management was more likely to initiate men's promotions, whereas women usually had to apply for a promotion or an open position themselves (Table 8.4).

Another problem arises when the institution relies upon career "ladders" or tracks to promotion. In the corporate world, job titles that are dominated by women are rarely part of an internal promotion ladder that leads to top management; when they are, they are more likely to be only to the level of managing other women (Baron, Davis-Blake, & Bielby, 1986).

In our workshops for women in academia, women reported a problem with some universities promoting very promising women on a "fast track" into middle management, often for the purposes of working with "special programs" (e.g., minority services). Although this looks like a career boost, they are subsequently passed over for further advancement. The traditional promotion track within academic leadership (to dean, provost, president) requires developing a scholarly reputation through publishing. A man who has devoted years to a single type of insect can be hailed as a great potential administrator because he has written three books, but a woman who has managed diverse clients, staff, and administrators, but who has not had time to publish research, is "too specialized." The fast-track areas of student services are not valued, and leadership within them is not recognized. If the leadership role involves women or minority affairs or helping students, there is further devaluing (see Perceptions, next section).

Education, special job-related training, and additional work experience are traditional keys to upward mobility. Yet a large study of managers in Australia demonstrated gender differences within this traditional track. Tharenou, Latimer, and Conroy (1994) tested influences on advancement with confirmatory modeling and found that although training and experience advanced all employees, the impact was more advantageous for men. Furthermore, men reported more access to training, which confirms Ragins and Sundstrom's (1989) observation of a process that groomed men for advancement through opportunities not offered to women.

Within the university, this systematic differential in career resources and advancement can be identified in various ways. Clark and Corcoran (1986) interviewed faculty and found what they termed an "accumulated disadvantage" for women, with fewer resources such as research support, travel funding, opportunities to review or edit journals, and so on.

How can the individual seeking promotion overcome these barriers? Aisenberg and Harrington (1988) observed that women in academia think in terms of jobs as opposed to a career strategy. Women have not, for example, created plans for where they want to be in 5 years. Aisenberg and Harrington suggested career counseling should be a priority for long-term success. Many of the women they interviewed credited a mentor or other person with giving them that extra push to publish their first article or to go after a job or a promotion. This support was not provided by the university; rather, it occurred through informal interactions, often among peers. Aisenberg and Harrington concluded that "the factor of support— received or not received—appears to be critical to the course of a woman's professional development" (p. 50).

Aisenberg and Harrington also note that women do not always play by the rules of the academic game. Some women are not aware of the rules; other women know the formal and informal rules but flatly refuse to follow them. Women who are repulsed by the current institutional politics, or who find the policies in conflict with the interests that are important to them, are faced with a difficult dilemma. One solution is to become adept at the game in order to secure a position or promotion, and then work from within to influence change. This choice should be made with eyes open, however, to the possible kinds of stress one will experience along the way (a stress often counterbalanced by the ultimate joys of creating change).

A number of academic and professional organizations have addressed these barriers. On most campuses, one can find an organization of women who work together across job titles and "levels" to create the informal and formal networks that had been missing for them. Within most professions, journals and academic organizations associated with women's studies have offered the professional experience not available in some more traditional areas. Because of the number of women who maintain ties to women's organizations in addition to their "home" fields, these groups can be quite strong. For example, within the American Psychological Association, the Division of the Psychology of Women is the fourth largest division, and a number of past (and future) presidents have begun their path to success by learning the ropes within the division. The annual Summer Institute for Women in Higher Education Administration, now in its 25th year, offers specialized training for highly promising administrators or potential administrators.

It is obligatory that individuals, however, work to make the systems on their own campuses and within their disciplines apply the guidelines equitably to men and women. A constant watch should be kept on the distribution of resources, including opportunities for training or advancement, and when an imbalance appears, it should be addressed. When selecting service commitments, we should place at high priority the campus committees responsible for funding internal research grants, for example. These can be the most important source for the future scholarly development of an assistant professor, yet we often dismiss this kind of service as work-intensive. At a national level, we must become reviewers for funding agencies, journals, and awards committees so that women can achieve the kinds of resources they deserve. And in our informal networks, we must provide encouragement for women and minorities to promote themselves, to use the resources that are available to them to overcome those that are not.

CONCERNS ABOUT BIASED PERCEPTIONS

Women and minorities often believe that an evaluation has been unfair, but the peer and academic evaluation systems that permeate academia sometimes make it hard to demonstrate bias in a direct fashion. In this section, we will discuss three common biases based on institutional or individual perceptions that have the effect of keeping women and minorities "stuck to the floor" or "walled in," and we will recommend strategies for dealing with them.

Devaluation of Competence

There is a substantial literature in psychology, reviewed in Lott (1985), that shows how work that is performed by or attributed to a woman is devalued when compared to the same work performed by or attributed to a man. Lott identified dozens of studies in which either college students or potential employers evaluate, describe, assign pay or reward to, perform tasks for, or select for a hypothetical or an actual job, equivalent male and female stimulus people (or work assigned to them). Although the results with college students are less strong, the results with real-world employers are quite consistent: Women are rated lower, given poorer evaluations, and are less likely to be hired than are men. This devaluation of competence can be overcome with such additional information as a successful achievement, but

> the general conclusion from studies in a variety of settings . . . is that a woman's success is more likely to be explained by external factors like luck or ease of task, or by high effort, an internal but stable factor, whereas a man's success is more likely to be attributed to high ability. (Lott, 1985, p. 51)

Despite such lowered expectations, women are not allowed to fail as much as men: "Men are said to fail because of bad luck, a hard task, or low effort, whereas women are said to fail because of low ability" (p. 51).

Has this situation changed? Unfortunately, recent studies suggest not. Melamed (1995) reviewed studies that demonstrated that up to 75% of the gender gap in salaries cannot be explained by factors other than sex discrimination. Melamed went a step further and examined career success among 451 British employees. She found that 55% of the gender gap in managerial level was attributable to sex discrimination when she controlled for ability ("human capital"), personality, demographics, career choices, organizational structure, and labor market forces.

A recent study of a Swedish peer review system demonstrates this bias most clearly in academia. Wenneras and Wold (1997) obtained records (through the Freedom of the Press Act) of applications and scores from the peer reviewers for a prestigious fellowship. In spite of the fact that women represented almost half of the applicants (52 of 114), only one quarter of the 20 fellowships were awarded to women. These fellowships are supposed to be awarded on the basis of scientific productivity and competence, and the relevance and quality of the proposal. The evaluations included numerical "scores" for scientific productivity/competence, and the authors were able to separate out this variable for evaluation.

Wenneras and Wold generated several objective measures of each applicant's productivity, not only counting the number of publications but also taking into account first authorships and journal prestige (citations) to create an "impact measure." They then regressed the impact measure and gender onto the average score assigned by the reviewers. The results were stunning: Women were given lower competence scores across the board, regardless of scientific productivity or impact. In fact, the most productive group of women, whose impact score was above 99, was assigned a slightly lower score than men who had an impact score of 20-39—in other words, a woman needed to be nearly three times more productive than a man to achieve the same score! Added to this was a strong bias for a candidate that the reviewer knew. A professional affiliation with a candidate increased the competence score the reviewer gave that candidate. Wenneras and Wold point out that these biases occurred in a country thought to be the best in the world in terms of equal opportunities for men and women, which leaves us to wonder what we would observe if similar decisions in our own system were more open to scrutiny. Certainly, it demonstrates the fallibility of "peer review."

There are three strategies to apply if one suspects that this sort of devaluation has taken place. One is to establish an "objective" statement of your competency. Review the publication records of comparable men/nonminorities, including the kinds of factors described above (number of citations of the journal, the article, etc.), in comparison to your own. A second is to copy the key articles described above and send them to your department chair, dean, or whoever may be in a position to overrule an unfair decision.

The third takes advantage of the affiliation bias, as well as Lott's (1985) observation that familiarity helps to negate the devaluing of women's competence. Getting to know professionals in the field, through a variety of informal and formal networks, seems to have great potential for countering bias. Such opportunities may be found in teaching groups and committee assignments, or by joining in departmental social events on a regular basis.

Another strategy sometimes used with success is to bring in the media to assist you in your fight. In the case of the first author, a lead newspaper article quoting from the decision of the Equal Employment Opportunity Commission about her denial of promotion ("Female teacher wins bias complaint," 1990) led to public outrage and, it was rumored, was responsible for internal administrative changes. A faculty member denied tenure in the College of Business at another institution created a full-time media blitz by faxing information around the country. Ultimately, her case (which was particularly outrageous) was covered on national television and in national magazines, and she won tenure and promotion—and taught many of us about an important new ally: the media.

"Women's Work"

A second, often-discussed type of bias relates to the area in which one works. In nonacademic spheres, success for women has historically occurred only in specific industries or sectors that were justified as "women's work": nursing, teaching, and social work (Sachs, Chrisler, & Devlin, 1992). These (not) coincidentally are the same areas in which opportunities for career success are more limited (Melamed, 1995); in academia, these departments often have "glass walls" around them, even through the dean's level.

There is no question that "women's work" (e.g., nursing, education, women's studies) is not as highly paid (and presumably not as highly valued) as "men's work" (e.g., business, engineering). Within a discipline such as psychology, researchers who address topics that are traditionally "appropriate" for women—development and gerontology, for example—are more often women and are paid less than are researchers who study topics such as physiological or mathematical psychology (Cantor et al., 1995). This bias emerges in evaluations of women's scholarship, both for academic advancement and for promotion into management, when a person who publishes in one of the less valued fields (e.g., women's studies) is presumed to be less intelligent, less accomplished, or less productive (e.g., Grant & Ward, 1991).

Some have suggested that social norms regarding the division of labor (women in the house, taking care of others; men as breadwinners) permeate the system as well. Although no researchers have documented the specifics, leaders to whom we have talked support an implication of this perceptual bias. We would hypothesize that people who lead programs or departments concerned with women and minorities, or programs designed to "help others," are not perceived as having the same skills as people who lead academic departments or more "mainstream" programs (although there are no data to suggest that leaders in these fields are any less effective than those in other areas). These roles, often filled by women or minorities, may be denigrated in various ways.

1. The leader is effective more as a role model (i.e., having the same gender or skin color) than as an administrator.
2. The leader would not be an administrator if he or she did not have the right physical characteristics.
3. Helping behaviors are innate feminine skills and do not translate into leadership of "real" academics.

Even the methods one uses can lead to differential perceptions of competence: For example, within sociology and psychology, a researcher who collects qualitative data may be considered less scholarly than someone who collects quantitative data (Grant & Ward, 1991). Women who use even the most carefully crafted and rigorously applied qualitative methodology find their work denigrated; even if the work is published, a department may choose not to count it toward promotion or other decisions. (The first author experienced this in two different academic departments and has observed problematic treatment of students who attempt to do qualitative work.)

Counteracting such a bias requires more research on the part of the individual, but it may be important to do early and often in one's career. In terms of review or job searches, documenting number of publications is not sufficient; it is important to annotate publication lists with information about the journal's significance, the role one played (if not the first author), the rejection rate of articles by that journal, and perhaps a statement about the importance of the findings. Although this would be unusual information for inclusion in a standard introductory-level job search vitae, it is critical for anyone who is preparing a dossier for review or promotion or for consideration for a move into administration.

When seeking outside letters of recommendation, it is helpful to look beyond one's own field and get "affirmation" from someone in one of the disciplines considered more "serious." There are always allies on a campus, and one needs only one or two letters to demonstrate that her scholarship is judged as competent by "outsiders."

CONCERNS ABOUT THE INSTITUTIONAL ENVIRONMENT

Each institution and discipline has a set of informal and formal rules that constitutes its culture. This culture can either enhance an individual's growth or create barriers to growth. Caplan's (1993) "Checklist for Woman-Positive Institutions" lists many of these cultural characteristics. We have selected three aspects of the culture for special mention.

Discrimination and Harassment

In this volume, Benokraitis has identified multiple forms of subtle sex discrimination, and Lott and Rocchio have discussed the extent of sexual harassment on campus. These experiences have an extraordinary impact on the long-term success of women, particularly minority women, when the institutional environment is nonsupportive. Quina and Romenesko (1993) cited a June 1992 report of exit interviews done with faculty women and minorities leaving the University of Wisconsin (UW) system. The responses clearly showed the influence of gender bias and harassment on women's career paths (Table 8.5). Women who left their jobs (including tenured women!) identified extensive barriers, including substantial levels of discrimination and harassment. We urge readers not to forget the pain and humiliation those experiences created for their victims (see Quina, 1996), and to take action to fight discrimination and harassment in all their forms.

Tokenism

Kanter (1977) discussed the problems experienced by anyone who is a minority in a majority group. There are two sorts of reactions, that,

TABLE 8.5   UW Systemwide Departure Rates

Departure rates			
Minority women	7.7%	Minority men	6.3%
Nonminority women	7.1%	Nonminority men	5.3%

Reasons given by women	
Nonsupportive Work Environment	*Discrimination and harassment*
9.5% of tenured	7.1% of tenured
13.4% of nontenured	4.1% of nontenured

although they seem contradictory, somehow manage to co-occur all too easily. One is that the token stands out and is noticed more for any problems, atypical behaviors, errors, and so on. Her clothing, hair style, speech, and behavior become the subject of review. (In the tenure case mentioned earlier that gained national media attention, a sweater the candidate wore to a Christmas party received a full paragraph of formal critique!)

At the same time, she is isolated, ignored, and left out of both formal and informal activities and networks, as discussed above. Yoder (1985) documented these phenomena among women in the first coeducational class at West Point. When the person is perceived to be an "affirmative action" candidate, she comes further prepackaged with a set of myths about affirmative action, not the least of which is a presumption that she is there because of her skin color or gender and is therefore not qualified (Plous, 1996).

The literature suggests that women who comprise less than 15% of a total level in an organization can be labeled as tokens, as they are not viewed as individuals but rather as symbols of women (Kanter, 1977). Thus, the first step toward eliminating this cultural distinction is to hire more women.

However, until jobs are more readily available and more readily filled by women, overcoming tokenism remains difficult for many women. Women have adopted various coping strategies, from attempting to fit in with "the guys" better than other men do to constantly calling attention to the everyday slights. Over time, tokenism does fade, but it is important to document in a diary specific examples of differential treatment and to make sure that one's evaluators have access to specific side-by-side comparisons of specific accomplishments with nonminority male comparators where possible.

Family Leave and Child Care

Universities have not been well known for family-friendly leave policies. Even though men's roles in child rearing have become acceptable, it is primarily women who bear the responsibility. Given the increasing numbers of women in professional careers and dual career couples in academia, family issues are important concerns for many women (Norrell & Norrell, 1996). Aisenberg and Harrington (1988) referred to the "consistent struggle to integrate work and family life, not to give one up for the other" (p. 154).

Norrell and Norrell (1996) reviewed parental leave policies currently in practice at higher education institutions. The prevailing attitudes were based on the older model of "no leave." A new approach would require communication among faculty and administrators who, in reality, often share needs and a recognition of the benefits for the community. And family-friendly policies can benefit the entire university mission. For example, a campus child care center can provide opportunities for parent outreach, student teaching opportunities, and research opportunities for a variety of departments, in addition to quality child care close to the employee's worksite.

New and creative ideas for tenure and promotion accommodations may be specific to the institution. Some have a "stop the clock" policy and do not count leave time toward tenure review. Although males may perceive a threat to the quality of work and females do not, there is a reported perception that women are delaying childbirth until after receiving tenure. The Norrells noted that there seemed to be no notable change in policies despite the fact that more women are serving on promotion and tenure committees.

Perhaps, as Aisenberg and Harrington (1988) suggested, it is necessary to recognize that child care is not a woman's issue, "it is a family issue, a human issue, a quality of life issue" (p. 154). Men and women and institutions must work toward an integration of family and professional lives for the benefit of all.

FUTURE CONCERNS

In interviews, most successful career women attributed their success to exceptional achievements and excellent communication skills, and they described themselves as success-driven workaholics and adept risk takers (Mainiero, 1994). In the 1987 Working Women Survey (in Williams, 1989), female executives identified the following success factors:

1. Superstar Track Record (identified winners who stood out);
2. Superior People Skills (supervisory skills and ability to get cooperation from subordinates);
3. Career Courage (taking risks for advancement);
4. A Passion for Success (determination);
5. Miscellaneous Factors (smart and confident).

These are skills that are important for either male or female executives. Mainiero (1994) described a high level of political savvy in women who made it to the top in *Fortune 500* companies. These women were exceptional at building and maintaining relationships to get results. However, they did not always follow a traditional path; it was suggested that part of their savvy was speaking directly and taking risks that may have run counter to the company norms—for example, successfully applying cooperative strategies and team approaches.

Although most of these women have broken through the glass ceiling in their organization, they are still the exception. This is important to acknowledge when considering strategies both at the organizational and personal levels. It is also important to note that these women were politically savvy because they knew how to stay informed and use that information to their advantage.

Empowerment

Cantor and Bernay (1992) interviewed women political leaders and devised a series of exercises for finding and being effective with one's own sense of power. They offer a "Leadership Equation: Leadership = Competent Self + Creative Aggression + WomanPower" (p. 17) that is, they believe, achievable by many women. The book is well worth reading for the stories of women leaders as well as the literature and exercises. Another helpful resource is *The Organizational Woman: Power and Paradox* (Haslett, Geis, & Carter, 1992).

What can the organization do to enhance leadership? In 1992, the DOL recognized helpful efforts by some companies whose personnel divisions or human resource departments were "empowered" to initiate actions to recognize employee potential, track their progress, and assist women in planning their career strategies. Empowering organizations are in better positions to provide information and support services based on an employee's own goals rather than on stereotyped assumptions. Furthermore, they must work to make sure that "empowerment" recognizes the individual's own cultural and personal situation and values. Rather than trying to transform the individual into a "corporate man," the process should be one of mutual growth and change (Thomas, 1991).

The DOL (1992) recognized companies who had developed support programs to assist employees to fulfill educational and experiential requirements. In the past, open positions may have required a particular experience. A woman applicant may not have had the experience because the opportunity was never made available to her, and consequently, she was denied a promotion. This is also true in academia, where women are not afforded the time for research and publications that is necessary to achieve tenure and move up in rank. Williams (1989) made a similar recommendation based on her research on Black women college administrators: "Institutions must develop in-house plans for training and upgrading of all employees, particularly women of color" (p. 111). In reality, this makes good sense for all organizations. Muller (1994) described empowerment as "a process of acknowledging the latent potency of others and assisting them to act purposely and assertively to reach his or her growth potential" (p. 81). This empowering support can take place through mentoring, career counseling, networking, and outreach efforts to younger women. Developing strong support systems and networks can encourage more women to take similar actions that could lead to career advancement.

Kelly (1993) urged more aggressive activities to tap the talent of women and minority employees so that they may be qualified and ready for promotions. He suggested that the onus be on managers (or, in academia, senior faculty and administrators) to take it upon themselves to seek out and encourage every individual to achieve his or her potential within the organization.

Those in leadership or helping positions need to give feedback to women and include them in all communications, share information, keep resumé files, and contact women who have demonstrated performance or who have the potential for performance (Kelly, 1993; "Reaching past the glass ceiling," 1993; Williams, 1989; Wilson, 1989). Leaders must be able to recognize and develop talent to its full potential and to support risk taking, particularly for the person who does not yet behave like a superstar.

The Next Generation

Many more women are now on campus in a variety of roles. We cannot assume that members of "Generation X" are going to want what older women have sought, or are going to find the same paths open to them. We know that many attitudes have indeed changed; many young women do not feel like aliens in the academy, and they come to graduate school with a clear sense of purpose. On the other hand, in the current era of downsizing, we can assume that they will have to work harder and achieve more than the women who came before them.

It is crucial that we not attempt to impose our own needs and experiences on the next generation, but rather that we listen to their voices and help them fill the needs they experience. The results of one study point to an important action. Johnsrud and Wunsch (1991) compared junior to senior women faculty. Although, for the most part, they had the same issues, the junior faculty felt more personal security (e.g., less sexual harassment threat) than the senior faculty (evidence of our success!). A surprising finding, however, was that junior faculty wanted assistance with the immediate problems of publishing, as opposed to long-term issues such as tenure clocks. Those of us who have been in the field a long time may forget how difficult it is to put pen to paper in the face of so many other demands, to cope with rejection by journals, or even to decide where to send a paper. We need to listen, and then to fill the roles that will most empower our future leaders. Inviting coauthorship that truly benefits our younger colleagues (as opposed to "using them" to do our work), sharing our own experiences, and just plain encouragement and support are important first steps.

We also need to target younger women in nontraditional areas. The 1992 DOL report acknowledged the paucity of women in math, science, and engineering that complicates the promotion process in areas that rely heavily on those competencies. Companies have attempted to address this issue through specialized grant programs for high school students, including internships, job shadowing, mentoring, and other outreach efforts. Colleges and universities could benefit from similar outreach programs, which might include faculty working with high school students in quantitative analysis, research, writing, and sharing technical expertise. It is a beginning for the "Pipeline for Progress" in academia.

Cantor and Bernay (1992) included in their book a special section called "empowering messages to give your daughters":

1. you are loved and special;
2. you can do anything you want;
3. you can take risks;
4. you can use and enjoy your Creative Aggression;
5. you are entitled to dream of greatness. (p. 230)

Words for us all, children or adults.

SUMMARY: STRATEGIES FOR EXPOSING AND BREAKING THE CEILING

1. To bring the glass ceiling to visibility to those not underneath it, collect more and better data, both quantitative and qualitative.
2. In identifying intervention strategies, focus on changing the institution, not on changing women and minorities.
3. Create and cherish informal networks. Join campus women's organizations, get together with other women (including secretarial staff!) in your unit or department just to have fun, develop tenure support groups, and always act in a trustworthy way.
4. Do not be timid about analyses. Draw parallels between sex discrimination, sexual harassment, and sexual assault (see Quina, 1996). Speak out on behalf of others, and identify and name subtle as well as blatant discrimination.
5. Organize and find allies in addressing the glass ceiling effect. One advantage of publicly funded institutions is that when all else fails, one may go outside to sympathetic legislators and media to draw attention to problems. Likewise, make institutional change the priority of someone other than only women, including strong administrative leadership and alliances within existing governing systems.
6. Consider more comprehensive revisions of academia and its management. Thomas's (1991) "management for diversity" suggests mutual mentoring of managers and employees, in preference to making diverse employees conform to a single style. This and other exciting new models for management and leadership should be explored.

REFERENCES

Aisenberg, N., & Harrington, M. (1988). *Women of academe: Outsiders in the sacred grove.* Amherst: University of Massachusetts Press.

Astin, H. S., & Leland, C. (1991). *Women of influence, women of vision: A cross-generational study of leaders and social change.* San Francisco: Jossey-Bass.

Baron, J. N., Davis-Blake, A., & Bielby, W. T. (1986). The structure of opportunity: How promotion ladders vary within and among organizations. *Administrative Science Quarterly, 31,* 248-273.

Cannings, K., & Montmarquette, C. (1991). Managerial momentum: A simultaneous model of the career progress of male and female managers. *Industrial and Labor Relations Review, 44,* 212-228.

Cantor, D. W., Astin, H. S., Bernay, T. M., Fox, R. E., Goodheart, C. D., Hall, C. C., Kenkel, M. B., Mednick, M. T., & Pion, G. M. (1995). *Report of the task force on the changing composition of psychology.* Washington, DC: American Psychological Association.

Cantor, D.W., & Bernay, T. (1992). *Women in power: The secrets of leadership.* Boston: Houghton Mifflin.

Caplan, P. J. (1993). *Lifting a ton of feathers: A woman's guide to surviving in the academic world.* Toronto: University of Toronto Press.

Clark, S. M., & Corcoran, M. (1986). Perspectives on the professional socialization of women faculty: A case of accumulative disadvantage. *Journal of Higher Education, 57,* 20-43.

Female teacher wins bias complaint against URI. (1990, February 14). *Providence Journal Bulletin,* p. A-3.

Grant, L., & Ward, K. B. (1991). Gender and publishing in sociology. *Gender & Society, 5,* 207-223.

Haslett, B. J., Geis, F. L., & Carter, M. R. (1992). *The organizational woman: Power and paradox.* Norwood, NJ: Ablex.

Johnsrud, L. K., & Wunsch, M. (1991). Junior and senior faculty women: Commonalities and differences in perceptions of academic life. *Psychological Reports, 69,* 879-886.

Kanter, R. M. (1977). *Men and women of the corporation.* New York: Basic Books.

Kelly, P. (1993, October). Conduct a glass ceiling self-audit now. *HR Magazine,* pp. 76-80.

Latham, R. (1989). *Promotion by gender/race.* Providence, RI: RI Department of Education Report.

Lie, S. S., Malik, L., & Harris, D. (Eds.). (1994). *The gender gap in higher education.* Philadelphia: Kogan Page.

Lott, B. (1985). The devaluation of women's competence. *Journal of Social Issues, 41*(4), 43-60.

Mainiero, L. A. (1994). On breaking the glass ceiling: The political seasoning of powerful women executives. *Organizational Dynamics, 22*(4), 5-20.

Masland, S. (1993). *A look at the composition of executive committees at the UWM campus.* Milwaukee: University of Wisconsin-Milwaukee.

Melamed, T. (1995). Barriers to women's career success: Human capital, career choices, structural determinants, or simply sex discrimination. *Applied Psychology: An International Review, 44,* 295-314.

Miner, V., & Longino, H. E. (Eds.). (1987). *Competition: A feminist taboo?* New York: The Feminist Press.

Muller, L. E. (1994). Toward an understanding of empowerment: A study of six women leaders. *Journal of Humanistic Education and Development, 33,* 75-82.

Norrell, J. E., & Norrell, T. H. (1996). Faculty and family policies in higher education. *Journal of Family Issues, 17*, 204-226.

Plous, S. (1996). Ten myths about affirmative action. *Journal of Social Issues, 52*, 25-32.

Quina, K. (1996). Sexual harassment and rape: A continuum of exploitation. In M. A. Paludi (Ed.), *Sexual harassment on college campuses* (pp. 183-198). Albany: State University of New York Press.

Quina, K., Cotter, M., & Adler, E. S. (1992). *Report card for the 1990s: A report on the status of girls and women in Rhode Island education.* Providence, RI: RI Commission on Women [available from first author].

Quina, K., & Jackson, N. (1996). *Report card for the 1990s: An update.* Providence, RI: RI Commission on Women [available from first author].

Quina, K., & Romenesko, K. (1993). *Assessing the glass ceiling in higher education* [Report to the U.S. Department of Labor]. Milwaukee: University of Wisconsin, Center for Women's Studies.

Ragins, B. R., & Sundstrom, E. (1989). Gender and power in organizations: A longitudinal perspective. *Psychological Bulletin, 105*(1), 51-88.

Reaching past the glass ceiling. (1993, Winter). *BNAC Communicator*, p. 1.

Riger, S., & Galligan, P. (1980). Women in management: An exploration of competing paradigms. *American Psychologist, 35*(1), 902-910.

Sachs, R., Chrisler, J. C., & Devlin, A. S. (1992). Biographic and personal characteristics of women in management. *Journal of Vocational Behavior, 41*, 89-100.

Tharenou, P., Latimer, S., & Conroy, D. (1994). How do you make it to the top? An examination of influences on women's and men's managerial advancement. *Academy of Management Journal, 37*, 899-931.

Thomas, H. R. (1991). *Beyond race and power: Unleashing the power of your total work force by managing diversity.* New York: Amacom.

Tinsley, A., Secor, C., & Kaplan, S. (Eds.). (1984). Women in higher education administration. *New Directions for Higher Education* [No. 45]. New York: Jossey-Bass.

U.S. Department of Labor. (1991). *A report on the Glass Ceiling Initiative.* Washington, DC: U.S. Government Printing Office.

U.S. Department of Labor. (1992). *Pipelines of progress.* Washington, DC: Government Printing Office.

Wechsler, H. (1995). *The NEA 1995 Almanac of Higher Education.* Washington, DC: NEA Publishing.

Wenneras, C., & Wold, A. (1997). Nepotism and sexism in peer-review. *Nature, 387*, 341-343.

Williams, A. (1989). Research on Black women administrators: Descriptive and interview data. *Sex Roles, 21*, 99-112.

Wilson, R. (1989). Women of color in academic administration: Trends, progress, and barriers. *Sex Roles, 21*, 85-97.

Yoder, J.D. (1985). An academic woman as a token. *Journal of Social Issues, 41*(1), 61-72.

Creating a Feminist Mentoring Network

Mary Zahm

I have several feminist mentors who provide me with support, guidance, and opportunities for personal and professional development. These women—and my relationship with them—are very different. Nevertheless, each has taught me how to profit from a mentoring relationship and how to become a successful mentor. How did these relationships begin? How have they evolved?

My first feminist mentoring relationship began when one of my psychology professors at Roger Williams University asked me where I was planning to study for my master's degree, as if it were an outcome to be expected. When I explained that I had just started college and was not sure if I could attend graduate school, she pointed out that I was an excellent student and encouraged me to consider going on. She invited me to travel with her to the annual meeting of the Eastern Psychological Association, where I saw first-hand how exciting being a professional psychologist could be. We still attend that annual meeting together, and she remains a source of support and guidance. She has recommended me to teach courses at her university and generously shares her syllabi and teaching tips. She also proofread early drafts of chapters for my book and offered excellent suggestions for improvements.

My second feminist mentoring relationship began when I enrolled in a master's program at Rhode Island College, and my advisor invited me to work on a research project with her. I took advantage of that opportunity and became coauthor of a paper that was presented at the annual meeting of the American Psychological Association. Now I was hooked on research, and—thanks to her sound advice—I applied for admission to a doctoral program in experimental psychology. I maintained contact with my advisor over the years as we are both members of the Rhode Island Association for Women in Psychology. She has always responded promptly whenever I needed a letter of recommendation and has provided me with the opportunity to teach courses in psychology and women's studies at her college. Our relationship has recently evolved into a working partnership; we are writing a book together on empowering women in transition.

239

The third mentoring relationship is with my former major professor. Our relationship began when she invited me to become her graduate student at the University of Rhode Island—with the stipulation that I would focus my research on factors that impact the lives of nontraditional women students, like me, who were in transition from home to work. I accepted her offer and began a relationship that has continued to evolve and deepen since that day. She is an excellent role model of a feminist professional psychologist and has provided me with many opportunities for personal and professional development.

My major professor included me in professional activities in every capacity, from stuffing mail for local professional meetings to helping her coordinate regional and national meetings. She encouraged me to join and become an active member of feminist professional organizations. She involved me in her research activities and thereby empowered me to produce scholarly papers and present them at regional and national professional meetings. She nominated me for awards. She invited me to team-teach courses with her so that I could gain teaching experience. Upon graduation, she hired me to teach courses when appropriate. Today, years (dare I say decades?) after our major professor-student relationship began, we consider ourselves to be each other's role model, mentor, and friend. To me, that is how a successful major professor-protégée relationship should evolve.

After a 13-year career as a human factors psychologist in industry, I am now teaching psychology at Bristol Community College. Now, I am in a position to provide support and guidance to many women in transition. How can I be a feminist role model and successful mentor?

My own experiences with generous feminist women have led me to think about what mentoring and role modeling mean. It seems to me that the characteristics of a successful feminist mentor include the following:

- Role modeling feminist professional behavior
- Providing accurate feedback to students concerning their academic performance
- Offering support and guidance to students concerning their program requirements and professional development
- Promptly providing requested letters of recommendation
- Through guided participation in a variety of scholarly activities, generously introducing students to the professional world of psychology
- Sharing professional expertise and lessons learned from experience

- Introducing students to leaders in their fields, which helps them to launch their careers as professional psychologists
- Nominating students for awards
- Involving students in both the daily "how is it done" as well as the glory when it is done well
- Allowing the major professor-student relationship to evolve into a reciprocal, collegial one

I am fortunate to have a network of feminist mentors. I actively pursue and nurture these relationships because I respect these three women and value the support and guidance they are willing to offer me. If you want to create your own feminist network, I encourage you to do the following:

- Join feminist professional organizations and participate in professional activities at which you might meet potential mentors
- Reach out to women who are already achieving the goals you hope to accomplish and ask them how you might pursue a similar career path
- When they inquire, inform potential mentors of your career interests and goals
- Ask knowledgeable mentors and colleagues for specific information concerning your career goals
- Ask mentors for specific assistance, such as writing letters of recommendation, and provide them with the information they need to expedite the task
- Introduce your mentors and students to one another in order to form a network of people who can share information and resources
- Keep mentors apprised of your progress, interests, goals, and accomplishments, and express a genuine interest in theirs
- Accept offers for professional collaboration that will provide desired experiences
- Remain in contact with your mentors and encourage mutually supportive, collegial relationships

The Pro Forma Review That Wasn't

Anonymous

Everyone assured me that the second-year review was strictly pro forma. No files were to be constructed; no outside evaluations requested. The department chair would simply write a letter to the administration to request that the untenured person's contract be extended. Nothing to worry about, I was told by the Dean of the Faculty, my department colleagues, and other faculty (both senior and junior); save your concern for the important third-year and tenure reviews. This is what I was told, but it is not what happened to me.

At the end of a monthly department meeting, at the close of the routine business noted on the agenda, the untenured faculty were asked to leave so that the tenured faculty could discuss a personnel matter. We left, glad for a few extra minutes at the end of the day. I had no idea that the "personnel matter" my colleagues were discussing was my future. I went off to a meeting with some students who were conducting research projects under my supervision.

When I returned to our building an hour or so later, I found the senior woman in my department (we were three in a department of nine) pacing the hall waiting for me. It was after 7 p.m., and everyone else had gone home. She looked angry. She said, "I need to speak to you right now." My heart started pounding, and I fumbled with my keys as I tried to unlock my office door. I wondered what I could have done to upset her. I did not want her to be angry with me. I liked and respected her, and she was really my only friend in the department at that time.

She shut the door firmly behind us, and I fell into my chair panicked. She said, "Something went terribly wrong in the meeting after you left. I didn't see it coming. I don't know what to do, and I'm so mad at [X and Y] that I could kill them!" She then proceeded to tell me that the matter they had discussed was whether or not to renew my contract. Two of the senior men in the department recommended against it. They didn't like the way I taught my courses; a few students had complained to them that I was too strict. Besides, they said, I was cold, unfriendly, and didn't seem to have a sense of humor. I wouldn't be a congenial colleague in the years ahead; I did not "fit in."

My friend and one of the other men argued that it was too soon to tell how good a teacher I would be; that students always complain about new faculty; that I was shy, not unfriendly; and that a better evaluation could be done the next year after they'd seen my third-year review file. The other two faculty at the meeting didn't say much. My friend was worried about them because she thought they could be convinced to vote against me, and, if they did, the Chair would write a letter recommending against my contract extension. They would vote in a week. "What should I do?" I asked. "I don't know," she said. "I've never been any good at political maneuvering. Any advice I gave you would probably be wrong. I'm sorry."

When she left, I cried. Then I went home, too upset even to talk to my husband about what had happened. Just over a year ago, we'd sold our co-op apartment in another state and left the community where we had lots of friends and many attachments. We'd bought a house; he'd changed jobs. How could I tell him that I might be out of work in a few months?

I had no classes the next day, and I decided to stay at home and think about my predicament. I realized how important it was that my friend told me what had happened. She broke confidentiality to do so, and if the others found out, they'd never forgive her. I decided that they wouldn't learn about it from me. I called a colleague I've known for a long time, a woman I very much admired who was well respected in our field. I knew she had been denied tenure earlier in her career, and I thought she would be sympathetic to my situation. When I told her what had happened, her response startled me. "Boy, are you lucky!" she said. "What do you mean?" I replied. "They're trying to fire me!" "I mean that you know who your enemies are already, so you can do something about it. I had to wait six years to find out who my enemies were; by then, it was too late."

Our conversation was not what I had expected, but by the end of the day, I realized that she'd given me the right advice. "I know who my enemies are," I told myself, "and I can do something about it." I decided to spend the rest of the week before the vote speaking to each of my colleagues individually. I decided to make appointments with everyone, tenured and untenured (I even spoke to the secretary because I knew she'd have to type the Chair's letter). In these meetings, I would invite them to ask me any questions they wanted about my courses, my teaching philosophy, my scholarly projects, and so on. I would encourage them to share with me any concerns they had about my progress. I would assure them that I wanted their advice in order to improve my performance. I would not let on that I already knew who had complaints and what they were.

The next day, I got to campus early and began leaving messages for everyone to request appointments. I ran into the Chair in the morning. She appeared anxious and asked me to come into her office. She told me that several members of the department had concerns about my performance. She could not tell me who had concerns or what they were, but said that she had to gather additional information in preparation for writing her letter. "Just tell me about your concerns then," I said. "Please ask me any questions you have." The conversation was very difficult for both of us. Before I left her office,

I told her of my plans to have a similar conversation with each member of the department. She looked surprised and urged me not to do that. But I had already put my plan in motion, and I was determined to follow through.

That week was the most difficult week of my life. All of the meetings were hard for me, but especially the ones that took place in my opponents' offices. I took notes. I urged them to tell me more. I answered all their questions as best I could. I struggled not to cry. I lived through it. They voted to extend my contract, and the Chair wrote a balanced letter. I had won the battle, but the war was still in progress.

I believe that my tactics succeeded in part because my presence in their offices intimidated them, which is probably why I was urged not to be so direct. I was assertive. I admitted there might be problems, and I indicated a willingness to correct them. It is difficult to vote against someone who is so obviously trying to improve. I had handled the "objective" complaints; now I had to work on the "subjective" ones. I had to find a way to make them like me.

I began clipping articles and cartoons related to my colleagues' specialties and leaving them in their mailboxes. I made sure I said hello as warmly as possible each time I saw them. When I walked into the next department meeting, I saw "my enemies" sitting near each other, with one chair in between them. I forced myself to take that chair. I chatted with them before and after the meeting, and I never missed another chance to sit with one or both of them. I asked them for advice; I asked them to lunch. For months, the sight of them upset me, and I often felt insincere in my overtures to them, but I kept up my spirits by repeating what had become my mantra: "I know who my enemies are, and I can do something about it."

A year later, when I assembled my third-year review file, everyone in the department gave me a good review. Three years later, they all recommended me for tenure, and 3 years after that, everyone recommended me for promotion to full professor. My strongest letters came from my former enemies. I say "former enemies" because, to my surprise, we've become good friends. In fact, they are the only ones among my current department colleagues with whom I socialize off campus. Getting to know them personally was good for my career and good for my ego. I learned, for example, that X never thinks anyone is as good as they ought to be and that Y is so pro-student that a single complaint about a grade can turn him against someone at least temporarily.

I hope what my readers will take from this tale is that it is possible to turn around a bad situation if one acts immediately and assertively. Some of what happened to me was lucky (my friend broke confidentiality; I telephoned the right colleague), but some of what happened could be done by anyone. Ask for feedback about your performance, solicit advice, be friendly to everyone (but especially to those you sense don't like you), be assertive, show you have a sense of humor, follow your instincts. You may think that playing up to senior colleagues is a distraction from the teaching, research, and service that ought to be occupying your time, and you may be right. You may call my behavior obsequious, but I call it taking charge of my own career.

Part IV

Taking Charge
and Taking Care

9 Standing Up, Talking Back, and Taking Charge

Strategies and Outcomes in Collective Action Against Sexual Harassment

Bernice Lott
Lisa M. Rocchio

The large number of empirical and theoretical papers, books, workshops, and conferences devoted to the subject of sexual harassment, beginning in the mid-1970s, attests to the fact that it has come to be viewed as a phenomenon of concern to government, law, business, and education, as well as the target of active pressures for social change. At the same time, however, a clear backlash is currently apparent in efforts to trivialize sexual harassment and to ridicule or pathologize those who are concerned with it.

Illustrative of such a backlash are two articles that appeared on the very same day in our hometown newspaper, the *Providence Journal Bulletin*. The first, a very brief news item, was headlined "All work, no play" (July 25, 1996, p. G1), and it communicated the presumably humorous report

AUTHORS' NOTE: Portions of this chapter appear in Lott, B., & Rocchio, L. M. (1997). Individual and collective action: Social approaches and remedies for sexist discrimination. In H. Landrine & E. A. Klonoff (Eds.), *Discrimination against women: Prevalence, consequences, remedies* (pp. 148-171). Thousand Oaks, CA: Sage.

that "asking someone you work with for a date can be dangerous." Why? Because federal and state laws permit a worker to file a grievance "if there's been an unwanted advance, an offer of work-related incentives, use of obscene or unwanted references to sex or attempted unwanted physical attention." The implication of this item, as is clear from its headline, is that someone who is troubled by such commonplace and presumably innocuous behaviors is silly or mean. In another section of the paper was a column entitled "Feminism and the morality police" by a sociologist from the Johns Hopkins University Institute for Policy Studies (Kelly, 1996). She warns the reader that there has been a dangerous expansion of the meaning of sexual harassment so that "almost any behavior can be construed" as such. She argues that there is now a "new Inquisition" and "morality police" that enable people with "hurt feelings" to charge others unfairly with sexual harassment. Such critics seem to us to be less concerned with the acts that define harassment than with protecting misunderstood perpetrators.

Those who give serious attention to the issue of sexual harassment are aware of its legal definition, which has guided both judicial decisions and policies and procedures adopted by public and private organizations. Under Title VII of the Civil Rights Act of 1964, discrimination on the basis of sex is prohibited. Both *sexual harassment* and *gender harassment* have been interpreted as forms of sex discrimination. The Interim Interpretative Guidelines on Sex Discrimination issued in 1980 by the Equal Employment Opportunity Commission (EEOC) suggested that sexual harassment is of two general types:

1. *Quid pro quo,* which occurs when an attempt is made to coerce an individual into sexual cooperation by promises of rewards or threats of punishment
2. The creation of a *hostile environment,* one that is pervaded by offensive, degrading, or intimidating behavior (cf. Fitzgerald, 1996a, p. 44)

These guidelines were first articulated in the context of employment but have been used to interpret Title IX of the Education Amendments of 1972, which prohibits sex discrimination in education. As noted by Fitzgerald (1996a), "In practice, educational institutions have generally adopted the EEOC Guidelines and extended them to include the situation of students" (p. 44). In a statement published in 1993, EEOC made clear that gender harassment is also prohibited in the workplace, giving as examples "epithets, slurs, taunts, and gestures, the display or distribution of obscene or pornographic materials; gender-based hazing; and threatening, intimidating or hostile acts" (Fitzgerald, 1996a, p. 51). Hostile behaviors directed against women in general because of their gender, in addition to sexual harassment of individuals, have both come to be defined and regarded as sex discrimination.

With respect to the prevalence of sexual harassment, large-scale studies have focused primarily on particular workplace settings or on college students (usually undergraduates). A prevalence rate for sexual harassment of undergraduate women is typically reported "in the 30% range," a figure on which there is substantial agreement "despite considerable methodological variation" (Koss et al., 1994, p. 126). Overall estimates from studies of working women have ranged from 50% (the Merit Systems studies of federal workers and the Gutek study of a sample of the Los Angeles workforce) to 17.5% (the National Victim Center Study) but, as noted by Koss et al. (1994), the latter survey "inquired only about harassment by supervisors and bosses, and counted as harassment only those instances that the respondent herself labeled as harassment . . . [and thus] the results likely represent a significant underestimate" (p. 125). Few studies have focused specifically on the prevalence of sexual harassment experienced by college professors and graduate students. One such study (Fitzgerald et al., 1988) of women faculty, staff, and administrators of a public university in the midwest found that more than half of the women faculty had experienced some form of gender harassment (e.g., offensive stories, jokes, or comments; staring or ogling; sexist remarks about women), and more than 20% had reported being the object of unwanted sexual advances or attention.

Critics of the attention given to sexual harassment (e.g., Paglia, 1994; Roiphe, 1993) enjoy considerable media attention but do not seriously address questions about the antecedents, correlates, or consequences of sexually harassing behavior. Indeed, a discussion of the complex, far-reaching consequences of sexual harassment is not often found in either the popular or scientific literature despite the enormous significance of the issue. If only sexually harassing behaviors were indeed trivial, as claimed in the new backlash, or easily ignored and shrugged off as "that's life," as girls and women have been taught to do, we could all stop talking about it. Unfortunately, that is not the case, as indicated by social science data and the reported experiences of women from varied backgrounds and in diverse situations.

Elsewhere, one of us (Lott, 1996) has used a social learning theory analysis to propose that experiencing sexual harassment has a wide range of serious outcomes for women. Sexual harassment

1. reinforces beliefs about personal vulnerability;
2. contributes to anxiety and self-doubt;
3. increases ambivalence toward heterosexuality by increasing the ambiguity of men's sexual behaviors and the confusion between interpreting them as expressions of sexual interest or power;
4. encourages women to believe that they are not "good" (i.e., virtuous) or not competent if they are not skillful enough to avoid harassment (Stanko, 1985);
5. makes it necessary for women to learn ways of avoiding or escaping from sexually harassing behaviors or situations, responses that may seriously conflict, compete, or interfere with going to classes, enhancing work status, earning a paycheck, or engaging in positive interpersonal relationships; and
6. serves to maintain power inequalities between women and men. Fiske and Glick (1995) have noted that, like stereotypes, "harassment similarly derogates, debilitates, and disadvantages the less powerful" (p. 110).

There are reciprocal and equally serious and far-reaching consequences for the men who engage in harassing behaviors. Those who get away with it (for whom there are no negative sanctions)

1. are reinforced for their behavior, which increases the likelihood of it being repeated under similar circumstances;
2. learn that they are powerful, which increases the likelihood that they will continue to exert power in sexual and related situations; and
3. become confused about the distinction between what is a "normal" expression of sexual interest (i.e., what is culturally acceptable) and what is deviant or aberrant (Stanko, 1985).

Such consequences affect men's behavior toward women and how men feel about and interact with women.

It is because the outcomes for both women and men have widespread and complex social significance that it is essential to try to answer the question of "what to do." Despite the increased attention that has been given to sexual harassment, to studying its incidence and proposing legal and organizational remedies, there is still enormous resistance to the subject by both men and women. As one of us has suggested elsewhere

(Lott, 1996), we resist talking about sexual harassment because the subject taps the hidden experiences of so many women and men, because resolutions of the problems seem so out of reach, and because the behaviors we need to examine are so ubiquitous. We do not want to believe that our professors or colleagues or boyfriends want to hurt or demean us. Men do not want to see themselves as villainous harassers or insensitive louts, and women do not want to see ourselves as victims, or as losing the little power we may have by criticizing or threatening the more powerful. We fear there will be negative outcomes from identifying and countering incidents of sexual harassment–outcomes that extend from being perceived as poor sports or complainers, through loss of relationships, to serious economic or professional reprisals.

REMEDIES

Organizational Changes

The strategies for dealing with sexual harassment that are most often discussed are ones that focus on top-down organizational changes instituted by well-meaning or lawsuit-avoiding employers or supervisors. These include the development of policies and grievance procedures, educational workshops, and open discussions of differences between women and men in interpretations of, and attitudes toward, harassing behavior (e.g., Comer, 1992).

The law provides remedies for individuals who can now bring suit against people and organizations on charges of sexual harassment, which is interpreted as a subclass of sex discrimination. What federal and state regulations have done with regard to sexual harassment is, as noted by Barak (1992), to "create a sanction system" that defines such harassment as "unacceptable conduct" and in this way sends a "philosophical and psychological message" (p. 818). The story of how the courts have dealt with such suits is a fascinating and complex one (see, for example, Fitzgerald, 1996c). One result of the legal actions that have been taken is that educational institutions and other employers have been either encouraged or mandated to develop policies and procedures that are designed to prevent (or decrease) sexual harassment and also to punish transgressors (Fitzgerald, 1996b). To accomplish the latter, a woman who has been subjected to harassment must report the incident(s) to those able to provide negative sanctions. And therein lies the problem. All who have studied the current situation agree that bringing a harasser "to justice" through formal (or informal) grievance procedures is a strategy seldom adopted by women (Bingham & Scherer, 1993; Booth-Butterfield, 1991; Riger, 1991).

Acting on their belief that prevention is the most effective way to eliminate sexual harassment, the federal EEOC recommended in 1986 that, in addition to developing appropriate sanctions for substantiated incidents of sexual harassment, organizations should use education, voice strong disapproval, and provide information about employee and student rights and about specific steps to be taken in reporting incidents (cf. Perry, 1993). Some (e.g., Gutek, 1985) have suggested that, regardless of whether grievance procedures are used, sexual harassment is likely to decrease in organizations (large or small) in which it is made clear by management that such behavior is not acceptable, is not regarded as normative, and that a sexualized work environment is inappropriate. As noted by Fiske and Glick (1995), "If those in authority communicated that stereotyping and harassment will not be tolerated and that this is a standard central to the organization's mission, then such policies have optimal impact" (p. 112).

Some empirical data support such a proposition. For example, in two studies of large national samples, Pryor, Giedd, and Williams (1995) obtained evidence "that local social norms, as indexed by the perceived attitudes of local management, influence the incidence of sexual harassment" (p. 73). Women were less likely to report sexual harassment in work situations where men saw it as less socially permissible and in work situations in which public display of sexually explicit materials degrading to women was discouraged.

In our view, sexual harassment is inextricably tied to the power imbalance between women and men and to the existence of sexism. Sexism can be conceptualized as including negative or ambivalent attitudes toward women (prejudice); widely shared beliefs about women's capacities, interests, and ways of behaving (stereotypes); and actions or norms that exclude, distance, or undermine women (discrimination).

> Sexual harassment is part of living in a sexist culture . . . in which women expect to be the targets of sexual jokes and innuendo as well as the receivers of positive sexual attention. Sexual harassment is deeply enmeshed in the relationships between women and men that we have been taught are natural. (Lott, 1996, p. 231)

Thus, proposed solutions need to include a wide range of efforts to enhance or ensure gender equity. Riger (1991), for example, argues that "extensive efforts at prevention need to be mounted at the individual, situational, and organizational level" (p. 503).

Individual Responses

Another group of strategies reported in the literature are those used by individual women as they attempt to respond to incidents of harassment on their own. Bingham and Scherer (1993) surveyed faculty and staff at a midwestern university and found that the most frequent personal response to sexual harassment was talking to the harasser. This was also the response most associated with satisfaction regarding outcome. Lower levels of satisfaction with situation outcome were associated with work climates that were perceived as "harassment-prone" or harassment encouraging.

In a study of responses to sexist (unfair) treatment, Lott, Asquith, and Doyon (1996) found that of 262 women (heterogeneous with respect to ethnicity and age) in their sample, 39.3% reported having ignored sexist incidents, 26.2% reported that they had confronted the sexist person directly, 22.1% said they left the place where the incident occurred, and 20.9% said they avoided further interaction with the unfair/sexist person. These same four ways of responding were the ones reported most frequently by women of color younger and older than 30 and by European American women younger and older than 30 with one exception: the younger European American women reported that they made jokes more frequently than they avoided the sexist person. These data suggest that, with the exception of direct confrontation, the most typical responses to harassment by women across broad age and ethnicity categories are ones of either acceptance or avoidance.

Yount (1991) spent more than 5 months observing and examining, through interviews and group discussion, the strategies a sample of women coal miners had developed to manage and cope with sexual harassment on the job. Coal mines are settings in which interactions have typically been "highly sexual and jocular" (p. 399), in which the presence of women workers was not welcomed, and in which "stereotyped conceptions . . . were used by antagonistic bosses and workers to justify discrimination in training and assignment opportunities offered to women on the grounds that female workers were impediments to production, safety, and morale" (p. 401). Thus, it is not surprising that the women miners found sexual

harassment to be a commonplace experience. Yount identified and catego-
rized three dominant strategies that the women workers appeared to have
developed: that of the "lady," the "flirt," and the "tomboy." The "ladies,"
who by and large were the older women workers, tended to disengage from
the men, to keep their distance, to avoid using profanity or engaging in any
behavior that might be interpreted as suggestive, and to emphasize by their
appearance and manners that they were "ladies." The consequences for
them were twofold: They were the targets of the least amount of come-ons,
teasing, and sexual harassment, but they also accepted the least prestigious
and remunerative jobs. The "flirts" were younger and single, and, as
defensive measures, they feigned flattery when they were the targets of the
men's sexual razzing. The consequences to them were that they became
perceived as the "embodiment of the female stereotype, . . . as particularly
lacking in potential and were given the fewest opportunities to develop job
skills and to establish social and self-identities as miners" (p. 410). The
"tomboys" were also single but generally older than the "flirts." They
attempted to separate themselves from the female stereotype, to focus on
their status as coal miners, to develop a "thick skin," and to respond to
harassment with humor, comebacks, sexual talk of their own, or reprocica-
tion. A major problem with these strategies is that the "tomboys" tended
to be considered "sluts" or sexually promiscuous, as women who violated
the sexual double standard, and they were thus subjected by some men to
intensified and escalated harassment.

The results of this intensive study of women coal miners seem to us to
be clearly applicable to other work settings—to factories, offices, and
universities. What the findings indicate is that individual strategies are not
likely to be effective, may have unanticipated negative consequences for
the workplace, and may even lead to increased sexual harassment. Women
who try to deal with sexual harassment on their own, regardless of what
they do, seem to be in a no-win situation. However, a woman who
considers formal complaints, filing charges, and using the procedures
available in her organization tends to be discouraged from doing so by the
anticipation of the time and energy that such a response will entail, the
strong possibility of retaliation by the more powerful man she is accusing,
being perceived as a victim, and not effecting change in her general
workplace environment even if she succeeds in having a single harasser
punished.

Informal, Collective Action

Strategies that are rarely mentioned are collective, grassroots efforts that mobilize the women involved to work together to change the social climate of their immediate environments. While we await and work for widespread and large-scale social changes in the direction of gender equity and top-down organizational changes, women need to develop for ourselves collective strategies matched to our particular situations that will effectively reduce the sexual harassment we experience in the everyday world at our places of work, training, and education. Such an approach was adopted by a group of women graduate students and faculty in the Department of Psychology at the University of Rhode Island.

The strategies developed and implemented by this group of women are an example of an informal grassroots effort. These strategies were developed within a particular historical, geographical, political, and social context and so would need to be adapted to the special circumstances of other groups interested in taking similar actions. What follows is a description of the context, formation, process, actions, and consequences of this group in the hope that other groups may find the information helpful.

WASH (WOMEN AGAINST SEXUAL HARASSMENT): A CASE STUDY

Like other colleges and universities that receive federal dollars for any purpose, our university has a sexual harassment policy ("Sexual Harassment Policy," 1988) that prohibits sexual harassment as a form of sex discrimination. Following the guidelines of the EEOC, sexual harassment is defined in our university's policy as

> unwelcome sexual advances, requests for sexual favors, and other verbal or physical conduct of a sexual nature . . . when (1) submission to such conduct is made either explicitly or implicitly a . . . condition of instruction, employment, or otherwise full participation in University life; (2) submission or rejection . . . is used as a basis for evaluation . . . ; or (3) such conduct has the purpose or effect of unreasonably interfering with an individual's performance or creating an intimidating, hostile, or offensive University environment.

The university promises to take "prompt action to investigate and redress sexual harassment" and prohibits retaliation against people who bring such complaints.

With respect to the steps to be taken by an individual who wishes such "prompt action," our university, like others, is required to prepare and publish a set of procedures. Although the policy quoted above has remained the same since 1988, the complaint process has undergone revision. The current set of procedures is now generic, that is, it applies to complaints of "discrimination/ harassment on the basis of race, sex, religion, age, color, creed, national origin, disability and sexual orientation" ("The Discrimination Complaint Process," 1994), and the document describing the procedures consists of eight single-spaced pages. In a pamphlet produced for campus distribution ("Sexual Harassment," 1994), the final section, entitled "What Can You Do About Sexual Harassment?" advises the reader that the university has a pool of advocates "to offer support and provide information," and that those who believe they have been sexually harassed "are encouraged to contact an advocate." How to make such contact is not specified, but a list of relevant campus offices is provided. The obstacles to effecting prompt action, to changing the behavior of individual harassers or the social climate of a particular workplace or educational environment, seem formidable.

How WASH Got Started

In the fall of 1991, allegations of sexual harassment against Judge Clarence Thomas were made public by Professor Anita Hill during the nationally televised Senate Judiciary Committee Hearings on his nomination to the Supreme Court. Although Judge Thomas was ultimately appointed to the Supreme Court, Professor Hill's testimony had an enormous impact on public awareness and concern about sexual harassment. Professor Hill's testimony and treatment by the Senate Committee and the media also made salient the powerful backlash that commonly occurs against any woman who publicly challenges her harasser. Efforts were made to denigrate Hill as a liar, as pathological, and as having fantasized about Thomas's attraction to her.

The impact of the Thomas confirmation hearings were easily observed on our campus. Classroom discussions were devoted to the topic, and students became more vocal about their own experiences with sexual harassment. Two feminist women professors, who believed in the potential

258

power and necessity of collective action and recognized that many students and faculty wanted both to speak and act, posted signs around the psychology department to announce a meeting open to all "women faculty, graduate students, and staff interested in sexual harassment." The initial meeting (and subsequent meetings) took place at the university Women's Center; the meeting time and place were posted in the psychology department newsletter as well as in signs in department corridors. This practice of open announcement of meetings was maintained for all meetings that followed.

Process

At the first meeting, we established important ground rules that were repeated at the beginning of each subsequent meeting. These rules were (a) no one could disclose the identity of attendees to people who were not present at meetings (although each woman was free to disclose her own attendance); (b) no one could disclose the exact number of attendees or the graduate programs from which they came; (c) no one could repeat anything discussed at a meeting, even to women who had attended previous meetings; and (d) if asked about a meeting, one should say that the meeting had been "well attended and numerous incidents of sexual harassment were discussed," but should not provide any other information.

Our efforts to protect the identity of WASH members who did not wish to be identified reduced the fear of graduate students and faculty members that by speaking and acting openly in response to departmental incidents of sexual harassment, they might antagonize other students or faculty and thus potentially jeopardize their careers. The desire to avoid open disclosure reflects realistic awareness and fear of possible retaliation as well as the damage done to self-confidence by personal experiences or observations of harassment. The confidentiality of our meetings and our focus on collective action worked together to emphasize that sexual harassment was a common experience for women and to reduce or eliminate risks to individuals. We believe that individual action is difficult to take, entails risks, and is often ineffective.

During the first meeting, in addition to establishing basic rules, we articulated the general goals of the group and agreed upon our group name "Women Against Sexual Harassment." WASH was to provide a safe and sympathetic forum in which to discuss incidents of harassment and to plan collective preventive, educational, and direct action strategies. We wanted to focus particularly on changing the normative culture within our department—social, teaching, mentoring, and supervision environment. We shared the conviction that only by organizing and working together could we effect social change. We also agreed that all actions taken by the group would be legal, socially responsible, and respectful of the rights of others.

The number of student and faculty attendees at WASH meetings varied considerably across meetings. Some members attended consistently; others attended only one or two meetings, or attended sporadically. Attendance was never taken, either formally or informally, and the group remained open in both practice and spirit. Occasionally, openly identified WASH members were asked whether undergraduates or women from other departments could attend, and these decisions were made by consensus of the group on a case-by-case basis. In an effort to protect the confidentiality and boundaries of the group, it was generally limited to graduate students, faculty, and staff of the Department of Psychology.

The decision to define our boundary in this way was based on the special relationship that exists between and among graduate students and faculty. Interaction between members of these two groups occurs on an almost daily basis and includes collaboration in classroom, research, and practice settings. WASH had arisen in response to concerns expressed by graduate students and faculty who were part of our particular departmental community about issues within that community. This community did not include undergraduates, whose interactions with faculty are typically far less frequent and intense; nor did this community include members of other departments. Other communities forming groups such as WASH will need to define their boundaries in accord with their own particular circumstances and needs.

Behaviors Discussed and Targeted by WASH

The incidents of harassment we discussed were varied and covered a wide range of behaviors. With respect to clinical supervision, issues discussed by WASH members included inappropriate personal disclosures by supervisors about sexual matters; asking supervisees for personal information not directly related to the client or issue being discussed; encouraging and enforcing sexist views of clients and their difficulties; encouragement by supervisors of flirtatious behavior with clients; and interpretation by supervisors of feminist viewpoints as indicative of "repression" or of being "uptight" or "conservative." Research-related issues included professors or teaching assistants asking undergraduate students in their classes for personal information under the guise of "research" without prior informed consent. Issues that were related to teaching included the selection of course materials that presented a consistently negative view of women; the use of primarily women in examples of client "pathology"; sexually inappropriate or demeaning class examples and "jokes"; focusing on a student's physical appearance or personal life in class; and the attribution of a student's or teaching assistant's complaints about any of the above as due to their pathology, discomfort with sexual material, or religious upbringing. In addition, we discussed a variety of comments that were made "casually" as "jokes" or comments in the hallway, such as greeting women students with "hey baby" or full-body hugs, and frequent comments about a student's physical appearance. We also discussed incidents where professors spoke "out of concern" to other colleagues about particular students with openly feminist views who "seemed to have problems with men." A terrifying incident in which one of our members returned to her office and found that an unknown male had left semen on her desk was also the subject of considerable attention and discussion.

Strategies Used by WASH at the Departmental Level

Our first group action was to publish a notice in the department newsletter that "the first meeting of Women Against Sexual Harassment (WASH) was well attended, and numerous incidents of sexual harassment were discussed." We announced the time and place of the next meeting and encouraged "all interested women faculty, graduate students, and staff" to attend. We specifically wanted to alert department members that sexual harassment within the department was being observed, discussed, and taken seriously.

Another early action was putting copies of the university's sexual harassment policy and procedures and related materials in student and faculty mailboxes and on a table in our department mailroom. In addition, we created a large "This Is Sexual Harassment" poster that was based on actual incidents that had occurred within our department. The approximately 5- × 2-foot poster defined harassment by use of examples, and each item was printed in large black letters. The poster was pinned to our mailroom bulletin board and remained undisturbed for 1 year. When it was defaced and ripped by people unknown, we replaced it with a smaller version, which attracted a small piece of rude graffiti but otherwise remained undisturbed in the department mailroom until there was a rearrangement of furniture and mail boxes. A small version has once again been placed on the bulletin board, but requires periodic replacement.

A small committee from WASH met with the department chair and requested that a sexual harassment workshop be conducted for faculty and graduate students (separately). The chair presented the proposal to the department faculty, who approved it, and two workshops were conducted by a university staff member who had never been asked to conduct such a workshop before (although it was part of her job description). The faculty workshop was well attended. The chair of the department had strongly recommended that faculty attend and had scheduled the workshop during a regular faculty meeting. The graduate student workshop was less well attended. The suggestion that students with graduate assistantships be required to attend a sexual harassment workshop was supported by the department chair but never implemented.

Strategies at the Individual Level

One professor agreed to meet with a small group of past and present teaching assistants to discuss complaints about women-demeaning examples and comments in an undergraduate class that he taught. Prior to this meeting, the larger WASH group helped the teaching assistants develop an agenda and rehearse a respectful and reasoned presentation to the professor.

One graduate student who wished to speak privately with a professor about his behavior in interactions with her received support and advice from WASH. Several members offered to wait near the professor's office while she met with him and to knock on his door at an agreed-upon time to assist her in keeping the meeting from being prolonged. This plan was developed during a WASH meeting, and the student was supported in her decision to act individually.

Similarly, another student was supported in her desire to file a formal complaint against a professor for making remarks so demeaning to women that the student decided that she could not continue to take the course. She wrote a letter of complaint to the professor and also filed a formal complaint, which led to a hearing in the Affirmative Action office. Resolution of the issue was informal, and guilt was not established, nor was any corrective action taken. This incident is an example of the problematic nature of formal procedures for dealing with sexual harassment.

As a final example of individual strategies, a small group of WASH students met with a professor about his use of a textbook that the students felt was extremely sexist. As a result, the professor raised the question of the book's sexism in his class and was convinced by the ensuing discussion not to use that book in subsequent semesters.

Strategies at the University Level

A letter was sent to the campus police department by WASH to communicate concerns regarding women's safety on campus. Soon after, several WASH members met with the new campus security director, and, following that meeting, new policies were issued about improved lighting on campus and the publication of incidents of violence in the student newspaper.

A letter was also sent by WASH to the university president regarding a decision to disband the university's Affirmative Action Sexual Harassment Subcommittee and to express our concern that revised sexual harassment policies and procedures had not been communicated to the campus community. We were not successful in our request that the Sexual Harassment Subcommittee be continued; our concerns about policies and procedures were simply forwarded by the president to the Affirmative Action Officer without any direct response from him to us.

Strategies at the Community Level

Several members gave a presentation about WASH at a local psychiatric hospital. The meeting was attended by a number of women staff at the hospital, and the focus was on strategies that they could develop and implement in their workplace. In addition, a workshop was conducted at a national conference of the Association for Women in Psychology on ways to eliminate sexual harassment within the academic community (Gregory, Minugh, Riedford, Rocchio, & Saris, 1993). The workshop presented WASH as a case study; it emphasized actions that were taken by members, problems that were encountered, and changes that were effected. Information about WASH has also been shared with wider audiences in a presentation to the higher education conference of the National Education Association (Lott, 1992) and in a book chapter (Lott, 1996).

The Impact of WASH: Backlash

From the beginning, we heard "grumbling" within the department that came from a variety of sources. Some students and faculty were overheard in conversations deriding the objectives of WASH and talking about the "witch hunt" that was going on against men within the department. Graduate students were sometimes asked, "You're not one of them, are you?" Some men professors complained openly that the department "wasn't what it used to be" and that they had to be "so careful with what they said these days because so much could be misinterpreted." At a graduate students' meeting, a male student asked the second author of this chapter (who was open about her membership in WASH) why men couldn't attend. He continued to push the issue and complained that WASH had "divided the department in two." The posted announcements of our meetings were occasionally torn down or had rude graffiti written on them.

These negative incidents and "grumblings" were relatively few in number and did not appear to be representative of the opinions of most of the department. There was, however, one major incident that resulted from a single breach of confidentiality within our group. A woman who attended one meeting reported to a male graduate student whom she was dating information that she claimed had been discussed about his behavior. This graduate student circulated a letter of complaint against WASH and two of its members to the entire department faculty, an administrator, and an attorney. The matter was ultimately resolved satisfactorily at a meeting between the two named WASH members, the woman who breached WASH's confidentiality, and the male graduate student, their respective advocates, the department chair, the clinical training director, and a third agreed-on "impartial" faculty member who moderated the meeting. We were able to use this meeting as an opportunity to address concerns raised by all the involved parties and to affirm WASH's right to maintain the confidentiality of its membership and discussions.

Positive Impact of WASH on Individual Members

Five former graduate student members of WASH, whom we approached, agreed to tell us how their experiences with WASH had changed or impacted them, both at the time of their involvement and subsequently. We were particularly interested in how WASH had prepared them to deal with sexist experiences in academia and other post-PhD work settings.

This is what *Woman 1* told us:

Watching the Hill-Thomas debate unfold was frustrating, very frustrating. Another day of watching a panel of White, middle-aged, upper-class men pose ridiculous questions to Anita Hill. Another day of listening to other women trash Anita Hill, suggesting she was either "delusional" or a "woman scorned." I grew angrier each day. Why was everyone finding it so hard to believe that Clarence Thomas sexually harassed Anita Hill? What Hill described was just another day in the life of many women everywhere.

Apparently, other graduate students were feeling the same way that I was. Many . . . had experienced or were currently experiencing sexual harassment. We were mad. We were sad. . . . I don't recall how many women attended that first meeting, but we filled up a room. . . . I was a first-year graduate student, so I didn't know many of the students there. I remember people saying that they were nervous about being at this meeting. Nervous about being identified as a potential "troublemaker" and how this might affect their relationships with faculty. We laid out some ground rules about confidentiality . . . and then we talked, and talked some more. We began meeting regularly. I can't tell you how much it meant to me to meet and talk with other women who shared my perspective.

We became a presence in the department. People took notice of "us." We posted information about sexual harassment. We held a sexual harassment workshop. . . . We got people thinking and talking, and I'd like to think our presence may have curtailed some sexually harassing behaviors. . . .

All in all, WASH was a major success. Being part of that group got us through a very difficult time. I believe my experiences as a student member of WASH affect my experiences today, as a professor. I discuss the issue of sexual harassment in my psychology classes. When approached by individual students . . . I tell them the truth. Don't expect to win sexual harassment suits. I don't advise them either way. . . . Most of the time, that's not what women are looking for anyway. Most of the time they are looking for someone to say, "No, you're not crazy. No, you're not blowing things out of proportion. Yes, it is insulting when a clinical psychology faculty member tells his students on the first day of class 'I can spot a sexual abuse victim within ten minutes of meeting them.' " The most valuable thing I've learned is that women must continue to support each other and challenge sexism. Individually, it's hard to take action. Collectively, it's hard to be ignored.

From *Woman 2* came the following:

I became involved with WASH in its second year. . . . [T]he group helped me in several ways. First, it allowed me to realize how prevalent sexual harassment is. I was shocked . . . after hearing of other members' personal experiences. The group also helped me to recognize sexual harassment as an offensive crime as opposed to flattery. Lastly, it helped me decide how to handle a personal case of sexual harassment. Members of the group listened very carefully while I presented them with a very complicated case. They helped me to identify the issues that would be involved were I to file a complaint, which I eventually chose not to do. Members of WASH supported my choice.

In my professional life as an academic, WASH has prepared me to face a working environment that may not be supportive of women . . . [and] may even be downright hostile to women. I now know what sexual harassment is, and the courses of action that are available to women who experience it. This knowledge will assist me personally and allow me to provide support, encouragement, and advice to students.

This is what *Woman 3* shared with us:

I experienced enormous changes as a result of my involvement with WASH, . . . an increased awareness of and sensitivity to the continuum of sexual harassment . . . [and] an increased sense of how hurtful and damaging sexual harassment can be. In addition, I am better equipped to recognize and label sexual harassment when it is brought to my attention by colleagues, and more able to sensitively discuss the situation with them. I also have an increased willingness to work for broader social change in the area of sexual harassment; for example, social action at the University level moved to a higher priority for me during my involvement with WASH.

On a more personal level, a veil of naiveté was lifted, never to fall again. WASH enabled me to label "difficult" or "uncomfortable" situations as sexual harassment and provided me with skills with which to handle such incidents. When an unknown man left semen on my office desk, the actions I took were largely a result of the support and information I received from WASH members. I contacted security [personnel], spoke with the department chair, requested information about other such incidents on campus, requested that a notice of the incident be placed in the [department] newsletter to warn my colleagues, and took it upon myself to personally speak with professors and students who had offices in the vicinity of mine.

. . . I developed a well of strength as a result of my experience with WASH. The faculty members were good models for how to make a difference within the University. . . . It was so significant, helpful, and powerful to me to have faculty members who were able to instill in students the courage and strength to make a difference. The WASH discussions were so validating, and, in many ways, WASH was for me a support group. Yet it was so much more, and I will always have the strength that I gained from breaking the silence about sexual harassment and academic incest.

Here is the voice of *Woman 4*:

WASH . . . had an enormous impact on me both as a graduate student and now as a full-time faculty person at a small liberal arts college. . . . Before the formation of this group, I was aware of sexual harassment in academe, but WASH greatly increased my awareness . . . , particularly regarding the more subtle aspects of sexism in the classroom. On a number of occasions, I had been upset by professors who repeatedly used sexist examples in their classes, but I don't think I fully recognized this as a form of harassment until WASH. Some of our most productive meetings involved defining/illustrating the many forms of sexual harassment and brainstorming strategies for change.

Eventually, I was one of a small group of students who initiated a meeting with a professor to discuss his behavior. Although I was very nervous about the possible repercussions of this meeting, this was an incredibly powerful experience for me. I learned a lot about how to fight back against harassers as well as the need for women to unite on this issue. Listening to the experiences of other graduate students and faculty reinforced my understanding of harassment as a way to maintain power over women. Within our group, some . . . were less willing to take public action than others, and our meetings also enhanced my sensitivity for women who choose not to speak out against their harassers. Through WASH, I developed a deeper understanding of the complex issues which influence both whether and how an individual takes action, and I came to appreciate decisions and opinions which differed from my own.

As a junior faculty person . . . I am much more likely to "speak up" when someone makes an inappropriate remark, and I believe this is a direct result of my WASH participation. For example, I recently participated in a debate regarding the importance of a multicultural curriculum. My debate partner (another woman) and I disagreed with the opposing team (two men) regarding the format of our presentation. The opposing team threatened that if we did not abide by their format, we would be perceived as less persuasive because we are women. My partner and I vehemently disagreed with our male colleagues, and I know, in part, my WASH participation helped to identify their behavior as unacceptable and harassing. Simply put, I am stronger and better prepared to deal with sexual harassment. I am no longer afraid.

And one final voice, that of *Woman 5*:

My involvement with WASH from its inception was truly transformational. I was a feminist who was very aware of sexual harassment, yet, like many women, I had difficulty labeling my interactions with an "inappropriate, but perhaps well-intentioned" professor as sexual harassment. Coming together with a group of strong and supportive women was empowering and uplifting. I gained personal strength both from the guidance I received . . . and the guidance I was able to give.

The two most important lessons I learned . . . were the importance of labeling even subtle harassment as sexual harassment and the power of collective action. Even in the face of a breach of confidentiality, I was able to . . . [act] powerfully and with a tremendous amount of support and guidance was able to advocate for myself and for WASH. As a group, we did so much more than support each other as we discussed the rampant and excruciatingly painful incidents of sexual harassment in our department; we created change! Our actions dramatically altered the departmental environment, and many of these changes have endured, even nearly 6 years later.

Now, as I work in both academic and clinical settings, I am much more confident about the resources I have available in the face of harassment. I am better equipped to strategize and no longer feel guilty, self-blaming, or tolerant of such incidents. In addition, I feel better able to counsel and advise others, as well as simply listen and support them as they struggle with their own experiences of sexual harassment. I have the tools necessary to label and fight sexual harassment in whatever work setting I may find myself, and an awareness of the many options available to me in addition to silence and individual solutions.

Overall Accomplishments

We believe that WASH was effective in raising the level of awareness of sexual harassment within our department and in raising the consciousness of individual faculty members about such issues. We also educated ourselves and others in our community by discussing our objectives, actions, and strategies. During the course of an American Psychological Association (APA) site visit to the clinical program at our university, some faculty and students spoke openly about WASH and its activities. In the written site review, our APA visitors specifically mentioned WASH as a source of positive contributions to the department.

In our view, the general atmosphere of our department was significantly and constructively altered by the existence and activities of WASH. The overall incidence of sexual harassment appears to have decreased significantly, and the most overt examples of sexual harassment seem to have been eliminated. WASH's success can be measured in part by the fact that the group stopped meeting when interest in it waned. The group was active from the fall of 1991 to the spring of 1994, by which time there appeared to be no further need for the group. We will have to wait and see how long the "immunization" effect of WASH will last.

CONCLUSIONS

We have presented this description of the formation and work of WASH as an example of how informal, collective strategies can be used to effect social change in a small community. A small group within our department decided to address a community problem by "standing up" and implementing small efforts to deal with the problem's various manifestations. Weick (1984) has argued that one reason social problems are difficult to solve is because "people define these problems in ways that overwhelm their ability to do anything about them. Changing the scale of a problem can change the quality of resources directed at it" (p. 48). If we redefine a social problem as a series of small tasks that can be accomplished, then a social problem becomes amenable to change by less than superhuman effort. Taking such a step-by-step approach to a major social problem like sexual harassment permits us to concentrate on "small wins" and may temper the tendency to feel overwhelmed by the enormity and complexity of such a wide-ranging and multifaceted issue.

It was toward this objective that the work of WASH was directed. Other groups tackling problems of sexual harassment within their small communities will have to do their own analyses of their particular circumstances and devise their own strategies suited to their historical, political, and social situation. We believe that there were some factors that were crucial to our success and that should be considered by other groups formed with similar objectives. These factors are adherence to strict confidentiality regarding who attends meetings and what is discussed; the use of strategies that are legal, ethical, and respectful of all people involved; and respect for the right of each woman to decide how to respond (or not to respond) to her situation.

Women forming groups for collective action will have to consider the specific features of their own work environments, the probability of negative reactions, and so on. Undoubtedly, the presence of at least two strong feminist and tenured faculty women contributed to WASH's success. In other settings, there may not be supportive women at different levels, and group members may feel safer if all attendees are peers.

We have found that informal, collective strategies can effect change. The specific strategies and targeted goals will, of course, vary from setting to setting, but there are alternatives to doing nothing, or to following the slow and often ineffectual formal procedures set up by large organizations, or to individual solutions that have low probabilities of success and high probabilities of negative repercussions.

REFERENCES

All work, no play. (1996, July 25). *Providence Journal Bulletin*, p. G1.

Barak, A. (1992). Combatting sexual harassment. *American Psychologist, 47*, 818-819.

Bingham, S. G., & Scherer, L. L. (1993). Factors associated with responses to sexual harassment and satisfaction with outcome. *Sex Roles, 29*, 239-269.

Booth-Butterfield, M. (1991, February). *Information seeking, sexual harassment, and notification in organizations.* Unpublished manuscript, Department of Communication Studies, West Virginia University, Morgantown.

Comer, D. R. (1992). Exploring gender-based differences to combat sexual harassment. *American Psychologist, 47,* 819.

The discrimination complaint process. (1994, August 2). Kingston: Affirmative Action Office, University of Rhode Island.

Fiske, S. T., & Glick, P. (1995). Ambivalence and stereotypes cause sexual harassment: A theory with implications for organizational change. *Journal of Social Issues, 51*(1), 97-115.

Fitzgerald, L. F. (1996a). Definitions of sexual harassment. In B. Lott & M. E. Reilly (Eds.), *Combatting sexual harassment in higher education* (pp. 42-54). Washington, DC: National Education Association.

Fitzgerald, L. F. (1996b). Institutional policies and procedures. In B. Lott & M. E. Reilly (Eds.), *Combatting sexual harassment in higher education* (pp. 129-140). Washington, DC: National Education Association.

Fitzgerald, L. F. (1996c). The legal context of sexual harassment. In B. Lott & M. E. Reilly (Eds.), *Combatting sexual harassment in higher education* (pp. 110-128). Washington, DC: National Education Association.

Fitzgerald, L. F., Shullman, S. L., Bailey, N., Richards, M., Swecker, J., Gold, Y., Ormerod, S. J., & Weitzman, L. (1988). The incidence and dimensions of sexual harassment in academia and the workplace. *Journal of Vocational Behavior, 32,* 152-175.

Gregory, C., Minugh, P. A., Riedford, M., Rocchio, L. M., & Saris, R. (1993, March). *Women against sexual harassment (WASH) unite: Working to eliminate sexual harassment from the academic community.* Workshop presented at the national meeting of the Association for Women in Psychology, Atlanta, GA.

Gutek, B. A. (1985). *Sex and the workplace.* San Francisco: Jossey-Bass.

Kelly, M. P. F. (1996, July 25). Feminism and the morality police. *Providence Journal Bulletin,* p. B6.

Koss, M. P., Goodman, L. A., Browne, A., Fitzgerald, L. F., Keita, G. P., & Russo, N. F. (1994). *No safe haven: Male violence against women at home, at work, and in the community.* Washington, DC: American Psychological Association.

Lott, B. (1992, February). *Sexual harassment on campus: Issues, problems, consequences, and remedies.* Paper presented at the meeting of the National Education Association Higher Education Conference, San Diego, CA.

Lott, B. (1996). Sexual harassment: Consequences and remedies. In B. Lott & M. E. Reilly (Eds.), *Combatting sexual harassment in higher education* (pp. 229-244). Washington, DC: National Education Association.

Lott, B., Asquith, K., & Doyon, T. (1996). *Women's responses to personal experiences of sexist discrimination related to ethnicity and age.* Unpublished manuscript, Department of Psychology, University of Rhode Island, Kingston, RI.

Paglia, C. (1994). *Vamps and tramps: New essays.* New York: Vintage.

Perry, N. W. (1993). Sexual harassment on campus: Are your actions actionable? *Journal of College Student Development, 34,* 406-410.

Pryor, J. B., Giedd, J. L., & Williams, K. B. (1995). A social psychological model for predicting sexual harassment. *Journal of Social Issues, 51*(1), 69-84.

Riger, S. (1991). Gender dilemmas in sexual harassment policies and procedures. *American Psychologist, 46,* 497-505.

Roiphe, K. (1993). *The morning after: Sex, fear and feminism on campus.* Boston: Little, Brown.

Sexual harassment. (1994, February). Kingston: University of Rhode Island Publications Office.

Sexual harassment policy. (1988, September). Kingston: Affirmative Action Office, University of Rhode Island.

Stanko, E. A. (1985). *Intimate intrusions: Women's experience of male violence*. London: Routledge & Kegan Paul.

Weick, K. E. (1984). Small wins: Redefining the scale of social problems. *American Psychologist, 39*, 40-49.

Yount, K. R. (1991). Ladies, flirts, and tomboys: Strategies for managing sexual harassment in an underground coal mine. *Journal of Contemporary Ethnography, 19*, 396-422.

What I've Learned About Addressing Sexual Harassment, Protecting Students, *and* Keeping a Job

Maryka Biaggio

As I write this essay, I am beginning my 21st year as an academic. I have held appointments at three different institutions: two state universities and one independent university. Of course, I also spent 4 years in undergraduate school and another 4 in graduate school. Unfortunately, as both a student and an academic, I have known students who have been sexually harassed by faculty. Difficult as these experiences have been, I do think I have learned from them, and I hope to offer here some suggestions for the benefit of other faculty and students.

To address sexual harassment effectively, faculty must have a good understanding of this topic. Many resources can provide a good foundation, including the excellent book *Sexual Harassment on College Campuses* (Paludi, 1996). The focus in this essay is on providing some specific strategies for faculty who are attempting to address sexual harassment of students. For the most part, these strategies are long-term. Sexual harassment is not an uncommon occurrence in academia, but addressing it is far from straightforward. Women faculty are often put in the position of advocating for students because students often turn to women faculty when they are harassed. So it is important to be prepared for this eventuality, and I have four general suggestions:

1. Build alliances. It is essential for all faculty, but especially for new faculty, to nurture relationships and alliances with other faculty, men and women alike, who understand the problems of sexual harassment and power differentials between faculty and students. It is simply not advisable to try to

navigate the murky political waters and administrative channels of academia without having good relationships with colleagues, both inside and outside of one's department. Building alliances with colleagues is not the same as building friendships. We must all work with colleagues whom we wouldn't necessarily choose for friends. Find out who has power in your department and your institution (hint: it's not always the people with administrative titles), and make efforts to work with these people. Seek them out for counsel, volunteer for projects on which they are working, and make yourself known to them. Such alliances can be indispensable when you need to advocate for students.

2. Know your university's governance structure and policies for addressing sexual harassment. Most universities have now developed policies for addressing sexual harassment. Review these policies, know to whom reports should be made, and see if you can garner some history about how complaints have been processed in the past. If there is a need to develop or update the policy, know how to maneuver within the governance system so as to facilitate a successful outcome. It is generally desirable to have a committee of people who represent various constituencies actually develop a draft and bring it for review through the governance structure. That way, the policy cannot be discounted as one person's political agenda. And it is also important that the members of this committee have some institutional support and understand the institution's history of addressing sexual harassment and sensitive issues in general. In this way, potential obstacles can be anticipated, and possibly neutralized, by engaging in consultation with obstructionist elements as the policy is being drafted. If obstructionists are listened to and taken seriously, they may even become advocates for a policy that they believe they have helped forge.

3. Foster a climate that does not tolerate sexual harassment. Certainly, it is far more desirable to prevent sexual harassment than to mop up after the miseries of individual incidents. By all means, try to implement preventive measures. It is the university administration's responsibility to publicize the sexual harassment policy, and this in itself can have a deterring effect. (So, if you've nurtured those alliances with people in the administrative realm, you can encourage them to get the word out on campus.) But education about sexual harassment can foster better understanding, not just among possible offenders but among students, who generally feel empowered by clear public statements about the unacceptability of sexual harassment. And as academ-

ics, we can do something about preventive education. If your university has an invited speaker series, or if your department has faculty presentations, take advantage of these opportunities. Forums such as these can be ideal for presentations on the negative impact of sexual harassment on students or on the importance of maintaining appropriate boundaries in faculty-student relationships. Even the most conservative or skeptical faculty are not likely to argue against efforts to educate, so this can be a powerful tool in raising awareness on your campus.

4. Be judicious in dealing with revelations from individual students. It is not unusual for women faculty, regardless of their rank or position, to be the recipients of student complaints. But there are great costs that students may have to endure in the course of revealing that they have been harassed. They may be labeled as troublemakers by faculty, shunned by their peers, or retaliated against by their harasser. It is not surprising that student silence, especially in the face of subtle forms of harassment, is still the norm. Thus, it is important to move cautiously and thoughtfully when approached by a student. The first consideration should be for the student's safety and well-being. Faculty advocates should gain a good understanding of the student's experience, and then carefully think through possible actions, discuss these with the student, and help the student anticipate consequences of the various actions. Care must be taken to respect the student's circumstances, and this means that students should have as much knowledge as possible of what to expect before they decide how to proceed. It is important that faculty advocates have a good understanding of sexual harassment issues and their institution's policy in order to assist individual students effectively.

These are some strategies that I have found helpful in addressing sexual harassment. Of course, one must be flexible in applying strategies to particular circumstances. However, caution, care, and consultation are always prudent when dealing with a problem as sensitive as sexual harassment.

REFERENCE

Paludi, M. (Ed.). (1996). *Sexual harassment on college campuses: Abusing the ivory power*. Albany: State University of New York Press.

10 Coping With Adversity

Linda L. Carli

Academic careers are very attractive. They provide faculty with freedom to pursue their own individual interests, considerable autonomy and control over their work, and opportunities for intellectual creativity and growth (Sorcinelli, 1994). Even during the pretenure years, most faculty view academic work as intrinsically rewarding and report a strong commitment to an academic career, even as they report increased dissatisfaction with their salaries and job security (Olsen & Sorcinelli, 1992).

In spite of the many attractions of academic work, the academy does have its drawbacks. Jobs in the academy are inherently stressful (Gmelch, 1984, 1996; Melendez & de Guzman, 1983). A recent study of faculty from a variety of disciplines revealed that they experience serious levels of stress from their jobs, stress caused by too heavy workloads, inadequate salaries, time pressures, and lack of career advancement (Gmelch, 1996). Role ambiguity, uncertainty about what constitutes excellence in academic work, and ambiguity about how faculty are evaluated exacerbate the stress (Gmelch, 1984; Seldin, 1987). The challenges of the academy affect both male and female professors. Yet as I have reported previously (Carli, 1997), the stresses experienced by female faculty are different in both quantity and quality from those experienced by men. In fact, many of the major sources of stress reported by faculty affect women more than men. What are the stresses experienced by women faculty, how do women respond to these stressful experiences, and what can they do to cope better?

SOURCES OF PROFESSIONAL STRESS
FOR WOMEN FACULTY

One of the attractions of an academic career is the belief that the academy is a meritocracy. Unfortunately, the academy does not operate as a meritocracy, particularly for women (Simeone, 1987). Although today, women make up a larger percentage of faculty at colleges and universities than in the past (Hamermesh, 1996; West, 1995), they receive promotions and tenure less often than do men (Nettles & Perna, 1995; Sandler & Hall, 1986). In spite of affirmative action, the increased presence of women, and the development of feminist teaching and women's studies programs on college campuses, only 46% of full-time female faculty are tenured, the same percentage as in 1975 (West, 1995). Men continue to earn about 28% more than women, after adjusting for age and for the number of hours worked per week (Hamermesh, 1996). The gender gap in pay exists even among full-time male and female faculty and even when controlling for their level of productivity, their experience and education, and the characteristics of the college or university at which they work (Nettles & Perna, 1995). Moreover, this gap has not improved in decades (West, 1995) and actually increases with increasing rank ("Women Profs," 1996).

In addition to receiving fewer promotions and lower salaries compared with men, women take longer to attain promotions (Hensel, 1991); have greater teaching commitments (Caplan, 1993); have more "caretaking" service commitments, such as advising students (see Chrisler, Herr, & Murstein, this volume); and are increasingly being hired for temporary, part-time, and non-tenure-track positions (Dagg & Thompson, 1988; Hensel, 1991). As a result of these discriminatory practices, women are overrepresented in the lower ranks of the profession, as instructors and assistant professors (Zimbler, 1994). Furthermore, the percentage of women at particular colleges and universities drops as the status of the institution increases; the highest percentage of women, relative to men, occurs in 2-year colleges and the lowest in research universities (West, 1995). Women in the academy are clearly hitting a "glass ceiling."

The situation is particularly dire for African Americans and other women of color whose status in the profession has been relatively unaffected by affirmative action policies (Gajec, 1993) and who continue to be underrepresented in the academy in general and less likely to be tenured or promoted (Hatchett & Bermudez, 1997; Nettles & Perna, 1995). Currently, Black women represent 2.3% of all full-time faculty; Asian women, 1.3%; Hispanic women, 0.8%; and Native American women, only 0.2% (Zimbler, 1994). Moreover, although it is often argued that ethnic minorities have an advantage in the academic job market (see Collins, this volume), recent research findings indicate that few minority candidates are actively pursued by academic institutions. Instead, those with the greatest advantage in attaining desirable jobs are heterosexual White males (Smith, 1996).

Discrimination in pay, promotion, and job status are not the only sources of stress for women in the academy. They also experience other forms of discrimination in their daily interactions with colleagues and students. Female professors have reported that their colleagues subject them to sexist jokes and comments, disparage their scholarship and the scholarship of other women, ignore them and exclude them from important networks, behave condescendingly to them, and even sexually harass them (Caplan, 1993; Fitzgerald, 1996; Grauerholz, 1996; Sandler & Hall, 1993; Simeone, 1987). Even the stresses associated with ambiguous role require-ments are likely to be more serious for women than for men. High-status jobs, such as academic positions (Gmelch, 1984; Seldin, 1987) and posi-tions in upper management (London & Strumpf, 1983), typically have particularly ambiguous criteria. Unfortunately, the more ambiguous the criteria for evaluations, the more sex-biased the evaluations and the more the evaluations unfairly favor men (Nieva & Gutek, 1980). For example, one study revealed that male faculty tend to view high levels of research productivity in women faculty as more professional but less feminine than more modest levels of research productivity (Wiley & Crittenden, 1992). Hence, women can be devalued for producing too little scholarship or too much. Of course, the idea that an academic could produce too much scholarship contradicts the standard of the ideal college professor, a contradiction that would rarely be applied to a man.

If colleagues are biased in their evaluations of female academics, so are students. Students expect women faculty to demonstrate more inter-personal warmth, concern, and support than they expect from their male faculty (Basow, this volume; Bennett, 1982; Langbein, 1994). Students give higher evaluations to their male than their female professors (Hensel, 1991; Langbein, 1994), overestimate the performance of male professors and underestimate the performance of female professors (Dobbins, Cardy, & Truxillo, 1986), consider male professors to be more competent and better teachers (Basow & Silberg, 1987; Sandler & Hall, 1993), expect more challenge and expertise from male professors and more availability and care from their female professors (Burns-Glover & Veith, 1995), and penalize female faculty more than male faculty for giving bad grades (Langbein, 1994).

Several studies have found that male students show higher levels of discrimination than do female students. They evaluate female faculty more harshly (Basow, 1995) and are more disruptive in the classes of female faculty (Brooks, 1982) than are women students. In addition, women faculty experience sexual harassment by male students (Grauerholz, 1996). Some of this hostility may be due to male students' discomfort with competence in women. In fact, research has shown that male college students are *more* influenced by a tentative than an assertive woman, even though they consider a tentative woman to be less competent (Carli, 1990b). They report that the competent woman is less likeable and more threatening, and consequently are more resistant to her influence attempts. Unfortunately, this creates a double bind for women faculty, who can be devalued for being either too competent or not competent enough.

Clearly, women in the academy have good reason to feel stressed. In fact, they do report higher levels of work-related stress than do men; this is particularly so for married women professors (Gmelch, Wilke, & Lovrich, 1986).

Although there has been little research that specifically examines the coping strategies of female academics, their experience of sex discrimination in an already stressful environment puts them at risk for burnout and depression. To say that it is stressful to be overworked, underpaid, denied tenure or promotion, sexually harassed by students, or demeaned by colleagues clearly understates the level of emotional distress these experiences cause. What are some reactions to these stresses?

REACTIONS TO GENDER-RELATED
PROFESSIONAL STRESSES

Denial

Even though women may frequently experience discrimination in the academy, they may not recognize it when it occurs. In fact, establishing bias in hiring and promotion typically requires the use of aggregate data that summarize the history of hiring or promotion at a particular institution or in the field in general. Many women are unaware of the pervasiveness and subtlety of gender discrimination in the academy or how their experience compares with that of their male and female peers. Consequently, women who experience discrimination may not only fail to recognize it, but instead may assume that their experience is unique and attribute it to bad luck or to mistakes on their part (Carli, 1990a). I have witnessed this a number of times. In one instance, it occurred when I made a presentation as part of a panel of women academics discussing gender discrimination in the academy. As part of my presentation, I described an incident in which a woman who had come up for tenure discovered that some of the materials she had submitted to the tenure committee had mysteriously disappeared from her file. After describing this incident, I discovered that many of the women in the audience and some of those on the panel had experienced the same thing; parts of their files, student evaluations, letters of support, books, or articles had mysteriously disappeared when they had come up for reappointment, tenure, or promotion. Clearly, the phenomenon of the "missing file materials" could hardly be considered unique, yet many of the women who had had this experience had assumed it was, in fact, just that. This assumption that one's negative experiences are unique creates a feeling of unique vulnerability, the sense that one is particularly vulnerable to unusual misfortunes; feelings of unique vulnerability, in turn, increase the risk of low self-esteem and depression (Perloff, 1983).

Women professors recognize that there is gender discrimination in the academy (Reid, 1987). However, it is often difficult for women to recognize that they themselves are victims of gender discrimination, even when they recognize that gender discrimination occurs to other women (Crosby, 1982). Again, it is easier to recognize discrimination with aggregate data but quite difficult to recognize it in an individual case. As Caplan (1993) has pointed out, discrimination is particularly hard to recognize in the academy, which is typically perceived as an institution that emphasizes objectivity, fairness, the pursuit of knowledge, and merit as a basis for evaluation. When assessing whether she is being treated equitably at her job, a woman might find reasons to explain why her pay is lower, her teaching load higher, or her job conditions less favorable than that of a man, reasons that are idiosyncratic and have little to do with gender discrimination. For example, one woman discovered that she had received less research money from her institution than a male colleague and assumed it was because she had poorer negotiation skills. Perhaps she had been a less effective negotiator, or perhaps she had been the victim of gender discrimination. It is always possible to come up with some post hoc explanation for differential treatment in an individual case, and thereby deny discrimination. Moreover, women may fail to attribute their experiences to discrimination because recognizing that one is a victim of discrimination is quite aversive (Crosby, 1982). Women who acknowledge that they are discriminated against must also acknowledge that they lack control and that their colleagues and institutions are treating them unfairly.

Lower Feelings of Entitlement

A factor that contributes to denial is women's lower feelings of entitlement. Studies of reward allocation reveal that women typically take smaller rewards for themselves than men do and are satisfied with lower levels of reward than men are (Major, 1987). These differences occur because women expect fewer rewards from their jobs, a realistic expectation, and because they compare their job experiences to those of other women rather than to those of men (Crosby, 1982; Moore, 1992). Consequently, the lower job rewards that women receive seem reasonable and fair to them. Furthermore, given the tight job market, faculty may feel privileged just to have an academic position. I know of one woman who teaches a course or two at several different colleges during the same semester and earns an average of less than $3,000 per course. Even when teaching eight courses per year, she receives no benefits and a relatively small salary. Yet she is not unhappy about her job situation; rather, she feels fortunate to have found work in academia.

Women's lower feelings of entitlement are not due solely to their lower expectations and their lack of awareness that they are personally underpaid. Even when they feel individually deprived, that is, underpaid or undercompensated, women academics, and other women as well, do not feel as entitled to greater compensation as men do (Moore, 1992). In a recent study, Moore (1994) examined feelings of pay entitlement among male and female academics. She found that men's feelings of entitlement depended on perceived individual deprivation; the more personally underpaid the men thought they were, the more they felt entitled to increased pay. For women, on the other hand, feeling personally underpaid had no effect on entitlement. Moreover, feelings of group deprivation, the belief that one's group is undercompensated, is not only more common among women (Crosby, 1982; Moore, 1992), but in female academics is also associated with *lower* feelings of entitlement (Moore, 1994). The more women faculty believe that other similar faculty are underpaid, the less pay they feel entitled to receive. This lower feeling of entitlement among women has been attributed to the lower status of women in our society that causes them to receive and expect lower rewards (Moore, 1994).

Self-Blame

One reaction to major life stresses is self-blame, that is, taking personal responsibility for causing or contributing to the stress. Research on working women, for example, reveals that about one quarter of them hold themselves responsible for being sexually harassed (Jensen & Gutek, 1982). In the academy, women professors report greater stress as a result of being self-critical and imposing excessively high standards for themselves than do their male colleagues (Gmelch et al., 1986). They also report greater stress about their perceived lack of scholarly productivity (Gmelch, 1993) and their feelings of lower self-efficacy with regard to their research ability than do male faculty (Holahan & Holahan, 1987; Landino, 1988; Schoen & Winocur, 1988). In effect, when compared with men, women are less confident in their scholarship, hold themselves to higher standards relative to their actual performance, and are more self-critical when they don't achieve those standards. This self-criticism is not justified; when controlling for education, type of research, experience, and type of institution, women actually have *higher* levels of scholarly productivity than men do (Nettles & Perna, 1995).

Blaming one's behavior for negative events typically leads to better adjustment and coping when it increases feelings of control, as well as increasing confidence that the negative event can be avoided in the future (Janoff-Bulman, 1992). In such cases, individuals can change their behaviors in order to avoid experiencing the negative events again in the future. However, self-blame sometimes leads to worse coping (e.g., Frazier & Shauben, 1994), particularly when it is associated with feeling guilty and angry at oneself (Montada, 1992). In the case of academics, and women academics especially, much self-blame focuses on personal lack of career advancement and scholarly productivity (Gmelch, 1993). Because many of the factors that lead to women's lack of advancement are chronic conditions that are out of women's personal control, self-blame may not be a particularly beneficial coping strategy. If, for example, a woman blamed her relatively low student evaluations on her poor teaching technique but they were really caused by gender discrimination, she might invest time and energy to improve her teaching, but her evaluations would continue to be low. This situation would not lead to increased feelings of control and confidence but to increased self-blame and, over time, a sense of futility. For chronic, uncontrollable stresses, self-blame, particularly blaming one's character, is associated with stress, depression, learned helplessness, and poorer coping (see Janoff-Bulman, 1979; Peterson & Seligman, 1983).

Reduced Feelings of Control

Research results indicate that men's attributions for success and failure are more internal than women's. A meta-analytic review of laboratory research findings revealed that men make stronger attributions to ability than women do, and women make stronger attributions to luck than men do (Whitley, McHugh, & Frieze, 1986). Although data are mixed, there is some evidence that women may attribute success, in particular, to external factors. For example, some studies have found that working women tend to discount success at work as due to luck or other external factors (Deaux & Farris, 1977; Heilman & Kram, 1978). This tendency of women to view success as externally determined has also been found for women in the academy. When asked to explain the success of the best known people in their fields, female professors make fewer internal and more external attributions than male professors do (Fox & Ferri, 1992). Women professors also view success in the academy, in general, as not based on merit (Reid, 1987). It appears, then, that women perceive outcomes, particularly successful outcomes, to be less controllable than men do, probably because for women, outcomes are less controllable. Whether this pattern of attributions is beneficial or harmful to women is unclear. Although perceived control has been linked to well-being and physical and mental health, maintaining high perceived control when events are not really controllable actually leads to impaired health (Shapiro, Schwartz, & Astin, 1996). In general, women might benefit most from focusing their attention on coping strategies that are within their control, strategies that can reduce professional stress and improve the quality of their work lives. At the same time, they should recognize that it is sex discrimination, rather than lack of merit, that prevents women academics from achieving the same levels of success as men.

Coping Styles

Research on working women reveals that they typically rely on problem-focused coping more than emotion-focused coping to deal with stress (McDonald & Korabik, 1991). Emotion-focused coping involves regulating one's emotional reactions to stress-inducing events. It can be distinguished from problem-focused coping, which involves taking action to change the events themselves (Folkman & Lazarus, 1980). Women academics also report using more problem-focused coping than emotion-focused coping to deal with conflicts between their different roles; in addition, women academics who use active coping strategies (whether problem-focused or emotion-focused) tend to be more satisfied than those who cope in a more passive manner (Amatea & Fong-Beyette, 1987). Active strategies involve doing something to deal with the source of the stress, whereas passive strategies involve avoiding or denying the source of the stress (Billings & Moos, 1981). Given these results, women faculty might benefit from taking action to deal with the many gender-related stresses of the academy.

COPING STRATEGIES

Seek Social Support

Women often rely on social support as a coping strategy (Thoits, 1991). In the academy, two significant sources of social support are networks and mentors. Because advancement in the academy depends not only on hard work and achievement, but also on having advocates, inside information, and direction and encouragement (Hall & Sandler, 1983), having a network or mentor can be very helpful in overcoming gender discrimination. Mentors can also be particularly beneficial to the advancement of women of color (Dasher-Alston, 1997).

Women faculty desire a mentor who is competent and honest and who provides critical feedback and support (Knox & McGovern, 1988). They report that having a mentor with a rank of full professor provides more power or leverage in helping them advance in their careers than having a mentor with a lower rank; on the other hand, they receive more emotional support from a mentor with an assistant professorship than one with a higher rank (Struthers, 1995).

Be aware that just because a woman's formal position is high in status does not mean that she is or feels very powerful. I once asked a small favor of a woman full professor at a very prestigious university. Even though she was very well known and extremely successful, she told me she was not powerful enough in her position to help me. A man of the same rank at the same university granted my request without hesitation. In the academy, as in other occupations, women in high-status positions may not have the same power, resources, or influence as men at the same rank.

Having several mentors, each of whom performs different roles, can be an effective way for faculty to have their needs met without overburdening any one mentor or sacrificing one benefit for another. Indeed, Hall and Sandler (1983) view a mentor as anyone, from those with higher status than the protégée through peers and subordinates, who can in some way help the protégée in her career. This definition of mentoring is quite similar to the strategy of networking.

Informal mentoring or networking can be as effective for women faculty as a formal mentoring relationship (Cormier, Lust, Palmer, & Wood, 1997). There are many advantages of belonging to such networks. They can provide emotional support in dealing with stress; professional support when you come up for review in your department; advice on how to deal with work-related problems; and information about a variety of issues, including teaching, job hunting, publishing, grant applications, coping with difficult colleagues or students, and informal norms in your institution or discipline. Networking is also an effective way to identify gender discrimination and reduce feelings of unique vulnerability and isolation. For example, Caplan (1993) described a situation in which a group of women discovered that they were being similarly exploited by one senior male professor in their department. Before forming their network, each woman had assumed that her experience was unique and had complied with the man's unreasonable demands. After learning in their group how he systematically took advantage of women, they no longer let him exploit them.

There are many ways to create and promote networks. Some examples include developing informal relationships with other faculty both inside and outside their departments, forming friendships with other women faculty at the same rank or in the same family situation, maintaining connections with colleagues from graduate school, attending professional conferences to meet faculty with similar professional interests, sending copies of articles or paper presentations to other scholars who have similar research interests, contacting other researchers to ask them about (and compliment them on) their work, asking colleagues from one's department or institution to lunch, attending college-sponsored events that faculty and administrators from other departments are likely to attend, offering to give or receive feedback on manuscripts, sharing syllabi and teaching ideas with or requesting them from faculty who have similar teaching interests, requesting suggestions on teaching or research from other faculty, serving with other faculty and administrators on college committees, exercising or engaging in other leisure activities with colleagues, and using e-mail to keep in touch.

Networks should include faculty of all ranks, as well as administrators and staff. It would be a mistake to assume that certain people are not powerful enough to establish a relationship. For example, I know of a faculty member whose office is rarely cleaned and who has to wait for extended periods to have equipment repaired, all because he has been uncivil to the maintenance staff at his institution.

Networks should also include individuals from outside one's own institution. This can be particularly important when a woman experiences a major stress, such as being denied reappointment or tenure. Rather than offering help, many people respond to a victimization by avoiding or blaming the victim (Herbert & Dunkel-Schetter, 1992); this is especially likely to occur when observers find the victimization to be personally threatening. When a woman has been denied tenure or reappointment or has had some other major conflict at her institution, people who previously supported her may be too fearful to continue that support. For example, one woman who failed to get reappointed to her teaching position, in spite of an excellent teaching and research record, told me that many colleagues at her institution, including coauthors of some of her research papers, would no longer interact with her. She felt even more distressed by their lack of social support than by losing her job. In such cases, having a network outside one's institution is crucial.

Use Time Efficiently

It is not surprising that female academics report more stress than their male colleagues over having too much work and too little time (Gmelch et al., 1986). Lack of time for scholarship is a particular problem, especially with the high teaching and service demands on women faculty. A recent survey of female assistant professors revealed that they believed that devoting too much time to teaching is a serious impediment to getting tenure (Finkel & Olswang, 1996). Another survey revealed that female faculty were, in fact, devoting almost twice as much time to teaching as to research (Stark-Adamec, Robinson, & Loutzenhiser, 1993). Clearly, inequitable working conditions, such as above-average teaching and service demands, contribute to some of the time pressures for women. Nevertheless, effective time management can help increase productivity and reduce stress.

According to Gmelch (1996), many faculty exacerbate their time pressures by devoting too much time to urgent tasks and too little time to important ones. Because important tasks, such as planning research, writing an article, or developing a new course, typically have no immediate deadline, they can be put off in favor of more urgent tasks. Gmelch argues that many of our urgent tasks are quite unimportant to us personally, yet they manage to take up much of our time. Examples of urgent but unimportant tasks include attending meetings, going through mail, reading and answering e-mail messages, dealing with drop-in visitors, and taking nuisance phone calls. Important tasks can also become urgent if we procrastinate long enough, which creates intense time pressure. Finally, faculty also waste time with matters that are neither important nor urgent, such as reading junk mail or gossiping.

To avoid spending too much time in an "urgent" mode, which can cause high stress, and to spend more time on important tasks, women faculty must examine how they spend their time and eliminate tasks that are truly unimportant to them. In addition, Gmelch (1993) advocates that faculty identify their goals in the areas of teaching, research, and service, and the important tasks that will help them achieve those goals. Women faculty should set aside uninterrupted time each week or, ideally, each day to work on those tasks, preferably devoting to them the most productive time during the day.

Reduce Role Ambiguity

Given that a major cause of faculty stress is role ambiguity, one way to reduce that stress is to obtain as much information as possible about your institution. What are the norms? Serving on many committees never got anyone tenured or promoted. Nevertheless, it would be a mistake to serve on too few committees. The key is to know how much service is normative. Similarly, how many courses are typically taught in your department, and how many advisees on average are assigned to each faculty member? Knowing this will prevent you from being exploited with excessive teaching or advising, in addition to ensuring that you are doing your fair share. What is considered good teaching in your department and at your institution? Are lectures normative, or are discussions? What do typical exams look like? At some schools, in some departments, multiple-choice exams are considered highly objective; at others, they are derided as reflecting nothing but rote memory. What constitutes research productivity in your institution? Does your department merely count the number of publications; are they concerned with the length of published papers; do they consider only peer-reviewed publications; or do they, as in one department I know, weight each publication by a status score assigned to different journals? Knowing the standards ahead of time can forewarn you that some of your publications may be discounted by your department and can help you decide whether to invest your energies in writing up a large number of less prestigious papers or a small number of more prestigious ones. Other important norms concern dress and expectations about how much faculty interact with each other and with students after work hours.

Knowing the norms at your institution and following them can make it difficult for those who are evaluating you to make unfair criticisms of you. Because norms in the academy are often unstated and ambiguous, and because they can change over time, it is best to obtain documentation about the rules and standards at your institution. It is possible to document even verbal communications. For example, I have a colleague who documents the verbal advice she receives from her chair and dean by sending them memos reiterating their recommendations and asking them whether she has accurately represented their positions.

Not knowing institutional norms can result in unexpected negative evaluations. For example, at one institution, a woman professor was not reappointed for being too good a teacher. Her student evaluations were so high that members of her department thought that she was "mothering" her students and grading them too easily. At that same institution, another woman was denied tenure for having low evaluations, presumably because she was too tough and inaccessible. In both cases, the women were criticized for having grades that were too far from the norm. In general, it is best to assign grades that are about average for your department or, if anything, to give grades that are somewhat tougher than average, but not excessively so. Grades that are too generous will create the impression that

287

your courses lack rigor. Grades that are too stringent can upset not only students and their parents, but colleagues and college administrators as well (Gose, 1997).

Another means of reducing ambiguity is to get clear and explicit feedback on your performance. Evaluations in the academy are often infrequent and vague (Gmelch, 1984; Seldin, 1987). Formal written evaluations, when they occur, are very important because they are often the only feedback faculty get and because they are written and are therefore permanent. When evaluations are negative, they should contain specific recommendations for improvement. If the feedback is unfairly critical, respond to the criticism in writing. If it is too vague, request clearer and more explicit feedback. Ambiguous or vague evaluations make it possible for an apparently supportive department suddenly to withdraw its support. Recently, a female professor was not reappointed after receiving a very negative evaluation from her department that primarily criticized her for doing research on a topic that was not rigorous enough. The professor was completely surprised by the evaluation because she had received no previous evidence that the department was displeased with her work. In fact, her research topic had never changed and apparently had been rigorous enough to get her the job at her institution. The rigor, or lack of rigor, of her research area had simply never been mentioned in earlier evaluations.

Negotiate Effectively

Professors undoubtedly negotiate every day, with their students about deadlines or whether a grade is fair, with their chairs about which courses they should teach or which department committee they should join, with other faculty about when to schedule meetings, with journal editors about when a review should be due, with secretaries about the typing up and copying of an exam, with librarians about obtaining a rush interlibrary loan request or ordering a needed book, or with maintenance staff about a defective office light or a leaky pipe. Although everyone negotiates, not everyone negotiates well. Effective negotiation is particularly important in situations that contribute to the stresses experienced by women academics, such as when a faculty member is being sexually harassed and wants the harassment to stop, or when she has received an unfair evaluation and wants it to be revised. It is also important for issues involving money or resources, such as obtaining a salary increase, money for research, extra travel money, and so on (see Rose & Danner, this volume).

Effective negotiation involves preparation: identifying your goals and the goals of the other party; determining what alternatives you have if you cannot realize a mutually satisfying solution; and obtaining clear, objective criteria with which to evaluate possible solutions. Preparation can also make you more confident in your ability to negotiate, and that, in itself, is associated with more successful outcomes (Lewicki, Litterer, Minton, & Saunders, 1994), as well as reduced anxiety and stress. The first step, identifying goals, may seem obvious, but it is not uncommon for people to lose sight of what they want when in the middle of a negotiation. One woman professor who wanted a position as chair turned down such an offer because the salary was not quite as high as she wanted. She failed to achieve her primary goal of becoming a chair because she became distracted by haggling over salary, an issue that was, in fact, not as important to her.

In addition to identifying your own goals, it is just as important to identify the goals and interests of the other party (Ury, 1991). What does the other party need or want, and how can that party's needs be met while also meeting your own? Better yet, are there commonalities or similarities between your goals and those of the other party? For example, if you are applying for an academic position in a department that offers a course that no one else is willing or able to teach, and you have already successfully taught it, it is clear that your goals and one of the goals of the department overlap. In this negotiation, you should be sure to emphasize your ability and desire to teach the course.

Sometimes, the other parties will reveal their goals, either subtly or directly, but often they do not. Consequently, you should do research ahead of time to identify those goals. Use whatever resources you have to learn more about the other party, including your friends and colleagues, newspapers, college or university publications such as annual reports, and past employees. You may discover, for example, that your president and dean have been criticized for not distributing research money more equitably among the different departments at your institution. Or you may discover that your chair is being pressured to increase class sizes to accommodate an unusually large entering first-year class. Knowing the goals of the other party will help you to identify areas of common interest.

People often enter negotiations with no idea what they would do if they failed to come to a satisfactory agreement. This is a common and grave error and one that can lead to increased stress should the negotiation not be successful. According to Fisher, Ury, and Patton (1991), all negotiators should determine in advance their best alternative in case they cannot reach agreement with the other party. Having this alternative, or BATNA (best alternative to a negotiated agreement), particularly an attractive BATNA, increases one's bargaining power. For example, when negotiating for better job conditions in your department, having decided that you would be willing to accept another job offer puts you in a strong position to bargain. If your BATNA is not very attractive, knowing this ahead of time will prevent you from being too rigid or rejecting solutions too quickly. Think carefully about your BATNA. Rather than consider a myriad of possible alternatives, force yourself to identify the best one, and then you will be better prepared to consider how attractive the negotiated solution is. It is crucial to have identified your BATNA ahead of time so that you remain aware both of your relative power in the negotiation and of your options should the negotiation fail.

To best determine what a fair solution would be, your preparations must include obtaining objective criteria to evaluate those solutions and to support your arguments. When negotiating with your institution for research funds, it is useful to know how much money other faculty have received in the past; when negotiating for improvements in your institution's maternity leave policy, it is useful to know that most other comparable institutions have more generous policies. Recently, I used objective criteria effectively to deal with a disgruntled student who was unhappy with her grade on a late paper. By presenting her with a copy of my college's policy on dealing with late papers, I was able to show her that the penalty I applied was actually less stringent than average and more than fair.

Only after thorough preparation should you enter the actual negotiation. During the negotiation, do not lose sight of your goals. Use your evidence and documentation to support your arguments. Be sure to listen carefully to the other party to identify goals that you may have missed in your research. Before rejecting or accepting the offers of the other party, consider carefully whether your goals are being met. The other party may suggest a satisfactory solution that you had not thought of. Finally, remain confident in your ability to negotiate well.

Dealing With Difficult Students or Colleagues

There are a number of ways of responding to sexist or hostile behavior on the part of students or colleagues. One is to confront them and tell them why their behavior is inappropriate. This is probably most effective with individuals who are exhibiting the behavior unwittingly and who probably would be embarrassed to have it brought to their attention. Individuals who deliberately intend to cause insult are less likely to change in response to a confrontation. For these individuals, and for cases of sexual harassment, records should be kept to document the nature of the harassment or discrimination, its frequency, and your response. Explicitly rejecting the harasser's attentions, such as writing a note to the harasser to explain that you want him to stop his offensive behavior, can make it easier to prove that sexual harassment occurred, should you ever decide to file charges.

Disruptive behavior in the classroom can cause women faculty great stress and can interfere with students' opportunities to learn. Many female faculty have described incidents in which a student had made derisive or hostile comments to them; talked or slept during the class; continually attacked or dismissed the course material; or conveyed dissatisfaction nonverbally by frowning, head shaking, smirking, or laughing during class (Sandler, Silverberg, & Hall, 1996). In one instance, classroom tensions escalated such that an entire class of students ultimately stormed out during the middle of a physics lecture because their female professor had made an error while writing on the blackboard. Ideally, disruptive classroom behavior should be addressed before it contaminates the entire class.

One way to avoid problems is to display good humor and warmth in the classroom. Research results suggest that students respond favorably to female professors who use humor and are friendly and helpful (Van Giffen, 1990). Women who convey a high degree of competence can be threatening, particularly to men, unless that competence is combined with warmth (Carli, LaFleur, & Loeber, 1995). As a result, women faculty who convey both competence and warmth are viewed as more effective teachers and are rated more highly than those who do not (Basow, this volume; Kierstead, D'Agostino, & Dill, 1988; Martin, 1984; Statham, Richardson, & Cook, 1991).

In dealing with specific instances of disruptiveness, confronting the problem directly can be effective. For example, when students talk or giggle in my classes, I immediately ask them if they have a question or if they have something they would like to share with the class. Often, they actually do have a question. When students shake their heads or show other signs of displeasure, I take them aside after class and tell them that they seem uncomfortable during my lectures and that their signs of discomfort are a distraction to me. Usually, they respond with surprise that I notice them at all (somehow students often feel invisible) and typically they apologize for distracting me. When I make a mistake while writing on the board, I make a joke about it that is not too self-deprecating.

Give Yourself Credit

Many women feel uncomfortable "blowing their own horn." Yet self-promotion is, to some extent, essential to advancement. Your colleagues may have no idea of your achievements unless you tell them. Mention articles accepted for publication. Save copies of thank-you notes from students who particularly enjoyed your course and share them with your chair. Let your accomplishments come up in casual conversation.

Keep a careful record of your teaching, research, and service achievements, including objective evidence of the quality of your work (e.g., how frequently your papers are cited, your teaching evaluation scores). Compile a dossier of your articles, teaching tools, flattering letters from research colleagues or students, and other materials, and add to it regularly. When you come up for tenure or promotion, your file will already be prepared. The dossier can also be used to support your case if you believe you have been unjustly treated. In addition to demonstrating your accomplishments to others, the dossier can remind you of just how good you are.

Finally, it is important not to give up in the face of criticism. Editors have mentioned to me informally that women are less likely than men to revise and resubmit journal articles. Perhaps this occurs because, as I have already noted, women academics tend to be more self-critical and have lower levels of entitlement than men. Regardless of the reason, the result is that women may be reducing their scholarly productivity.

Receiving negative feedback can be daunting. Nevertheless, for many competitive journals, it is not uncommon for authors to receive an initial rejection with an invitation to revise and resubmit the manuscript. Even though reviews are often severe, and even hostile, that does not mean that the manuscript is not worthy of publication. Some manuscripts have been revised multiple times before being accepted by some top-ranked journals. So do not give up; revise and resubmit.

I have also found it helpful to talk directly with journal or book editors about reviewers' comments, particularly when they are unclear, contradictory, or biased. Often, in a one-to-one conversation, editors are much more revealing about which of the reviewer's comments must be taken seriously and which can be ignored.

CONCLUSION

In this chapter, I discussed some of the causes of professional stress in women academics, ways in which women may respond to these stresses, and coping strategies to deal with the stress effectively. Most of the professional stresses experienced by academics—lack of advancement, excessive teaching demands, low salaries, receiving ambiguous feedback about performance, sexual harassment, and hostile or discriminatory inter-actions with colleagues and students—affect women more than men. In response to these stresses, women may deny that they are experiencing gender discrimination and blame themselves for their stressful working conditions. They may also feel less entitled to better pay and other benefits than their male colleagues, and less control over their successes and achievements. These are natural reactions to stress but are not the most effective means of coping.

I have outlined the following coping strategies to help women deal with the professional stresses of the academy:

1. Obtain social support in the form of networks and mentors.
2. Use time more efficiently to eliminate unimportant tasks, and devote blocks of time each day or week to important ones.
3. Reduce the ambiguity of your academic position by determining the norms at your institution and documenting them.
4. Use effective negotiation techniques when seeking improved work conditions or attempting to resolve conflict.
5. Document instances of discrimination by colleagues and students. Confront faculty and students who behave inappropriately. Use humor and warmth in the classroom.
6. Document your achievements and take credit for your successes. Do not give up in the face of criticism.

Finally, be aware that the academy is not a true meritocracy. Our success, or lack of success, will be affected by factors that are beyond our control. For us to cope effectively, we must recognize this gender bias. We must also recognize what factors we can control and take what action we can to improve working conditions for ourselves and all women in the academy.

REFERENCES

Amatea, E. S., & Fong-Beyette, M. L. (1987). Through a different lens: Examining profes-sional women's interrole coping by focus and mode. *Sex Roles, 17,* 237-252.

Basow, S. A. (1995). Students' evaluations of college professors: When gender matters. *Journal of Educational Psychology, 87,* 656-665.

Basow, S. A., & Silberg, N. T. (1987). Student evaluations of college professors: Are female and male professors rated differently? *Journal of Educational Psychology, 79,* 308-314.

Bennett, S. K. (1982). Student perceptions and expectations for male and female instructors: Evidence relating to the question of gender bias in teaching evaluations. *Journal of Educational Psychology, 74,* 170-179.

Billings, A. G., & Moos, R. (1981). The role of coping responses and social resources in attenuating the stress of life events. *Journal of Behavioral Medicine, 4,* 139-157.

Brooks, V. R. (1982). Sex differences in student dominance behavior in female and male professors' classrooms. *Sex Roles, 8,* 683-690.

Burns-Glover, A. L., & Veith, D. J. (1995). Revisiting gender and teaching evaluations: Sex still makes a difference. *Journal of Social Behavior and Personality, 10,* 69-80.

Caplan, P. J. (1993). *Lifting a ton of feathers: A woman's guide to surviving in the academic world.* Toronto: University of Toronto Press.

Carli, L. L. (1990a; October). *Coping with victimization: Theory and research.* Paper presented at the 1990-91 Colloquium Series of the Bunting Institute for Research and Advanced Studies, Radcliffe College, Harvard University, Cambridge, MA.

Carli, L. L. (1990b). Gender, language, and influence. *Journal of Personality and Social Psychology, 59,* 941-951.

Carli, L. L. (1997, January). *Gender-related stresses in the academy.* Paper presented at the 10th Annual International Conference on Women in Higher Education, Fort Worth, TX.

Carli, L. L., LaFleur, S., & Loeber, C. (1995). Gender, nonverbal behavior, and influence. *Journal of Personality and Social Psychology, 68,* 1030-1041.

Cormier, P., Lust, P., Palmer, K., & Wood, C. (1997, January). *Mentoring for women at Longwood College.* Paper presented at the International Conference on Women in Higher Education, Fort Worth, TX.

Crosby, F. (1982). *Relative deprivation and working women.* New York: Oxford University Press.

Dagg, A. I., & Thompson, P. J. (1988). *Miseducation: Women and Canadian universities.* Toronto: OISE Press.

Dasher-Alston, R. M. (1997, January). *Mentoring women of color: Opening the drawbridge to the ivory tower.* Paper presented at the International Conference on Women in Higher Education, Fort Worth, TX.

Deaux, K., & Farris, E. (1977). Attributing causes for one's own performance: The effects of sex norms and outcome. *Journal of Research in Personality, 11,* 59-72.

Dobbins, G. H., Cardy, R. L., & Truxillo, D. M. (1986). Effect of ratee sex and purpose of appraisal on the accuracy of performance evaluations. *Basic and Applied Social Psychology, 7,* 225-241.

Finkel, S. K., & Olswang, S. G. (1996). Child rearing as a career impediment to women assistant professors. *Review of Higher Education, 19,* 123-139.

Fisher, R., Ury, W., & Patton, B. (1991). *Getting to yes: Negotiating agreement without giving in* (2nd ed.). New York: Penguin.

Fitzgerald, L. F. (1996). The prevalence of sexual harassment. In B. Lott & M. E. Reilly (Eds.), *Combatting sexual harassment in higher education* (pp. 55-68). Washington, DC: National Education Association.

Folkman, S., & Lazarus, R. S. (1980). An analysis of coping in a middle-aged community sample. *Journal of Health and Social Behavior, 21,* 219-239.

Fox, M., & Ferri, V. (1992). Women, men, and their attributions for success in academe. *Social Psychology Quarterly, 55,* 257-271.

Frazier, P., & Shauben, L. (1994). Causal attributions and recovery from rape and other stressful life events. *Journal of Social and Clinical Psychology, 13*, 1-14.

Gajec, L. C. (1993). *The status of Hispanic females in Michigan higher educational institutions as faculty, administrators, and supervisors.* Unpublished doctoral dissertation, Wayne State University.

Gmelch, W. H. (1984, July). Pressures of the professoriate: Individual and institutional coping strategies. In T. B. Massey (Ed.), *Proceedings of the Tenth International Conference on Improving University Teaching* (pp. 119-131). College Park: University of Maryland University College.

Gmelch, W. H. (1993). *Coping with faculty stress.* Newbury Park, CA: Sage.

Gmelch, W. H. (1996, September-October). It's about time. *Academe, 82*, 22-26.

Gmelch, W. H., Wilke, P. K., & Lovrich, N. P. (1986). Dimensions of stress among university faculty: Factor analytic results from a national study. *Research in Higher Education, 24*, 266-286.

Gose, B. (1997, July 25). Efforts to curb grade inflation get an F from many critics. *Chronicle of Higher Education,* p. A41.

Grauerholz, E. (1996). Sexual harassment in the academy: The case of women professors. In M. Stockdale (Ed.), *Sexual harassment in the workplace: Perspectives, frontiers, and response strategies* (pp. 29-50). Thousand Oaks, CA: Sage.

Hall, R. M., & Sandler, B. R. (1983). *Academic mentoring for women students and faculty: A new look at an old way to get ahead.* Washington, DC: Association of American Colleges.

Hamermesh, D. S. (1996, March-April). Not so bad: The annual report on the economic status of the profession. *Academe, 82*, 14-108.

Hatchett, B. F., & Bermudez, D. O. O. (1997, January). *Barriers and facilitators to successful attainment: African American women in academia.* Paper presented at the International Conference on Women in Higher Education, Fort Worth, TX.

Heilman, M. E., & Kram, K. E. (1978). Self-derogating behavior in women—fixed or flexible: The effect of co-workers' sex. *Organizational Behavior and Human Performance, 22*, 497-507.

Hensel, N. (1991). *Realizing gender equality in higher education: The need to integrate work/family issues* (ASHE-ERIC Higher Education Rep. No. 2). Washington, DC: George Washington School of Education and Human Development.

Herbert, T. B., & Dunkel-Schetter, C. (1992). Negative social reactions to victims: An overview of responses and their determinants. In L. Montada, S. Filipp, & M. J. Lerner (Eds.), *Life crises and experiences of loss in adulthood* (pp. 497-518). Hillsdale, NJ: Lawrence Erlbaum.

Holahan, C. K., & Holahan, C. J. (1987). Self-efficacy, social support, and depression in aging: A longitudinal analysis. *Journal of Gerontology, 42*, 65-68.

Janoff-Bulman, R. (1979). Characterological versus behavioral self-blame: Inquiries into depression and rape. *Journal of Personality and Social Psychology, 37*, 1798-1809.

Janoff-Bulman, R. (1992). *Shattered assumptions: Toward a new psychology of trauma.* New York: Free Press.

Jensen, I., & Gutek, B. A. (1982). Attributions and assignment of responsibility for sexual harassment. *Journal of Social Issues, 38*, 121-136.

Kierstead, D., D'Agostino, P., & Dill, H. (1988). Sex role stereotyping of college professors: Bias in students' ratings of instructors. *Journal of Educational Psychology, 80*, 342-344.

Knox, P. L., & McGovern, T. V. (1988). Mentoring women in academia. *Teaching of Psychology, 15*, 39-41.

Landino, R. A. (1988). Self-efficacy in university faculty. *Journal of Vocational Behavior, 33*, 1-14.

Langbein, L. I. (1994). The validity of student evaluations of teaching. *Political Science and Politics, 27,* 545-553.

Lewicki, R. J., Litterer, J. A., Minton, J. W., & Saunders, D. M. (1994). *Negotiation* (2nd ed.). Burr Ridge, IL: Irwin.

London, M., & Strumpf, S. A. (1983). Effects of candidate characteristics on management promotion decisions: An experimental study. *Personnel Psychology, 36,* 241-259.

Major, B. (1987). Gender, justice, and the psychology of entitlement. In P. Shaver & C. Hendrick (Eds.), *Sex and gender* (pp. 124-148). Newbury Park, CA: Sage.

Martin, E. (1984). Power and authority in the classroom: Sexist stereotypes in teaching evaluations. *Signs, 9,* 482-492.

McDonald, L. M., & Korabik, K. (1991). Sources of stress and ways of coping among male and female managers. *Journal of Social Behavior and Personality, 6,* 185-198.

Melendez, W. A., & de Guzman, R. M. (1983). *Burnout: The new academic disease* (ASHE-ERIC Higher Education Research Rep. No. 9). Washington, DC: Association for the Study of Higher Education.

Montada, L. (1992). Attributions of responsibility for losses and perceived injustice. In L. Montada, S. Filipp, & M. J. Lerner (Eds.), *Life crises and experiences of loss in adulthood* (pp. 133-161). Hillsdale, NJ: Lawrence Erlbaum.

Moore, D. (1992). *Labor market segmentation and its implications.* New York: Garland.

Moore, D. (1994). Entitlement as an epistemic problem: Do women think like men? *Journal of Social Behavior and Personality, 9,* 665-684.

Nettles, M. T., & Perna, L. W. (1995, November). *Sex and race differences in faculty salaries, tenure, rank & productivity: Why, on average, do women, African Americans, and Hispanics have lower salaries, tenure and rank?* Paper presented at the annual meeting of the Association for the Study of Higher Education, Orlando, FL.

Nieva, V. F., & Gutek, B. A. (1980). Sex effects on evaluation. *Academy of Management Review, 5,* 267-276.

Olsen, D., & Sorcinelli, M. D. (1992). The pretenure years: A longitudinal perspective. *New Directions for Teaching and Learning, 50,* 15-25.

Perloff, L. S. (1983). Perceptions of vulnerability to victimization. *Journal of Social Issues, 39,* 41-61.

Peterson, C., & Seligman, M. E. P. (1983). Learned helplessness and victimization. *Journal of Social Issues, 39,* 103-116.

Reid, P. T. (1987). Perceptions of sex discrimination among female university faculty and staff. *Psychology of Women Quarterly, 11,* 123-128.

Sandler, B. R., & Hall, R. M. (1986). *The campus climate revisited: Chilly for women faculty, administrators, and graduate students.* Washington, DC: Association of American Colleges.

Sandler, B. R., & Hall, R. M. (1993). *Women faculty at work in the classroom, or, why it still hurts to be a woman in labor.* Washington, DC: Center for Women Policy Studies.

Sandler, B. R., Silverberg, L. A., & Hall, R. M. (1996). *The chilly classroom climate: A guide to improve the education of women.* Washington, DC: National Association for Women in Education.

Schoen, L. G., & Winocur, S. (1988). An investigation of the self-efficacy of male and female academics. *Journal of Vocational Behavior, 32,* 307-320.

Seldin, P. (1987). Research findings on the causes of academic stress. *New Directions for Teaching and Learning, 29,* 13-21.

Shapiro, D. H., Schwartz, C. E., & Astin, J. A. (1996). Controlling ourselves, controlling our world: Psychology's role in understanding positive and negative consequences of seeking and gaining control. *American Psychologist, 51,* 1213-1230.

Simeone, A. (1987). *Academic women: Working towards equality*. South Hadley, MA: Bergin & Garvey.

Smith, D. G. (1996, September 6). Faculty diversity when jobs are scarce: Debunking the myths. *Chronicle of Higher Education*, p. B3.

Sorcinelli, M. D. (1994). Effective approaches to new faculty development. *Journal of Counseling & Development, 72*, 474-479.

Stark-Adamec, C., Robinson, T. P., & Loutzenhiser, L. (1993). Faculty women's allocations of time. *Perceptual and Motor Skills, 77*, 689-690.

Statham, A., Richardson, L., & Cook, J. (1991). *Gender and university teaching: A negotiated difference*. Albany: State University of New York Press.

Struthers, N. J. (1995). Differences in mentoring: A function of gender or organizational rank? *Journal of Social Behavior and Personality, 10*, 265-272.

Thoits, P. A. (1991). Gender differences in coping with emotional distress. In J. Eckenrode (Ed.), *The social context of coping* (pp. 107-138). New York: Plenum.

Ury, W. L. (1991). *Getting past no: Negotiating with difficult people*. New York: Bantam.

Van Giffen, K. (1990). Influence of professor gender and perceived use of humor on course evaluations. *International Journal of Humor Research, 3*, 65-73.

West, M. S. (1995, July-August). Women faculty: Frozen in time. *Academe, 81*, 26-29.

Whitley, B. E., Jr., McHugh, M. C., & Frieze, I. H. (1986). Assessing the theoretical models for sex differences in causal attributions of success and failure. In J. S. Hyde, & M. C. Linn (Eds.), *The psychology of gender: Advances through meta-analysis* (pp. 102-135). Baltimore: Johns Hopkins University.

Wiley, M. G., & Crittenden, K. S. (1992). By your attributions you shall be known: Consequences of attributional accounts for professional and gender identities. *Sex Roles, 27*, 259-276.

Women profs still earn less. (1996, Fall). *About Women on Campus, 4*, 5.

Zimbler, L. (1994). *Faculty and instructional staff—What are they and what do they do?* Washington, DC: U.S. Department of Education, Office of Education, Research and Improvement.

"Do Unto Others . . ."

Regina Bento

I can still remember my first rejection letter. Dripping with sarcasm, it not only rejected the paper I had submitted for a conference, but it also seemed to reject me as a person. It froze me for 3 years in a bad case of writer's block, until I eventually thawed my way out of it. This freezing and unfreezing process is what I would like to share with you, in the hope that it will help you deal a little better with receiving (and writing!) rejection letters.

Let me start by saying that the paper should have been rejected. It was too long, not exactly earth shaking, and it had been submitted to a highly competitive major conference in my field. As an international doctoral student, this was my first formal paper submission in the United States and I had no clue about the process. But the review I received did not teach me these lessons, which I learned only much later, once I had healed from it. Instead of discussing what made the paper wrong for the conference, the review was a sour diatribe, a name-calling exercise where the reviewer wondered what sort of idiot would dare submit such long-winded, badly written junk to such an exalted conference.

The freezing effect of the letter was compounded by factors in my own personal history. As a Latina, both my culture of origin and my gender role in that culture had taught me that negative feedback should be targeted only at behaviors or outcomes, not people. Throughout my professional life, any criticism had always been offered in a thoroughly professional way.

But the experience of being a newly arrived international PhD student in the United States had produced a curious ambivalence in how I expected to be treated by others. In the doctoral program I received as much respect, or more, as I had been used to in my country. Top U.S. schools had actively recruited me, due to my extremely high scores in the GMAT and GRE and to a very successful academic record. I went on to become the only person in several years to have a perfect GPA in the tough doctoral program of one of the most elite schools in the United States—MIT. Outside the protective walls of the school, however, I had found out for the first time in my life what it meant to be a minority. My foreign accent triggered discrimination episodes in the supermarket, in stores, on the phone, and in the playground where I took my children. Over and over, I got from the external environment the insidious message that I was worthless, that I did not quite belong, and that my academic success was either a fluke or an undeserved by-product of affirmative action. By the time that rejection letter, arrived I was ready to doubt myself, ready to accept the end of my lucky ride, ready to be "unmasked" as a fake. To make things even worse, by the time I got that letter I was also isolated from my support group of professors and friends at school (I moved to the West Coast as soon as I reached the dissertation stage).

If I received that letter today, I would probably toss it in the trash can, mentally refer the reviewer for therapy, and seek advice from colleagues before resubmitting the paper to some other publication outlet. Back then, I just froze. I developed such a bad case of writer's block that I even felt insecure when writing simple notes to my kids' teachers in preschool. I extended my dissertation's literature review and data analysis for much longer than necessary, just to postpone the dreaded task of writing it. I did not submit a paper for a conference or journal during the following 3 years.

The unfreezing process happened slowly. As a new faculty member at the University of California, Riverside, the experience of being highly successful in teaching boosted my self-esteem and stimulated my intellectual curiosity as a researcher. I started attending junior faculty workshops, and in one of them, I found out that a female scholar whom I really admired had also suffered a 3-year writer's block, but had survived it to become one of the most creative and recognized researchers in her field. Similar experiences were reported in an excellent book by Cummings and Frost about the objective and subjective aspects of publishing in the organizational sciences (Cummings & Frost, 1985).

Boosted by those war stories and by sharing my work with colleagues, I started trying some "safe" submissions. First, I built some confidence by submitting to conferences that required only abstracts. Next, I started submitting to journals where the reviews were done by members of the editorial board, and where the editors closely monitored the quality of the reviews. Finally, I learned to read reviews as tools: If they helped improve the manuscript, I used them; if they didn't, I discarded them.

I also developed a helpful psychological device for starting new writing projects in order to overcome the block of looking at a blank computer screen. During the "frozen" years, whenever I started to write something, I could feel that nasty anonymous reviewer peering over my shoulder and ridiculing all I wrote. As a result, I would spend hours writing and rewriting the first paragraph until I would finally give up the whole thing in total desperation, thus accumulating one more experience of failure. Part of the unfreezing process was to be more selective in my choice of invisible audiences. Whenever I'm writing a first draft, I visualize the reader as someone who is interested in the subject, thinks as I do, and can be helped by what I have to say. The idea in that first draft is to just get the ideas written down, as if I were writing an essay in an exam with a time limit. In the second draft, confident that I already have accomplished "something," I change the invisible audience to someone not too interested or knowledgeable in the topic, whose attention I have to attract and maintain by focusing on relevance and form. In subsequent drafts, the invisible audience becomes more and more challenging, until I am ready to share the paper with real people.

One other thing that helped the unfreezing process was to become an anonymous reviewer myself. In the doctoral program, I had written many reviews of books and articles for class assignments, but I knew that the author would never read them. Those assignments were for my own benefit, not the authors'. When I later started writing actual professional reviews, I realized they required a very different approach. I thought long and hard about what had hurt me most in that first rejection letter: the lack of respect for me as a person, and the lack of any objective ideas on what was wrong with the paper, or what could be done to improve it.

In order to treat the author as I would like to be treated, I write reviews as if the author were a good friend who has asked me for honest feedback on how to make the best use of the work embodied in the manuscript. As a friend, I try to make sure that even the most negative thing I have to say about the work will not easily be misread as criticism of the author. As a friend, I also try to provide as much feedback as possible on both content and form. It would be disrespectful, and a disservice to the author, if I ignored the weaknesses I perceive in the manuscript and failed to indicate how I thought they could be overcome. It takes me much longer to write a rejection letter than it does a revise/ resubmit or an acceptance letter. But that is infinitely better than running the risk of sending out the type of hasty and nasty review that might freeze an author for years, keeping him or her from trying again.

As a reviewer, I try to send the letter I would want to receive as an author. As an author, I try to send out the type of work I would want to receive as a reviewer. In publishing as in life, "Do unto others . . ." is really not a bad idea.

REFERENCE

Cummings, L.L., & Frost, P. (1985). *Publishing in the organizational sciences*. Homewood, IL: R. D. Irwin.

La Llorona in Academe

Ester Ruiz Rodriguez

There is a Mexican myth about a woman who slays her children and tosses them into a body of water. She then spends eternity wailing and wandering, lost and alone on the waterways of the world as she searches for her children.

On many occasions I have felt a kinship with La Llorona (the crying lady), as I wander lost through the halls of academe, moaning my fate as I search for the ever elusive prize of tenure.

I wondered as I approached the end of my second year, and had been informed of yet another change in my teaching schedule, whether I would ever adjust to the continually changing schedules. How was I supposed to get any writing done when I had to teach different courses each semester? Maybe I didn't belong in academia. Or, maybe I should think about a career in the community college. As the semester ended, I was discouraged, frustrated, and too drained to do any writing, which my tenured colleagues suggested I needed to do during the summer.

As I spoke with two friends, graduates of the same doctoral program and also in assistant professor positions, I became aware that they were experiencing similar feelings. They felt lost and overwhelmed, and were questioning whether academia was meant for them. I had just finished studying for my licensing exam in psychology, and I remembered that some research had demonstrated that misery not only likes company, but misery likes miserable company. We decided to go on a vacation and be miserable together.

As it turns out, that was one of our most beneficial decisions. We went to Puerto Peñasco, Mexico. Laying by the ocean rejuvenated our spirits. Talking about the similarities of our difficulties helped us to recognize that we were not alone in our misery, and three bright women should be able to figure out what to do. We would not settle for a fate similar to La Llorona.

We initiated brainstorming regarding what would help at this stage of our careers. Once we began this brainstorming process, there was no stopping us. We all had so many suggestions. Unfortunately, most of our ideas concerned things that were not under our control. Another day at the beach laying out in the sun, and our laments assumed a different pitch. We had managed somehow to externalize our misery. Now, we were lamenting the lack of support available from our departments. The Mexican sun worked its miracle again, and we began to brainstorm about where we might find this support. Once again, we felt an infusion of energy. At about this point, we recognized that we were helping ourselves to feel better. We were supporting each other, and we resolved to continue to do so.

We made an agreement to continue to take vacations together to beautiful places and support each other in our writing endeavors. We began by writing down our goals and sharing them with each other. Next, we identified and listed ongoing writing projects and projects on the back burners. We reviewed each other's goals to ensure that they were realistic. We also helped each other set a realistic time frame for our projects and to come up with solutions to our other problems.

These working vacations, aside from being tax deductible, have been extremely helpful in many ways. First, each of us has two accessible reviewers for any writing that we do. Second, we are able to discuss issues and concerns regarding controversial subject matter. Third, because we review our writing goals and progress toward tenure each time we meet, we get an immediate sense of how we are doing, and we reward ourselves for progress made. Finally, we can still lament our fate and, like La Llorona, moan on the water, but we know that it will be a time-limited moaning. Because as soon as we come in from the sun, we will have to write. Unlike La Llorona, we won't have to wait an eternity to find what we seek.

Afterword

Mary Gray

Several years ago, a student of mine from Greece came into my office after the semester break. She brought with her a small statue of an owl, a replica of one in the National Museum in Athens. Giving it to me, she said that I had become a role model for her, a figure whom she wanted to emulate and whose characteristics were embodied in Athena, symbolized by this owl. I was very touched. Since then, others have seen this owl and have brought me other owls; prowling the street markets and souks of a new city with a goal in mind adds to the pleasure, and in that way I have myself added to my collection of owls. Now I am surrounded by cloisonné from China, scrap metal from Brazil, malachite from Kenya, silver from Mexico, verdite from South Africa, peat from Ireland, camel bone from the Arabian peninsula, ceramics and wood from dozens of countries, all in the form of owls. In the midst of all of this, how do I envision myself as a present-day Athena? How am I armed? What can I learn from the authors of this volume?

First of all, we must not forget that the core of Athena's power was her wisdom. Wisdom is not just knowledge, important though that is. Judgment, reflection, experience, and a personal center of self-confidence are also components of Athena's strength. To develop any of these is not an easy task; to put them together in an appropriate balance as the basis for a successful career in academe seems daunting. But as with most worthwhile goals, the key is to move a step at a time.

If we are to arm ourselves as Athena, what should we choose as our weapons? Clearly, there is no one answer for everyone, but there are some general themes. Let me start with something close to my heart. In her reflections, Mary K. Madsen says, "Math anxiety is not befitting an administrator." Nor, I would argue, the successful academic. To bargain successfully for an initial salary package and for subsequent advancement,

303

to put together a proposal to secure funding for one's projects, to serve on important committees in one's institution and in professional organizations, indeed, in many cases, to conduct one's own research, quantitative skills—at a minimum quantitative literacy—are a requirement. Not everyone comes initially to academe with these, but it is never too late to start acquiring them. There are few characteristics that diminish a woman faculty member's image in the eyes of her colleagues more than a demonstrated ignorance of figures—especially when they have dollar signs attached. You may have been let off the hook throughout your academic career by being told that "girls aren't good at math," but it isn't true. Moreover, ease with numbers is a "guy thing" that is consistently used as a putdown.

In fact, at every stage, women opt out of opportunities by choosing a less quantitatively oriented path. For the most part, the best paying faculty positions are those that rely on quantitative skills. Even when women choose a nominally quantitative field—economics, business, computer science—they cluster in the "softer" areas. But even though not everyone wants to concentrate on finance or computational complexity (thank goodness!), even though one is a poet or historian of art, to be adequately armed in the academic arena, one needs to be able to construct a budget, read a balance sheet, and, alas, perhaps understand the statistics of discrimination.

I came to academe well prepared on the quantitative side, but I found that there were, nonetheless, gaps in my arsenal of weapons. A nice part about academe is that the skills you lack are, for the most part, all around you to be learned. In the late 1970s, I worked on pension equity issues as a statistician, only to find the army of lawyers representing the insurance industry condescendingly explaining that I didn't understand the law. My chief failure seemed to be that I thought giving different benefits to men and women just because they happened to be men or women was classifying them on the basis of sex (clearly illegal), whereas the lawyers thought it was classifying them on the basis of longevity (not illegal). So I went to law school, and by the time the case got to the Supreme Court, I was able to make my argument as a lawyer in an amicus brief. Fortunately, the Court agreed.

Similarly, I have found over the years that my language skills were seriously deficient, and that to be an effective participant in many of the professional and voluntary activities that I enjoy, I needed to learn some more languages. So I did. And, of course, nearly everyone of my generation has faced learning to use information technology in ways that revolutionize one's teaching and research. And what of simply the ability to start writing—in any language? It is bad enough to agonize over writing up the results of one's research, but woe to the academic who has trouble writing the endless memos required to accomplish the simplest of tasks. Just being able to get started is a valuable, indeed indispensable, tool. The art of skillful negotiating on behalf of yourself, your research, your students, and your department marks you as a formidable player on the academic field. Each of these skills is an arrow in the quiver of an Athena, adding to her knowledge and wisdom, and each is something that can, though often through much effort, be acquired.

And what about the art of saying "no"? I have often contemplated replacing my message on my voice mail, at least at home, with "No!" That would take care of those requesting that I serve on yet another committee or give still another talk, as well as those who want me to donate to this or that worthy cause or to sign up for a different long-distance telephone service. That not only students but colleagues, administrators, and family members consider the time of a male faculty member sacrosanct but your time to be theirs is distressingly true. Several authors in this volume speak of distinguishing the important from the merely urgent, and that is truly a weapon with which I long to be well armed.

Another substantial weapon is the ability to recognize one's limitations. Not every rejection letter is based on discrimination—maybe your research actually could be more thorough, your analysis more penetrating, your writing clearer. Sometimes, you lose out on a job or a promotion because someone else is better; sometimes, what appears to be harassment is genuine interest or concern. Would that we were all granted the wisdom to recognize easily which is which. And would that we were all able to decide which things are worth fighting for at all costs and from which struggles we need to walk away to save our careers and our sanity.

Advice about finding mentors, support groups, or networks is invaluable. We all need to know what it takes to succeed at the task at hand—finishing a dissertation, finding a job, negotiating a salary, getting tenure—and it varies from discipline to discipline, from institution to institution. Read what the faculty manual says about requirements for tenure, and then find someone who will tell you what it *really* takes.

In general, women have long engaged in the kind of cross-disciplinary research and teaching that is now figuring in the strategic plans of most colleges and universities; being somewhat isolated in their own departments, they have often sought collaborators from elsewhere in the university. Many of us have taught in interdisciplinary programs and stretched our research to encompass insights and techniques from beyond the traditional paradigms. Such initiatives are now a hot area at most institutions, and here we are, armed with our experience and expertise. But it will very likely be necessary to point out to male newcomers to this kind of collaborative effort that we are old hands at it and, moreover, are prepared to take leadership roles.

I find it discouraging that there are still glass ceilings—for some to be promoted to full professor, for others to break into the top research institutions, for others to be president of a major university. The numbers in each of these above-the-ceiling categories are discouragingly small, long after there have been enough women in academe to form an adequate pool for such advancement. But then I look back to see whence we have come and believe that if we arm ourselves as this volume's authors suggest, the current glass ceilings will shatter, as have those of the past, for our daughters if not for ourselves. At a recent meeting of a professional society to which I have belonged for more than 30 years, a male colleague told me that he often relates an experience of mine as evidence of what a single persistent person can do. Some 25 years ago, a small group of women in this society became aware of the paucity of women speakers at professional meetings, the dearth of women members on the governing council of the organization, the total absence of women from the editorial boards of the field's major journals. We thought that the governing council ought to take some action, and so I decided to go and observe this council in action. I was met at the door of the meeting room by the then-president of the organization and told that the meeting was open only to members of the council. Having researched the issue in advance, I was able to reply that the bylaws stated differently. "Oh," he said, "it's a gentlemen's agreement." "Oh good," said I, "I'm no gentleman, so I can stay." Ever since then, the meetings have been open. We have had several women presidents and vice presidents of the organization, myself included; nearly every journal has at least one woman editor, and no meeting fails to have women among its invited speakers. And best of all, the percentage of PhDs in the field going to women has increased from 6% to more than 20%. And should there be a hint of backsliding, the organization of which I was the founding president, the Association for Women in Mathematics, is right there to keep up the pressure.

That there is a less than admirable side to Athena I might concede, but as I stare at my newly acquired antique ivory owl, I salute the power, the wisdom, the perseverance, the skillful maneuvering that makes Athena a worthy model for today's women faculty.

Index

AAUW. *See* American Association of University Women
Abdul-Wakeel, A., 141
Abrami, P. C., 142, 146
Abramson, J., 112
Abramson, L., 138
Abramson, P., 138
ACE (American Council on Education), 110, 189
Adler, E. S., 217, 221, 222
Adler, N. E., 118
Administration. *See* Sex discrimination, organizational; Women faculty, leadership
Admissions:
gatekeeping in, 12-13
sex discrimination and, 12-13
Adversity coping skills, xviii
academic careers, positives of, 275
academic careers, stresses of, 275
case examples of, 297-302
conclusions regarding, 293
difficult students or colleagues, dealing with, 290-292
give yourself credit, 292
negotiate effectively, 288-290
professional stress sources and, 276-278
reduce role ambiguity, 286-288
seek social support, 283-284
stress reactions and
denial reaction, 278-280

lower feelings of entitlement, 280-281
reduced feelings of control, 282
self-blame reaction, 281-282
use time effectively, 285-286
Affirmative action, ban on:
female enrollment and, 22
minority enrollment and, 28
Affirmative action, resistance to, xvi
administrative discrimination and, 13
competition theory and
AAUP survey data and, 48, 54-55
40% solution concept and, 53-54
increased scrutiny, in academe, 50
intergroup relations and, 48-49
performance pressure and, 50-51
pressures on minorities, in organizations, 49-50
social isolation and, 51
stereotypes and, 51-53
conclusions regarding, 69-70
contact theory and
authorities and prescriptions for civility, 64-65
competition and, 60-61
competition, for resources, 61-62
competition, for tenure, 62-63
dissimilarity and similarity and, 63-64
professional networking and, 59-60
status, numbers, rank, and, 56-58
status, salary and, 58-59

About the Authors

Susan A. Basow, PhD, is the Charles A. Dana Professor and Head of Psychology at Lafayette College in Easton, PA. She received her PhD in psychology from Brandeis University in 1973. She is a Fellow of the American Psychological Association and a licensed psychologist. She has written a well-known textbook that is now in its third edition, *Gender: Stereotypes and Roles* and is particularly interested in how gender affects our appraisals of self and others. She has published numerous articles on gender issues in student evaluations, as well as on attitudes toward women's bodies. She served for 7 years as Coordinator of the women's studies program at Lafayette College, a program she helped found.

Nijole V. Benokraitis, PhD, is Professor of Sociology in the Division of Criminology, Criminal Justice, and Social Policy at the University of Baltimore. She has served as both Chair and Graduate Program Director of the Department of Sociology and has chaired numerous university committees. She has published five books, many book chapters, and numerous articles on such topics as affirmative action, sex discrimination, subtle sexism, marriage and the family, and institutional racism.

Regina Bento, MD, PhD, is Associate Professor of Management at the Merrick School of Business, University of Baltimore. She received her PhD from Massachusetts Institute of Technology and her MD from the Federal University of Rio de Janeiro. She is chair of a universitywide committee for teaching enhancement at the University of Baltimore and a Faculty Associate at the Hoffberger Center for Professional Ethics and at the Center for International and Comparative Law. Dr. Bento is a member of the editorial board of the *Journal of Business Ethics*, has been on the editorial board of the *Journal of Information Technology Management*, and has served as a reviewer for numerous professional books, journals, and conferences. Dr. Bento's published work includes an award-winning book; several book chapters; several articles in journals such as *Human Resource Management Journal, Journal of Managerial Psychology, Information and Management*, and others; as well as numerous business cases, proceedings, and other publications. Her scholarly work has followed four interrelated research streams: behavioral issues in the management of end-user computing; unintentional bias in the allocation of organizational rewards; values, culture and organizational rewards; and teamwork and information technology in higher education.

Maryka Biaggio, PhD, is Professor and Coordinator of Admissions at the School of Professional Psychology at Pacific University in Oregon. She is currently Secretary/Treasurer of the National Council of Schools and Programs and Professional Psychology. She has served as a member of the Association for Women in Psychology Implementation Collective and was the Coordinator of the Association's 1996 annual conference in Portland, Oregon. Her areas of expertise include sexual harassment, gay/lesbian issues, and dual relationship ethical issues.

Linda L. Carli, PhD, Visiting Associate Professor, Department of Psychology, Wellesley College, does research in the areas of gender, interaction, and communication; gender and social influence; and coping with adversity. Her achievements include numerous presentations and publications on psychology of gender, and she has received grants to support her research. In addition, she has actively mentored many students and developed and participated in a variety of workshops and programs on diversity for business, government agencies, and academic institutions. She has developed 10 different courses on the psychology of women and has won an award for her teaching. Dr. Carli serves on the editorial board of *Social Psychology Quarterly* and reviews articles for many journals in psychology.

Joan C. Chrisler, PhD, is Professor of Psychology at Connecticut College. She is President of the Connecticut Conference of the American Association of University Professors and has previously served as president of the New England Psychological Association and Coordinator of the Association for Women in Psychology. She has been active in several other professional associations as an officer, board member, or committee chair and is a Fellow of the American Psychological Association. She has published extensively on the psychology of women and gender and is especially known for her work on women's health, menstruation, weight, and body image. She is coeditor of *Lectures on the Psychology of Women, Variations on a Theme: Diversity and the Psychology of Women,* and *New Directions in Feminist Psychology.* She has been honored for her professional service by the New England Psychological Association and by AWP, which presented her with the Christine Ladd-Franklin Award and a Distinguished Publication Award.

Lynn H. Collins, PhD, a clinical psychologist in the Department of Psychology at La Salle University, received her BS from Duke University and her PhD from Ohio State University. She is a Fellow of the American Psychological Society and the Maryland Psychological Association and has been an officer of the New England Psychological Association, the Association for Women in Psychology, and the Baltimore Psychological Association. Dr. Collins serves on the Board of Directors of the Eastern Psychological Association. She publishes in the areas of childhood social skills, gender, psychopathology, and pedagogy, and is a Consulting Editor for *Psychological Assessment* and a Contributing Editor for *Journal of Genetic Psychology* and *Genetic, Social, and General Psychology Monographs.* Her specialty areas are anxiety disorders, cognitive behavioral therapy, gender, and international psychology.

Maureen Cotter is an EdD candidate at Johnson and Wales University. She earned her BS in physical education at Rhode Island College, her MS in physical education at the University of Rhode Island, and her MEd in secondary administration education at Providence College. She has been a physical education teacher, high school coach, and regional gender equity specialist. For the past 10 years, she has served on the Education Committee of the Rhode Island Commission on Women, where she facilitated the Educators' Colloquium on Gender Equity and co-coordinated the Title IX Report Card project and the Glass Ceiling in Higher Education Task Force.

Mona J. E. Danner, PhD, is Assistant Professor of Sociology and Criminal Justice and Graduate Program Director at Old Dominion University in Norfolk, Virginia. She is President-Elect of the University Women's Caucus and active in the ODU women's studies program and the American Society of Criminology's Division on Women and Crime. Her areas of interest include social inequality (gender, ethnicity/race, class, nation); criminal justice; and women globally. She is currently engaged in research on gender and the process of negotiating the academic contract. In 1995, she visited Beijing, China, where she presented her research on social indicators of gender inequality at the NGO Forum held in conjunction with the United Nations Conference on Women.

Michelle R. Dunlap, PhD, is a social psychologist and Assistant Professor of Human Development at Connecticut College. Her leadership roles within academe and professional organizations include Steering Committee member of the New England Psychological Association and Co-Chair of the Program Committee for the 1998 annual conference of the Association for Women in Psychology. Dr. Dunlap's areas of expertise include social and personality development, social psychology, multicultural developmental issues, and service-learning.

Chris D. Erickson, PhD, is Assistant Professor of Counseling Psychology at Temple University. Her research focuses on the career development experiences of women, including the professional development of women in academia. She has published and presented her research internationally and is currently conducting research on adolescent vocational problem solving.

Alberta M. Gloria, PhD, is Assistant Professor of Counseling Psychology at the University of Wisconsin-Madison. In addition to her research on cultural congruity and academic persistence of Chicano/Latinos, she has published and presented nationally on the psychosociocultural influences on racial/ethnic minority students in higher education. She is on the editorial board of the *Journal of Multicultural Counseling and Development* and is Secretary of the Section on Ethnic and Racial Diversity of Division 17 (Counseling Psychology) of the American Psychological Association.

Mary Gray, PhD, JD, is Professor of Mathematics and Statistics at American University and a member of the District of Columbia and the U.S. Supreme Court Bars. She is a Fellow of the American Association for the Advancement of Science and a recipient of its Lifetime Mentor Award. She has published extensively in statistics, mathematics, mathematics education, women in science, educational and employment equity, intellectual property law, and opera. Her involvement in pay equity includes salary studies for more than 30 colleges and universities. She has served several terms as Chair of her department and has also chaired the University Senate, the women's studies program, and numerous faculty committees. She was the founding President of the Association for Women in Mathematics, Vice President of the American Mathematical Society, President of the Women's Equity Action League, and Chair of Committee W on the Status of Women in the Profession for the American Association of University Professors.

Linda Herr, MA, is Professor of Theater and Dean of Academic Programs at Connecticut College. She has served as Chair of the Department of Theater and as Acting Director of the Gender and Women's Studies program and is associated with the Eugene O'Neill Center's National Theater Institute and with Primary Stages. She has long been active in faculty governance and has served on most of the major campus committees. She studied theater in New York and Chicago; she has acted and directed professionally as well as on campus. Her areas of expertise include Eugene O'Neill's dramas and the works of feminist playwrights.

Bernice Lott, PhD, is Professor Emerita of Psychology and Women's Studies at the University of Rhode Island and is a former Dean of University College. She has taught at the University of Colorado and Kentucky State College and been a visiting scholar/professor at Brown University's Center for Research and Teaching on Women, Stanford University's Institute for Research on Women and Gender, the Department of Psychology of Waikato University in New Zealand, and the University of Hawaii at Manoa. She has received her university's Excellence Award for scholarly achievement, served as president of Division 35 (The Psychology of Women) of the American Psychological Association (APA), and has been honored for scholarly teaching and social policy contributions by the Association for Women in Psychology, APA's Committee on Women, and APA's Division 35. She is the author of numerous theoretical and empirical articles, chapters, and books on issues relevant to women, including her book, *Women's Lives: Themes and Variations in Gender Learning.* Her latest books are *The Social Psychology of Interpersonal Discrimination*, coedited with her former student, Diane Maluso, and *Combatting Sexual Harassment in Higher Education,* coedited with Mary Ellen Reilly. Her areas of interest are interpersonal discrimination; the intersections among gender, ethnicity, and social class; multicultural issues; and the social psychology of poverty.

Mary K. Madsen, RN, PhD, FAAMR, is Associate Professor of Nursing, Director of the Interdisciplinary Rehabilitation Clinic, and Director of the Health Care Administration Program at the University of Wisconsin-Milwaukee. She has a long history of faculty governance and administrative work at the university. She has served on many faculty committees, as Chair of the Health Maintenance Department of the School of Nursing and of the Department of Health Sciences, School of Allied Health Professions, and as Assistant Vice Chancellor for Academic Affairs. She is an active researcher and writer and has received a number of grants to support her work.

Nelly K. Murstein, PhD, is Hannah K. Hafkesbrink Professor of French at Connecticut College. She has served several terms as Chair of the Department of French and Italian. She has long been active in faculty governance and has served in a wide variety of capacities, most notably on the Faculty Steering Committee and Conference Committee, the Advisory Committee on Tenure, Promotion, and Termination of Appointments, and as Acting Chair of the Department of Dance. She is an active member of the Modern Language Association and the American Association of Teachers of French, and she currently serves as Chair of the Board of Directors of Mystic Paper Beasts, a mask-pantomimic performance group. Her areas of expertise are modern French literature and French theater.

Loraine K. Obler, PhD, is Distinguished Professor in the Program in Speech and Hearing Sciences and Program in Linguistics, and Ombuds Officer of the City University of New York Graduate School. Her leadership roles within academe and professional organizations include serving as Spokesperson and Coordinator of the Association for Women in Psychology. Dr. Obler's areas of expertise are neurolinguistics, bilingualism, language in aging and dementia, neuropsychology of talent, and dyslexia.

Clare Porac, PhD, is Professor of Psychology at the University of Victoria in British Columbia. She is a Fellow of the American Psychological Association, the American Psychological Society, and the Canadian Psychological Association. She is currently Director of the Canadian Psychological Association and President of the University of Victoria Faculty Association.

She is also a member of the Canadian Association of University Teachers Academic Freedom and Tenure Committee. Her areas of expertise include human visual perception and sensorimotor coordination, particularly as it relates to right- and left-handedness. She is currently completing the requirements for the Certificate in Conflict Resolution at the Justice Institute in New Westminister, British Columbia.

Kathryn Quina, PhD, is Professor of Psychology and Women's Studies at the University of Rhode Island. She specializes in gender equity in education, instructional quality, sexual abuse, and HIV risk in women and is currently leading a research team that evaluates interventions for incarcerated women. She has coauthored or coedited three books and has published numerous chapters and articles in her areas of expertise. She has co-coordinated studies of gender equity on two campuses, co-coordinated the Rhode Island Commission on Women's Title IX Report Card project and the Glass Ceiling in Higher Education Task Force, and has served in leadership roles in the American Psychological Association, Association for Women in Psychology, and the New England Psychological Association.

Lisa M. Rocchio, PhD, earned her doctorate in clinical psychology from the University of Rhode Island. She is currently in independent practice in Johnston and North Kingstown, Rhode Island. Her areas of expertise include interpersonal violence, feminist therapy, and eating disorders. She has served as Chair of the Association for Women in Psychology's Student Caucus and Co-Coordinator of the Rhode Island chapter of AWP. She has taught courses in psychology and women's studies at Providence College and at the University of Rhode Island.

Ester Ruiz Rodriguez, PhD, is Assistant Professor of Nursing at Arizona State University, where she teaches personality and counseling theory courses and supervises counseling practica for psychiatric nurse practitioners. She received her doctoral degree in counseling psychology in 1994 and has pursued a research program in cross-cultural issues and Latino health. More recent research projects have included psychological separation and worldview, ethnic identity and adjustment, domestic violence in pregnant Latinas, and strengths and limitations of Mexican American families. In addition, she has established a strong relationship with the metropolitan Phoenix Latino community, where she is frequently invited to speak at programs designed to motivate racial/ethnic students to pursue higher education. She serves on several advisory boards and holds executive board positions in several professional organizations. She also provides psychological services as a practitioner and consultant.

Kim Romenesko, MA, is Senior Administrative Program Specialist with the Center for Women's Studies at the University of Wisconsin–Milwaukee, where she collaborates with faculty and staff to fulfill the Center's research, instructional, and public service missions. She earned her BS and MA in sociology from the University of Wisconsin–Milwaukee. Over the past 8 years, she has helped coordinate more than 100 lectures, seminars, workshops, and symposia on topics relevant to women's studies research and teaching, including the Breaking the Glass Ceiling project funded by the Chicago Women's Bureau of the Department of Labor.

Suzanna Rose, PhD, is Professor of Psychology and Women's and Gender Studies at the University of Missouri-St. Louis, where she served as Director of Women's Studies for several years. Nationally, she has been an active member of the Association for Women in Psychology since the 1970s and served it in various leadership roles. In 1992, she was awarded the Christine Ladd-Franklin award for feminist activism in psychology by AWP. She is a Fellow of the American Psychological Association. In 1997, she was one of the coordinators of the National Women's Studies Association conference held in St. Louis. In addition to her national service, Dr. Rose, who edited *Career Guide for Women Scholars,* has been a career consultant to women faculty at different universities. The Critical Career Development Workshop she developed is aimed specifically at helping women develop effective strategies for research and publishing. Her primary research concerns how gender, sexual orientation, and race affect personal relationships, including colleague relations, friendships, and romantic relationships.

Ellin Kofsky Scholnick, PhD, is Professor of Psychology and Special Assistant to the President on Women's Issues at the University of Maryland. She has served as Secretary-Treasurer of the Developmental Psychology Division of the American Psychological Association, President of the Jean Piaget Society, and as Associate Editor of *Child Development* and *Developmental Psychology.* She is currently Series Editor of the Jean Piaget Society Symposium series. Her research focuses on the development of reasoning and planning skills and the role of parent-child conversation in fostering conceptual development.

Joann Claire Silverberg, PhD, Associate Professor of Classics at Connecticut College, has been acting Chair of the Department of Classics, Director of Women's Studies, and represented the college on the Faculty Steering and Conference Committee and the Academic and Administrative Procedures Committee. She is currently on the Board of Directors of the Classical Association of Connecticut. Her areas of expertise include Latin and Greek language and literature, ancient comedy, ancient love poetry, ancient historiography, women in antiquity, and linguistics.

Ethel Morgan Smith, PhD, is Assistant Professor of English at West Virginia University, where she teaches African American literature and creative writing. She is presently a Fulbright scholar in African American Literature at the University of Tübingen in Germany. She is the recipient of the following awards: the National Endowment for the Humanities (NEH) Summer Seminar, the Virginia Foundation Grant for the Humanities and Public Policy, and a Dupont Fellowship. She has recently completed a narrative on the history of the Hollins Community, a small African American community that has existed since 1842, and she is looking for a publisher for her novel, *A Walk in the Park*.

Mary Zahm, PhD, is Assistant Professor of Psychology at Bristol Community College in Fall River, Massachusetts. She is Regional Coordinator for the Rhode Island Association for Women in Psychology and a member of the planning committee for the 1999 Association for Women in Psychology conference. Her areas of expertise include psychology of women, human development, personal adjustment, and human factors.